THE

SIMPLY GOURMET DIABETES

COOKBOOK

THE
SIMPLY GOURMET DIABETES
COOKBOOK

**Easy, Healthy Recipes and Menus for
People with Diabetes and Those Who Love Them**

MARY DONKERSLOOT, R.D.

Originally published as *The Everyday Gourmet Diabetes Cookbook*

THREE RIVERS PRESS/NEW YORK

Dedicated to Father Joseph Kerwin

Grateful acknowledgment is made to the following for permission to reprint previously published material: *The New York Times*, "Losing Count of Calories as Plates Fill Up," by Marion Burros, copyright © 1997 by The New York Times Co. Reprinted by permission. The American Diabetes Association and The American Dietetic Association for the Food Exchange Lists © 1995 American Diabetes Association and The American Dietetic Association.

Published by Three Rivers Press, 201 East 50th Street, New York, New York 10022.
Member of the Crown Publishing Group.

Originally published as The Everyday Gourmet Diabetes Cookbook *in hardcover by* Clarkson Potter/Publishers *in 1998.*

THE EVERYDAY GOURMET *is a registered trademark of Kathleen Perry. This book is in no way affiliated with* THE EVERYDAY GOURMET.

THREE RIVERS PRESS *is a registered trademark of Random House, Inc.*

Random House, Inc. New York, Toronto, London, Sydney, Auckland
www.randomhouse.com

Printed in the United States of America
Design by Julie E. Baker

Library of Congress Cataloging-in-Publication Data
Donkersloot, Mary.
    The simply gourmet diabetes cookbook : easy, healthy recipes and menus for people with diabetes and those who love them / Mary Donkersloot.
        First ed. published: New York: Clarkson Potter Publishers, 1998.
        Includes bibliographical references and index.
        1. Diabetes—Diet therapy—Recipes.   I. Title.
    RC662.D585   1999
    616.4'620654—dc21   99-18309
                            CIP

ISBN 0-609-80514-2

10 9 8 7 6 5 4 3 2 1
First Paperback Edition

CONTENTS

ACKNOWLEDGMENTS

I've dedicated this book to Father Joe Kerwin. He gave me a part-time job as his cook at age fifteen, which introduced me to the connection between food and health, and in particular, diabetes. This set the stage for me to choose to become a nutritionist, a career that has been most fulfilling.

I thank my agent, Maureen Lasher, for encouraging me to take on this project, and I appreciate the enthusiastic support of my editor, Katie Workman. They both believed in this project wholeheartedly, and made it even more fun to work on.

Anne Albertine, one of America's most talented professional chefs, passed on her creative culinary genius, which inspired many of the recipes in this book. Sara Jaye assisted me daily, testing recipes and calculating all the nutritional analyses; her talent, artfulness, and pleasant manner brought joy and great food into my kitchen. I also thank Brigit Binns for her expertise in recipe development and Jonah Hadary for helping me launch this project.

Many of my colleagues who are experts in the field of nutrition have been generous with their precious time, reviewing specific chapters and giving valuable comments and suggestions: Madelyn Wheeler, M.S., R.D., F.A.D.A., C.D.E., who reviewed all the diabetic exchange and carbohydrate choice values; Robert Antonacci, M.S.; Gerald Bernstein, M.D.; Betty Brackenridge, R.D., S.C.E.; Candy Cumming, M.S., R.D.; Margo Denke, M.D.; Susan Dopart Diercks, M.S., R.D.; Lynn Guiducci, R.D.; Fran Kaufman, M.D.; Karmeen Kulkarni, C.D.E., M.S., R.D.; Kelly Van Horn, R.D.; and Larry Verity, Ph.D.

Special thanks to all of those at Clarkson Potter who turned this manuscript into a beautiful book, including Erica Youngren, Marysarah Quinn, Julie Baker, Andrea Connolly Peabbles, and Joan Denman.

And thanks to my husband, Steve Proffitt.

As we enter the twenty-first century, the syndrome of diabetes mellitus is going to explode upon us. This disease state that has never captured the imagination of the American public and therefore has not been a major political force will dominate in the next few decades. There is no immediate cure, so we have to pay attention to what needs to be done now. Diabetes is the most expensive disease to this country—$138 billion a year—costing more than heart disease or cancer and representing 15 percent of our national expenditure on health care. It is the fourth leading cause of death but it is woefully underfunded for research. Diabetes is still the leading cause of blindness, kidney failure, and nontraumatic limb loss. It is all preventable. In my mind, the single greatest advance since the discovery of insulin has been our ability to educate people with diabetes. We now know for sure, as established by the DCCT (Diabetes Complications and Control Trial) that normalization of blood glucose can prevent complications. This appears to be the case in both type I and type II diabetes.

Diabetes can be viewed as a balance of opposing forces trying to maintain enough glucose in the blood to service the brain, an organ that utilizes only glucose. On the one hand, the liver is capable of producing glucose all day long, driven by hormones such as glucagon, cortisol, adrenaline, and growth hormone. Only insulin moderates what the liver produces. When the balance favors the hormones, the blood glucose level rises. When insulin is present, it falls. The syndrome of diabetes occurs when there is either insufficient insulin or abundant insulin but insulin that can't work. As I said, in this century the single most important advance in managing diabetes since the discovery of insulin is our ability to educate and monitor our own blood glucose levels.

In *The Simply Gourmet Diabetes Cookbook,* Mary Donkersloot takes on that educational challenge. She presents the physiological issues in a most understandable way that allows the readers to have a clear picture of why they need to do certain things. The foundation of treatment for type II diabetes is good living. That means weight control through diet and exercise before embarking into pharmacology. Both weight loss and exercise have been shown to increase the number and sensitivity of receptors to insulin on different cells. Since insulin resistance is the hallmark of type II diabetes, reversing it will make a substantial difference. You can return to this book again and again to reinforce your knowledge. She helps you make fewer calories an adventure and allows you to be in control of your lives and your blood glucose.

—Gerald Bernstein, M.D.
    associated clinical professor of medicine,
    Albert Einstein College of Medicine, New York;
    director of the Beth Israel Diabetes Management Program;
    and president of the American Diabetes Association

To manage type I diabetes successfully requires an understanding of how insulin, activity, and nutrition interact to affect blood glucose levels. People with diabetes must learn not only the basic principles of diabetes management but they must also understand how to adjust their regimen to achieve optimal blood glucose control, since this has been shown to improve outcome and prevent long-term complications. Many innovations have been developed and many recommendations have been made over the past several years to make diabetes management easier and more realistic. Perhaps none has been as important to the day-to-day life of someone with diabetes as the 1994 American Diabetes Association (ADA) Nutrition Recommendations and Principles for People with Diabetes Mellitus.

At the heart of the ADA nutrition recommendations is the realization that nutrition plans need to be individualized and humanized. The concept that someone with diabetes could become sugar-free was abandoned—anyone who had worked in the field knew the folly of telling a child with diabetes that he or she could never have birthday cake again or stay up late and eat a pizza. Since each person with diabetes is different, nutrition plans were no longer standardized by age or weight, but rather made for the individual—taking into account the needs of growing children, the desires of those who wanted to loose weight, and specific dietary preferences. Most important was the concept that patients could learn to adjust their intake and to balance it with their activity level and their insulin dosage. It was encouraging to see that this could truly lead to optimal blood glucose control.

One of the main principles to emerge from the ADA recommendations was that of carbohydrate counting. Carbohydrate counting emphasizes the importance of the total grams of carbohydrate—rather than the type of carbohydrate—and the fact that carbohydrate is what truly affects postprandial blood glucose concentrations. By understanding how to read recipes and food labels, how to exchange one carbohydrate for another, and how to distribute these carbohydrates through the daily meal plan, it becomes easier to take multiple daily injections of insulin using carbohydrate-to-insulin ratios to improve blood glucose control. And finally those previously forbidden carbohydrates—eaten by most people anyway—can be put into the meal plan without the consequence of having to accuse someone of cheating.

As a pediatric endocrinologist and as director of the Children's Hospital Los Angeles Diabetes Center, I welcome this cookbook as a wonderful resource for people with type I diabetes. It is not only a cookbook but an overview of diabetes nutrition. It allows patients and their families the chance to enjoy true culinary delights, and to have the ability to meticulously manage their diabetes by utilizing the carbohydrate counting component of this cookbook. It gives recipes for great eating, and the reward will be the ability to improve blood glucose control today as well as to enjoy a healthier tomorrow.

—Francine Ratner Kaufman, M.D.
associate professor of Pediatrics,
University of Southern California School of Medicine;
director of the Comprehensive Diabetes Center,
Children's Hospital, Los Angeles, California; and board
member of the American Diabetes Association

INTRODUCTION

I was raised in a large family on a farm in Iowa where cooking was just another part of life. As I grew into my teens, I took a part–time job cooking for the local priest, Father Joe Kerwin, who had diabetes. I worked with Father Joe's dietitian, and learned how to prepare meals in keeping with the diabetic diet as it was then defined—rather strict, and quite different from the foods my mother cooked. He avoided sugar like the plague and ate special diet foods that often tasted terrible. Twenty years have passed and I am now a registered dietitian myself. I work with hundreds of people with diabetes and their families in my Beverly Hills nutrition practice, teaching them a far more liberal philosophy of diabetes diet management than I knew from my job cooking for Father Joe.

Last year, Father Joe, at the age of seventy, retired to Florida. I visited him shortly after he moved, and was saddened to learn that he'd had an argument with one of his closest friends. She was angry with him for eating dessert at a dinner party, as she believed sugar was completely off-limits for people with diabetes. She felt as if he was sabotaging his health in the days of his long-awaited retirement.

Both of them were unaware that a moderate amount of sugar is acceptable in the diet when diabetes is under control. Father Joe's diabetes was well managed; he kept his carbohydrate intake in check and consistent, and he walked two miles every day. With his diabetes under control, having some dessert as part of his carbohydrate allowance would have been okay. In fact, he restricted himself unnecessarily, and his friend's well-meaning but misdirected advice only worsened his guilt.

I realized that similar conflicts were probably erupting in many other families as well. Through work with people with diabetes, I knew that many of them are unaware of the new diabetic guidelines. This experience with Father Joe and his friend just made it hit home.

GOOD NEWS FOR PEOPLE WITH DIABETES

Statistics from the American Diabetes Association indicate that 16 million Americans have either type I or type II diabetes (each type is explained in detail on pages 6–10).

Diet is the cornerstone of treatment for both types of diabetes, so it's good news when new research suggests a different way of looking at diet. At one time, people with diabetes were taught to avoid sugar at all costs, but new research indicates that carbohydrates affect blood glucose levels similarly, whether they come from sugars or starches. The amount of carbohydrates, not the source, appears to be the major factor in determining the effect of food on blood glucose levels. In 1994, the American Diabetes Association released the fifth edition of the nutrition guidelines for people with both types of diabetes. These guidelines are fully outlined in chapter 1, but the basic message is this: *A high level of sugar in the blood is the enemy in diabetes. A moderate amount of sugar in the diet is not.* But for years, the message was to avoid sugar, or at least that's what people heard. Now many people with diabetes have a hard time believing it's okay to eat *some* sugar.

AN UNHEARD MESSAGE

Because these revised guidelines seem to contradict the commonly held beliefs about diet and diabetes, they have not been widely understood, either by people with diabetes, or by many of the people who treat them. The net result is that many people unnecessarily deprive themselves of an occasional sweet, or, reacting to overly restrictive dietary guidelines with the same classic response most people have to a strict diet—go on binges. While the real problem may be eating too much food—whether it is bread, fruit, meat, or fat (most overweight people don't overeat vegetables)—people with diabetes often focus on avoiding sugar. The new wisdom concentrates on eating a healthy diet rich in variety, instead of focusing on sugar intake alone. You can include foods such as sugar and fat in a healthy, well-balanced diet and still maintain good blood glucose control. I believe that, armed with this new knowledge, many people with diabetes will be better able to control both their disease and their natural cravings for sugar. The result will be improved management of diabetes and a more enjoyable style of eating. You'll read more about this in part 1.

PART ONE

NEW BASICS

SMART MOVES FOR MANAGING DIABETES

CHAPTER 1

THE NEW GUIDELINES AND HOW TO ACHIEVE THEM

When someone is told they have diabetes, one of their first fears is that they will have to give up many of their favorite foods. Perhaps the most exciting piece of news about the New Guidelines is that no food is off-limits. The meal plan you and your dietitian create will include a certain amount of carbohydrates, expressed in grams, choices, or exchanges. One carbohydrate choice or one starch exchange is equal to 15 grams of carbohydrates. *Remember, the total amount of carbohydrates eaten is the priority, rather than the source of carbohydrate.* Therefore, one carbohydrate choice can be a starch, fruit, milk, or dessert and is the serving size that supplies 15 grams of carbohydrates.

Carbohydrates are the main focus, because diabetes is a disease where the body is unable to break down and use carbohydrates properly. The result is hyperglycemia—an abnormally high amount of glucose in the blood, which spills over into the urine. To understand diabetes, and hyperglycemia, you must understand how your body turns food into energy, and how diabetes affects that process. *When you eat, food breaks down into a form of sugar, called glucose, the body's main fuel.* Glucose enters the bloodstream and the level of glucose in your blood begins to rise. When an increase in glucose is sensed, the body sends a signal to your pancreas. The pancreas then makes insulin and sends it into the bloodstream. *Insulin is like a key that allows blood glucose to cross from the bloodstream into the body's cells.* Once the glucose is inside the cell, your body converts the glucose into energy. *So insulin effectively lowers the level of blood glucose by letting glucose leave the bloodstream and go into the cells.* When this all happens the way it should, you have the energy for a full and active life.

In people who have diabetes, this system doesn't work. Glucose builds up in the bloodstream instead of going into the cells of the body. The kidneys are unable to handle the excess glucose in the blood, and in most cases, it spills into the urine. Uncontrolled diabetes—consistently high blood glucose levels—can eventually cause damage to small blood vessels and complications in the heart, kidneys, eyes, and nerves. It also increases the risk for heart disease two to four times and more than doubles the risk of a stroke. The two main categories of diabetes (type I, when the body makes little or no insulin, and type II, when the body makes insulin, but cannot use it) are caused by different problems but are similar in their symptoms and outcomes.

TYPE I DIABETES

People with type I diabetes don't produce an adequate amount of insulin (the hormone that helps sugar move from the bloodstream into the muscles). They usually develop the disease in childhood and need insulin injections; thus, the disease is also called juvenile diabetes. They make up 10 percent of the diabetic population. Type I, or juvenile, diabetes occurs mainly in children and in thin people under forty, while type II usually occurs in late adulthood, or sometimes earlier in people who are obese. Although both types, if left untreated, share the symptom of high levels of glucose in the blood, the causes of the two types are unrelated.

Type I diabetes is an autoimmune disease process. The individual with type I destroys his or her own insulin-producing beta cells which are located in the pancreas. In type I, the chief abnormality lies within the immune system, which treats the insulin-producing beta cells as if they were foreign and mounts a full-blown assault to wipe out the effective beta cell population. *The person with type I diabetes has virtually no ability to make insulin. Consequently, the only treatment is to take insulin, and at the present time the only way to do that is by needle injection or IV infusion.*

Boys and girls are equally prone to juvenile-onset diabetes, and most are thin. Diabetes among children and teenagers is often triggered by a childhood infection, such as a virus. For a time, the virus may mask the diabetes as the parents associate their child's symptoms with the fever. The first appearance of diabetes often seems sudden and dramatic. Also, all children's blood sugar levels fluctuate much more than adults' due to their greater physical activity and the needs of their growing bodies. The following are some of the main indications of diabetes in children:

- **Increased passing of urine:** Often the earliest clue to diabetes is an increase in the amount or frequency of urination. Bed-wetting can sometimes be a hint that a child may have diabetes.

- **Constant thirst:** To keep up with the loss of urine, people with diabetes drink more fluids. If a child has lots of sweetened liquids, such as soft drinks or fruit juice, the extra sugar may accelerate the development of symptoms.
- **Sudden weight loss:** Because of the body's inability to use sugar for energy, children with diabetes usually lose or fail to gain weight until they are treated.
- **Unsatisfied hunger:** This may occur even when the child is eating plenty of food. Once again, the sweets such as candy, cookies, and pastries may make the symptoms worse.
- **Cessation of growth:** A child with diabetes may not grow according to standard growth patterns. When insulin therapy has started, they will usually catch up and resume normal growth.
- **Irritability:** This can be a very early sign of diabetes. As the emotions of children can fluctuate dramatically, parents may not notice a change in their behavior immediately. If a happy, contented baby suddenly becomes much more fussy and needs more frequent diaper changes, you should consider diabetes as a possible cause.
- **Ketoacidosis or coma:** Usually children are diagnosed before they get to this stage. However, some types of illnesses (such as flu, diarrhea, or pneumonia) may quickly bring on a state of coma. The lack of insulin reserves causes ketosis, a condition resulting from an accumulation of fat by-products called ketones in the blood. When plenty of insulin is available, fat is either completely broken down or stored by the body. But when fat is burned without insulin being available, a lot of fat gets converted into ketones. A build-up of these acid by-products causes ketoacidosis which can lead to life-threatening consequences such as coma. The earliest clues to ketoacidosis and coma may be rapid breathing, nausea, and sleepiness. Untreated, the child may lapse into a coma from which he or she can't be awakened easily.

TYPE II DIABETES

Type II, or adult-onset diabetes is much more common, affecting 90 percent of all people with diabetes. These people produce insulin but either don't make enough or can't use it properly. Type II is often preventable or controllable through diet and exercise. It is hereditary. If one of your parents has it, it is likely you will get it, too, particularly if both you and your parent are obese. Most people with this tendency do not develop the disease until they are at least 35 years old; many are well into middle age before they develop symptoms. *With this type of diabetes, the insulin-producing cells of the pancreas are not damaged and there is no immune attack.* In some cases, insulin is still manufactured by the pancreas, but perhaps not enough to cover the body's need. *In most cases, however, especially in those people with diabetes who are older and overweight, the pancreas continues to produce plenty of insulin, often much more than normal, but the cells are unable to use it efficiently.*

The reason is a shortage of insulin receptors, areas on the cell membranes that allow insulin to enter the cell walls. A whole cell, for example, normally has about thirty thousand receptors, of which about 10 percent, or three thousand, are at work at any one time. Research has found that, in a susceptible person, overeating and a large weight gain increases the production of insulin, which in turn causes a reduction in the number of receptors. *Plentiful insulin floats uselessly in the blood, unable to penetrate the cells, while sugar piles up but cannot be used, and is filtered by the kidneys into the urine.*

This type of diabetes can often be controlled with diet and exercise, or diet and exercise combined with oral hypoglycemic drugs that stimulate the release of insulin or lower blood sugar levels. As reviewed in chapter 6 on managing weight, a ten- or twenty-pound weight loss may be enough to make symptoms go away. People with type II diabetes are generally not automatically obligated to take insulin injections like their type I counterparts, although some people with type II diabetes may require insulin injections to supplement their own supply. The following are common symptoms of type II diabetes:

- **Feeling very tired:** The earliest clue to diabetes in adults is a vague feeling that things are not quite right. That may include a lack of energy, feeling tired more easily, thinking less clearly, and forgetfulness.
- **Increased passing of urine:** If there is a high level of sugar in your blood, you will need to get rid of it by producing more urine. The need to urinate more often than usual, particularly during the night, may be an early clue to diabetes.

- **Constant thirst:** If you're urinating more frequently, you'll need to replace the fluid lost, and are likely to feel excess thirst. Some people report the urge to drink fluids every 15 to 30 minutes when they are developing diabetes.
- **Sudden weight loss:** Although people with adult-type diabetes are usually overweight, they sometimes seem to lose a little weight before they are first treated by a doctor, since they are losing sugar, a source of calories, in the urine.
- **Blurred vision:** The accumulation of sugar and sugar metabolic by-products and its accompanying fluid in the lens of the eye can cause swelling and fuzzy vision. When the lens is swollen it takes longer to change the focus from near to distant vision. Fortunately, these abnormalities can be completely corrected by restoring the blood sugar to normal levels.

If you or someone you love has diabetes, you have a new focus in your life—to keep blood glucose levels as close to normal as possible. You will have regular appointments with your health care team and will monitor your own blood sugar on a daily basis. According to Francine Kaufman, M.D., director of the Comprehensive Diabetes Center at Children's Hospital, Los Angeles, "Targeted blood glucose levels vary with age, and specific goals must be determined by your health care team. We set targets and then measure the hemoglobin A-1 C, which is a measure of blood glucose levels over a period of time. It's like a report card on how the patient is really doing." Some of the blood glucose ranges that Dr. Kaufman uses in her clinic are, for adult type II diabetes, between 70 and 110 mg/dl (milligram per deciliter) glucose upon awakening in the morning and between 140 and 180 mg/dl glucose two hours after a meal. Children with type I diabetes have different blood glucose goals, depending on their age and developmental abilities. For example, for infants and toddlers, it's 120 to 220 mg/dl. For preschool-age kids, it's 100 to 200 mg/dl, whereas school-age children may be safe with a tighter control of 80 to 160. For adults with type I diabetes, blood glucose goals are also individualized but may be set at 80 to 150 mg/dl. *Since blood glucose goals are determined on an individual basis, these numbers can only be considered examples. Be sure to discuss your specific goal with your health care team.*

It's not always easy to keep blood glucose in line, but this book can help.

For many years, it was thought that this tight control was not too important as long as you felt well and functioned normally. Today we know differently. The Diabetes Control and Complication Trial (DCCT), a nationwide ten-year study involving more than 1400 patients with type I diabetes, looked to see just how important keeping blood sugars under control is in preventing complications. The results of that study, released in June 1993, show that it is critically important. Those individuals who kept their blood sugars as close to normal as possible using the guidelines outlined in this chapter reduced their risk of diabetic eye disease (retinopathy) by 76 percent, their risk of kidney disease by 35 to 56 percent, and their risk of nerve damage by 60 percent.

Of course, life isn't always fair, and there are no guarantees. Some people who seem to pay little attention to their diet never develop complications, while others who take great care do get them in later years. But, for the most part, it is true that greater control of blood sugar levels means a better, healthier, longer life.

Nobody's perfect, and you won't be either, but remember, if poor control rather than just an occasional slipup becomes your pattern, you will undoubtedly pay the price later. *All the health problems associated with diabetes are hastened and exacerbated by poor blood glucose level control.*

Living with diabetes means a constant balancing act between the food you eat, the insulin you produce yourself or take by injection, and the exercise you get. Insulin allows you to burn the food you eat for energy to fuel your body. If you eat more food, you will need more insulin. If you eat less food, you will require less insulin. Exercise helps the muscles use insulin better. So if you exercise, you'll need less insulin, whether it's coming from your own pancreas or an injection. You can read more about exercise in chapter 7.

THE GOALS OF THE NEW DIABETES GUIDELINES

By eating the right foods, in the appropriate amounts, at the right time, and keeping good exercise habits, people with diabetes will improve their overall health, as well as reduce their risk of complications. These goals are outlined by the American Diabetes Association. Here's what you're actually trying to achieve:

1. Maintain near-normal blood glucose levels by balancing food intake with exercise and, in some cases, medicine.
2. Achieve optimal levels of cholesterol and triglycerides in your blood. People with diabetes are four times as likely to have heart disease, strokes, and vascular problems in their legs, kidneys, and eyes. Following the eating style recommended in this book can help avoid these serious complications by lowering your cholesterol and triglyceride levels or fats in the blood.
3. Eat the amount of food that will allow you to maintain a reasonable weight. That means the weight that you and your doctor agree is achievable and maintainable both short and long term. In my early days as a dietitian, I calculated a weight goal based on my client's height and frame size. Not anymore. If you are overweight, just start by losing ten to twenty pounds. No matter what your starting weight, you may lower your blood sugars, as well as your cholesterol and triglyceride levels and even your blood pressure, by simply decreasing your weight by this amount.
4. Prevent, delay, or treat nutrition-related risk factors and complications. This includes acute problems such as low blood sugar, the flu, as well as long-term potential problems such as nephropathy (kidney disease), neuropathy (nerve problems), hypertension (high blood pressure), and cardiovascular disease (heart disease).
5. Keep in good overall health. The dietary guidelines outlined for healthy Americans also pertain to people with diabetes.

DIETARY GUIDELINES

Lower the Fat in Your Diet

Less fat means a decreased risk of coronary artery disease and the intake of fewer calories, which will help control body weight. The American Heart Association and the National Cholesterol Education Program (NCEP) recommend reducing total fat intake to 30 percent or less of calories from fat, and reducing saturated fat to 10 percent or less. When your dietitian gives you your food plan, it will likely include a recommendation for the amount of calories and fat grams you should take in daily. If you know how many calories you need, you can use the chart on page 14 to determine your daily fat goal.

There's No Such Thing as a Diabetic Diet

I tell my patients that the diet I follow myself is very much like the one recommended for anyone with diabetes. It's simply a low-fat diet based on the principles of variety, moderation, and balance. The only difference is that diets planned for individuals with diabetes need greater consistency in the *amounts* and *types* of food eaten, and care in the timing of meals and snacks, especially if insulin is taken.

Diabetes is a chronic disease with serious consequences and complications if not kept under control. If you have diabetes, you must watch what you eat, get regular exercise, and in some cases take oral medication or inject insulin. And as yet, there is no cure. But the good thing is that there is something you can do! Unlike many other diseases, diabetes is one whose effects depend on the simple choices you make each day in your life. If you learn about it and make a few lifestyle changes, you may experience fewer symptoms and side effects of diabetes, and be able to decrease or even eliminate your need for medications. All this, just by eating sensibly and watching the timing of your food intake! This book will be your road map to better blood glucose control.

Eating suitable meals at regular mealtimes will help avoid very high or low blood glucose levels and long-term complications associated with diabetes. Healthy eating guidelines for the person with diabetes coincide nicely with a standard, healthy diet as spelled out in the 1995 U.S. Dietary Guidelines for all healthy Americans:

1. Eat a variety of foods.
2. Balance the food you eat with physical activity. Maintain or improve your weight.
3. Choose a diet with plenty of grain products, vegetables, and fruits.
4. Choose a diet low in fat, saturated fat, and cholesterol.
5. Choose a diet moderate in sugar.
6. Choose a diet moderate in salt and sodium.
7. If you drink alcoholic beverages, do so in moderation.

This chapter explains how the new guidelines change the management of diabetes through diet. You'll find a complete rundown of the new guidelines, a review of the latest research, and an explanation of the role of specific nutrients, including carbohydrates, protein, fat, fiber, sugar, salt, and alcohol.

Chapter 3 introduces carbohydrate counting, which is the latest approach to meal planning. *Carbohydrate counting is one of the most precise and adaptable ways to manage meals and keep blood sugar (glucose levels) in control. In fact, once you get the hang of it, it can add a lot of freedom to your choices.* For those on insulin and, in particular, those using an insulin pump, carbohydrate counting is recommended for tighter control of blood glucose level. It also works very well as a weight management tool. The new diabetes guidelines lend themselves to carbohydrate counting, and the menus and recipes in this book will help you implement the personalized food plan that you work out with your dietitian.

Sample meal plans—for those who take insulin and for those who do not —in chapter 4 provide individuals with diabetes guidelines to eating in the real world—in restaurants, with families, on the go—without straying from a heathful eating plan. Use the menu plans to help incorporate the recipes in this book into your daily meals, as well as for special holiday occasions.

Part 2 contains more than 200 recipes that fit perfectly into a diabetes-friendly diet. But be prepared to share—these are tasty and easy recipes with a gourmet flair that will please everyone. They are made using ingredients and cooking techniques known as the "new basics"—ones that many Americans are already moving toward. Cooks can cut back on saturated fat by using olive oil or canola instead of butter (I don't use butter or margarine in any of these recipes), or using egg whites instead of whole eggs when possible. Everyone, especially those with diabetes, should eat more vegetables, in salads, side dishes, or even entrees. Desserts are being prepared with less fat and sugar than their original counterparts. In *The Simply Gourmet Diabetes Cookbook,* you'll learn all the secrets of low-fat cooking and baking, and you'll love our Chicken Pot Pie, Teriyaki Flank Steak, Seafood Enchiladas, and Apple Tarts in Phyllo, and you'll never feel the need to go back to your old high-fat ways.

In Exchange Lists for Meal Planning, you'll find the American Dietetic Association's revised version of the diabetic exchanges, lists of food groups including dairy, fruits, vegetables, bread and grains, proteins, fats, and treats. These new exchanges divide meats into very lean, lean, medium-fat, and high-fat meats. The portion sizes of each will be listed so that you can fit them into your food plan, whether you use carbohydrate counting, or follow a meal plan based on the exchange system. You'll also find various resources for mail-order sources for hard-to-find food products, books that may be helpful in managing diabetes, and organizations that provide additional support for people with diabetes.

Below are the basic changes in the diet guidelines for people with diabetes:

	Old Guidelines	New Guidelines
Primary Goal of Treatment	Weight loss was the primary nutrition goal for people with type II diabetes.	Achieve and maintain near-normal blood glucose and blood fat levels, including cholesterol, low- and high-density lipoproteins, and triglycerides.
Sugar	Sucrose, or table sugar, and other sources of simple sugar were avoided and replaced with complex starches.	Sucrose, or table sugar, can be included in moderation as part of the carbohydrate allotment in a diabetic meal plan.
Fat	All fat intake was limited to 30 percent of total calories: saturated fats less than 10 percent, polyunsaturated fats up to 10 percent, and the rest (10 to 15 percent) as monounsaturated fats.	Modify total fat intake and recognize that saturated fats are the primary culprit in raising blood cholesterol. Understand that monounsaturated fats may actually play a positive role as part of a low-fat diet, particularly if triglycerides and VLDL cholesterol are the primary concerns, and that omega-3 (fish oils) have an antiplatelet clotting effect and actually lower triglycerides and cholesterol.

	Old Guidelines	New Guidelines
Weight goals	Determined an ideal weight based on height and weight charts and pressured people to achieve it. Since this weight goal was difficult or impossible to attain and maintain, it led to failure and frustration.	Losing 10 or 20 pounds may be enough to improve diabetes control, especially in type II diabetes. Strive for a healthy and reasonable weight that can be maintained.
Meal planning approaches	Preplanned printed diet sheets provided rigid food recommendations.	Individualized meal plans are created, based on food preferences, lifestyle, medication, and complications. The newest meal planning approach is carbohydrate counting, which gives priority to the total amount of carbohydrates eaten rather than the source of the carbohydrate.
Food groups	Exchange lists included seven groups of foods: starch, meat, vegetable, fruit, milk, fat, and "other carbohydrates" for occasional use.	The "other carbohydrate" list is expanded. Vegetables, unless three or more servings are eaten at one meal, are free. A section of very lean meats has been added to the meat list, and fats are divided by saturation. About one-third more foods are included, among them such newer food products as low-fat or nonfat food, vegetarian foods, and ethnic foods.

So let's get going. The next step is to learn more about diabetes and the new diet guidelines in order to reap the substantial benefits that the right diet can deliver.

Eat Less Saturated Fat

Reduce your fat intake from saturated sources, such as meat, dairy products, and baked goods. This is one of the most important things you can do to keep your cholesterol and triglycerides in line. The recipes and menu plans help you *automatically* reduce saturated fat intake to less than 10 percent of total daily calories. Studies show that saturated fats promote the most dangerous forms of cholesterol build-up and have two times more cholesterol-raising potential than dietary cholesterol itself.

Limit Cholesterol

For those with normal blood cholesterol levels, the cholesterol level in the diabetic diet is limited to less than 300 milligrams per day, the same as for healthy Americans. But if your cholesterol is elevated, you'll probably be advised to limit your intake to 200 milligrams a day. You'll find the cholesterol content listed in each recipe in this book. For more information on fat and cholesterol, refer to chapter 5, Managing Fat and Cholesterol.

Have Adequate, but Not Excessive Protein

Protein builds and repairs muscle tissue. In diabetes, protein also affects blood sugar levels. About 60 percent of protein is converted to glucose, but at a much slower rate than carbohydrate is converted to glucose. Consequently, protein has a stabilizing effect on blood sugar. *If you include a protein source along with your carbohydrate in your meal, your blood sugar is likely to have less of a rise than if you eat carbohydrate alone.* This is particularly true for those with type II diabetes.

Obviously, we need protein, but many meat-eating Americans get more than they need, sometimes even too much. The protein in your food plan which has been created by your dietitian probably contributes between 10 and 20 percent of your total calories. That's enough for building and repairing muscle tissue as well as a balance to keep blood sugars in check, but extra protein may work the kidneys harder as they try to get rid of protein waste products. Research has shown that keeping dietary protein within the recommended levels and eating more protein from nonanimal sources (beans, grains, vegetables) may prevent or delay diabetic nephropathy (kidney disease). If you have been told by your doctor or dietitian to limit protein, you'll want to pay special attention to the protein content listed in each recipe, and plan your meals accordingly.

Another concern with protein is that many foods high in protein are also high in fat. The recipes that follow emphasize protein sources that are *not* high in saturated fat or total fat. Your meal plan probably includes protein at each meal, but the portions are likely to be three to four ounces per meal, or up to nine to fifteen ounces total daily. You may be encouraged to eat fish three to four times per week, since it is the lowest in saturated fat and is a source of the omega-3 fatty acids that may play a protective role in the prevention of heart disease. The skinless white meat of poultry is the next leanest option, with lean meats trimmed of visible fat and minimal marbling also on the list. Everything that is grown contains protein, although in smaller amounts than in animal sources. So bread, rice, pasta, and other grains contribute protein to the diet. Vegetable sources of protein also include legumes (dried peas, beans, and lentils), which also provide soluble fiber—a bonus, since this kind of fiber may help lower cholesterol. Cook legumes with minimal fat, ideally olive oil, which is monounsaturated, if fat is used. Low-fat or nonfat dairy products—cheese, milk, and yogurt—are other protein foods that are also included in the recipes and menu plans.

Concentrate on Complex Carbohydrates

Everyone, including people with diabetes, should eat a good amount of complex carbohydrates. In fact, complex carbohydrates such as grains, beans, and starchy vegetables should form the basis of your diet, with animal proteins taking up less of your plate. That's because complex carbohydrates are the best source of energy and contain more nutrition in the form of vitamins, minerals, and fiber. They also help you to feel full and satisfied.

Preliminary research from the Harvard School of Public Health published in the *Journal of the American Medical Association* in February 1997 also makes a case for choosing whole-grain carbohydrates over refined ones. In the study, more than 65,000 nurses ages 40 to 65 were quizzed about their dietary practices over a ten-year period. Results indicate that eating a lot of white bread, soft drinks, white rice, and potatoes may set the stage for diabetes. Based on dietary questionnaires, researchers calculated each woman's total fiber intake as well as the type of fiber (as cereal, fruit, or vegetable fiber) and the number of servings of carbohydrate-rich foods eaten. They also took note of the glycemic index, a relative measure of how food raises blood sugar. Foods with the highest glycemic load (those most likely to raise blood sugar) included white bread, mashed potatoes, French fries, and low-fiber cold cereals.

The researchers concluded that women who ate less than 2.5 grams of cereal fiber and who also consumed the highest glycemic load were two and a half times more likely to develop type II diabetes than women eating the lowest glycemic load and the highest cereal fiber intake (more than 5.8 grams per day). The Harvard research supports the hypothesis that a steady diet of high-glycemic-load foods puts a chronic demand for more insulin on the pancreas. If it is able to respond, there's no consequence. But some people may be insulin-resistant, meaning that their insulin isn't as effective as it should be, and not know it. For them, this added stress could trigger diabetes sooner than it might otherwise develop.

More research will certainly look further at this issue, but in the meantime, choosing more whole grains over refined ones may offer protection from diabetes, especially for those with a family history of the disease. Read more about how to do this in chapter 2 on carbohydrates.

Limit Sodium

People differ in their sensitivity to sodium and its effect on blood pressure. High blood pressure is more common in people with type II diabetes, and people with type II diabetes are more sodium-sensitive than the general public. Therefore, it is wise to be moderate in your sodium intake. In general, keeping it less than 3000 milligrams per day is recommended. If you have high blood pressure, 2400 milligrams of sodium or less is recommended.

A teaspoon of salt contains 2300 milligrams of sodium. Check food labels for sodium content of food. A single serving of food that contains more than 400 milligrams of sodium or entrees with more than 800 milligrams of sodium are significant sources.

The new labeling laws from the FDA mandate that a low-sodium food must have 140 milligrams of sodium or less per serving. This is useful information for those on low-sodium diets who seek alternatives to typically salty processed foods such as canned tomatoes, broth, and soups. Less sodium comes naturally with less processed foods—fresh fruits, vegetables, whole grains, legumes, and unprocessed meats, cooked with moderate salt, are all safe.

Get an Adequate Amount of Vitamins and Minerals

Individuals with diabetes who are in good health generally have nutritional needs that are addressed by the recommended dietary allowances (RDAs) designed for the general population. However, many medical problems associated with diabetes can affect nutritional needs. For example, poorly controlled diabetes may result in excessive loss of water-soluble vitamins and minerals. For those with marginal vitamin C intake and vascular fragility, a supplement of vitamin C (500 mg to 1 g/day) may be recommended.

There are other complications of diabetes that may also benefit from supplements. Magnesium depletion has been associated with insulin insensitivity, and may improve with oral supplementation. Older patients in general, including those with diabetes, should be encouraged to take at least 1000 mg of calcium per day to prevent osteoporosis. (Few of my clients are willing to drink the 4 cups of milk or eat 4 servings of yogurt a day to meet that need.) For patients with diabetic neuropathy (damage to nerves), a two-month trial of thiamin, vitamin B_1 (50 mg/day), or vitamin B_6 (50 mg/day) may be considered. Finally, individuals with diabetes, especially those with poor blood glucose control, are at high risk of zinc deficiency. At present, no clear guidelines exist for supplementation, but zinc supplements have been shown to help heal leg ulcers in uncontrolled studies of elderly subjects. Before taking any supplement, check with your doctor.

At one time, taking chromium supplements was popular among people with diabetes, but only a severe chromium deficiency can lead to elevated blood glucose levels, and people with diabetes do not tend to be chromium-deficient. In three double-blind studies, in which people with diabetes received a chromium supplement, the supplement had no effect on blood glucose control.

Those people who are at risk for not getting enough vitamins and minerals because of limited food choices or tolerance include the following groups: dieters consuming less than 1200 calories per day, vegans who omit all animal food, the elderly, pregnant and lactating women, women who have very heavy menstrual bleeding, people taking medications that affect vitamin or mineral status, or those who have ongoing kidney disease.

Aside from preventing deficiencies, certain vitamins and minerals are being considered protective against developing disease. Antioxidants such as vitamins A, C, and E, and selenium, for example, may prevent fats in the blood from oxidizing and then depositing in the wall of the arteries. And the B vitamin folic acid and vitamin B_6 may prevent heart disease by reducing homocysteine levels in the blood. Homocysteine is an intermediate substance produced during the breakdown of two amino acids, a process requiring several B vitamins. Although homocysteine is toxic to the blood vessel walls and is therefore a risk factor for heart disease, it is not normally present in the blood. If there is a genetic inability to process it, certain B vitamins may help, B_6 and folic acid in particular.

Many people are taking these different types of supplements as pills, or as additives to their foods. You must discuss vitamin and mineral supplementation with your doctor or health care practitioner. While it's true, theoretically, that it is possible to meet the recommended dietary allowances of various nutrients by eating a balanced diet including a wide variety of foods, many of us don't consume such a diet on a regular day-to-day basis. Surveys bear this out, showing less-than-adequate intake of fresh fruits and vegetables, as well as dairy products in particular, resulting in lower intakes of such nutrients as vitamin A, vitamin C, and calcium. Even people who consistently eat a healthy low-fat diet often take vitamin supplements as a sort of "insurance," to make certain they're getting the proper level of vitamins and minerals.

Limit Alcohol

Alcohol intake is permitted in moderation for people with diabetes. If you choose to drink, you'll do best to drink moderately. Whether you are on insulin or not, two drinks once or twice a week are all that are recommended.

There are certain precautions that people with diabetes should consider. First, because alcohol causes the blood sugar to drop, it's important to eat food when drinking. Do not skip meals or snacks. Even if your blood glucose levels are high at bedtime, if you've been drinking alcohol, you should eat your bedtime snack because alcohol may lower the blood glucose level during sleep. This hypoglycemic effect may last for up to twelve hours after you drink. ***Beware of alcohol's ability to throw off your blood glucose control in general.*** If you have frequent hypoglycemic reactions, you'll do best to avoid alcohol.

Excessive alcohol consumption may cause other problems beyond hypoglycemia. It is notorious for raising triglyceride levels in some people with diabetes. Since it is a concentrated source of calories, it can also lead to weight gain and the elevated cholesterol levels that are a consequence of being overweight.

Alcohol is actually absorbed like a fat, and some dietitians recommend that their patients who follow the diabetic exchanges substitute alcohol for a fat exchange.

THINKING IT THROUGH

Over the years I've found that those who are most successful in adopting new and improved eating habits are those who carefully consider each change they make. Begin now to set realistic goals for a given time period. In the following chapters, you'll find supporting information you can use to achieve those goals.

CHAPTER 2

UNDERSTANDING THE CARBOHYDRATE CONNECTION

Many people think of carbohydrates as the potato in the meat-and-potato diet. But carbohydrates are a lot more than just bread, pasta, and bananas. Carbohydrates make up a huge range of foods, from table sugar to rolled oats, and like most things in life, they range from simple to complex.

Carbohydrates are our main source of energy and should form the basis of all our diets, whether we have diabetes or not. The amount of carbohydrates in your plan will vary, but expect around half of your calories to come from these sources. The exact amount will depend on your calorie need, blood glucose control, and lipid levels, and will be determined by your doctor or dietitian.

There are four different types of carbohydrates: sugars, starches, fiber, and sugar alcohols. The simplest carbohydrates are made up of one or two sugar or glucose molecules. Starches, or complex carbohydrates, are larger molecules, called complex because they are made of long chains of glucose molecules, more than a hundred in many cases. Fiber is also complex in chemical structure with long molecules. But unlike starches, fibers cannot be digested. As you'll see, these indigestible fibers in foods like whole grains, fresh fruit, and vegetables play numerous important roles in the body. Finally, sugar alcohols are sugars that are only partially metabolized and therefore contribute fewer calories to our bodies than regular sugar.

The digestive process breaks down both the simple and complex carbohydrates into glucose for absorption from the small intestine. The glucose then is distributed by the bloodstream to the muscle cells for fuel, and to the liver for storage in fat cells. It is a commonly held belief that sugars in foods, both added and naturally occurring, are rapidly absorbed and lead to hyperglycemia and increased need for insulin. However, as outlined in the New Guidelines in chapter 1, recent studies show that, gram per gram, simple sugars like table sugar do not raise blood glucose any more quickly than do other carbohydrates, like bread, potatoes, or pasta.

Many factors influence how quickly a food is digested. First, keep in mind that we tend to eat mixed meals with several different foods, not just one food. It may take more time for the body to digest a meal with a large amount of fat or fiber or lots or raw foods. Your blood glucose level at the time you eat and how much diabetes medication is in your body can also play a significant role in how quickly the food raises blood glucose levels.

Here's the bottom line: The total amount of carbohydrates, as well as the total amount of food eaten, has more of an effect on blood glucose levels than the source of the carbohydrate. This chapter reviews the many sources of carbohydrates and helps you effectively manage them in your diet so you'll have an easier time keeping your blood glucose levels in the proper range. By eating the right amount of complex carbohydrates, you can learn how to make room for a little dessert.

START WITH STARCHES

Starches include breads, cereals, pasta, muffins, crackers, legumes, starchy vegetables (like potatoes, peas, and corn), and other vegetables. They are the ideal type of carbohydrate for all of us because they are a good source of glucose, the body's fuel source. Starches also contribute fiber and vitamins and minerals, and they have very little fat, saturated fat, or cholesterol. Of course, they do raise your blood glucose more than meats and fats, so you must pay special attention to the portion size. If you eat more than is recommended in your plan, you'll need to adjust your medication or your exercise or both. You'll see just how to work these tasty foods into your diet in chapter 3, which discusses carbohydrate counting.

If you follow nutrition in the news media, you may have noticed that starches or complex carbohydrates, as they are now known, have had a history of going in and out of fashion over the last several decades. In the seventies, many people believed that starches were "fattening," a misconception that has resurfaced (as trends often do) in the nineties. If you wanted to lose weight, you stopped eating bread and potatoes. The fact is, blaming an individual food for extra pounds is too simplistic. It's the total quantity of calories that counts. When we eat beyond our calorie needs, whether it's the bread or the butter, it will lead to excess body weight.

Let's take another look at why starches were thought to be "fattening." One reason is that starches were generally served laden with fat: cream sauce on pasta, butter on bread, and potatoes fried in oil. These added fats generally doubled or even tripled the calories of the starch. The second reason starches seemed troublesome is that these carbohydrates are likely to be overeaten. Have you ever been at a restaurant and eaten too much bread or tortilla chips before your meal arrived? Or have you been served a heaping plate of pasta, with or without a high-fat sauce, and ended up cleaning your plate and walking (or waddling) away feeling stuffed to the gills? It's easy to do. That's why the main focus of your meal plan is being aware of carbohydrates. It's what raises blood sugar, and it's easy to overeat.

The image of starches took a turn for the better in the eighties, when health professionals and the media convinced everyone (well, almost everyone) that fat was the culprit in the diets of those who were overweight, not starches. The tremendous attention given to fats did put an appropriate focus on the high-fat diets of many Americans. And there were positive results. People started to add less fat to their foods and choose less fatty meats and dairy products. Perhaps the most drastic response was from the packaged-food industry, which filled our grocery stores with reduced-fat and fat-free products. Many of these helped a lot of people eat less fat. But low-fat diets didn't always result in weight loss, because although the fats were reduced, the carbohydrates were often present in greater amounts, resulting in virtually no change in calories eaten. In addition, many people gave themselves permission to overeat such new fat-free goodies as muffins, cookies, cakes, and pies. After all, they reasoned, they're fat-free, not realizing that all those fat-free carbohydrates were not by any means calorie-free.

I've had many clients, particularly women with small frames, saying they had cut out all fat and were still struggling with their weight. After some probing, I'd discover they were overeating foods like pasta, rice, bagels, and fat-free baked goods. It was a case of too much of a good thing. Yes, high-fat diets contribute excess calories. But so, too, does eating four to six carbohydrate choices at a meal when you only needed two or three.

Eating too many complex carbohydrates is a particular problem in people with diabetes, because very low-fat, high-complex-carbohydrate diets can cause triglyceride levels to rise abnormally high. So what's the answer? ***People with diabetes must know how many carbohydrate choices per meal and per day they should eat (always emphasizing whole grains), and measure and keep track of their intake, on paper or in their heads.*** Yes, it can be a nuisance, but it will pay off in better health. And now that the rules about what you can eat have been liberalized, it's easier than ever to enjoy a wide-ranging and appealing diet that will make you feel better today and tomorrow.

DON'T FORGET TO EAT YOUR VEGETABLES

If you're like most Americans, you depend heavily on foods such as breads, rice, and pastas for carbohydrates. The more you eat, the greater the rise in your blood sugar. But there's an easy way to counter that problem. Just give vegetables a more prominent role on your plate. Consider that a cup of broccoli, for example (5 grams of carbohydrate and 25 calories), causes less of a rise in blood sugar than an equal amount of pasta (30 grams of carbohydrate and nearly 200 calories).

Many vegetables have so few carbohydrates and calories per serving that they are considered "free" foods when carbohydrate counting (eaten in reasonable amounts, of course). Among these foods are cabbage, celery, cucumber, green onions, lettuce, mushrooms, spinach, tomatoes, cauliflower, and zucchini. For a more complete rundown, see the American Dietetic Association's Exchange Lists for Meal Planning. The added bonus is that these foods are also high in vitamins, minerals, and fiber. They provide a modest addition of protein, and a negligible amount of fat, if any. However, not all vegetables are free foods. Corn, peas, potatoes, and winter squash are some examples of this group. Although they are vegetables, their carbohydrate content qualifies them to be counted as starches. They provide great variety in the diet, which helps to assure a good balance of vitamins, minerals, and fiber.

FIND THE FIBER

Any food that is plant-based contains fiber. Foods derived from animal sources such as meat, dairy products, and fats do not contain fiber. Fiber is not a single thing—it's a hodgepodge of substances, including celluloses, hemicelluloses, lignins, pectins, and more. In order to get the benefits of all the different fibers, it's best to have an eating pattern based on a variety of vegetables, fruits, and cereals along with beans and whole grains. The fibers in foods are divided into two main categories—those that are soluble in water and those that are not.

Soluble fiber: The ads for oatmeal proclaim that oats lower cholesterol, which may reduce the risk of heart disease. And it's true! Oats contain a fiber called beta glucan that acts like an army of little sponges to help soak up cholesterol and take it out of the body. Research suggests that 3 grams of soluble fiber per day may lower cholesterol levels by 5 to 6 percent, depending on your starting blood cholesterol. To get the 3 grams from oatmeal, you must eat ¾ cup dry oatmeal or 1½ cups cooked oatmeal. This is three carbohydrate choices, and if that's more than your limit at breakfast, try the hot oat bran cereal, which provides beta glucan in a more concentrated form. Just one cup of cooked oat bran provides the 3 grams of soluble fiber.

Other foods that contain soluble fiber include legumes such as beans and peas, as well as certain fruits and vegetables. However, not all soluble fiber contains beta glucan. Most of the research has been done on oats, so that's what we know best, but it appears that barley and rye may also contain beta glucan, the water-soluble fiber that binds with cholesterol in the intestine and prevents it from being absorbed into the bloodstream. The type of soluble fiber in fruits and vegetables probably does not have the same cholesterol-lowering effect. They do, however, contain valuable vitamins and minerals and should also be included in the diet.

Insoluble fiber: This type of fiber, which can be found in wheat and corn bran, whole grains, and some vegetables such as corn, peas, green beans, and broccoli, is most likely to help one keep regular bowel habits and prevent constipation. Because this fiber increases the bulk of the stool, the elimination process happens more quickly and easily. Such fiber also reduces the risk of colon cancer by diluting carcinogens and, again, shortening the time it takes to remove the stool from the body, giving any carcinogen less time to act.

It was once thought that insoluble fibers might also help to control blood glucose levels. However, more recent studies indicate that the amount of fiber required to achieve that result is higher than what one would normally eat. According to Susan Dopart Diercks, M.S., R.D., a nutrition and exercise consultant in Santa Monica, California, blood glucose can have a mind of its own, and it's not always easy to predict the response. "Different people may vary in their reactions to the same foods," says Diercks. "Potatoes may cause more of a rise in one person and rice may cause a greater increase in someone else."

The different reactions of blood sugars to different kinds of carbohydrates may be a result of several factors, including the fat and fiber content of the meal, lots of raw foods in the meal that take more time to digest, and eating slowly. The amount of your blood glucose level at the time of the meal and the amount of diabetes medication also have an impact on how high a food causes your blood glucose to rise.

So when you test your blood glucose after a meal, you may discover a different effect from eating 100 percent whole-grain bread versus white bread, or from eating an orange as opposed to drinking 4 ounces of orange juice. There are many good reasons to choose the higher fiber option as mentioned above, and if it has a positive effect on your blood glucose, consider it a bonus!

Achieving a high-fiber diet: Most experts recommend a fiber intake of 20 to 35 grams a day (most Americans get only around 10 grams of fiber per day) from both soluble and insoluble sources. Increase your fiber gradually instead of making drastic changes. Many of my clients have been able to double their fiber intake by making simple substitutions. Here are some ways to increase the fiber in your diet:

- Have oatmeal or other whole-grain cereals at breakfast.
- Choose whole-grain breads, corn tortillas, corn bread, rye bread, and pumpernickel bread.
- Eat brown rice instead of white rice.
- Eat more vegetables beyond salad greens, including broccoli, carrots, cauliflower, cabbage, zucchini, and green beans.
- Eat legumes several times a week. Try split pea or black bean soup, make a lentil salad, or simply top your green salad with a few garbanzo beans.
- Choose fresh fruits (unpeeled, when possible) rather than fruit juices or canned fruit.

Some people choose to take a fiber supplement, such as Metamucil or other fiber-filled drinks. These can be helpful in relieving constipation if regular foods aren't enough. According to Judith Marlett, Ph.D., R.D., a professor of nutritional sciences at the University of Wisconsin, Madison, most of the foods that contain fiber only contain small amounts. The best way to increase fiber intake and at the same time get all the vitamins and minerals you need is to eat more servings of fiber-rich foods. Try to vary your choices. But take note: adding a concentrated fiber source to a diet of limited variety may produce a higher-fiber diet, but the total diet may not be nutritionally adequate.

The maximum amount of fiber that is tolerable has never been determined, although over 50 grams may cause gastrointestinal discomfort in some individuals. As you work toward increasing the fiber in your diet, drink plenty of water to help prevent this.

Eat a combination of soluble and insoluble fibers to receive all the benefits (the chart below outlines these two kinds of fibers). Since people with diabetes have a higher risk of heart disease, they may tend to overemphasize the cholesterol-lowering oat products. But don't rely on a large bowl of cereal in the morning for *all* your fiber. Although that's a good start, ignoring the wheat products is not a good idea—you'll miss out on their protective effects. As you can see from the chart beginning on the facing page, some foods contain both types of fiber (such as legumes, oatmeal, and cab-

ALL FIBER IS NOT THE SAME

The Differences Between Soluble and Insoluble Fiber
Soluble and insoluble fiber are the two basic types of dietary fiber important for good health.

Soluble Fiber	Insoluble Fiber
• Dissolves in water and is partially absorbed into the bloodstream through the lower digestive tract.	• Does not dissolve in water and is not readily absorbed by the body.
• Lowers blood cholesterol levels by preventing absorption of cholesterol-like particles in the digestive tract.	• Promotes regularity and helps bowel function.
• Prolongs digestion, providing energy over longer spans of time.	• Stimulates smooth, efficient movement of food through the digestive system.
• Found in oats, beans, and other legumes, barley, and some fruits.	• Found in wheat bran, whole-grain products, oats, most vegetables, and fruits.

bage). Here you can kill two birds with one stone, as they say. Some of the recipes in this book that contain both include Blueberry Corn Muffins, Baked Oatmeal, Colcannon (mashed potatoes with cabbage), White Bean or Lentil Soup, Two-Bean Burritos, and Lentil Salad with Goat Cheese and Sun-Dried Tomatoes.

Try to consume 4 to 5 choices a day of fiber-containing foods. Vary your choices. Remember, both types of fiber provide a sensation of fullness after a meal, which may help counteract overeating. The chart below shows some common foods and the kinds of fibers they contain.

Fiber Content of Commonly Eaten Foods

Food	Serving Size	Soluble Fiber (grams)	Insoluble Fiber (grams)	Total Fiber (grams)
Grains				
Barley, pearled, cooked	½ cup	1.2	2.7	3.9
Bread, white	1 slice	0.2	0.6	0.8
Bread, whole wheat	1 slice	0.3	2.2	2.5
Corn bread	2½″ square	0.2	2.1	2.3
Oat bran, uncooked	½ cup dry	3.0	5.0	8.0
Oatmeal, cooked	1 cup	1.9	1.8	3.7
Rice, brown, cooked	⅓ cup	0	0.6	0.6
Rice, white, cooked	⅓ cup	0	0.2	0.2
Shredded Wheat	1 biscuit	0.3	2.4	2.7
Pasta	½ cup	0.2	0.8	1.0
Wheat bran, All-bran	½ cup	1.0	11.0	12.0
Fruits				
Apple with skin	1 small	0.4	2.6	3.0
Banana	1 small	0.5	1.3	1.8
Cantaloupe	1 cup	0.2	1.0	1.2
Orange	1 small	0.5	1.7	2.2
Grapes	17 small	0	0.8	0.8
Peach with skin	1 medium	1.0	2.0	3.0
Pear with skin	1 medium	0.7	3.9	4.6
Grapefruit, peeled	½ medium	0.3	1.1	1.4
Strawberries	1¼ cups	0.8	2.5	3.3

Food	Serving Size	Soluble Fiber (grams)	Insoluble Fiber (grams)	Total Fiber (grams)
Vegetables				
Broccoli, cooked	½ cup	0.2	1.7	1.9
Carrots, raw or cooked	1 medium or ½ cup	0.4	1.5	1.9
Cauliflower, cooked	½ cup	0.2	1.0	1.2
Corn, whole-kernel, cooked	½ cup	0.1	1.5	1.6
Green beans, drained	½ cup	0.3	1.2	1.5
Potato, baked, with skin	1 small (3 oz.)	0.5	1.5	2.0
Tomato, raw	1 average	0.2	0.6	0.8
Lettuce, leaf or iceberg	1 cup, shredded	0	0.7	0.7
Legumes				
Black-eyed peas, cooked	½ cup	0.2	2.3	2.5
Kidney beans, cooked	½ cup	1.0	3.5	4.5
Lima beans, cooked	⅔ cup	0.7	3.9	4.6
Peas, green, cooked	½ cup	0.3	2.8	3.1
Pinto beans, cooked	½ cup	0.2	2.9	3.1
Great Northern beans, cooked	½ cup	0.3	7.9	8.2

Source: J. A. Marlett and T-F. Cheung, "Data Base and Quick Methods of Assessing Typical Dietary Fiber Intake Using Data for 228 Commonly Consumed Foods," *Journal of American Dietetic Association* (1997).

A SWEETER LIFE FOR THOSE WITH DIABETES

Previously, ice cream, cookies, and other sweets were considered off-limits to people with diabetes. ***Now research has consistently shown that common table sugar and other sugars when consumed separately or as part of a meal or snack do not have a greater impact on blood glucose levels than other car-bohydrates.*** These advances in understanding the effects of different foods on blood glucose have made sweet foods an acceptable part of the diabetes meal plan. Just make sure you include them according to the guidelines: Eat sweets in small portions occasionally and learn what they do to your blood glucose.

If you're planning to have a dessert after dinner, eliminate the starch or adjust the amount of starch you eat with your entree. You could have, for example, a piece of chicken or fish and a salad and/or a vegetable, passing on the potato, rice, or pasta. By doing that, you've made more room for dessert. If you do include sweets in your diet, it is still a good idea to keep them limited.

Most sweets—ice cream, cakes, pies, cookies, and candy bars—also have fats. It's the fats that add most of the extra calories. If you need to lose weight or have trouble with blood fats, sweets can cause problems for you.

You may know that sugar comes in many forms and is called many different names on food labels. A product may claim "no sugar added" while it still contains sugarlike products such as high-fructose corn syrup, fructose, corn syrup, honey, lactose, maltose, mannitol, sorbitol, xylitol, or molasses. All of these contain sugar and your guide will be the carbohydrate listing on the label. Each 15 grams is counted as a carbohydrate choice. Sugars are divided into two categories, those with calories (caloric) and those with no or negligible calories (noncaloric), called sugar substitutes. Here's a review of both.

Fructose

The naturally occurring sugar in fruit and honey is called fructose. Fructose has a lower glycemic response, a relative measure of how food raises blood glucose. But this fact does not make fructose more or less recommended as a sweetener. Fructose, honey, and fruit juice concentrates raise blood glucose just as white sugar does. Don't be fooled by the familiar claim on baked goods and frozen desserts stating that they are "fruit-juice sweetened with no sugar added." The nutrition guidelines say that one is no better than the other. They have about the same number of calories and, other than fructose, raise blood glucose at a similar rate. Although fructose does raise blood glucose more slowly, some evidence exists that it may also raise blood cholesterol levels, a high price to pay.

Sucrose

Sucrose is the common table sugar so familiar to us all. Made of sugar-cane or sugar beets, it is available granulated, cubed, or powdered and provides calories without nutrients. Now that you know that gram for gram, table sugar does not raise the blood glucose any more quickly than do other carbohydrates, like cereal, bread, or pasta, you can make your choice about how to spend your carbohydrate budget. You'll want to base your decision on your personal diabetes goals. If your blood sugar is not in good control and your glycated hemoglobin is higher than you want it to be, pass on the sweets. If you need to lose weight, be sure to budget for the sweets so that eating them does not put you over your calorie limit. And finally, if your blood fats are elevated, particularly your triglycerides, you may want to limit sweets. When you eat a sweet, you may want to test your blood sugar to see what effect it has. You might find that the same quantity of ice cream has less effect than frozen yogurt. That could be because the ice cream has more fat, which can slow the rise of blood glucose, even though the frozen yogurt has more carbohydrates.

Sugar Alcohols

The sugar alcohols, including sorbitol and mannitol, are chemically reduced carbohydrates, commonly used as sweeteners in products like chewing gum, toothpaste, and mouthwash because they provide a cooling effect in the mouth and they don't promote tooth decay.

Sugar alcohols are not widely used in other foods because they are only about half as sweet as sucrose and too much would be required in order to reach the level of sweetness we expect in certain foods. That means that if you replaced sugar with sugar alcohols, you'd be consuming more calories and would be more likely to experience some side effects, such as minor intestinal problems.

Sugar Substitutes

Although common table sugar is now acceptable as part of the diabetes meal plan under the new guidelines, you may still want to keep low-calorie, sugar-free foods and beverages around as part of your strategy for keeping blood sugars in line. Since they generally provide no carbohydrates that need to be counted, there is more room in the diet for other carbohydrate sources of one's choosing.

Some individuals have come to prefer the substitute to the real thing. Many of my clients prefer diet soft drinks over regular soft drinks, would rather sweeten their coffee with a sugar substitute, and are perfectly content with artificially sweetened yogurt, pudding, and frozen desserts. This satisfies their sweet tooth without counting as a carbohydrate choice. The chart below shows the carbohydrates you'll save if you continue to use your favorite sugar substitute.

Carbohydrates Saved by Using Sugar-free Products

Product	Carbohydrates (g)	Carbohydrates (g) with Sugar Substitute
Soft drink (12 oz.)	35	0
Dry mix lemonade (1 cup)	17	0 to 2
Black coffee (1 cup) with		
1 teaspoon sugar	5	0
Strawberry yogurt (1 cup)	32	18
Vanilla ice cream (½ cup)	14	11
Gelatin dessert (½ cup)	19	0
Chocolate pudding (½ cup)	23	8

Sugar substitutes on the market include saccharin, aspartame, and acesulfame-K.

Saccharin

One of the sweeteners that's been around for over 100 years is saccharin, popular because it is 300 times sweeter than sugar. Since it is not broken down by the body and is excreted in the urine, it provides sweetness without calories. It comes in liquid, powder, or tablet form, and can be found under many brand names, beginning with the most popular Sweet'n Low®, and also Sprinkle Sweet®, Sweet-10®, Sugar Twin®, and Weight Watchers® Sweet'ner. Saccharin is heat-stable and used by food manufacturers in many products, including beverages, baked goods, jams, processed fruits, salad dressings, and sauces.

For more than 50 years, saccharin was the mainstay of diabetic diets. Then, in a 1972 study, rats were fed exceedingly high doses of saccharin (the equivalent of 1250 cans of diet soda a day) and they developed bladder tumors. In response, the FDA took saccharin off the list of food additives "generally recognized as safe." At that point, saccharin was the only artificial sweetener on the U.S. market—and there was a public outcry from people with diabetes and others. That study has now been widely discounted and saccharin is back on the market. Over 30 human studies and 14 animal studies have found no harm in using saccharin. In fact, a recent 23-year study with monkeys done at the University of Nebraska found no evidence that saccharin causes cancer or tumors of any kind.

Aspartame

Aspartame is an artificial sweetener composed of two amino acids: aspartic acid and phenylalanine. It is very low in calories and tastes very similar to sugar. Since it is about 180 times sweeter than sugar, only a small amount of it must be used to obtain the same sweetness of sugar, resulting in an insignificant number of calories.

NutraSweet® is the trade name for one manufacturer's line of products that contain aspartame. It is sold in a powdered form that uses a filler with carbohydrates and calories. There are currently four different products from the NutraSweet company made of aspartame. The most popular are the Equal packets, each with the sweetening power of 2 teaspoons of sugar. For convenience, this product can be purchased in tablet form or in a pouch called Equal Measure®. Most recently, the company has come out with Equal Spoonful® which comes in a jar and measures just like sugar. Its formula is less concentrated, so it can be substituted teaspoon for teaspoon for sugar.

Equal can be used nicely to sweeten beverages or top fruit. Because it tends to break down when heated, it is somewhat limited in baking. Prolonged cooking, probably over twenty minutes, at high heat levels may result in some loss of sweetness. It works best in stovetop cooking, because it can be added after foods are heated. The recipe for Lemon Tart in the dessert chapter, for example, can be sweetened with Equal after the filling has thickened and cooled, and it is the best lemon tart I've ever tasted. However, I've tried NutraSweet unsuccessfully with cookies and muffins.

According to the manufacturer, there are many recipes in which Nutra-Sweet can be used for baking. For a free collection of recipes write to the NutraSweet Center, listed in Resources. NutraSweet is used in over 6000 products, including sugar-free soft drinks and gum.

As with saccharin, the safety of aspartame has also been questioned. Court rulings and governmental agencies have generally agreed that if you have a sensitivity or negative reaction to it, of course it makes sense to avoid it. Since NutraSweet contains phenylalanine, it should not be used by persons with phenylketonuria (PKU), a rare disease.

Acesulfame-K

Acesulfame-K (also called Ace-K; K is the symbol for potassium) is a noncaloric artificial sweetener that is 200 times sweeter than sugar. It was approved for use in the United States in 1988. The big advantage of Ace-K is that it retains its sweetness when heated, so it can be used for cooking and baking. However, it does not impart the correct texture to baked goods when used alone, so some sugar is often used along with Ace-K. Many people report that it also has a slight bitter aftertaste when used in large amounts. It is sold in the United States as Sunett or Sweet One. Watch for it on food labels for tabletop sweeteners, dry beverage mixes, chewing gum, and dessert and pudding mixes, alone or in combination with calorie- and carbohydrate-containing sugars. It is now waiting to be approved for use in soft drinks, which is the biggest use of sweeteners.

How to Replace Sugar with Sugar Substitutes

Sugar	Aspartame	Saccharin	Acesulfame-K
2 tsp.	1 packet	⅕ tsp.	1 packet
1 tbs.	1½ packets	⅓ tsp.	1¼ packets
¼ cup	6 packets	3 packets	3 packets
⅓ cup	8 packets	4 packets	4 packets
½ cup	12 packets	6 packets	6 packets
⅔ cup	16 packets	8 packets	8 packets
¾ cup	18 packets	9 packets	9 packets
1 cup	24 packets	12 packets	12 packets

Cooking and Baking with Sugar Substitutes

The savings in carbohydrates and calories makes it tempting to start replacing *all* the sugar in recipes with sugar substitutes, but there are limitations to what these sweeteners can do. Sugar is a necessary component in many baked goods, such as breads, pastries, and cookies, not only for its flavor, but also for the texture and color it imparts. A chemical reaction takes place between sugar and other ingredients that does not occur with artificial sweeteners. Therefore, for best results in most recipes, try reducing the sugar used in the recipe and replacing the removed sugar with a substitute. By replacing only part of the sugar, you can maintain the texture-enhancing properties of the real sugar, and have the sweetness of a sugar substitute with fewer carbohydrates. Keep in mind that this may not work with all recipes, and a little trial and error will help you determine which recipes respond to the substitution best.

CHAPTER 3
CARBOHYDRATE COUNTING: YOUR KEY TO BETTER CONTROL

Calculating a diabetic meal plan comes easily to a dietitian but is often much harder for the individual or family to put into practice. While it may seem daunting to learn a new system, it's easier and will save time and energy in the long run, perhaps with better results. For many people, carbohydrate counting is an easier alternative to the somewhat complicated diabetes exchange lists.

Carbohydrate counting is based on the understanding that the carbohydrate in the food you eat is the main factor that continues to cause your blood sugars to increase after a meal. If you take in excess carbohydrate beyond what your body is able to respond to (either with or without diabetes medication), your blood glucose level will rise too high.

For example, a typical breakfast plan might include one slice of toast and one whole banana which equals 3 carbohydrate choices, or 45 grams of carbohydrate. If a person with diabetes usually ate this amount of food, but occasionally added ¾ cup of unsweetened cereal with a cup of milk, his blood sugar would rise much higher because of the additional carbohydrates. By counting how many carbohydrates you eat, you'll have a better idea of where your blood glucose is going.

The new nutritional guidelines lend themselves to carbohydrate counting. That's because **carbohydrate counting gives priority to the total amount of carbohydrate eaten, rather than the source of carbohydrate.** Therefore, one carbohydrate choice can be a starch, fruit, milk, or dessert at the serving size that supplies 15 grams of carbohydrate. *You begin to see how counting carbohydrates will help the person with diabetes liberalize their diet and still keep their blood sugar in line. For those who take insulin and have chosen intensive diabetes management using multiple daily insulin injections or an insulin pump, carbohydrate counting is especially useful.* In fact, it's been speculated that for people with diabetes who take insulin shots in particular, carbohydrate counting leads to tighter control of blood sugar than relying on exchange lists. But people with all types of diabetes can use this approach. It is even used by some of my patients who do not have diabetes but feel they've been overeating starches and want to manage carbohydrates in order to control their weight. The recipes in this book list carbohydrate values along with the exchange values, making them a welcome resource for all those who have switched over to carbohydrate counting. What follows is a brief review of just how to use carbohydrate counting to manage blood sugar levels.

BEGIN WITH A FOOD PLAN

You and your dietitian will decide how many carbohydrates you can eat each day and how to distribute the carbohydrate foods you eat among your daily meals and snacks. *Consistency is one of the most important factors in managing blood glucose. If you try to eat a similar amount of carbohydrates each day for breakfast, lunch, and so on, it will be easier for your body's insulin to do its job, helping glucose to enter the cells.* If you eat 45 grams of carbohydrates one day for lunch and the next day you eat 90 grams of carbohydrates, you'll need more insulin prior to the meal with more carbohydrates. Although you need not eat the same food, if you eat a similar *amount* of carbohydrate at each meal, it will help you to keep your blood glucose within the target range. That way, you can figure out the correct dose of insulin to keep your blood glucose in good control.

Your food plan will tell you either how many carbohydrate choices you can eat per meal or how many carbohydrate grams you can eat. Either way, 1 carbohydrate choice equals 15 grams of carbohydrate. In general, try to stay within 5 grams, plus or minus, of your carbohydrate goal at each meal and snack. For example:

1 carbohydrate choice = 15 grams of carbohydrate = ⅓ cup rice
2 carbohydrate choices = 30 grams of carbohydrate = ⅔ cup rice
3 carbohydrate choices = 45 grams of carbohydrate = 1 cup rice

A CASE IN POINT

At the age of 69, John was diagnosed with type II diabetes. Over the past 1½ years he and his dietitian have worked together to normalize his blood sugar levels. John is 6 feet 4 inches tall and he weighed 210 to 215 pounds when he first went to visit his dietitian. He was in fairly good shape from playing tennis four times a week, but his blood sugar levels were out of control. He decided he would learn how to count carbohydrates in order to improve them. He agreed to monitor his blood glucose four times a day.

In the beginning, John was eating a whole bagel for breakfast. Two hours after eating it, his blood sugar levels were 220. His dietitian suggested he weigh the bagel, and it turned out to be 4 ounces, or 4 carbohydrate choices. So the next day he tried eating only half of the bagel and adding an egg for a bit of protein and fat. Two hours after that breakfast, his blood sugar was 120. He learned that if he ate two carbohydrate choices instead of four and added protein, his blood sugar dropped to within the normal range. He found the Morningstar Farms Grillers, a vegetarian sausage with twice the protein of an egg and only 5 grams of carbohydrates, also worked as a substitute for the egg. He did not need a midmorning snack.

For lunch, John keeps his carbohydrate choices to 2 or 3. He prefers to eat a sandwich which he makes at home, but occasionally when he's out, he has a hamburger or a grilled chicken burger. If the bread or bun is big, over his goal of 2 or 3 ounces, he simply leaves some of it behind. It's a small price to pay for keeping blood sugars in the normal range.

His afternoon snack is a handful of nuts, about an ounce, or the amount in two small airline bags. This gives him fat, protein, and a half of a carbohydrate choice. Some days he substitutes a piece of beef jerky or a slice of low-fat cheese and a piece of fruit. Occasionally he likes to treat himself to two 1-ounce Snickers candy bars with about 15 grams of carbohydrates each. Two hours after eating them, he tests his blood sugar, and it is generally still in the normal range of 140 to 180. The highest his blood sugar goes up these days is 140. He is usually between 80 and 120 two hours after a meal.

For dinner, John's carbohydrate goal is 3 servings. He enjoys a pretty typical meal, including about 6 ounces meat, fish, or chicken, 1 cup of rice or 1½ cups pasta or a good-sized potato (about 9 ounces), the amount of carbohydrate equal to 3 servings, along with a vegetable and a salad.

In paying attention to what he eats, John has lost about 20 pounds, settling in at about 190. He added walking to his exercise regimen because the start-and-stop nature of tennis doesn't give him the optimal cardiac/aerobic benefit that a one-hour walk does. His hemoglobin A-1-C has gone from 13 down to a range of 5.3 to 7.2, indicating that his average blood sugar over a period of time is in the normal range.

PORTION SIZES

As you may already know, *accurately assessing portion sizes is very important if you're to be successful matching carbohydrate intake to insulin demand.* For example, ½ cup cooked oatmeal, ½ banana, ⅓ cup rice, and 1 cup milk are all one carbohydrate choice, or 15 grams of carbohydrates. Start by measuring your foods like cereals, pasta, and soups in measuring cups. Weigh such foods as fruits, breads, and baked goods on a kitchen scale. Your food label is likely to give both a weight and a volume measure so you can decide which measure to use.

With plenty of practice, you'll learn which portion sizes equal 15 grams of carbohydrates, and will be able to count your intake accordingly. You can then eyeball certain foods to estimate portion size, but it's still a good idea to check with a measure or scale from time to time, once a week or so.

DON'T FORGET BEVERAGES

In case you thought that beverages were just something to wash down the real food, think again. Any drink containing sugar raises your blood glucose, whether it comes from added sugar or natural fruit juice. Check the carbohydrate content of your drinks, including soda, juice, sweetened tea, or sports drinks by looking at the nutrition facts on the label.

IF YOU'VE GOT A SWEET TOOTH

And who doesn't? Just because you have diabetes, doesn't mean you're not going to have cravings that don't coincide with your perfectly balanced meal plan. While you aim for a balanced diet, you're probably going to continue to include sugary foods from time to time. Here's your chance to learn how to accommodate them with the least amount of disturbance of your blood sugar. Betty Brackenridge, a registered dietitian and diabetes educator from Learning Prescriptions in Gilbert, Arizona, has been using the carbohydrate counting system for many years. According to Betty, "I started using carbohydrate counting so my patients could enjoy their 'splurge foods' without sending their blood sugar sky high—way before sweets were smiled upon by all the diabetes diet experts. After all, high blood sugar is the enemy, not particular foods. A blood sugar level of 400 is equally harmful whether it came from a piece of pecan pie or a bowl of rice. Now we use carbohydrate counting as well to keep all foods in balance with insulin—the sweet and the not-so-sweet."

PROTEIN AND FAT

Just because we are focusing on counting carbohydrate to manage diabetes doesn't mean that you don't need to pay attention to how much protein and fat you eat. Remember, if you eat too much of anything—carbohydrate, protein, or fat—it will cause your blood sugar to go up. And in addition, common sense tells you that if you eat too much oil or meat, it will lead to weight gain. But immediately after a meal, you do not observe a rise in blood glucose from protein and fat the way you do from carbohydrates. That's because only 60 percent of protein and 10 percent of fat is converted to glucose, and this conversion takes longer than carbohydrate. Fat slows digestion of sugar and helps stabilize blood sugar. But it doesn't take very much fat to have this effect, and the best fat is monounsaturated, from olive or vegetable oils. For details on how much and what kind of fat to eat, refer to chapter 5. Your protein needs are reviewed in chapter 1 as part of the New Guidelines.

If you're familiar with the diabetic exchanges, they can help you estimate carbohydrate content of food. Just keep in mind that one carbohydrate choice is 15 grams of carbohydrate. Then round up or down to make it fit:

> 1 carbohydrate choice = 1 starch exchange (15 grams)
> or 1 fruit exchange (15 grams)
> or 1 milk exchange (12 grams)

The exchange lists for meal planning are listed in the Resources section at the back of this book.

Of course, life is not simple, and neither are foods. Most foods are combinations of carbohydrates, proteins, and fats. Here is a list of how they fit together:

	Carbohydrate	Protein	Fat
3 oz. lean meat	0	21	9
½ cup fruit	15	0	0
½ cup vegetable	5	2	0
8 oz. skim milk	12	8	0
⅓ cup black beans	15	3	0
⅓ cup rice	15	3	trace
½ cup pasta	15	3	trace
1 tablespoon peanut butter	6	7	8
1 teaspoon oil	0	0	5

The more you use the carbohydrate counting system, the more familiar you will become with the carbohydrate values of the foods you eat. Fortunately, most packaged foods are labeled. For example, you can check the nutrition facts panel on your cereal box. Weigh or measure how much cereal you put in your bowl and compare it to the amount listed on the label. Make the adjustment in your calculation. (See the example on the facing page.)

Although the nutrition panel lists the different types of carbohydrates, including fibers and sugars, for the purposes of carbohydrate counting, you need to pay attention only to total carbohydrate. Since 1¼ cups of oat bran equal 41 grams of carbohydrates, if you eat only half that amount, or about ⅔ cup, you'll be getting about 20 grams of carbohydrates, which is considered one carbohydrate choice.

WHEN A FOOD IS FREE

If a food has less than 5 grams of carbohydrates, it is labeled a "free" food, and is not counted against your carbohydrate allotment. An example of this is ½ cup of broccoli, which is 5 grams of carbohydrates. But if you eat 1½ cups of broccoli, that is 3 times 5 grams, or 15 grams, and then the broccoli is considered one carbohydrate choice, or 15 grams of carbohydrate. *Free foods have enough carbohydrate to affect your blood glucose*

Oatmeal Squares
Nutrition Facts

Serving Size 1 cup (56 g)

Servings Per Container about 8

Amount Per Serving

Calories 220   Calories from fat 25

	% Daily Value*
Total Fat 2.5 g	4%
Saturated Fat 0.5 g	2%
Polyunsaturated Fat 1 g	
Monounsaturated Fat 1 g	
Cholesterol 0 mg	
Sodium 260 mg	11%
Potassium 230 g	7%
Total Carbohydrate 43 g	14%
Other Carbohydrate 30 g	
Dietary Fiber 4 g	17%
Soluble Fiber 2 g	
Insoluble Fiber 2 g	
Sugars 9 g	
Protein 7 g	

levels when you eat large portions. Check the free foods listed with the exchange values in the back of this book, but be sure you are consuming them in the portions indicated.

One of my patients, Barbara, frequently ate the grilled vegetable salad at the Ivy, a popular Los Angeles restaurant. When she checked her blood glucose level two hours after that meal, the level was above her target range of 100 mg/dl (milligrams per deciliter) to 150 mg/dl. I asked her to bring the salad into my office at her next appointment so we could weigh and measure exactly how many carbohydrates it contained and how she should count it. (It was so delicious, it ended up as a recipe in the salad section of this book—see page 196). The salad consisted of a bed of romaine salad greens and cabbage, with 4 ounces of shrimp, ¼ cup corn, asparagus, zucchini, and tomato. The salad greens, cabbage, asparagus, zucchini, and tomato are usually considered free foods, with only 2 grams of carbohydrate per cup. But when we measured the amount of these vegetables in total, there were 7 cups, or 14 grams. Barbara used her own fat-free dressing back at the office, which she considered a free food. But the Nutrition Facts on the label of the dressing listed a serving size of 2 tablespoons, which included 10 grams of carbohydrate. Barbara was actually using 4 tablespoons of the dressing, which came out to 20 grams of carbohydrate, over 1 carbohydrate choice. Barbara used the ratio of 10 grams of carbohydrate for each single unit of regular insulin. Because she hadn't counted the salad greens and the accurate amount of dressing, she was short by 34 grams, or two carbohydrate choices, therefore requiring three additional units of regular insulin. By increasing her dose, Barbara was able to keep her blood glucose in the target range of 100 mg/dl to 150 mg/dl.

Carefully review your food intake, exercise, and post-meal blood glucose. Identify patterns in the ups and downs of your blood glucose and take action to correct the highs and the lows. Do you always have a high blood glucose after eating pizza? You may need to cut your pizza intake back by a slice and add a salad; or you may need to increase your insulin dose. We all overeat occasionally, and you can compensate with more insulin on occasion. But don't make a habit of it or you'll find your weight creeping up.

For those who have chosen intensive insulin diabetes management using multiple daily insulin injections or an insulin pump, you can use your food and blood glucose records to fine-tune your diabetes management by adjusting short-acting insulin according to anticipated carbohydrate intake and physical activity. This approach will need to be orchestrated by your own health care team, and is beyond the scope of this book.

In the Resources section in the back of the book, you'll find several publications that explain carbohydrate counting in greater detail and provide the carbohydrate content of foods.

CHAPTER 4

THE MENU PLANS: EVERYDAY EATING

Now that you have been introduced to carbohydrate counting, let's look at how we put food together for daily meal plans. *Each person should have his own personalized meal plan tailored to meet the foods he likes and the lifestyle he leads.* Your exercise and activity patterns directly affect the amount of carbohydrates you need at each meal. Figuring out how many carbohydrates you need takes into consideration meals eaten at home, those in restaurants, as well as snacks and the occasional feasts. *Your meal plan or pattern should be determined by a registered dietitian or a certified diabetes educator, who will work with you to determine how many carbohydrates, proteins, and fats you should eat at each meal.*

The meal plan in this book is based on the concept of carbohydrate counting, as described in the previous chapter, with a certain number of carbohydrate choices per meal. The carbohydrate choices are based on 15 grams of carbohydrate per choice, and on an even distribution of carbohydrates throughout the day. What follows is a seven-day menu plan which includes many of the recipes in this book, based on three levels—1200, 1500, and 1800 calories. These are meant to be helpful guides. Check with your dietitian to find the calorie level that is right for you.

All meals in these menus are combinations of carbohydrates, proteins, and fats. Carbohydrates provide about half of the calories needed per day, and they have the greatest impact on your blood sugar. That's why we count them. Protein makes up 15 to 20 percent of calories, and I've emphasized proteins low in saturated fat. The remaining calories are from fat, again emphasizing monounsaturated fats whenever possible. Even though I have kept the calories from fat low, if you need more calories and do not have a triglyceride or cholesterol problem, you can add monounsaturated or polyunsaturated fats such as nuts, olive oil, or avocados. As long as you don't eat beyond your calorie needs, you can probably eat these additional fats in moderation without raising fats in the blood. Most important, the carbohydrates must be distributed evenly throughout the day in both meals and snacks.

BREAKFAST

Breakfast literally means to "break the fast," and that has special significance to individuals with diabetes. It's important to start the day with a combination of foods that will keep your blood sugar in a good range throughout the morning. The correct balance of carbohydrates, protein, and fat at breakfast helps you maintain optimal blood sugars. Blood sugar and insulin levels are relatively low in the morning because your stomach is empty and your food is digested. This is particularly true if you have not overeaten the night before.

Always check your blood sugar in the morning. Sometimes the liver releases sugar during the night, which may account for an elevated blood sugar reading. Many of the typical breakfast foods such as toast, bagels, and hot or cold cereals are high in carbohydrates and low in fat and protein. They tend to digest fairly quickly and turn into glucose, raising your blood sugar. This lack of fat and protein in many breakfasts allows these foods to cause an even greater surge in blood sugar. Here's how: One of the nutritional virtues of fat is to slow down the pace of digestion in the stomach. When there is little or no fat in the gastrointestinal tract, these high-carbohydrate foods rush from the intestines into the blood as though they were race cars headed to the finish line, resulting in a rapid increase in blood sugars.

Protein has a different role, although, like fat, it also helps to stabilize the blood glucose level. The sugar or starch in your meal is converted almost entirely into glucose fairly quickly. Only about 60 percent of protein is converted to blood sugar, and it's converted more slowly. Protein plays an important role in blood sugar levels because of that delay. After your carbohydrates have been converted to energy, the protein kicks in to prevent your blood sugar from dropping.

Your breakfast should include a balance of carbohydrates, protein, and fat. Here are some combinations that might fit into your plan:

1. Cereal, fruit, milk
2. Cheese or cottage cheese, fruit, bread
3. English muffin, fruit, peanut butter, or cheese
4. Egg, egg white, or egg substitute, bread, fruit

The upcoming menus give seven specific examples of breakfast, and you'll find recipes for many of them in the book. By testing your blood sugar levels two hours after breakfast, you'll learn what suits your particular nutritional needs, and can adjust accordingly.

Some of my clients have observed that when their morning carbohydrate is fruit juice, their blood sugar may rise higher than if they have a slice of toast or a banana. Although carefully measuring your carbohydrate is always important, it is especially important at breakfast. If you eat too many carbohydrates at breakfast, your blood sugar is likely to remain high for too long in the day. How much you need to eat will vary, depending on your needs. If you're a small woman, you'll need to eat less than a tall man or a growing teenager. Again, your dietitian will help you to determine your calorie level.

LUNCH AND DINNER

The quantity and type of food eaten at lunch and dinner (or dinner and supper, as we call it back on the farm) should be the same. Depending again on your calorie need, you may have 3 to 4 ounces of protein and 3 to 4 carbohydrate choices. If you're a small woman, 2 or 3 carbohydrate choices may be enough. If you're a large man or an active teenager, you'll need more. Your plan will be your guide, and your blood sugar readings will confirm the need for changes.

SNACKS

Every person with diabetes is different. You may or may not need snacks at various times. If your blood sugar dips too low between meals, you'll need to include a snack. Test your blood sugar between meals and at bedtime to make the determination. Most likely, if your blood sugar is over 150 mg/dl percent, your health care practitioner will tell you that you don't need a snack. If you don't *need* a snack but *want* a snack, consider a non-caloric beverage or choose a food from the list of free foods on page 413. My client John enjoys a cup of low-sodium chicken broth mid-morning and finds it the perfect choice to tide him over till lunchtime. Figure out these numbers, and make your choice accordingly.

PORTION SIZES

Because carbohydrates are what cause the blood sugar to go up the most quickly, it is essential that they be measured. Check the lists to see examples of a carbohydrate choice containing 15 grams of carbohydrate. A piece of fruit may have more than 15 grams of carbohydrate. For instance, a 3-inch piece of banana has 15 grams and 8 strawberries has 15 grams. A larger fruit may be closer to 25 grams of carbohydrate. Learn your fruit servings and count them accordingly.

You'll also want to become familiar with portion sizes from the starch group. Some of the most common are rice (⅓ cup), pasta (½ cup), or bread (1 ounce). If you plan to eat 2 carbohydrate choices at dinner, then learn what ⅔ cup of rice or 1 cup of pasta looks like. Buy a scale to weigh the bread. If you do it often enough at home, you'll be better able to estimate accurately when you're eating out in a restaurant.

DAY ONE

	Calorie Level		
	1200	1500	1800
BREAKFAST			
Eggs and Spinach in	1	1 to 2	2
Pita★	½	1	2
Orange, 1 medium	1	1	1
Olive oil	0	1 tsp.	1 tsp.
LUNCH			
(Sandwich)★			
Bread	2	2	2
Avocado	¼	⅓	½
Low-fat Swiss cheese	2 oz.	2 oz.	2 oz.
Pimiento	1	1	1
Melon	0	½ cup	1 cup
DINNER			
Garlic Shrimp★	4 to 5	6 to 8	8
Cold Sesame Noodles★	¾ cup	1 cup	1 cup
Snow Pea/Yellow/Mushroom Salad★	1 cup	1 cup	1½ cups
Olive oil	1 tsp.	2 tsp.	2 tsp.
SNACK			
Hot air popcorn	3 cups	3 cups	6 cups
Sugar-free hot cocoa made with skim milk	8 oz.	8 oz.	8 oz.

Notes: Whether you use real eggs, egg substitute, or egg whites depends on your blood fats. Ask your dietitian or health care practitioner which is most suited to you. Pita bread varies in size. Make sure you read the label and count the number of carbohydrate choices. Avocados are a good source of monounsaturated fat, the kind that is preferred as a fat source. The sandwich incorporates several vegetables—including cucumber, bell pepper, and onion—all of which increase fiber, vitamins, minerals, and flavor. In the dinner, be aware that the way the noodles are cooked makes a difference in carbohydrate content. The longer pasta cooks, the more water it absorbs and the lower its carbohydrate count. One cup of al dente pasta contains 44 grams of carbohydrate, whereas 1 cup of pasta cooked until very tender contains only 32 grams carbohydrate.

★Recipes in book.

DAY TWO

	Calorie Level		
BREAKFAST	1200	1500	1800
Oatmeal★ (cooked in milk)	½ cup cooked	1 cup cooked	1 cup cooked
Milk, nonfat	1 cup	1 cup	1 cup
Raisins	0	2 tbs.	2 tbs.
LUNCH			
Lentil Soup★	¾ cup	1 cup	1½ cups
Lamb Meatballs★	2	2	3
Apple	1	1	1
DINNER			
Chicken Piccata★	1 breast (4 oz.)	1 breast (4 oz.)	1½ breasts (6 oz.)
Garlicky Seasoned Rice★	⅔ cup	⅔ cup	1 cup
Stir-fried Spinach★	1 cup	1 cup	1 cup
Additional olive oil	0	0	1 tsp.
SNACK			
Cereal	½ cup	½ cup	½ cup
Milk, nonfat	¾ cup	1 cup	1 cup
Banana	0	0	3-inch piece

Notes: Oatmeal contains soluble fiber that can help lower cholesterol. Cooking it in milk increases the protein, which helps level out blood sugars later in the morning. Lentil soup varies in its carbohydrate value, depending on how much water is added to the soup. Just remember, ⅓ cup of cooked lentils is a 15-gram carbohydrate serving. The spinach listed here is 11 grams of carbohydrates, and should therefore be counted as a carbohydrate.

★Recipes in book.

DAY THREE

	Calorie Level		
BREAKFAST	1200	1500	1800
Bagel (2 oz.)	½	1	1
Lox (smoked salmon) or ham	2 oz.	2 oz.	2 oz.
Cucumber Salad★ or sliced cucumber and tomato	Free	Free	Free
Light cream cheese	1 tbs.	2 tbs.	2 tbs.
LUNCH			
Corn, Chicken, and Noodle Soup★	2 cups	2 cups	2 cups
Saltine (or equivalent) crackers	0	0	6
1 carrot	1	1	1
1 orange	0	1	1
DINNER			
Cuban Picadillo★ or turkey with raisins	4 oz.	4 oz.	5 oz.
Tortilla, 8-inch	1	2	2
Zucchini sautéed in 1 teaspoon olive oil	¾ cup	¾ cup	1½ cups
SNACK			
Low-fat frozen yogurt	6 oz.	6 oz.	6 oz.
Nuts (almonds)	0	0	1 oz. or 24

Notes: Check the weight of your bagel. If it is 3 ounces instead of 2, count it as 3 carbohydrate choices, or slice it in thirds and eat only 2 slices, saving the remainder for later. Frozen yogurt varies widely from brand to brand in its nutritional attributes. If you choose one that is sweetened with a nonnutritive sweetener such as aspartame, you'll have fewer carbohydrates. Just determine your portion size from your food plan.

★*Recipes in book.*

DAY FOUR

	Calorie Level		
	1200	1500	1800
BREAKFAST			
Cottage cheese (1% fat)	½ cup	½ cup	1 cup
Fruit, peach	1	1	1
Peanuts, dry roasted	1 oz.	1 oz.	1 oz.
LUNCH			
Ceviche★ with diced avocado	¾ cup	1 cup	1 cup
Saltine crackers	6	6	6
Viennese Brownies★	1	1	2
DINNER			
Easy Roast Chicken★	4 oz.	4 oz.	4 oz.
Potato	1 cup	1½ cups	1½ cups
Carrot	1	2	2
Onion	Free	Free	Free
SNACK			
Graham cracker squares	3	3	6
Milk or yogurt, nonfat	1 cup	1 cup	1 cup

Notes: One ounce of peanuts provides 6 grams of carbohydrates, 6 grams of protein, and 14 grams of fat, mostly monounsaturated. Still, that fat content contributes a significant amount of calories, and therefore nuts should be eaten in moderate portions as listed here. The brownies included at lunch prove how the new guidelines can work, allowing a concentrated sweet as part of a meal while staying within the total carbohydrate goal.

★Recipes in book.

DAY FIVE

	Calorie Level		
BREAKFAST	**1200**	**1500**	**1800**
French Toast★	1 slice	2 slices	2 slices
Maple syrup (reduced-calorie, no sugar added)	2 tbs.	¼ cup	¼ cup
Milk	1 cup	1 cup	1 cup
LUNCH			
Chinese Chicken Salad★	2½ cups	3½ cups	3½ cups
Roll or tortilla or cracker	1 serving	1 serving	2 servings
Fruit, mandarin oranges	½ cup	½ cup	½ cup
DINNER			
Japanese Glazed Salmon★	3 oz.	4 oz.	6 oz.
Seasoned Sticky Rice★	⅔ cup	1 cup	1 cup
Steamed asparagus (12 spears)	1 cup	1 cup	1 cup
Olive oil for asparagus	0	1 tsp.	1 tsp.
SNACK			
Peanuts	1 oz.	1 oz.	2 oz.
Fruit	1	1	1

Notes: Two tablespoons of S & W reduced-calorie, no sugar added syrup contains 15 grams of carbohydrate, so is counted as 1 carbohydrate choice. If you elect to use real maple syrup, the same amount has closer to 2 carbohydrate choices. When you eat a large salad, as is on the menu for lunch, it is generally recommended that you count the greens as 1 carbohydrate choice, unlike when you eat a smaller, dinner-sized salad, in which case it need not be counted and is considered free. The message here is that large portions of free foods must be counted.

★Recipes in book.

DAY SIX

	Calorie Level		
BREAKFAST	1200	1500	1800
Cereal	1 carb.	2 carb.	2 carb.
Fruit	1	1	1
Milk, nonfat	½ cup	1 cup	1 cup
LUNCH			
Tuna Salad Sandwich★			
Tuna	3 oz.	4 oz.	4 oz.
Bread	2	2	2
Fat-free mayonnaise	Free	Free	Free
1 tsp. olive oil	1	1	1
Vegetable	Free	Free	Free
Fruit	1	1	1
DINNER			
Barbecue Chicken Pizza★	1 slice	1½ slices	2 slices
Basic green salad with	1 to 2 cups	1 to 2 cups	1 to 2 cups
Vinaigrette	2 tbs.	2 to 3 tbs.	3 tbs.
SNACK			
Blueberry Corn Muffin★	1	1	1
Milk	½ cup	1 cup	1 cup
Ham, chicken, or turkey	0	0	2 oz.

Notes: Cereals vary in their carbohydrate content. For example, a 1½-cup serving of puffed wheat or puffed rice has 15 grams of carbohydrate, or 1 carbohydrate choice. A ½-cup serving of bran flakes also provides 1 carbohydrate choice. Check the label of your brand. If you decide to order out for pizza instead of making your own, request that your pizza be topped with vegetables such as onion, garlic, bell pepper, or sliced tomatoes. Order a low-fat protein like chicken rather than pepperoni or sausage. Order light or low-fat cheese if it's available, or simply order less cheese to keep the fat content in check. Limit yourself to one small slice, or two at the most, and round out the meal with a salad.

★Recipes in book.

DAY SEVEN

	Calorie Level		
BREAKFAST	1200	1500	1800
Blueberry Muffin★	0	1	1
or English muffin	½	1	1
(+ 1 tsp. margarine)			
Milk, nonfat	1 cup	1 cup	1 cup
Cheese, low fat	1 oz.	2 oz.	2 oz.
LUNCH			
Curried Turkey Salad★	1 cup	2 cups	2½ cups
Roll	1	1	1
DINNER			
Spaghetti Pomodoro★			
Pasta	½ cup	¾ cup	1 cup
Sauce	¼ cup	⅓ cup	½ cup
Chicken sausage	1 oz.	2 oz.	3 oz.
Basic Green Salad with Balsamic Vinaigrette★	1 cup	1 cup	1 cup
SNACK			
Crackers, saltines	6	6	12
Peanut butter	1 tbs.	2 tbs.	2 tbs.
Milk, nonfat	½ cup	½ cup	1 cup

Notes: See the note for pasta, Day 1, to determine portion size. When eating pasta, include a protein in the meal as well. Look for a sausage that is lower in fat, and remember that just because it's made from chicken doesn't necessarily mean it has less fat.

★*Recipes in book.*

MENUS FOR ALL OCCASIONS

Here you will find a wide variety of menus. Some are perfect for easy weekday family meals, while others are great for special celebrations. The carbohydrate content of each meal is listed in grams and in choices to help you determine how it will fit into your meal plan. By following the menus, you will achieve a good balance of carbohydrate, protein, and fat, although you'll have to adjust portion sizes to meet your individual carbohydrate and calorie allowance. Unless otherwise indicated, the menu items are based on a single serving of a recipe. Non-recipe items include a specific portion size.

If you have type II diabetes, weight loss is likely to be a top priority for you. Using the menus here won't help bring your blood glucose under control if you eat too much food. The recipes in this book are all low in fat to help you lose weight and to allow your body to more effectively use the insulin it is producing. These menus focus on eliminating or greatly reducing high-fat, high-calorie items and replacing them with lower fat foods. High-fiber foods may help you feel more full and still lose weight because you are consuming fewer overall calories. Those people who are on insulin must pay attention to specific eating times. Although low blood glucose levels are less likely in those taking oral hypoglycemic agents, reactions can occur if you eat irregularly or skip meals.

DINNER FOR 6 OR 8

Poached Salmon with Tomato-Lemon Sauce (page 218) served over
   Sautéed Cucumbers (page 333)
Warm Spinach Salad (page 189)
Saffron-Scented Basmati Rice (page 339)
Chocolate-Orange Biscotti (page 377)

CALORIES, 630; CARBOHYDRATES, 63 GRAMS; CARBOHYDRATE CHOICES, 4.

AL FRESCO DINNER

Grilled Fish with Pico de Gallo (page 226)
Grilled Asparagus (page 328)
Garlicky Seasoned Rice (page 338)
White Bean Hummus with Pita Bread (page 153)

CALORIES, 520; CARBOHYDRATES, 61 GRAMS; CARBOHYDRATE CHOICES, 4.

WEEKEND LUNCH

Grilled Portobello Burgers (page 307)

Honeydew Melon, 1 cup cubed

CALORIES, 280; CARBOHYDRATES, 51 GRAMS; CARBOHYDRATE CHOICES, 3½.

COCKTAILS AND HORS D'OEUVRES

Tomato and Mozzarella Salad with Basil (Caprese) (page 182)

Fruit and Prosciutto Wraps (page 147)

Tapenade on Bruschetta (page 152)

Spinach Quiche (page 128)

Strawberries in Yogurt and Brown Sugar (page 367)

CALORIES, 550; CARBOHYDRATES, 62 GRAMS; CARBOHYDRATE CHOICES, 4.

MEXICAN DO-AHEAD DINNER

Seafood Enchiladas (page 238)

Refried Pinto Beans (page 322)

Jicama and Carrot Salad with Lime (page 186)

CALORIES, 420; CARBOHYDRATES, 49 GRAMS; CARBOHYDRATE CHOICES, 3½.

PERFECT PICNIC

Easy Roast Chicken (page 258)

Sugar Snap Peas with Potato and Parsley Sauté (page 354)

Viennese Brownies (page 384)

CALORIES, 400; CARBOHYDRATES, 36 GRAMS; CARBOHYDRATE CHOICES, 2½.

BREAKFAST IN BED

Fresh-squeezed orange juice, 8 ounces

Spinach Quiche (page 128)

Morningstar Farms Grillers or sausage, 1 serving

CALORIES, 440; CARBOHYDRATES, 50 GRAMS; CARBOHYDRATE CHOICES, 3½.

SUMMER SUNDAY BACKYARD BRUNCH

Chili-Rubbed Barbecue Chicken (page 254)

Mom's Potato Salad Revisited (page 203)

Sesame-Ginger Slaw (page 191)

CALORIES, 380; CARBOHYDRATES, 50 GRAMS; CARBOHYDRATE CHOICES, 3½.

BIRTHDAY PARTY FOR 50 ADULTS

Grilled Chicken Fajitas (page 256)

Chipotle Black Beans, half serving (page 323)

Flour tortilla, 1 medium

Espresso Angel Food Cake with Chocolate Sauce (page 370)

CALORIES, 580; CARBOHYDRATES, 76 GRAMS; CARBOHYDRATE CHOICES, 5.

BIRTHDAY PARTY FOR 15 KIDS

Barbecued Chicken Pizza (page 292)

Raw carrot, 1 whole

Mocha Angel Cake Roll (page 374)

CALORIES, 310; CARBOHYDRATES, 47 GRAMS; CARBOHYDRATE CHOICES, 3.

QUIET NEW YEAR'S EVE FOR 8

Céleri Rémoulade (page 179)

Roast Loin of Pork with Garlic (page 272)

Herb-Scented Roasted Potatoes (page 357)

Caramelized Carrots and Parsnips with Orange Zest (page 336)

Pears Baked in Marsala (page 361)

CALORIES, 550; CARBOHYDRATES, 49 GRAMS; CARBOHYDRATE CHOICES, 3½.

MIDWEEK CHINESE SUPPER

Ground Turkey with Ginger, Hoisin, and Green Onions (page 265)

Flour tortilla, 1 medium

Grilled Eggplant with Spicy Soy Marinade (page 329)

CALORIES, 430; CARBOHYDRATES, 47 GRAMS; CARBOHYDRATE CHOICES, 3.

PIZZA FOR GROWN-UPS

3 Pizza Nouveau

- Pizza Margarita (page 290)
- Pizza with Roasted Red Pepper, Chicken Sausage, and Cilantro (page 291)
- Barbecued Chicken Pizza (page 292)

Basic Green Salad with Vinaigrette (page 177)

2 slices of pizza and a salad:

CALORIES, 535; CARBOHYDRATES, 53–64 GRAMS; CARBOHYDRATE CHOICES, 4.

MORE THAN LUCK POTLUCK DINNER

Pork Tenderloins with Port Sauce, Prunes, and Apricots (page 271)

Colcannon (page 332)

Chopped Belgian Endive Salad (page 188)

CALORIES, 590; CARBOHYDRATES, 63 GRAMS; CARBOHYDRATE CHOICES, 4.

THANKSGIVING DINNER

Artichoke Soup, half serving (page 159)

Roast Turkey, Italian-Style (page 266)

Parsnip-Potato Puree, half serving (page 355)

Pumpkin Pie (page 380)

CALORIES, 530; CARBOHYDRATES, 62 GRAMS; CARBOHYDRATE CHOICES, 4.

CHRISTMAS DINNER

Oysters on the Half Shell with Tequila, Habanero, Lime Juice, and Cilantro (page 136)

Osso Bucco (page 274)

Brussels Sprouts with Chestnuts (page 335)

Saffron-Scented Basmati Rice, half serving (page 339)

Lemon Tart (page 364)

CALORIES, 810; CARBOHYDRATES, 72 GRAMS; CARBOHYDRATE CHOICES, 5.

NEW YEAR'S DAY–DAY AFTER PARTY

White Bean Soup (page 174)

Baby Shrimp Salad with Dill (page 199)

Warm Spinach Salad (page 189)

Chocolate Sandwich Cookies (page 378)

CALORIES, 440; CARBOHYDRATES, 43 GRAMS; CARBOHYDRATE CHOICES, 3.

SEVEN QUICK WORKDAY MEALS

Day One
Corn and Chicken Noodle Soup, two servings (page 169)
Waldorf Salad with Fennel (page 193)
CALORIES, 310; CARBOHYDRATES, 46 GRAMS; CARBOHYDRATE CHOICES, 3.

Day Two
Chicken Marsala (page 243) with ⅔ cup rice
Zucchini sautéed in olive oil and garlic, ½ cup
CALORIES, 390; CARBOHYDRATES, 42 GRAMS; CARBOHYDRATE CHOICES, 3.

Day Three
Swordfish Steaks with Lemon, Capers, and Cracked Pepper (page 225)
Lemon Pesto Spaghettini (page 294)
Steamed broccoli, 1 cup florets
CALORIES, 535; CARBOHYDRATES, 50 GRAMS; CARBOHYDRATE CHOICES, 3½.

Day Four
Easy Roast Chicken (page 258)
Rosemary Polenta Squares (page 353) or
    Herb-Scented Roasted Potatoes (page 357)
Basic Green Salad with Vinaigrette (page 177)
CALORIES, 440; CARBOHYDRATES, 46 GRAMS; CARBOHYDRATE CHOICES, 3.

Day Five
Santa Fe Shrimp Skewer (page 231) with ½ cup rice
Sliced tomato, 1 whole
CALORIES, 246; CARBOHYDRATES, 48 GRAMS; CARBOHYDRATE CHOICES, 3.

Day Six
Spaghettini Pomodoro (page 295)
Basic Green Salad with Vinaigrette (page 177)
CALORIES, 330; CARBOHYDRATES, 48 GRAMS; CARBOHYDRATE CHOICES, 3.

Day Seven
Chinese Chicken Salad (page 200)
Fresh fruit
CALORIES, 320; CARBOHYDRATES, 28 GRAMS; CARBOHYDRATE CHOICES, 2.

SEVEN VEGETARIAN DINNERS

Day One
Ratatouille (page 334)

Garlic toast, 1 slice

CALORIES, 250; CARBOHYDRATES, 47 GRAMS; CARBOHYDRATE CHOICES, 3.

Day Two
Risotto with Red Beans and Sage (page 346)

Basic Green Salad with Vinaigrette (page 177)

CALORIES, 370; CARBOHYDRATES, 54 GRAMS; CARBOHYDRATE CHOICES, 3½.

Day Three
Spinach and Potato Dumplings, two servings (page 142)

Coleslaw with Apple (page 192)

CALORIES, 290; CARBOHYDRATES, 47 GRAMS; CARBOHYDRATE CHOICES, 3.

Day Four
Tomato-Bread Salad (page 197)

Creamy Celery Soup (page 171)

CALORIES, 300; CARBOHYDRATES, 41 GRAMS; CARBOHYDRATE CHOICES, 2½.

Day Five
Baked Stuffed Shells with Spinach-Herb Filling (page 301)

Spaghetti Squash with Gremolata (page 325)

CALORIES, 410; CARBOHYDRATES, 57 GRAMS; CARBOHYDRATE CHOICES, 4.

Day Six
Pissaladière (page 286)

Strawberry Spinach Salad (page 190)

CALORIES, 330; CARBOHYDRATES, 47 GRAMS; CARBOHYDRATE CHOICES, 3.

Day Seven
Vegetable Fried Rice, 2 servings (page 344)

Refried Pinto Beans, 2 servings (page 322)

Grilled Portobello Mushrooms (page 133)

CALORIES, 360; CARBOHYDRATES, 56 GRAMS; CARBOHYDRATE CHOICES, 4.

CHAPTER 5

MANAGING FAT AND CHOLESTEROL

People with diabetes are more likely to die of heart disease than of anything else. They tend to have lower HDLs, the so-called good cholesterol, and higher LDLs, the form of cholesterol that clogs arteries. That may not be the only reason, but the fact is, they are two to four times more vulnerable to heart disease than people without diabetes. Some physicians believe the risk is so great that they frequently recommend that people with adult-onset diabetes include cholesterol-lowering drugs as part of their treatment.

But before we jump ahead to drug therapy, diet must be the first line of defense. In fact, even those who are already taking cholesterol-lowering medications will have better results with the right diet. ***Research shows that the types and quantity of dietary fat and cholesterol eaten are related directly to the development of heart disease.*** Eating too much of *any* kind of fat contributes to weight gain, since fat contains more than twice the number of calories per gram than protein and carbohydrate. Decreasing our fat intake aids in weight loss, which in turn helps you achieve better blood glucose control. Better blood glucose control in turn will lower the levels of certain bad fats in your bloodstream.

THE RIGHT BALANCE OF FAT

While too much fat can make us fat, too little leaves us without a sense of satisfaction and can lead to overeating. For people with diabetes, too little fat may translate into eating more carbohydrates, which can elevate triglycerides. Americans typically eat a diet too high in fat. We like it because it adds a rich taste and texture to almost any food and it makes us feel full after a meal. But some people go overboard in avoiding fat, trying to eliminate all fat from their diets. In fact, a small amount of fat is needed to transport fat-soluble vitamins A, D, E, and K in the body and for an essential fatty acid that is required in order to make nerves and hormones. By understanding fats, you can learn how to balance them in your diet.

Fat, Cholesterol, and Your Heart

Cholesterol is a waxy white fat found naturally in your body. It's used to build brain and nerve cell walls, to make certain hormones, and it is a component of the bile that helps us digest our food. All the cholesterol we need for these important functions is made in our livers at a rate equivalent to eating about ten eggs a day, depending on genetics and diet. But we also get cholesterol from the foods we eat. Food sources high in cholesterol include egg yolks, organ meats (especially liver), and dairy fat. *The recommended dietary cholesterol intake from foods is 300 milligrams per day or less, and 200 milligrams per day if your cholesterol level is elevated.* Too much of it can clog your arteries and eventually choke off the supply of blood to the heart, which is the reason high cholesterol is a leading risk factor for heart disease.

Cholesterol is perhaps one of the most confusing pieces in the puzzle of fat and heart disease. *Although there is a definite link between high levels of cholesterol in the blood and heart disease, the cholesterol in the food you eat is not the only factor in elevating blood cholesterol levels. An even greater culprit is saturated fat.* Take shrimp, for example. It's a high-cholesterol food but has very little saturated fat, and it therefore is less likely to raise blood cholesterol levels than a cookie or a French fry, both of which have little or no cholesterol, but are likely to contain saturated fats. *Just remember—both cholesterol and saturated fat raise serum cholesterol, but saturated fat in food has the greatest negative effect on your blood cholesterol level.* That's one reason to eat more fish and less fatty meats.

THE CHOLESTEROL TRANSPORT SYSTEM

Being a fat, cholesterol is not soluble in blood, just as oil and water don't mix. Consequently, cholesterol relies on certain proteins to form carriers called lipoproteins, which ferry cholesterol throughout the body. The lipoproteins are categorized by their density, and are called low-density lipoproteins (LDL), high-density lipoproteins (HDL), and so on.

High-density lipoproteins (HDLs): High in protein and low in cholesterol, HDLs are like little vacuum cleaners going through your arteries sweeping out undesirable cholesterol, preventing it from clogging the arteries. The more HDL you've got, the better. Higher levels of HDLs in the blood actually reduce risk of heart disease. To raise your HDL, stop smoking, lose weight, and exercise. Don't eat a diet too low in fat; lowering total fat intake to below 30 percent of calories may lower your HDL. Just be sure to emphasize monounsaturated fats like olive oil and limit saturated fats from meats, full-fat dairy products, and baked goods.

Low-density lipoproteins (LDLs): Low in protein and high in cholesterol, LDLs have been dubbed the bad cholesterol because they carry cholesterol to the arteries where it deposits to form artery-clogging plaque that can lead to a heart attack or stroke. People with high levels of LDLs have a higher risk of heart disease. Researchers have been able to determine elements that help lower LDL, and these efforts nearly always work, at least to some degree. Here's the prescription: lose weight, exercise, eat less saturated fat and cholesterol, and eat more soluble fiber like oats and dried beans.

Triglycerides: Triglycerides are the fats floating in your blood. Although high levels of triglycerides are not good, it's not clear if it's the low HDL levels that always accompany triglycerides that are most problematic. We do know that your body produces more triglycerides when you consume too many simple sugars or carbohydrate foods or drink too much alcohol. When people with diabetes have not had proper blood glucose control, the level of triglycerides is likely to be elevated as well. According to Margo Denke, M.D., an endocrinologist and associate professor at University of Texas Southwestern Medical School, "substituting carbohydrate calories for fat calories may increase triglyceride levels." Denke advises that people with diabetes not rely too heavily on breads, cereals, rice, and pasta for their calories, with too little fat. "Stay within your plan for carbohydrates and unsaturated fats," Denke suggests, "and for those individuals with elevated triglycerides who are eating very low-fat, high-carbohydrate diets, I tell them to substitute a quarter cup of nuts for some carbohydrates in a day. As amazing as it seems, that fat may help to lower their triglycerides. About a tablespoon of monounsaturated oil like olive or canola may also do the trick." To summarize, to lower your triglycerides, lose weight, exercise, eat less saturated fat and cholesterol, and don't restrict your monounsaturated fat *too* severely.

KNOW YOUR BLOOD FAT LEVELS

Your doctor may have done the simple blood test that measures your triglycerides and the total cholesterol along with the breakdown of the HDL and LDL. To keep the numbers straight, remember that you want your low-density lipoprotein (LDL) to be low and your high-density lipoprotein (HDL) to be high. Here are some guidelines for reading your test results at age 18 and over from the National Heart, Lung, and Blood Institute:

Risk	Total Cholesterol	LDL	HDL	Triglycerides
High	240 or above	160 and above	less than 35	above 400
Borderline	200 to 239	130 to 159	N/A	200 to 399
Desirable	below 200	below 130	N/A	below 200

YOUR DAILY FAT INTAKE

So *how much* fat should you eat? That depends on your blood lipid levels, your blood sugar control, and your weight. The chart below shows how many grams you'll be eating if your diet provides 30 percent of calories from fat, with 10 percent of calories from saturated fat.

Daily Calorie Level	Maximum Grams of Total Fat	Maximum Grams of Saturated Fat
1000	33	11
1200	40	13
1400	47	16
1600	53	18
1800	60	20
2000	67	22
2200	73	24
2400	80	27
2600	87	29
2800	93	31
3000	100	33

How to Change the Fat Content of Your Meals

Check labels to see how many grams of fat are in the foods you eat. Eat more fish, at least three times a week. Eat the skinless white meat of chicken, and make sure the beef or pork you select is lean. Try to eat more meatless meals, substituting legumes. Limit added fats from toppings such as butter, margarine, or mayonnaise, and choose new low-fat or nonfat dairy products to replace excessive saturated fat, cholesterol, and calories from butterfat. Use olive oil or canola oil when cooking.

Studies show that for every point your cholesterol goes down, you have a 2 percent reduction in your risk of heart disease. Therefore, lowering your blood cholesterol about 10 to 15 percent will lower your risk of heart disease by 20 to 30 percent. Of course, this varies depending on your genetic makeup and former eating habits, but it's a pretty motivating and well-established statistic. If you've been eating a high-fat diet, you may see an even greater reduction.

THE DIFFERENT TYPES OF FAT

All fats and oils (liquid fats) are made up of different amounts of monounsaturated, polyunsaturated, and saturated fats. Each affects your blood cholesterol and triglycerides in different ways. That's because they are made of different types of building blocks, known as fatty acids. Fatty acids are simply long chains of carbon atoms with varying amounts of hydrogen and oxygen atoms attached. These fatty acids can be saturated, monounsaturated, or polyunsaturated, depending on their number of what chemists term "double bonds." Saturated fatty acids have no double bonds; "monos" have one double bond; and "polys" have more than one double bond.

All foods containing fats have mixtures of the different types of fatty acids, but one type invariably predominates, determining the effect the food will have on your blood fats. Following are the categories of fatty acids, their primary food sources, and descriptions of the impact they can have on your health.

Saturated fat: Saturated fat raises your blood cholesterol level more than anything else in your diet, even cholesterol itself. It comes primarily from meat and dairy products, including butter, cheese, whole milk, cream, ice cream, red meats, poultry, and lard. Exceptions to the animal fat rule are a few vegetable sources that are highly saturated, including coconut oil, palm oil, and cocoa butter (the fat in chocolate). Some fats have been chemically altered or hydrogenated so that they become saturated. These include shortening (like the original white, solid-at-room-temperature Crisco) and regular margarine. Here's how it stacks up for saturated fat:

- increases LDL—"bad cholesterol"
- increases total blood cholesterol
- may be linked to increased risk for heart disease and cancer

Monounsaturated fat: Today's most popular oil may also be the one that's best for people with diabetes. Olive oil is the oil highest in monounsaturated oils, followed by canola oil and peanut oil. Olives, nuts, and avocados are high in monounsaturated fat. For years, nutritionists told their clients that monounsaturated fat had a neutral effect on cholesterol—neither raising nor lowering blood levels of cholesterol. Research now suggests diets rich in monounsaturated fat may actually lower blood cholesterol even more than a diet that severely restricts total fat. As a bonus, it keeps the HDL from being lowered along with the LDL, unlike the polyunsaturated fats. My advice: as long as your total fat is around 30 percent of calories, use olive oil or canola oil for the fat in cooking, salad dressings, and so on. Of special importance to people with diabetes, the "monos" may also help to lower triglycerides.

To summarize, monounsaturated fat provides these benefits:

- decreases LDL—"bad cholesterol"
- protects HDL—"good cholesterol"
- decreases total blood cholesterol
- decreases triglycerides
- is less likely to oxidize (a process that may contribute to narrowing of the arteries)

Polyunsaturated fat: Found mostly in safflower oil, corn oil, cottonseed oil, soy oil, seed oils, polyunsaturated margarine, walnuts, and fish, this fat has long been touted for its role in lowering blood cholesterol. It is generally recommended that this fat make up 10 percent of your calories, or a third of your fat intake. The problem, as mentioned above, is that polyunsaturated fat not only lowers LDLs, the bad guys, but it also lowers the HDLs, the good guys.

If you replace saturated fat with polyunsaturated fat, you may find that it:

- decreases LDL—"bad cholesterol"
- decreases HDL—"good cholesterol"
- decreases total blood cholesterol
- is more likely to oxidize

Comparing Fat Sources

Current research indicates that monounsaturated fat is the best fat for people with diabetes, so look for fats with high amounts of monounsaturated fat to replace sources of saturated fat. (Remember, it's *replace,* not increase!) The richest sources of monounsaturated fat are olive oil and canola oil.

Fat/Oil	% Mono Fat	% Poly Fat	% Sat Fat	Cholesterol
Olive oil	77	9	14	0
Canola oil	62	32	6	0
Peanut oil	48	33	19	0
Margarine	49	32	19	0
Chicken fat	47	23	30	11
Vegetable shortening (Crisco)	43	25	26	0
Corn oil	25	62	13	0
Soybean oil	24	61	15	0
Safflower oil	12	79	9	0
Lard	47	10	43	12
Butter	28	4	68	33
Beef fat	44	5	51	14

Fish: I recommend that my patients eat fish at least three times a week. It tastes great and is low in saturated fats, with between 20 and 100 milligrams of cholesterol per three-ounce serving. Shellfish, although it is relatively high in cholesterol, does not seem to raise blood lipid levels. That may be because fish oils are also rich in a type of polyunsaturated fat. But they are really in a class of their own because they contain a unique brand of polyunsaturated fatty acids—the omega-3 type—not found in significant quantities elsewhere in common foods. Omega-3 fatty acids help prevent the formation of blood clots by acting as a sort of biological antifreeze, remaining fluid even at frigid temperatures. Consequently, the highest levels of omega-3 fatty acid are generally found in fish that live in cooler waters. Salmon, herring, albacore tuna, sardines, and mackerel are good examples, as you can see from the list on the following page.

Compared to the omega-6 fatty acids in vegetable oils, which contain two or three double bonds, omega-3 fatty acids are even more highly polyunsaturated, with five or six double bonds. Many fish feed on zooplankton—tiny water animals that eat microscopic floating plants called phytoplankton. We can thank the phytoplankton for manufacturing the omega-3 fatty acids that ultimately become part of fish cells and tissue. Predators like tuna and cod attain their omega-3s by dining on smaller fish that consume zoo plankton.

Some of my patients ask me about taking fish oil supplements. Unfortunately, in capsule form, fish oils have been shown to elevate blood glucose levels. This effect is currently under investigation.

The Omega-3 Fatty Acid Content of 3½-ounce Portions of Raw Fish (edible portions only)

Lean Fish (.5 g to 3.5 g fat per serving)	Omega-3s (milligrams)
Cod	
Atlantic	184
Pacific	215
Haddock	185
Hake	224
Pollack	
Walleye	372
Atlantic	421
Flatfish (flounder, sole)	199
Red snapper	311
Sea bass	595
Lake trout	568
Tilefish	430

Medium-Fat Fish (1.5 g to 6 g fat per serving)	Omega-3s (milligrams)
Bluefish	771
Striped bass	754
Catfish	373
Carp	352
Shark	843
Swordfish	639
Tuna	1173
Whiting or silver hake	224

High-Fat Fish (4 g to 10 g fat per serving)	Omega-3s (milligrams)
Mullet	325
Mackerel	2299
Whitefish	1258
Pompano	568
Salmon	
Atlantic	1436
coho	814
sockeye	1172
chinook	1355

FAT SUBSTITUTES

So what about finding fat substitutes to replace the saturated fats in our diets? Over twenty fat replacements are currently being used in food products. Carbohydrate-based fat replacers are more commonly used in salad dressings, baked goods, frozen dairy desserts, puddings, and chewing gums. They include dextrins, maltodextrins, modified food starches, polydextrose, cellulose, and gums. Their contribution to carbohydrate content of the product is reflected in the food label. Protein from milk or egg whites is also occasionally used as the base for fat replacers. In a process called microparticulation, the protein molecules are divided into very small particles that, when eaten, create a smooth mouth feel, mimicking fat.

Olestra is the newest fat replacer on the market, with the brand name Olean. It is made from soybean or cottonseed oil combined with sugar and processed in a special way so that it adds no calories. It can be used to replace fat in frying, sautéing, or baking foods. It is currently approved for use in the making of savory snacks, such as chips, pretzels, and crackers, but has been known to cause abdominal cramping and diarrhea in some individuals. Procter & Gamble, the company that manufacures olestra, is making their fat replacer available to snack food companies as well as testing it in Pringles, their own potato chips. Frito-Lay is expected to expand its current test marketing of olestra snacks nationwide in Ruffles, Lays, Doritos, and Tostitos in 1998. The Nabisco Company is also test marketing olestra in fat-free versions of Ritz and Wheat Thins.

CHAPTER 6

A SENSIBLE WAY TO CONTROL YOUR WEIGHT

Maintaining a healthy body weight is very important for people with diabetes. For those with type II diabetes, shedding pounds may lead to an improvement, or even disappearance, of the symptoms of diabetes. *For both types of diabetes, preventing and reversing weight gain improves blood sugar control and reduces the risk of cardiovascular disease, the major killer among diabetic individuals.* Losing weight permanently is a difficult task, but it is possible to succeed in weight loss, and this chapter will tell you how.

SETTING YOUR GOAL FOR WEIGHT LOSS

One of the important outcomes of the new guidelines for the diabetic diet relates to weight control. How much weight does the overweight person with type II diabetes need to lose in order to improve his or her condition? We now know that this person does not need to reach an "ideal" weight, a goal that is not only often unrealistic but unnecessary.

My patient Marilyn was 52 years old and newly diagnosed with type II diabetes. She weighed 220 pounds. Ten years ago, the Metropolitan Height/Weight Charts would likely be used to calculate her ideal body weight. But telling Marilyn that she should weigh 140 pounds would have been a setup for failure. The new guidelines suggest that Marilyn aim for a weight loss of 10 percent of her body weight, or 22 pounds, and then work on maintaining it.

Such modest weight losses have been shown to produce long-term improvements in glycemic control. In a study of overweight patients with type II diabetes, those who lost 15 to 30 pounds and maintained it for a year had long-term improvements in hemoglobin A-1 C, insulin, HDL cholesterol, and triglyceride levels.

CALORIE BALANCE

Many people who come to my office for weight management have no idea how many calories they eat in a day and how many they actually require. The first thing I do is to ask them about their typical eating habits so that together we can figure out what areas of their diet need adjusting. My client Lisa grew up in an Italian family and was used to eating large bowls of pasta with each meal. Lasagna with béchamel sauce was her favorite food. Lunches in restaurants often consisted of Caesar chicken salad with several pieces of bread and butter. We estimated her usual daily intake to be about 2500 to 3000 calories. Based on her height—five feet four inches—we figured she would maintain her weight at about 1400 calories per day (the formula: 1000 calories for the first five feet and 100 calories for each inch thereafter). She is now working on eating 1400 calories each day, then burning 700 calories total from exercise each week, with the goal to work up to burning 1500 to 2000 calories from exercise every week as her fitness level improves.

DESIGNING YOUR PERSONAL WEIGHT LOSS PLAN

Your dietitian will help you set up a plan with goals for calories, carbohydrate choices, and fat. You can work together to figure out how to include foods that taste good to you, meet the demands of your lifestyle, fulfill your nutritional needs, and help you achieve the best blood sugar control possible. You may find it helpful to develop menu plans, shopping lists, and other strategies to improve the quality of your diet and make sure you're eating the right amount of food. Refer to chapter 4 for sample menu plans designed especially for people with diabetes.

PORTION SIZES

Balancing food calories with physical exercise is essential to weight loss. Once you know how many calories you need, the next step is to learn about portion sizes. Experiment in your kitchen with measuring cups or a scale to become familiar with foods you commonly eat which you suspect may be problem areas. Check out 100 calories worth of rice, pasta, or potatoes. Put it on a plate so you'll be able to eyeball the amount you are served at a restaurant. Then you can figure out how much you want to include in that meal, and stay within your goal. If you've been using the American Dietetic Association Diabetic Exchange Lists to do your meal planning, you've probably noticed that some of the portion sizes are smaller than what you're used to seeing, and certainly smaller than what you are served in a restaurant. According to Candy Cumming, R.D., M.S., a weight loss counselor in San Diego, California, "Muffins listed in the exchanges or calorie books are 1940s portion sizes, about 1½ ounces, listed at 165 calories. But today's muffins are 5 to 6 ounces, so if you use the outdated portion size, you'll be off by about 500 calories. This miscalculation, whether it's applied to muffins, pasta, or any other food you eat, can sabotage your effort to lose weight."

THE IMPORTANCE OF SELF-MONITORING

By keeping records of your food, exercise, and blood glucose levels, you'll learn which foods are contributing most to your overall calorie and fat intake and be motivated to modify your food choices accordingly. My patients who learn to monitor their own plans are quickly able to identify problem areas and create solutions. It's almost as if they are becoming their own nutritionist. And in doing so, their eating program becomes one of freedom from rigid diets and structure that can sabotage even the most well-intentioned individual. Rather than relying on willpower, they find that they are meeting their goals with knowledge and planning.

As you develop a clear insight into your eating style, choices about which foods you want to eliminate or modify will begin to surface. Are you eating too much bread? Or are high-calorie desserts using up too much of your carbohydrate allowance? You will learn which foods are problems and which are not. Ironically, by having a structure and keeping track, you can vary your choices among your favorite foods while maintaining good control of your blood glucose.

This brings up another facet of the new, more flexible guidelines. They allow for the enjoyment of small amounts of food containing sucrose and other refined sugars by people whose diabetes is well controlled. Previously, ice cream, cookies, and other sweets were considered off-limits to people with diabetes. Advances in understanding the effects of different foods on blood sugar have now made sweet foods an acceptable part of the diabetes meal plan. For example, if you are allowed 3 carbohydrate choices at dinner, or 45 grams of carbohydrates, you can divide them among rice and a dessert, as long as the total grams are within 45. With this more flexible option, there is less of a sense of deprivation, which makes it easier to stick to a plan. This can help with overeating.

OVERCOMING OVEREATING

The advantage of a food plan that allows you to vary food choices each day is that you're not likely to get bored or feel restricted. For example, one night your carbohydrate choice is pasta, the next it's a potato, and on the following it's bread. This avoids a rigid diet structure that can end up backfiring.

The classic response many people have to a strict diet is to eventually go on a binge. According to Dr. Charles Portney, a psychiatrist based in Santa Monica, California, who counsels people with eating disorders, "The more you restrict, particularly early in the day, the more likely you are to binge. By putting yourself in a starvation mode, you're likely to slow your metabolism. The body responds to the physical and emotional deprivation of restriction with progressively less control, resulting in a binge of overeating when you finally let go."

So while an improvement in eating habits may well be in order, you need not adhere to overly restrictive dietary guidelines. By including an occasional sweet in the meal plan, many people with diabetes may avoid the cycle of restricting followed by overeating, and will be able to control both their disease and their natural cravings for sugar. The result will be improved management of diabetes.

Even for people without diabetes, severe food deprivation as a means of weight loss is counterproductive. Studies show that a restrictive diet regimen rarely results in long-term weight loss. Gradual changes in dietary patterns and physical activity levels appear to be better associated with maintenance. Learn to eat less fat in your diet. Focus on efforts to stop overeating. If you are eating too many starchy carbohydrates such as bread, pasta, or rice, cut back on them and work on developing a balance of starches with more vegetables and lean protein. Keep fruit servings to two or so a day, and limit high-calorie sweets, even if they are fat-free, sugar-free cookies, cakes, and crackers. Use the menu plans in chapter 4 as a guide to get you on track. But don't starve yourself.

One of my patients, Ed, reported in our first session that he never felt hungry. When mealtime rolled around, his wife would cook dinner or they would be at a restaurant, and he would eat because it was "time to eat." Consequently, he ate too much. We discovered he was eating too much at each meal, and when we cut back on his portion sizes, he began to experience normal hunger at mealtimes. According to Elyse Resch, M.S., R.D., and Evelyn Tribole, M.S., R.D., authors of *Intuitive Eating,* "The best way to manage weight is to pay attention to your body's cues to eat. A simple way to put it is eat when you're hungry and stop when you're full. If you tune in to what you really feel like eating, it will help you avoid feeling deprived and then overeating."

Your food plan will include goals for how many calories and carbohydrates you should aim for. ***Working in those favorite foods that you once thought were off-limits can keep you from going overboard with excessive amounts of foods that you were once not allowed.*** And remember, it doesn't take a large portion of food to satisfy a craving. Still, if there are foods which trigger overeating, you may want to avoid them. My client Cathy claimed that when there were chocolate chip cookies in her house, they called her name. She would eat them till they were gone. By switching to pre-portioned Weight Watchers frozen desserts, she was able to eat only the amount that was within her plan while satisfying her craving for sweets.

I have heard from many of my patients that they just don't have the willpower to lose weight. Perhaps willpower and fear of health consequences are not good motivators! Dr. John Foreyt, a psychologist and the director of the Behavioral Medical Research Center at Baylor College of Medicine, has identified the factors that appear to be associated with long-term success with weight control. As mentioned earlier, regular physical activity is at the top of the list. Second, having the support of family and friends who are eating the same healthy foods and exercising together each day can provide the support necessary for long-term success. Third is internal motivation. He finds that rather than thinking solely in terms of a number on the scale or the size of jeans you'd like to wear, you should focus on the behaviors you'll have to do in order to get there—i.e., the foods you will eat and activities you will carry out. Finally, let your indicators of success go beyond the scale as well. Think about how you want to feel after eating a meal. More energy? You bet. ***Eating moderately rather than overeating will result in small amounts of weight loss that give you not only more energy, but lower blood pressure, glucose, and lipids.***

EXERCISE GETS RESULTS

Your weight loss plan should include exercise. ***Studies show that people who combine diet with exercise are more likely to lose weight and keep it off than those who rely on either diet or exercise alone.*** As discussed in chapter 7, exercise helps maintain muscle mass, improves blood lipid profiles, and improves blood sugar control over the long term. In fact, studies that compare those who are successful with weight loss efforts versus those who are not show that the one consistent difference is the amount of exercise performed.

The exercise goal in weight loss programs is to increase energy (or calorie) expenditure, aiming for burning 1500 to 2000 calories per week through exercise. A good rule to remember is the following: Walking one mile uses 100 calories for a person weighing 150 pounds. If you weigh more or less, divide your weight by 150 and multiply that by 100. For example, a person weighing 300 pounds uses 200 calories per mile, whereas a person weighing 120 pounds uses 80 calories per mile.

I suggest that my patients begin with a short walk of 10 to 15 minutes 3 times a week, burning about 150 to 225 calories per week. After a few weeks, increase the distance until they are up to 2 miles a day 5 days a week, which brings them up to burning about 1000 calories per week. This may be enough to maintain weight, but in order to lose weight, continue to build distance until you burn 1500 to 2000 calories per week through exercise. If you walk 20 miles a week, you'll be using an extra 2000 calories. That would be about 3 miles a day, or a 1-hour walk 7 days a week. That's a great goal regardless of your weight. You don't need to do it all at once. Perhaps 30 minutes in the morning and 30 minutes in the evening is a good way to break it up. For more details, see chapter 7 on exercise.

CHAPTER 7

EXERCISE ESSENTIALS FOR PEOPLE WITH DIABETES

Exercise makes everything in the body work better. And that's especially important if you have diabetes. *Not only does regular exercise increase muscle mass and tone, and increase the body's metabolic rate, it also gives the muscle's cells a tune-up, which helps them burn sugar faster. Most people with diabetes who exercise regularly require less medication because exercise lowers their blood sugar.* If you have type II diabetes, exercise makes your body's own insulin work better. The effect of exercise on blood sugar can last from 12 to 72 hours.

Not only is exercise an important tool in managing your diabetes, it has been called the ultimate cure for obesity. By raising your metabolism, it helps you burn more calories, even in your sleep. If you're overweight and have type II diabetes, losing weight is an important way of getting your diabetes in better control. Of course, what you eat is also important. I tell my patients that the fitness/weight control equation is 50 percent exercise and 50 percent diet. Together they can help you reach and stay at your desired weight.

Regular exercise also improves blood flow and blood pressure by increasing the elasticity of your veins and arteries. It can even increase the number of blood vessels, thus decreasing the pressure needed to pump blood through your circulatory system. Regular exercise makes your heart and lungs stronger. If that's not enough to convince you to exercise, it's been documented that exercise can improve your mood, lower the tension in your body, and increase your energy level. You feel better about yourself when you exercise. If there were a pill that offered these tremendous physical and emotional benefits, people would be lining up to buy it. There is such a pill; it takes just 30 minutes a day to swallow!

SETTING UP YOUR EXERCISE PROGRAM

A successful exercise program begins with choosing an activity that you enjoy, one that can fit into your daily routine. Keep in mind, in the same way the food you eat must please your palate, the exercise you choose must be fun if you are going to look forward to it on a regular basis. If you like being outdoors, then choose an activity such as walking, jogging, or bicycling—and make it regular. If you prefer being indoors or are restricted by the weather, then check out classes at a community center or gym where you can swim, take a class, or walk or jog indoors. If you prefer exercising at home, alone and indoors, why not try a stationary bike or a videotape. When you find an exercise that you like, write it into your schedule. As with food, introducing variety can be helpful in sticking with a program. Make it a priority, and it will support your goal for getting and staying in good shape. And by all means, if you have diabetes, consult with your physician before you increase your physical activity.

Aerobic exercise is the preferred type of exercise for people with diabetes because it's what changes the chemistry in the cells to make them metabolize carbohydrates better. Aerobic exercise includes a variety of activities, including brisk walking, cycling, swimming, jogging—any activity that works major muscle groups and requires oxygen to keep the muscles going for 20 to 60 minutes per session. You'll generally require five or more of these exercise sessions each week to lose weight or improve fitness level and three to four times a week to maintain it. For improvement of glycemic control, exercise is recommended at least every other day. Shorter sessions do not produce the desired aerobic and metabolic benefits. However, if you've been inactive, you may have an increased risk for heart attack or stroke and may need to begin at a lower level. Work on *gradually* increasing the duration and frequency of exercise until you reach your desired level of fitness.

Your doctor or health care professional, preferably an exercise physiologist, can also help you choose the exercise that is right for you. Most of my patients find walking to be their exercise of choice. It's convenient and does not require any special equipment. All you need are a good pair of supportive shoes that fit well. You can walk anywhere, anytime. Make it a part of a daily exercise routine, along with using stairs rather than elevators and parking your car farther away from stores and your office than you do now.

HOW HARD SHOULD YOU EXERCISE?

In the beginning, keep in mind that you're in no big hurry. This is a long-term effort, not an overnight fad. If you choose walking as your activity, start by just going for a walk at a comfortable pace slightly above a stroll. In the beginning, try walking at least three times a week for 20 to 30 minutes each time. Exercise such as this—hard, but not too hard, and continuous for a minimum of 20 minutes—is better than weight lifting or "stop and start" exercises when it comes to improving blood sugars.

As you become more comfortable with exercise, you can get a bit more sophisticated. Measure your time. Use your car's odometer or the rule of ten city blocks to a mile (or twenty short city blocks if you're in New York City) to measure your route; see how long it takes you to walk a mile comfortably on flat ground. Chances are it'll take between 15 and 20 minutes. Build from there.

To get the best result, your walking should be aerobic. That means it must be strenuous enough to increase the heart rate to between 55 and 85 percent of your maximum heart rate, as determined by a standard maximum heart rate of 220 beats per minute and your age. Your target heart-rate zone is the heart rate at which you'll get the most benefits from exercise. It's simple to measure your target heart rate. After 5 minutes of exercising, count your pulse for 10 seconds, then multiply by 6 to get your beats per minute. Use the chart below to determine your target heart-rate zone. Please note that these values are estimates. Try to stay within the target zone according to your age.

Age	55% to 85% Beats per Minute
20	110–170
30	105–161
40	99–153
50	93–154
60	88–136
70	83–127
80 and above	77–119

If you have a problem finding your target heart rate, ask your doctor, exercise physiologist, or diabetes educator for help. Your doctor can also tell you if you are taking a medicine, such as beta blockers for the heart and blood pressure, which may prevent your heart rate from going up. If so, the heart-rate chart above will not apply to you. One goal is to work up to walking two miles a day, as often as possible, or at least every other day. Another way to look at it is, as you're able to walk up to your target level of intensity, you can walk longer till you reach 45 minutes to an hour, and then more often, up to five to seven days a week. With this exercise routine and wise food choices in moderate quantities, you'll be best able to lose body fat.

Although anaerobic exercise such as weight training does not benefit you in the same way as your aerobic activity, it also has pluses for people with diabetes. Brief and frequent weight-lifting sessions increase lean body mass (muscles), which in turn increases the calories you expend each day. Maintaining muscle mass and strength is essential to overall fitness and optimal diabetes management. According to Robert Antonacci, M.S., an exercise physiologist and president of Fitness Appraisal, Inc., in Carlsbad, California, "An effective strength training routine can be lifting one weight 8 to 10 times for each of five major muscle groups. Weakness and neuropathy commonly develop in the legs, back, chest, arm, and shoulders, so try to work these groups. It may take only 10 to 15 minutes every other day to increase lean body mass, strength, and bone density. You don't need go to a gym. Just purchase a few weights that you can work with easily at home."

If you have eye disease related to your diabetes (retinopathy), you need to do activities that will not raise your blood pressure too much. Weight training and higher-intensity aerobic exercise may increase your blood pressure, which in turn may make your retinopathy worse. Be sure to consult with your physician before participating in a weight-training program if you have this condition.

Dr. Larry Verity, Ph.D., Fellow, American College of Sports Medicine, and a professor of exercise physiology at San Diego State University, has had type I diabetes for twenty-two years and remains free of any complications, a testament to a daily routine that includes exercise and reasonable food choices. He's an expert at designing exercise prescriptions, particularly for those who have health concerns. According to Dr. Verity, "People with diabetes who have no complications should engage in sustained aerobic activity for 30 minutes at least five days and preferably seven days a week. This amount of exercise will help you achieve a more stable blood glucose, avoiding those peaks and valleys of blood glucose."

You may have heard about the much publicized report from the Centers for Disease Control which determined that start-and-stop exercising was also beneficial. According to Dr. Verity, "it was once thought that exercise must be continuous, but we now know that you will also receive benefits from 30 minutes of activity accumulated over the period of a day, say, for instance, in three 10-minute intervals. So if you don't have time to do 30 or 45 minutes of exercise, do what you can, even if it's 10 minutes. This level of activity has the greatest benefits for those individuals that are completely sedentary. For best results in achieving weight loss or improving diabetes, try to walk briskly or do some form of continuous aerobic activity for 30 minutes 5 days to 7 days a week."

MONITOR YOUR BLOOD GLUCOSE

Hypoglycemia is a significant threat to people who exercise while taking insulin or sulfonureas. People controlling non-insulin-dependent diabetes with meal planning and exercise alone aren't at risk for developing hypoglycemia, low blood sugar, when exercising. Talk to your doctor or diabetes educator about making changes. Even the day-to-day variations in your activity level may require you to adjust your food intake and/or insulin dosage.

However you increase your activity level, you must monitor your blood glucose. I suggest that my patients measure their blood glucose before and after exercise. If your blood glucose is low before or during exercise, have a snack to raise it. It's not uncommon to see a 250 milligram percent blood glucose reading go down to 150 milligram percent during or after exercise. Carry a snack to eat that contains real sugar. Hard candies like Life Savers, 4 to 6 ounces of juice or Gatorade, or glucose tablets are good choices. Check your local pharmacy for Z'Bars, candy bars specifically designed to increase blood glucose during a hypoglycemic episode. If your blood glucose becomes too low during or after exercise, and you feel shaky or light-headed, these rapidly acting sugars will help to quickly raise it. *Since any increase in physical activity can lower your blood glucose, you may need to change your meal plan or medication or both.* And don't forget to drink plenty of water before, during, and after exercise. It's the best way to hydrate your working muscles.

KEEPING EXERCISE SAFE

Begin your exercise session with a 10-minute warm-up. If you're going for a walk, that can mean simply walking slowly for the first 5 minutes, just enough to raise the core body temperature. Then do your stretching exercises for another 5 minutes. This will enhance flexibility and prevent injury. During the last 5 minutes of exercise, again, slow down your pace, and do a bit more stretching afterwards. The cool-down will facilitate removal of metabolic by-products, especially important if you have a heart problem. After exercise, much of your blood supply is pooled in your extremities. If you stop suddenly, your heart may be unable to pump enough of your blood back to your heart and brain. Cooling down allows for a gradual return of blood from the extremities to the heart.

Avoid vigorous exercise if it is too hot, humid, smoggy, or cold. The safest time for people with diabetes to exercise is 60 to 90 minutes after a meal. This helps to prevent the blood glucose from getting too high or too low and allows people taking insulin to decrease their dose if necessary. If you have tendency to develop low blood glucose levels following exercise, you may do better to exercise in the morning, either before or after taking medication and eating breakfast. At this time, post-exercise hypoglycemia appears to be less likely, and you're better able to detect any problem during normal waking hours.

DIABETES IDENTIFICATION

It's a good idea to keep diabetes identification with you at all times, either as a piece of jewelry or a wallet card. It is actually best to have both. Wallet cards have spaces for you to write your name and phone number and the name and phone number of your doctor. Jewelry (necklaces and bracelets) identifies you as having diabetes and may give a 1-800 number to call. Some also say what kind of medicine you take. Carrying these things will tell people what's wrong if you cannot talk and need help.

They could save your life. It is also wise to exercise with a buddy who is familiar with your diabetes.

If you have type I diabetes, do a urine ketone test if your blood sugar is higher than 240 mg/dl. If your urine ketones are high, do not exercise until levels are within the normal range again. Stop exercising and call your doctor if you start to have chest or leg pain. People with diabetes often lose feeling in their legs due to nerve damage. Injuries need immediate attention because if a person has poor circulation, an injury won't heal properly, and then there is a risk of gangrene. Check your feet for cuts, blisters, and reddened areas before and after each exercise session. You may want to keep a record of when and how long you exercise, so you can use the information to make adjustments to your diet or medication, if necessary.

CHAPTER 8

DINING OUT DOESN'T HAVE TO DO YOU IN

THE PROBLEM OF THE EVER-INCREASING PORTION SIZE

Trying to estimate how many carbohydrate choices or calories you eat in a restaurant is perhaps the greatest challenge of dining away from home. You have probably been taught by your dietitian to estimate portion sizes using the mental yardstick, based on measuring portions at home and becoming familiar with how that portion size looks on a plate or in a bowl. But you may be confounded by a trend in the restaurant world toward ever-larger portions. For instance, try to guess how much spaghetti is on a plate: 2 cups or 4½?

Since carbohydrates affect your blood glucose most significantly, we must pay particular attention to those foods. *One source of confusion is the likely gap between the amount of carbohydrate choices in your food plan and the amount you are likely to be served in a restaurant.* If your food plan suggests three carbohydrate choices for dinner, that is 1½ cups of cooked pasta, or 300 calories. But most restaurants typically serve 2½ cups of pasta, not to mention the bread and the sauce. That's at least five or six carbohydrate choices, or 800 calories. If you're trying to stay within your carbohydrate limit, it's important to do the arithmetic. While foods like pasta can fit easily into your plan, you will still gain weight or elevate your blood glucose if you eat them in overly large quantities.

I recently discussed this subject with an American executive who works for Intel in Japan. He was back in the United States for a visit and told me how shocked he was at the giant portions served in restaurants here. American restaurants are heaping huge quantities on plates in an effort to attract customers who demand more for their money. According to Jeffrey Prince, former communications director for the National Restaurant Association, even the plates in restaurants are bigger. Most restaurants used to buy 10- or 11-inch plates, but now, according to Prince, 12-inch plates are becoming standard.

Lisa Young, a registered dietitian who has run weight loss programs and is now a doctoral candidate at New York University, is writing her dissertation on portion size. Many servings on the diabetic exchange lists seem "like cocktail servings," she says, but notes that in real life, everything from bagels to restaurant main dishes is getting larger. On the exchange system, of course, although the serving sizes may be smaller than what you actually eat, you simply do the math. A meat exchange is one ounce, although your meal plan probably includes 3 or more ounces per meal; a starch exchange is ½ cup of cereal, but if you eat 1½ cups, you must count it as three carbohydrate choices or starch exchanges.

Young points out that the baked potato in the diabetic exchange chart lists at 3 ounces and is 80 calories. She insists that this size of a baking potato would never be served in a restaurant, and may even be hard to find in the supermarket. A more typical size is usually 6 to 8 ounces, which would count as two or three carbohydrate choices, and would boast anywhere from 160 to 240 calories, without any toppings.

Keep in mind that the "serving" sizes of the carbohydrate choices, or even those listed in my recipes, are not meant as recommendations. Your registered dietitian will determine how many carbohydrates you need at each meal and snack. You may eat more than the serving size listed; you may eat less. The objective is to be familiar with the carbohydrate values so you can determine how much fits into your particular plan. And most important, try to eat similar amounts of carbohydrates at similar times each day.

THE HIDDEN FATS AND CALORIES IN RESTAURANT FOODS

The next concern is what the large restaurant portion contains. Is the pizza topped with ½ cup of cheese or with 2 cups? Is there a tablespoon of oil in your pasta sauce or ½ cup? It's hard to tell what's in certain foods that are a combination of ingredients. Most calories and fat are hidden. This makes a strong case for ordering the simplest of meals: a baked potato rather than mashed potatoes; plain chicken or fish rather than chicken or fish in a heavy sauce. Avoid adding butter to bread or rolls. If you're trying to lose weight, you may get enough calories from your entree and can skip both bread and the butter. If you eat out frequently and consistently eat large portions with more fat in them than you're counting on, you're likely to have at least a significant rise in your blood glucose, if not in your overall body weight.

STRATEGIES FOR DEALING WITH LARGE PORTIONS

Whatever you order, keep in mind that a meal with all the trimmings is likely to be double what you need. The logical conclusion is to not eat everything on your plate. That may be a departure from your normal way of doing things, and it does take some practice, but it can be done. Start with ordering less. If you're at a restaurant, the food may taste better than you're used to, so you want to finish it. If you're out with family or friends, perhaps having a glass of wine and a jolly time, your inhibitions are down, and you are likely to overeat. In order to prevent your blood sugars from going through the roof, you must eat half, if you can, or order less. Here are some strategies that can help. Practice them until they become habits.

1. Check the list of appetizers. You may find one that will satisfy you as a meal. If you order a full entree, skip the appetizer altogether, or have a small salad with minimal vinaigrette dressing.
2. Order appetizer-sized portions of an entree.
3. Order salad and soup. If you're not very hungry or don't need the carbohydrates, order soup only or salad only, and go lightly on the dressing.
4. Pasta is a tricky meal to order in a restaurant, and I encourage people to proceed with caution. It is best to order a half portion. If it's not available, eat half and take the other half home. You probably already know to avoid a pasta with a cream sauce. It's just as important to limit the total quantity of pasta, even if it has a low-fat or fat-free sauce.
5. Share an entree with someone.
6. Skip the bread. If you can't control yourself, set it out of your reach or ask your waiter to take it away.
7. As soon as you're finished with half of your meal, ask your server to take your plate. Consider taking the rest home. It will make a nice lunch tomorrow.
8. After a meal where you've stayed within your limits, remind yourself of how good you feel. When you've eaten to the point that you feel uncomfortable, privately but consciously observe that it actually isn't fun to feel stuffed. Instead of flogging yourself and feeling guilty, just make up your mind to do it differently next time.

9. If you plan to have dessert, you may need to pass on both the bread and the rice, potato, or pasta, and instead order a nice plate of sautéed vegetables or a salad with your protein.

10. Control your alcohol intake. If your doctor has given you guidelines about alcohol limits, stick to them. Alcohol adds extra calories and stimulates the appetite, all the while decreasing your inhibitions. That may be just what you *don't* need in a restaurant situation.

Finally, beware of thinking that it's okay to overeat at a restaurant meal because it's a special occasion. According to Hope Warshaw, M.M.Sc., R.D., C.D.E., and author of *The Restaurant Companion: A Guide to Healthier Eating Out,* "Most Americans eat out an average of four times a week. It will be difficult to achieve your health and nutrition goals if there's always an opportunity to overeat." Warshaw's book offers tips on various cuisines, including Mexican, Chinese, Italian, Thai, Indian, and Middle Eastern. She even includes fast-food restaurants and lists carbohydrate values from many selections from all these menus. This is a valuable resource for helping you make the best selections when dining out.

Here are some helpful tips about specific foods.

BREAKFAST

- **Cold cereal:** Available almost anywhere, this is a good breakfast standby. Ask for nonfat or low-fat milk and try to select a whole-grain cereal. Shredded wheat is often available. Order fresh berries or melon on the side. It's a treat you may not always have at home. This breakfast provides more fiber and less fat than the egg breakfast. If you are traveling and have trouble with constipation, staying with cereal may help.

- **Eggs:** Go easy on eggs due to their high cholesterol content. But their protein content helps to keep blood sugars stable. Many restaurants offer egg substitutes or egg white omelets. Beware of the foods that accompany the egg—bacon, ham, sausage, hash browns, or fried potatoes—because they may add more fat than you need.

- **Oatmeal:** It would seem that there is nothing a restaurant could do to adulterate this wholesome food, and it is probably true (any added salt would be minor compared with a typical healthy day's intake of sodium). A half cup is equal to one carbohydrate choice. Milk or fruit toppings add carbohydrates as well. The benefit of oats for breakfast is that they contain soluble fiber that may help to lower cholesterol. See chapter 2 for details. This is a good breakfast; just add some yogurt or milk for protein.

- **French toast:** A typical order of French toast at a restaurant is likely to be six carbohydrate choices from the bread and over three carbohydrate choices (53 grams) from ¼ cup syrup. If you really want the French toast, figure out the number of carbohydrates you're allowed in the morning and portion it out. You may need to add an egg or a slice of lean ham for protein.

SALADS

Choosing a Caesar, chef, or cob salad as an entree may be eating a meal higher in calories than a sandwich. Beware of too much cheese, bacon, meats, and avocado. To slim down a spinach salad, ask the waiter or waitress to omit or limit cheese or bacon. Order light dressing or ask for dressing on the side. Instead of pouring the dressing on the salad, dip the tines of the fork lightly in the dressing before taking a forkful of salad. Use a tablespoon or two of dressing instead of a quarter or a half cup. Then look for a flavorful vinegar, such as a seasoned rice vinegar, or lemon wedges to add moisture. These minor requests make a major difference in the nutritional value of this potentially great lunch.

SOUPS

Bean, lentil, vegetable, minestrone, wonton, and chicken noodle are nice lunch alternatives. Because they are broth-based, they contain much less saturated fat than cream soups. Depending on your carbohydrate allowance, you may want a cup rather than a bowl. Ask the waiter or waitress about the soup. Can the onion soup be ordered without the cheese? Can the black bean soup be served without sour cream? Try a bowl of chili with beans, without added cheese. Is the chowder a tomato-based Manhattan-style (best choice) or a cream-based New England-style? If you're within your carbohydrate allowance, add a slice of bread or a few crackers so your blood sugar will be high enough during the afternoon.

BREADS

Breads are considered as one carbohydrate choice or exchange per ounce. Learn to estimate the carbohydrate value of a slice of bread at home. A typical slice of bread ranges from 1 to 2 ounces. One ounce or 30 grams provides one carbohydrate serving, or 15 grams of carbohydrate. But a pretzel from a street vendor can be as much as 5 ounces, or as much food as five slices of bread. Bagels are seldom 2 ounces, and are more likely 3 or 4 ounces. Large-sized 5- to 6-ounce muffins are common these days. Even when they're fat-free, you can still figure they're one carbohydrate choice or exchange per ounce—that's five or six carbohydrate choices!

SANDWICHES

Sandwiches are a good standby as a lunch option, but they vary tremendously in size. Find a deli or sandwich shop in your neighborhood where you can get the kind and amount of sandwich you want, even if it means you eat half one day and save the other half for the next day. That's what I do, but I always ask to have the sandwich cut in half and the two halves wrapped separately. The second half goes directly into my office refrigerator so I'm not tempted. Best choices are sliced turkey or chicken with lettuce, tomato, and mustard—hold the mayonnaise and cheese. For variety, lean ham or beef may occasionally be substituted if they are truly lean, and in the case of ham, if you can afford the sodium. Processed meats such as bologna, salami, and pastrami tend to be high in fat as well as sodium. Tuna and chicken salad should be selected only if they have little or no mayonnaise. Keep the sandwich moist by adding plenty of lettuce and tomatoes. Tomatoes in particular provide good nutrition and flavor without the fat or calories.

To figure out how many grams of carbohydrates are in a typical sandwich, ask your dietitian to help you dissect it. My client Fiana brought in a chicken wrap made in unleavened flat bread. It had 5 ounces of bread (five carbohydrate choices) and 4 ounces of chicken, with a few vegetables, and was 570 calories *without* the mayonnaise.

My husband brought me a sandwich from the Normandy Bakery, a French bistro near his office: a 6-ounce French roll (six carbohydrate choices) with 6 ounces of ham and mayonnaise. The total came to 650 calories. Remember, the biggest variable to affect your blood sugar is the bread. Eat only the amount of bread on your sandwich that is in your plan. If it's double what you need for lunch, eat only the protein and half the bread. Choosing familiar restaurants on most days helps take the guessing out of the carbohydrate value of your selection.

MEXICAN FOOD

Since traditional Mexican foods are primarily carbohydrates—rice, beans, tortillas, and chips—the best way to avoid *grande* blood glucose levels is to order à la carte. Fajitas are a good choice, because you can assemble your own burrito from a corn or flour tortilla that is baked, microwaved, or grilled, and not deep-fried like the crispy taco shells. Corn tortillas are generally made without fat, so any brand is fine. Some flour tortillas are made with lard, so look for the kind that are made with vegetable oil only—the amount easily fits into a low-fat diet. Pay attention to the tortilla size:

> 6-inch tortilla = 15 grams of carbohydrate
> 8-inch tortilla = 25 grams of carbohydrate
> 16-inch tortilla = 50 grams of carbohydrate

Avoid items with lots of cheese, sour cream, or guacamole in them. They can add up to high fat, high calories, and high blood sugars. Use light amounts of these for flavor. Instead, pour on the salsa, chopped tomato, and shredded lettuce. Skip the cheese or go easy on it. Decide whether you'd like to get your carbohydrate choice(s) from rice and beans, or a tortilla, or a combination of them. Here's a quick rule of thumb from Linn Guiducci, R.D., a pediatric nutrition specialist in Portland, Oregon, and the author of a series of nutrition topic sheets for children with diabetes. A soft-shell taco, 2 to 3 ounces of chicken, beef, and/or cheese and 1 cup of beans or rice (or a half cup of each) and vegetables (which are free) is 45 grams of carbohydrate, or three carbohydrate choices total.

How can you forget the chips? You certainly won't if they are sitting right in front of you. If you decide to eat 10 chips, figure they add about 15 grams of carbohydrate, or 1 carbohydrate choice. Enjoy a reasonable amount, and then set them slightly out of your reach, or at least move them to a different spot just to remind yourself that you no longer care to eat them. Make a decision and stick with it.

ITALIAN

One of the most popular Italian dishes, pasta, is also one of the easiest to overeat. Make sure you count ½ cup as 15 grams of carbohydrate. Try ordering a half portion or an appetizer-sized order of pasta as your main course if it is available, and choose a tomato-based marinara sauce or one with clams or seafood and vegetables.

When ordering meat in an Italian restaurant, choose veal piccata lightly sautéed with lemon, which is a better choice than veal Parmesan with breading and cheese. Chicken cacciatore is a good alternative to chicken Parmesan for the same reason: it is prepared in a tomato sauce without being breaded or fried first, and cheese generally is not added. Remember to ask for it to be cooked without the skin, or remove the skin before eating.

If you are ordering pizza, remember that a slice of pizza is probably around 500 calories per slice, with 15 to 45 grams of carbohydrate, or one to three carbohydrate choices, depending on the size and the thickness of the crust (most likely three, or even more if it's very thick or deep dish). Help yourself along by ordering a salad with Italian dressing. Eat the salad first and then slowly eat the pizza so you can stop before you've had too much. Your blood glucose will tell you how much pizza you can handle. Ask for light cheese, if available, to limit saturated fat calories.

CHINESE

The great part about Chinese or Thai food is the ease with which vegetables become a part of your meal, adding fiber, vitamins, and minerals and lots of flavor. Take advantage of it with shrimp and snow peas, Moo Goo Gai Pan (chicken with vegetables), or beef with broccoli. To make sure your beef with broccoli has more broccoli than beef, ask for it. Then request that it be prepared with minimal oil.

With Chinese food, the common practice is to order several items and share with the group. That's fine, but if you order an entree per person, you'll have too much food. Make one item a broth-based soup, another a salad, and perhaps another an all-vegetable Buddha's delight. You'll cut calories and fat by staying away from breaded and fried dishes like General Tso's Chicken, Lemon Chicken, and fried egg rolls. Ask for your dish to be prepared with minimal oil. To avoid overeating, stick with one plate of food. Second helpings may lead to more food than you need. Limit rice or skip it, if necessary, to stay within your carbohydrate goal. Remember, ⅓ cup rice is one carbohydrate choice, or 15 grams of carbohydrate.

CHICKEN

The popularity of chicken has spawned a host of roasted chicken restaurants where you can dine in or take home a roasted chicken along with a side dish or two. This can make an easy and healthy supper. Keep in mind that the white meat has less fat than the dark meat, and don't eat the skin, since it adds a teaspoon of fat per piece, or about 50 calories. When choosing side dishes, take advantage of low-calorie, high-fiber, vitamin-rich vegetables such as broccoli, green beans, or carrots. Starchy vegetables such as corn, winter squash, or mashed potatoes are also good options as long as you count them as a carbohydrate choice. Check with the restaurant about fats added to side dishes and avoid those with butter, a saturated fat.

FISH

Many of my clients prefer to order fish in a restaurant rather than cook it at home. I suggest you do both, as the oil in fish has many benefits. The Chart House, a popular national restaurant chain, specializes in fresh seafood and steak. "Our average dinner portion of fish is 8 to 9 ounces," says Leonard Delgado, director of restaurant food and beverage systems at the Chart House Restaurant. A 9-ounce piece of grilled salmon is about 630 calories, or about 70 calories per ounce. Top with lemon instead of tartar sauce or butter for a savings of about 50 calories per teaspoon. Take advantage of the appetizer menus for shrimp cocktail, steamed clams, or mussels. Avoid items that are breaded and fried.

STEAK

A steak was once thought to be the dieter's choice, but we now know that it's not the best choice by far if you're limiting saturated fat. You're better off with fish or chicken prepared without cream sauce, cheese, or butter. Remember the "better" the cut, the more marbled the meat, the more calories from fat, which is mostly saturated. Small 3- to 4-ounce portions of beef can be a part of a conscientious diet—just make sure it's lean. Flank, round, and sirloin are leaner than filet mignon or prime rib.

6-Ounce Portions	Fat Grams	Calories	Carb
London broil	12 to 16	320 to 360	0
New York strip	16	350	0
Filet mignon	16 to 20	350 to 400	0
Prime rib	40 to 50	400 to 500	0

FAST-FOOD RESTAURANTS

In an effort to bridge the gap between the ideal diet and the demands of our busy lives, a review of the best options at a few fast-foods restaurant may be helpful. This may be especially beneficial for young children and teens with type I diabetes. Their lifestyles make McDonald's, Burger King, and Taco Bell a fact of life. According to Lynn Guiducci, R.D., "the kid's meals give children about the right servings—a two- to three-ounce hamburger or cheeseburger, small fries, a little ketchup and mustard, and a milk to go with it, which roughly provides three carbohydrate choices, depending on the portion size of the individual restaurant. A side salad is a nice addition. A grilled chicken sandwich (not breaded), with lots of vegetables such as tomato, lettuce, and onions, a little barbecue sauce or ketchup, small fries, and a milk makes a quick, acceptable meal. A simple hamburger, taco, or sandwich and a diet drink or iced tea may keep carbohydrates at two or three choices."

As for teens, Guiducci says, "They naturally have bigger appetites and will most likely need more food and calories than the kid's meals will provide." She tries to encourage more meat or chicken in the meal and a little less bun. "So, for example," Guiducci recommends, "a quarter-pound hamburger or cheeseburger with one bun instead of a triple-decker bun, which usually provides fewer carbohydrates and also can be more filling." The size of the fries also makes a big difference in the carbohydrate count as well. A small order can be equal to approximately two carbohydrate choices, while a large order equals almost four choices.

Don't assume a trip through the salad bar will be lower in carbohydrates than a sandwich. It all depends on what you choose. Fruit and vegetables are sorely missing from most of these quick-service establishments, so make up for them at other meals or in snacks throughout the day. Low-fat milk provides the same amount of calcium and has two-thirds fewer calories than a shake, with only one carbohydrate choice in an 8-ounce carton. You'll do better to order a frozen yogurt cone at 120 calories and 1½ carbohydrate choices than a 16-ounce shake at McDonald's, which provides between 300 and 500 calories, or four to six carbohydrate choices.

Fish Sandwich: Don't fall for the notion that the fried fish sandwich at a fast-food restaurant is a better choice than the burger. Remember, breading acts as a grease sponge. As a rule of thumb, it doubles the calorie value. Here's how they compare:

	Calories	Fat	Carbohydrates
McDonald's Fish Sandwich	440	26	38
McDonald's Plain Hamburger	260	10	31

SOME SURPRISING FINDINGS

Here is a list of typical restaurant selections taken from a *New York Times* article by Marion Burros, reviewing New York University dietitian Lisa Young's research on portion sizes along with a few collected by the newspaper. Since the only listings are for calories and fat, I have estimated carbohydrate values.

	Calories	Fat	Carbohydrates
Hamburger and onion rings	1550	101	126
Lasagna	960	53	93
Caesar salad	660	46	30
Porterhouse steak dinner with baked potato, butter, vegetables, and salad	1860	125	69
Gnocchi	700	47	52
Fettuccine with creamed spinach	1050	82	98
Mixed salad	600	36	45
Focaccia club sandwich	1222	65	85
Risotto	1280	110	60

CHAPTER 9

STOCKING THE PANTRY

A home-cooked meal seems like a rare treat in this day and age. Many people frequently eat their lunches at work or at a restaurant, and over half of their weekly evening meals away from home. The tactical advantage to eating at home is that you have more control over the ingredients used to cook the food. For example, at home you can use olive oil rather than butter, and you can use less of it. Portion sizes are also better controlled. Many of my clients feel they are more likely to stay within their carbohydrate goals when they eat at home rather than at a restaurant. The cooking tips and guidelines for stocking your pantry outlined in this chapter will help you set up for a home-cooked meal and resist at least some of the temptation to order take-out, or to go out.

If you're already in the routine of making home-cooked meals and your cooking is fairly healthy, you may not need much help, and can proceed directly to the recipes for some new ideas. But if you're turning over a new leaf nutritionally, you may need a little extra help as you stock your pantry and replace some of your old cooking techniques with a few new ones. Prepare yourself for some of the best food you've ever eaten as you review the following tips and lists.

COOKING TIPS

Pasta: Any kind of commercially made pasta will turn out a nice dish. The fresh pasta from the deli case boils in 2 to 3 minutes, while the dried varieties may take 8 to 12 minutes. I tend to prefer dried pasta to fresh, unless I'm sure I'm going to cook it within a day or two. All the recipes in this book call for dried pasta.

In the effort to select whole-grain pasta, you may have to look beyond your local supermarket to a specialty or health food store. If the whole wheat spaghetti or linguine is too chewy for your taste, try Eden's 50/50 line of pastas. It's half whole wheat and half white flour. You won't know the difference, but your body will be better for it.

Pasta should always be cooked in a large pot of boiling water without a lid. It needs a stir from time to time. Oil and salt are *not* necessary when cooking pasta; the sauce will add plenty of flavor and moisture. If your pasta will be set aside prior to eating or assembly, rinse it and cover with plastic to prevent sticking or drying out. Remember, 2 ounces of dry pasta will yield 1 to 1½ cups cooked, depending on the type. When pasta cooks longer, it absorbs more water and has less carbohydrates per cup. That means that in order to keep carbohydrates at their lowest, dried pasta should be cooked for 12 to 14 minutes rather than 7 to 8 minutes, depending on the shape and without overcooking it, of course.

	Carbohydrate Grams
1 cup pasta cooked al dente	44
1 cup pasta cooked tender	32
2 cups pasta cooked al dente	88
2 cups pasta cooked tender	64

To translate, you save nearly 1 entire serving of carbohydrate per cup, and 2 servings of carbohydrate per 2 cups when you opt for pasta that has been cooked slightly longer.

Rice: Brown rice is higher in fiber, so choose it whenever you can. Basmati rice, available in both white and brown types, is my favorite. It has a rich, nutty flavor. Try substituting chicken broth for the water and add garlic for a new twist. Quick-cooking rice is an option, but the texture and flavor are not as good, in my opinion.

If you add salt to a pot of rice or cooked cereal, you might be interested to know that ⅛ teaspoon of salt contains about 300 milligrams of sodium. That is for the entire *pot* of rice. If there were four servings in that pot, each would have 75 milligrams of sodium, which fits well into the recommended sodium intake of 3000 milligrams, or 1000 milligrams per meal. If you are on a more restricted sodium diet, make the appropriate adjustments.

When I cook rice to serve with chicken or fish, I usually make a big pot so I can use the leftover rice the next day for one of my versions of fried rice (see page 344). Rice, pasta, couscous, and beans are great for "batch" cooks, who like to do their week's cooking on a Saturday or Sunday afternoon. A pot of black bean soup, lentil salad with goat cheese and sun-dried tomatoes, stuffed manicotti shells, couscous, and polenta are all great for reheating, packing in a lunch, or in some cases, eating cold.

Meat, poultry, or fish: If you keep chicken breasts, pork loin chops, or ground turkey in your freezer, particularly in individual portions, you can turn them into a meal in minutes using one of the recipes in this book. Fresh fish is delicate and generally does not freeze well (shrimp and scallops are exceptions), so I usually buy and cook it the same day or the very next day.

To sauté chicken, fish, meat, or even vegetables with less fat than traditional sautés, simply substitute a flavorful liquid for butter, margarine, or oil. Depending on the type of dish, choose from chicken, beef, or vegetable stock, vermouth, red or white wine, dry sherry, soy sauce, or water. Here's how:

1. Heat a nonstick sauté pan over medium-high heat and then add 2 teaspoons of oil.
2. When the oil is hot, add onion, garlic, peppers or other vegetables, meat or poultry and sauté, moving the pieces around with a spatula or wooden spoon.
3. Continue to sauté, stirring frequently. Add a tablespoon of the desired liquid as needed to keep from burning, each time using a spatula or wooden spoon to scrape up the glaze formed at the bottom of the pan.
4. To thicken a sauce, blend arrowroot, cornstarch, or flour with cold stock, water, or milk. Whisk it into the sauce and cook over low to medium heat until it thickens. For medium thickness, use 1 tablespoon of arrowroot per cup of liquid. If you use cornstarch, you'll need about 4 teaspoons, and if you use flour, you'll need closer to 2 tablespoons per cup of liquid to achieve the same thickening power.

Fresh vegetables: Many people get into the produce department, see all those great-looking, colorful fruits and vegetables, and buy enough for three weeks rather than three days. Buy only enough perishable vegetables (such as mushrooms, zucchini, broccoli, and salad greens) as you plan to use in the first half of the week. Whether they last through the rest of the week depends on how fresh they were when you bought them. Keep less perishable vegetables (potatoes, carrots, garlic, shallots, onions, and winter squash) on hand.

Some of my clients like to use the bags of prewashed salad greens, including romaine, spinach, and a wide variety of mixed greens. Vegetables all cut up and ready to stir-fry are also available, fresh or frozen. Use the guide below to sauté vegetables, or steam them if you like. But seasoning them is important. Just a touch of oil, garlic, and salt will keep them interesting. I've seen too many people who stopped eating vegetables altogether because they were bored with plain steamed vegetables and were too afraid to add *any* fat, thus missing out on all the vitamins, minerals, and fiber in vegetables just to save a teaspoon of oil. And remember, that small amount of oil may even be good for you if it's monounsaturated (olive or canola oil). The recipes in the vegetable and salad sections of the book will give you some new ideas for tempting vegetable treats.

Frozen vegetables and fruits: Peas and corn are quite good in the frozen form, as is spinach, which is used in several of my recipes including manicotti shells, quiche, and potato-spinach dumplings. Other frozen vegetables have a hard time competing with the flavor and texture of fresh, but they can help in a pinch. Nutritionally, they are fine, with only a slight amount of salt already added, usually about 50 milligrams per half cup.

I keep frozen blueberries, raspberries, strawberries, and mango on hand for smoothies, muffins, and toppings. Whenever my bananas get too ripe before they're eaten, into the freezer they go for smoothies or banana ice cream. Just peel them, cut them into chunks, put them in a plastic bag, and toss them in the freezer. Later you can drop them in a blender with an orange or other fruit along with some yogurt or buttermilk for an icy treat.

Canned beans, soups, vegetables, and fruits: Canned corn, peas, and green beans usually mean too great a sacrifice in taste and texture. Worse is their typical sodium content of around 250 milligrams per half cup. Rinsing these will help reduce sodium by about a third. I do have a bias, however, toward canned legume-type beans. Black, kidney, garbanzo, and pinto beans are great staples to use in salads, soups, or in main dishes.

Rinse beans well to remove about ⅓ of the sodium, or look for low-sodium beans if you are on a low-sodium diet. Mix a can of black beans with a cup or so of corn, and add some onion and bell pepper. Toss this mixture with a vinaigrette dressing and you have a terrific salad or an easy-to-carry lunch. A can of kidney beans added to leftover rice and seasoned with onion, celery, and garlic will make a version of the Cuban dish called Moros y Cristianos. Serve this with a nice tossed green salad with a few tomato slices and you have a great vegetarian dinner.

Canned water chestnuts, bamboo shoots, and baby corn are ideal for a stir-fry dish. Artichoke hearts and hearts of palm are a nice surprise in a salad, and may both be found packed in water rather than oil. Although fresh fruits are the best choices, the few canned varieties that work best include pineapples, cherries, applesauce, pears, and mandarin oranges. I've tried turning my Halloween pumpkins into pumpkin pie, but the water content varies too much. I find that canned pumpkin still makes the best pumpkin pie filling. See my recipe in the Desserts section.

Sauces and toppings: Food purists may shun bottled sauces such as spaghetti sauce and barbecue sauce, yet many admit they are mighty handy to have around. These include bottled spaghetti sauces, which are about ½ serving carbohydrate (7 grams) per ¼ cup. Barbecue sauce and various Asian sauces tend to be a little sweeter, and are generally used in smaller amounts. Salsa, horseradish, and various mustards are generally low enough in carbohydrates to be considered "free" foods when eaten in reasonable amounts. Look for reduced-sodium versions of condiments and sauces. Pass on the cream-based sauces due to their high saturated-fat content. You may find a pesto sauce in the deli case, made with olive oil, pine nuts, and basil; it's fine—just keep the portion to 1 or 2 teaspoons per cup of pasta.

Keep whole tomatoes, tomato paste, and tomato sauce on hand for chicken, rice, or other pasta dishes. Tomato paste is generally made without any salt added, and other tomato products can be purchased in the low-salt variety. Tomato paste, anchovy paste, and pesto can now be purchased in tubes, convenient for storage and using in small amounts.

Jams, jellies, and preserves can be used on toast, bagels, or English muffins in the morning, but you'll get fewer carbohydrates from low-sugar jams. Here's how they compare:

1 Tablespoon	Carbohydrate Grams
Regular preserves	13
Low-sugar jam	6
No-sugar jam	2

If you need fat in your breakfast for the extra satiety it provides, the best option is to add a teaspoon of oil to your breakfast bread and toast it on a pan or griddle or under a broiler. I suggest you avoid the margarine/butter debate altogether, as I have in my recipes, and use oil whenever possible. If you must use a spread, choose the option with the least amount of saturated fat, which is probably a soft, reduced-fat margarine in a tub. If you're stuck on butter, try "I Can't Believe It's Not Butter," which is a blend of butter and unsaturated oil.

Canned soups: You won't find cream of mushroom soup or any other such thing in my recipes, and for good reason. Many canned soups are loaded with sodium, fat, and artificial flavorings that are not as tasty as freshly seasoned sauces. I do, however, recommend canned chicken, beef, or vegetable broth (often referred to by cooks as stock), and suggest you choose the one that is labeled "100% fat-free with ⅓ less sodium." Of course, homemade broth is the best, but if you don't have the time, canned will do just fine.

New, more nutritionally acceptable soups that can be simply heated for a last-minute meal are becoming more available. These include the Progresso, Healthy Choice, and Campbell's home-style versions of minestrone, vegetable, chicken noodle, split pea, and lentil soups.

Bread products: When choosing breads, select those made with 100 percent whole grains. The more coarse, predominantly whole-grain, sprouted or cracked wheat varieties have more fiber, vitamins, and minerals. They may also cause a slower rise in blood glucose, although this is a subject currently under debate (see chapter 2). To assure that a bread is truly whole-grain, look for the words "whole grain" or "whole wheat" in the list of ingredients. Don't be fooled by bread labeled "whole wheat" that lists white flour as the first ingredient with caramel color or molasses added for color. Ingredients are listed in descending order by quantity, so whatever is listed first is present in the greatest amount. Descriptors on the front label indicating the bread is mostly unrefined grain include cracked wheat, made with whole grain, made with whole wheat, multi-grain, oat bran, oatmeal, pumpernickel, rye, seven-grain, or whole bran.

If you don't eat a lot of bread, keep it in the freezer. If you have too much bread on hand, and it's on its way to getting stale, make French toast (page 125). Vary bread choices, using pita, tortillas, bagels, or English muffins.

If you like to make pizza at home, and don't want to go to the trouble of making your own crust, pick up pizza crusts from your neighborhood pizza joint. I keep two or three of them in my freezer. Be sure to allow four to five hours to thaw. (You can't rush the thaw—adding heat will affect the yeast.) A crusty loaf of sourdough bread is another pizza crust option. Just cut it in half lengthwise and top with your tomato or pesto sauce, vegetables, and cheese. Remember that the more bread you use, the more carbohydrate choices to count.

Buy corn or flour tortillas made without lard or other saturated fats and stuff them with meat, seafood, beans, or low-fat cheese for a quick meal. Add vegetables for fiber and new flavors. Avoid folded crispy tortilla shells, which are fried. Heat soft tortillas in a nonstick pan or in a microwave, adding a bit of olive oil if needed.

Dairy: Keep plain nonfat or low-fat yogurt on hand for smoothies or as a topping on berries or melon. It's a great substitute for sour cream on fish or a baked potato or as a filling in a tortilla. Season with herb, garlic, lemon, or cilantro. Use artificially sweetened lemon yogurt as a dressing in a fruit salad or strawberry-flavored yogurt as a pie filling.

Buy part-skim mozzarella cheese or other reduced-fat cheese. Since regular cheeses are high in saturated fat, you may want to try some nondairy cheeses such as Tofu-rella. This tofu-based cheese comes in a yellow and a white cheese and is really quite good in sandwiches and salads.

Keep canned evaporated skim milk on hand for cooking—it's richer than fluid milk without the saturated fat. Although I prefer fresh buttermilk for baking, I keep dried buttermilk on hand as a backup.

Vinegars, oils, and salad dressings: I do not buy bottled salad dressing. In fact, I have a hard time eating it on a salad at a restaurant. It's so easy to make your own. Keep flavored vinegars on hand, including balsamic, tarragon, champagne, or raspberry. Mix and match the following ingredients for your salad dressings:

> Olive oil, preferably extra-virgin
> Vinegar—balsamic, seasoned or regular rice wine, or other
> Mustard—a good one such as Dijon
> Garlic, fresh, minced
> Shallot, scallion, or onion, chopped
> Sweetener (optional)
> Lemon

For my basic recipe for salad dressings, see page 177. If you prefer to purchase a low-fat or nonfat dressing, check the labels and try to keep your serving size to 5 grams of total fat per 2-tablespoon serving, with 0 grams of saturated fat. Watch how much you pour onto your salad.

Extra-virgin olive oil is best for salad dressings, but you may want to keep a "light" olive oil on hand. It has a lighter taste, perfect for those dishes that don't call for the stronger flavor, like sweet baked goods, Asian-influenced foods, or Mexican foods. You get the benefit of the monounsaturated fat in the olive oil without the olive oil flavor. Canola oil is the lowest in saturated fat, without a pronounced flavor, and there are many brands available now. Each oil has its advantage. Olive oil is highest in monounsaturated fat, while canola oil is lowest in saturated fat. Both fall within the acceptable guidelines for both saturated and monounsaturated fat, so I suggest stocking your pantry with both.

Cooking sprays: Nonstick vegetable oil cooking sprays are great for reducing fat and calories in the skillet, sauté pan, and baking dish. Their popularity has manufacturers filling the supermarket shelves with many different flavors, as well. Use butter-flavored Pam on corn on the cob or popcorn. Olive oil flavors can be used to grill vegetables. Remember, one serving of the cooking spray is $\frac{1}{3}$ second, and that is the amount that equals 0 grams of fat. If you hold your finger on the nozzle for 5 seconds, you'll get more—approximately $\frac{1}{4}$ teaspoon, or 20 calories. It *is* fat, after all, so, as always, be reasonable. Used wisely, the sprays are a convenient and ingenious invention, and they do make life a little simpler.

Seasonings and herbs: The most common seasonings used in my recipes are garlic, onion, lemon, wine, chicken broth, reduced-sodium soy sauce, and Dijon mustard. I also recommend fresh basil, thyme, and sage when appropriate, along with a few others. I have suggested salt and pepper "to taste" in many recipes. Of course, there is no need to add the salt if your taste buds have been trained not to require it or you are trying to cut back. I prefer using kosher salt, which is coarser-grained and has not been iodized. Consequently, it doesn't have the slightly acidic or bitter taste that you get from regular iodized salt. Because kosher salt is heavier and less dense, it's also a little less salty than regular salt. Again, suit your own tastes and health concerns.

FOOD CHECKLIST FOR DIABETIC GOURMET MEALS

Cooking healthy food doesn't have to take very much time if you keep your kitchen stocked with foods that can be easily turned into simple, delicious meals. It just requires planning and having the foods on hand, plus the ideas to put them together tastefully and simply. With the possible exception of certain types of fresh seafood, which appear only once or twice, all the ingredients called for here can be found in any well-equipped American supermarket. The quality of the dish will depend on the integrity of the ingredients used to make it. Always use the freshest and the best, which is not necessarily the most expensive. Shop farmers' markets for produce, and discount houses for canned goods and certain staples, snacks, and frozen items. Some of my patients request that I make a home visit to help them organize their kitchens. I literally go through their cupboards, refrigerators, freezers, and pantries to get rid of the junk and replace it with the good stuff.

Here's the checklist we use as a guide:

IN THE PANTRY

Pasta or noodles in various shapes: whole-grain spaghetti, manicotti shells, macaroni, bow ties, flat fettuccine noodles, etc.

Rice: brown, white, basmati (available in brown or white)

Couscous, polenta

Dried beans: black, kidney, lentil, small white, lima, split peas

Canned vegetables: black, kidney, garbanzo, pinto beans; vegetarian refried beans, water chestnuts, bamboo shoots, baby corn, artichoke hearts, hearts of palm

Canned fruits: pineapple, applesauce, mandarin oranges, no sugar added

Dried fruits: raisins, apricots, prunes, etc., no sugar added

Sauces, spreads, and condiments: bottled spaghetti sauces, salsa, ketchup, barbecue sauce, Dijon mustard—coarse grain and regular—horseradish, oriental sauces such as hoisin and plum sauce, Worcestershire sauce, sun-dried tomatoes, capers, red and white wine, vermouth, dry sherry for cooking (do not use cooking wine, which is lower quality and may have salt added), whole tomatoes, tomato paste, tomato sauce, jams, jellies, preserves, fruit spreads (no sugar added), peanut butter (old-fashioned variety)

Canned broth: reduced-sodium chicken, beef, and vegetable

Canned soups: reduced-fat minestrone, vegetable, chicken noodle, split pea, lentil

Canned pumpkin (one of the rare vegetables that is often better canned than fresh cooked)

Canned fish: tuna, crabmeat, salmon, anchovies, packed in water

Vinegars: balsamic, rice vinegar (seasoned and unseasoned), cider vinegar, and an assortment of seasoned vinegars such as raspberry, champagne, tarragon, or wine vinegar

Oils: olive oil, extra-virgin and regular, canola oil, peanut oil for stir-frying, and sesame oil, for occasional seasoning, nonstick cooking spray, regular flavor, olive oil, butter flavor, garlic flavor, etc., as you prefer

Salad dressings: fat-free, light, or reduced-fat mayonnaise or salad dressing

Seasonings and herbs: garlic, onion, lemon, reduced-sodium soy sauce, salt, kosher salt (my preference), pepper, whole peppercorns, seasoned salt (reduced-sodium salt and seasoned salt if on a restricted-sodium diet), various dried herbs

Evaporated skimmed milk

Sugar-free cocoa mix

Less perishable vegetables: onions, garlic, potatoes, carrots

Cereals: old-fashioned oatmeal (or rolled oats, economy size and individual packets!), grits, puffed rice, puffed wheat, wheat bran cereal

Snacks: graham crackers, rice cakes, pretzels, Fig or other Newtons, Lay's baked potato chips, Tostitos baked tortilla chips or Guiltless Gourmet oil-free tortilla chips

Baking ingredients: whole-wheat, all-purpose, and cake flours; baking powder, baking soda, cornstarch, cream of tartar, unflavored gelatin, sugar-free gelatin dessert and pudding mixes, cocoa powder, unsweetened, low-fat semisweet chocolate chips, various extracts: vanilla, lemon, almond, etc.

Sweeteners: sugar, artificial sweeteners, individual packets or bulk containers, honey, molasses, no-sugar-added maple-flavored syrup

IN THE FREEZER

Pizza crusts

Peas, corn, and other frozen vegetables

Peaches, cherries, berries, and other frozen fruits

Boneless, skinless chicken breasts

Extra-lean ground turkey or beef

Lean pork loin chops

Bananas that have been ripened, peeled, sliced, and stored in plastic bags

MAKING TWO MEALS OUT OF ONE

When you make the effort to cook a meal, plan to cook enough so there will be leftovers. You'll be glad you did the next day or so. If you plan to be home the next day or can pack a lunch to work, refrigerate the leftovers in containers with lids, plastic storage bags, or foil. Most people end up throwing part of their food away because they forget about it, get tired of eating the same thing night after night, or just end up not being home to eat it. If you have plans to be out the next day or so, simply freeze leftovers in individual containers for future lunches or quick dinners. There's nothing better than the opportunity to "heat and eat" a home-cooked meal on a night when you don't feel like cooking.

THE LOW-FAT TOOLS OF THE TRADE

There are a few kitchen basics that are a must for state-of-the-art cooking. Here are a few on my list:

Sharp knives: begin with a basic 8-inch chef's knife, a boning knife, and a paring knife

Nonstick sauté pans, casserole, baking pans, and cookie sheets make low-fat cooking and cleaning easy

Plastic spatulas, wooden spoons, and other utensils appropriate for use with nonstick cookware

Roasting rack to place in casserole for roasting meat or poultry

Food processor, for pureeing soups and sauces, chopping vegetables

Mini food processor, for making salad dressing and chopping garlic and such

Blender, for fruit smoothies

Kitchen scale

Salad spinner

Fat-skimming ladle

READ FOOD LABELS TO MAKE INFORMED CHOICES

If you have diabetes or are shopping for someone who does, chances are you're paying more attention to nutrition information on food labels than you once did. That's good. It's the perfect way to put nutrition knowledge into practice. Take, for example, a loaf of bread from your cupboard. It tells you how many grams of carbohydrates are in each slice, so you can figure out how many of your carbohydrate servings a slice will use. It also lists calories, protein, and fat, as well as how many grams of fiber and how much sugar or sodium a serving contains. These values are all compared to a standard based on a 2000-calorie per day diet called Daily Value. Whether you need more or less than the standard value of 2000 calories per day, it's a good reference point. Also listed are the key nutrients, vitamin A, vitamin

C, calcium, and iron. Ingredients are listed by weight in descending order, with those present in greatest amounts listed first, and so on.

SUGARS LISTED ON LABELS

Although the new diabetic guidelines focus more on the total carbohydrate rather than the source, you may still want to check the label for sugar. It's confusing, since there are many names for sugar, including corn syrup, dextrose, glucose, corn sweetener, sucrose, sugar, brown sugar, fructose, maltose, sorbitol, mannitol, honey, and fruit-juice concentrate.

The artificial or non-nutritive sweeteners will also be listed, although they do not increase the carbohydrate or calorie level. They are found in many products that will help the person with diabetes curb his carbohydrate intake. These include NutraSweet, saccharin, acesulfame-K. For more information about these helpful ingredients, refer to chapter 2 (page 32).

OTHER ADDITIVES

In addition to the foods, you'll also find listed the additives that are present to protect our food from spoilage, and add flavor or texture. Vitamins and minerals that fortify foods are also considered additives and will be included in the list. Many new fat-free products contain plant gums or sea-weed derivatives that have been safely used for centuries, like carrageenan.

Although we often think of additives in a negative way, they often bring clear benefits, particularly in the area of food safety. The vast majority are entirely safe. Sensitive individuals who have reactions to certain additives can read labels and avoid the offensive ingredient. Many people with asthma are sensitive to sulfites, for example.

I advise my clients to eat a variety of food to avoid an excess of some dietary elements and a deficit of others. If you are concerned about food additives, eat as many whole, unprocessed foods as possible, limiting mixes and convenience foods. Use fresh meat instead of cured or smoked meats. Eat fresh fruits, vegetables, nonfat dairy products, and whole grains for snacks instead of packaged snack foods.

HEALTHY TERMS NOW DEFINED

As part of the Nutrition Labeling and Education Act (NLEA) of 1990, the Food and Drug Administration gave quantitative definitions to words used that had been loosely defined in the past, such as *light* or *healthy*. A sampling of these descriptors is listed in the Appendix section of this book (page 420). Although these rules apply to packaged foods only, hopefully they may soon apply to foods made at restaurants as well.

HEALTH CLAIMS

In 1997, the FDA authorized the very first health claim on food labels, describing the relationship between a food or nutrient and the risk of a disease or health-related condition. Oat products containing at least .75 gram of soluble fiber per serving are now allowed to link their consumption with lower cholesterol levels, and a decreased risk of heart disease. The health claim must also meet certain low-fat requirements, which will prevent another version of the oat bran craze of the eighties, when oat bran was added to otherwise high-fat products like potato chips or fat-laden muffins. Other health claims that may be considered in the future could include some of the following pairs: calcium and osteoporosis; sodium and hypertension; saturated fat and cholesterol and coronary heart disease; fat and cancer; fruits and vegetables and cancer; folic acid and neural tube birth defects.

CHAPTER 10

TRAVELING IN STYLE

Many of us enjoy traveling, but for people with diabetes, it can be a frightening prospect—an extended period of time away from your trusted doctor, your medicine cabinet, and the safety net your family and friends provide. It's enough to make even the most avid traveler hesitate. Yet by simply following some basic safe travel guidelines, anyone with diabetes can enjoy vacations, business trips, or any extended period away from home without worry.

IDENTIFICATION

When traveling with diabetes, make sure you have some sort of identification on your person at all times, indicating you have diabetes. This is usually in the form of a bracelet or necklace with an internationally recognizable symbol. That way, if you are incapacitated for any reason, you will most likely receive the proper medical attention sooner than if those treating you were only speculating the cause of your symptoms. Also, carry diabetes identification cards in your wallet, luggage, and any carry-on bags, and give one to anyone you are traveling with. These can be obtained from the American Diabetes Association at 1-800-232-3472, and are helpful in emergency situations.

Another form of identification is a letter signed by your doctor stating your condition and the medication you require, along with an address and phone number where the doctor can be reached. This can be helpful at borders and airports, when a customs agent finds a carry-on full of syringes and needles.

SUPPLIES

Another consideration for those traveling with diabetes is the accessibility of necessary medicine and supplies. For example, if you're just going to Chicago for the weekend, you'll most likely be able to secure any emergency supplies you may need without a problem. However, if you're headed to Indonesia for three weeks, it's hard to say whether even aspirin will be readily available. The easiest way to ensure that you always have what you need is to bring it yourself. *Carry* **at least** *the supplies you'll need—insulin, glucagon, blood-testing equipment, prescription medicine, etc.—for the period you will be away, and it can't hurt to carry extra, just to be safe.*

In the case of airline travel, at least a portion of your medications should be with you in your carry-on luggage at all times. If a situation arises where you arrive at your destination but your luggage does not, you will have the supplies you need on hand. Also, all insulin should be carried with you, as any prolonged exposure to heat or cold, which can be the case in baggage compartments, can be detrimental.

Talk to your physician about what medications you take, what their generic names are, how much you need, and their availability in other countries. Also, have your physician or a local chapter of the American Diabetes Association give you a listing of English-speaking doctors and/or medical facilities located at your destination. You may also want to contact the American embassy or consulate in the area, as they can assist you in seeking medical attention.

Finally, remember to have some food and a sugar source handy at all times, and especially when it's harder to maintain your normal eating schedule, such as on planes, trains, buses, etc. You don't want to become hypoglycemic on an eight-hour bus trip from Mexico City to Acapulco without any hard candy or juice and without the language skills to ask for help in getting them. Check pharmacies for a source of Z'Bars, candy bars specifically designed to increase blood sugar during a hypoglycemic episode.

PLANNING

Planning is probably the most important aspect of traveling with diabetes. All the tips mentioned above require planning, and you guarantee yourself a trip free of anxiety by simply doing your homework.

One of the most common problems facing someone with diabetes is keeping meals and medication on schedule. This requires some forethought, because if you're crossing time zones, as in airplane travel, your schedule can be completely thrown off, thus exposing you to unnecessary and potentially dangerous stress. Speak with your physician about creating a schedule that fits your travel plans and disrupts your meals as little as possible.

Also, read up on your destination, particularly if it is foreign, to determine food and eating customs. If you are familiar with the food ahead of time, you will reduce your chances of having to order something you *think* might meet your carbohydrate requirements, without really being sure. Also, meal size and the times at which they are eaten can differ greatly from country to country. Austrians often eat a large, heavy lunch, much like an American dinner, and then enjoy a lighter dinner much later in the evening. This could really wreak havoc with your schedule. Plan ahead.

Finally, anticipate problems. No matter how well you plan your trip, circumstances beyond your control can still turn a dream vacation into a nightmare. Pack medication for diarrhea, as this is one of the most common ailments affecting travelers, and certainly one that can ruin a trip. Make sure you have any required immunizations taken care of before your departure date (many are required well before your trip, in order to ensure effectiveness), especially if you are traveling to tropical areas. Your doctor can tell you what is necessary depending on your destination. Also, make sure your traveling companions know of your condition. In the case of any unforeseeable emergencies, they will be better equipped to help you get proper medical attention.

Travel need not be stressful and anxiety-ridden, and by following the guidelines above, you can ensure that your diabetes won't get in the way of a pleasant trip.

CHAPTER 11

DEALING WITH EFFECTIVE SELF-MANAGEMENT OF DIABETES

CHILDREN WITH DIABETES

Diabetes affects everyone differently, and nowhere is this more evident than with children. Care for a child with diabetes must be tailored specifically not only for that child's *type* of diabetes but also for that *child*. Children are still developing physically, emotionally, and mentally, and diabetes can impact the normal developmental stages in ways that adult diabetic care does not provide for. To ensure that children receive the proper treatment that will maximize their quality of life, parents and caregivers should understand the unique effects diabetes has on individual children.

NORMALCY AND FLEXIBILITY

Normalcy *and* flexibility *are possibly the two most important words in the treatment of children with diabetes.* It can be difficult for any child with special needs to feel accepted if, for example, they are not allowed to eat what their friends eat or participate in popular sports and activities. Children with diabetes *do* have special considerations, but they should be taught as early as possible that their condition shouldn't prevent them from enjoying "normal" things. Rather, they must learn to enjoy those things in different ways.

For example, teach your child early on about the carbohydrate values of basic foods and the number of grams or choices to be eaten at each meal and snack. Children are quick learners, and the more children understand how the food they eat determines how much insulin they'll need to take, the better they'll feel about their abilities to handle their diabetes. You can breathe a little easier knowing that they are more capable of making informed decisions regarding their nutrition when you're not around to help. Meal plans for children are more flexible now and focus primarily on counting carbohydrates, as explained in chapter 3. They are easier, less time consuming, and more flexible than relying solely on the diabetic exchange lists. Also, don't regulate specific food choices as much as you regulate how and when your child is eating. If your son sees all his friends eating bologna sandwiches and he knows he is forbidden to do the same, this can chip away at his feelings of normalcy. However, if he knows that he can have that bologna sandwich as long as he regulates his total carbohydrate intake, there is one less reason for him to feel different, and he'll feel more in control of the situation.

This brings us to flexibility. When raising a child with diabetes, don't teach limitations, teach flexibility. Children—and adults, for that matter—respond much better to choices than to restrictions. Therefore, become aware of all options in a given situation and make sure that the child is aware of them also. It's hard enough getting any small child to eat nutritiously, and this can present some real concerns and stress for parents trying to maintain their child's normal blood glucose levels. Furthermore, children recognize this stress and can learn to manipulate parents or caregivers through their eating habits. Talk to your doctor and/or dietitian about what is acceptable for your child and what your alternatives are. By creating some flexibility for your child, you reduce your own stress and establish some reasonable guidelines for your child as well.

TEACH OTHERS, TEACH YOURSELF

You know what is necessary for maintaining your child's diabetes, but don't forget to keep those who have the most contact with your child—teachers, friends, and relatives—informed as well.

For school-age children, spend time with all the school officials who may come into contact with your child, such as teachers, administrators, nurses, to make them aware of your child's condition, and insure they are well-prepared to handle any emergencies. It is important to do this discreetly, however, so your child does not feel singled out. Schedule a private appointment with the teacher and discuss how to handle any changes from daily routines, such as parties or field trips, and what the day-to-day requirements are for your child. Discuss in particular how to spot hypoglycemia, a low blood glucose level (usually 70 milligrams per deciliter) that can lead to unconsciousness if untreated. Hypoglycemia can be caused by too much insulin, not enough food, a delayed meal, or the child simply participating in more activity than usual. Common symptoms include confusion, tiredness, shakiness, dizziness, headaches, and/or abrupt change in emotional state. Treatment requires quickly increasing blood glucose levels by eating rapidly absorbed sugars or injecting glucagon. This is important information for other school officials as well, not to mention your relatives and friends, and the parents of your child's playmates.

Your child can also teach others about his or her condition. Encourage your child to be honest and forthright about diabetes with people they feel comfortable with. Diabetes is nothing to be ashamed of, and your child should know this early on.

Finally, teach *yourself* about your child's diabetes. You are the one in control of how well equipped your child is to deal with diabetes. You must create an environment of openness and knowledge for yourself and your child. Let children know they are loved unconditionally. Create a positive emotional environment for your child and yourself, and try to eliminate unnecessary tension and stress. Remember first and foremost that this is a growing human being, with needs above and beyond those created by diabetes. Meeting those needs can be challenging, but seeing your child greet the world with knowledge and self-assurance makes the extra effort worthwhile.

THE ADULT

While adults need to worry less about developmental concerns, they have reproductive concerns, weight control issues, and ingrained habit changes to worry about. Also, diabetes affects men and women differently, so each individual really has to create his or her own personalized management plan in order to stay as healthy as possible. Fortunately, it sounds more complicated than it really is. Maintaining a strong relationship with your doctor and/or dietitian, as well as following some of the tips below, will allow you to more easily manage your diabetes.

Women

There are two aspects of diabetes that are more of a concern for women than men: weight control and GDM (gestational diabetes mellitus). It has been found that overweight women are more likely to develop type II diabetes, and since obesity is more prevalent in women than in men, women comprise a larger segment of newly diagnosed diabetes cases, not to mention having an increased susceptibility to heart disease, higher blood pressure, and poor reproductive health. Diabetes has also been known to lower good cholesterol (HDL) levels in women as well. Women must take special precautions when it comes to weight control and diet in general to ensure that their needs are met, and a dietitian can assist in assessing these individual needs. It is important for women, who often assume the caregiver role for others, to nurture themselves as well.

Women planning on becoming pregnant, or who already are, should be knowledgeable about GDM as well. GDM is characterized by high blood glucose levels during pregnancy and is diagnosed in approximately 90,000 pregnant women in the United States each year. The condition is often temporary, and women usually return to normal carbohydrate tolerance after delivery. However, GDM must be carefully managed to ensure the health of both the mother and the baby. Complications of GDM include an increased chance of the mother developing type II diabetes later in life, and high birth weight for the baby, resulting in cesarean delivery. GDM usually can't be prevented, and women who develop GDM in a first pregnancy are likely to have it again in later pregnancies. Remember, however, that GDM cannot be transferred to your baby. Again, develop a working relationship with your dietitian and physician so they can help you properly manage your condition and help you keep your blood glucose at a healthy level. Also, staying active always helps, whether pregnant or not, and can help ensure your baby's health.

Men

Just as women often assume the role of caregiver, men often assume the role of care receiver. That is to say, men are less likely to monitor their own eating habits, because they are less likely to be the one buying and preparing the food. When a man diagnosed with diabetes suddenly has to pay close attention to how and what he eats, he might be confronted with the necessity of learning skills he might not be entirely familiar with, like new cooking techniques or even shopping, because someone else always did it for him. Men who were previously not involved in their own food preparation must become knowledgeable about how their diet affects their diabetes. Most undoubtedly know that keeping blood glucose under control is key, but they may not know how certain foods factor into this. Wives, domestic partners, and family should all be ready to assist with this learning process. But remember, the man with diabetes is ultimately responsible for himself.

PART TWO

RECIPES

CHAPTER 12

BREAKFAST AND BRUNCH

Your mom was right when she told you that breakfast was the most important meal of the day. People who skip breakfast are likely to have more body fat, gain more weight (or lose less), and have high blood cholesterol levels. And for those who have diabetes, there are even more reasons to eat a healthy breakfast. The right combination of foods in the morning helps you avoid wide fluctuations in blood glucose and insulin levels during the rest of the day.

Breakfast should include carbohydrates for optimal blood glucose, protein to stabilize blood glucose, and, for satiety, some fat. Many people eat the same thing for breakfast most of the time, particularly during the week, with a variation only on the weekend. Here are a bunch of tasty breakfast ideas for those days when you feel like something new. The oatmeal with cinnamon or the Tropical Fruit Smoothie make fast weekday treats, and the Blueberry Corn Muffins, French Toast, or Spinach Quiche will kick off a leisurely Saturday or Sunday deliciously.

HIGH-PROTEIN OATS WITH CINNAMON

MAKES 2 SERVINGS

For a stick-to-your-ribs breakfast, try that old standby oatmeal. Oats contain soluble fiber that may help to lower cholesterol. Although ⅔ cup of oats contains about 3 grams of protein, you'll get an additional 7 grams of protein by cooking oats in milk. This can help stabilize blood glucose levels midmorning.

1½ cups nonfat milk
¼ teaspoon salt
⅔ cup old-fashioned rolled oats
¼ teaspoon ground cinnamon

¼ teaspoon ground allspice
2 teaspoons firmly packed brown
   sugar

1 In a medium saucepan, combine the milk and salt and bring to a boil.

2 Add the oats, reduce heat to low, and stir to combine. Simmer the mixture, stirring frequently, for about 5 minutes, until oat flakes are softened.

3 Serve the oatmeal in warmed bowls, sprinkled with cinnamon, allspice, and brown sugar.

PER SERVING					
CALORIES	180	CARBOHYDRATES (G)	30	CARBOHYDRATE CHOICES: 2	
FAT (G)	2	PROTEIN (G)	11	FOOD EXCHANGES PER SERVING: ½ SKIM	
CALORIES FROM FAT (%)	10	FIBER (G)	3	MILK, 1½ STARCH	
				LOW-SODIUM DIETS: OMIT SALT; INCREASE	
CHOLESTEROL (MG) LESS THAN 5		SODIUM (MG)	360	CINNAMON.	

BAKED OATMEAL

MAKES 8 SERVINGS

For oatmeal fans who want more protein in their breakfast, adding milk and egg white does the trick, making it somewhat like bread pudding. Since baked oatmeal keeps for several days in the refrigerator, you can make a batch on the weekend and reheat it during the week when you want a quick breakfast. Enjoy it with low-calorie, sugar-free pancake syrup.

Vegetable oil cooking spray
2¼ cups quick oats or 2¾ cups
    old-fashioned rolled oats
½ cup firmly packed brown sugar
1 teaspoon ground cinnamon
½ teaspoon salt (optional)
3⅓ cups skim milk

4 egg whites, slightly beaten, or
    ½ cup egg substitute
1 tablespoon vegetable oil
1 tablespoon vanilla
Sugar-free syrup, nonfat yogurt
    (optional)

1 Heat oven to 350°F. Spray an 8-inch square glass baking dish with vegetable oil cooking spray.

2 In large bowl, combine oats, brown sugar, cinnamon, and salt; mix well. In medium bowl, combine milk, egg whites, oil, and vanilla; mix well. Add to dry ingredients; mix until well blended.

3 Pour into prepared baking dish. Bake, uncovered, 55 to 60 minutes or until center is set and firm to the touch. Cool slightly before serving. Top with sugar-free syrup or yogurt, if desired. Store, covered, in refrigerator for 2 to 3 days.

PER SERVING					
CALORIES	200	CARBOHYDRATES (G)	33	CARBOHYDRATE CHOICES: 2	
FAT (G)	3.5	PROTEIN (G)	10	FOOD EXCHANGES PER SERVING: ½ SKIM	
CALORIES FROM FAT (%)	16	FIBER (G)	3	MILK, 2 STARCH	
CHOLESTEROL (MG)	0	SODIUM (MG)	220	LOW-SODIUM DIETS: OMIT SALT.	

WHOLE-GRAIN GRIDDLE CAKES

MAKES 8 PANCAKES

My husband raves about my pancakes. He can't believe they're so light and delicious, and they're fat-free! The secret, of course, is whipping the egg whites to compensate for the tenderizing effect that would otherwise be provided by egg yolk and oil. We take turns making them on Sunday mornings, and often have batter left over for hot, fresh pancakes again on Monday morning.

½ cup all-purpose flour
½ cup whole wheat flour
¼ teaspoon salt
1 teaspoon baking soda
4 large egg whites or 4 teaspoons egg
    white powder

1 tablespoon sugar
1½ cups buttermilk or nonfat yogurt
Vegetable oil cooking spray

1 Sift the all-purpose and whole wheat flours into a medium mixing bowl. Add the salt and baking soda, and stir together until evenly blended.

2 In another mixing bowl, using a perfectly clean whisk, whip the egg whites to soft peaks, gradually adding the sugar. If using egg white powder, first mix the powder with the sugar, then add 2 tablespoons plus 2 teaspoons of water to reconstitute them, and proceed to whip the egg white mixture.

3 Make a well in the center of the dry ingredients. Pour in the egg whites and the buttermilk and combine them with a few swift strokes, using a rubber spatula. (Ignore the lumps, which will go away during cooking.)

4 Heat a large nonstick skillet over medium heat and spray it lightly with vegetable oil cooking spray. When the pan is hot, ladle about ¼ cup of batter for each pancake and, in batches, cook the pancakes until they are brown underneath and the top is set, about 2 minutes. Flip the pancakes and continue cooking until golden, about 1 minute. Serve immediately with syrup or fruit topping.

PER TWO 4-INCH PANCAKES	BEFORE	AFTER			
CALORIES	200	160	CARBOHYDRATES (G)	28	CARBOHYDRATE CHOICES: 2
FAT (G)	6	1	PROTEIN (G)	10	FOOD EXCHANGES PER SERVING: 2 STARCH
CALORIES FROM FAT (%)	26	7	FIBER (G)	2	LOW-SODIUM DIETS: OMIT SALT.
CHOLESTEROL (MG)	120	LESS THAN 5	SODIUM (MG)	600	

OATCAKES WITH APPLESAUCE

MAKES 8 PANCAKES

If you use old-fashioned rolled oats, note their slightly longer soaking time. Also, if you elect to use powdered egg whites, they should be mixed with the flour, sugar, baking powder, and salt before they are added to the liquid ingredients. Because they are rather dense, these oatcakes take a little longer to cook than normal pancakes, but their hearty flavor and texture are very fortifying.

1½ cups nonfat milk
½ cup quick or old-fashioned
    rolled oats
2 large egg whites or 4 teaspoons
    powdered egg whites
1¼ cups all-purpose flour

2 teaspoons baking powder
¼ teaspoon salt
About 2 cups good-quality store-
    bought or homemade applesauce,
    for serving

1 In a bowl, combine ¼ cup of the milk with the oats, stir to moisten evenly, and let sit for 1 minute if using quick oats, 2 minutes for old-fashioned. Add the remaining milk and the egg whites to the oat mixture and mix together until evenly blended.

2 In a separate bowl, mix the flour, baking powder, and salt.

3 Add the dry ingredients to the oat mixture and stir together until well combined. (If using powdered egg whites, mix them in with the dry ingredients and increase milk by ¼ cup.)

4 Heat a nonstick griddle over medium heat and, when it is hot, ladle ¼ cup of batter onto the griddle for each oatcake (be sure not to crowd them; cook in two batches). Cook each oatcake until the top is bubbly, then turn to the other side and cook an equal amount of time. Transfer to a warm platter in the oven while you make the remaining oatcakes; serve with applesauce.

PER 5-INCH OATCAKE

CALORIES	110	CARBOHYDRATES (G)	21	CARBOHYDRATE CHOICES: 1½	
FAT (G)	.5	PROTEIN (G)	5	FOOD EXCHANGES PER SERVING: 1½ STARCH	
CALORIES FROM FAT (%)	5	FIBER (G)	1	LOW-SODIUM DIETS: ACCEPTABLE	
CHOLESTEROL (MG)	0	SODIUM (MG)	105		

PER 5-INCH OATCAKE WITH ¼ CUP APPLESAUCE

CALORIES	140	CARBOHYDRATES (G)	28	CARBOHYDRATE CHOICES: 2	
FAT (G)	.5	PROTEIN (G)	5	FOOD EXCHANGES PER SERVING: ½ STARCH,	
CALORIES FROM FAT (%)	4	FIBER (G)	2	½ FRUIT	
CHOLESTEROL (MG)	0	SODIUM (MG)	105	LOW-SODIUM DIETS: ACCEPTABLE	

BLUEBERRY CORN MUFFINS

MAKES 12 MUFFINS

These muffins are the best I've ever tasted. The combination of cornmeal and blueberries is terrific.

Vegetable oil cooking spray
1 cup all-purpose flour
1 cup yellow cornmeal
½ cup sugar
1 tablespoon baking powder
½ teaspoon baking soda

Pinch of salt
1 cup buttermilk
¼ cup canola oil
2 large egg whites, lightly beaten
1 cup fresh or thawed frozen
   blueberries

1 Place the rack in the center of the oven and preheat it to 400°F. Spray two non-stick 6-cup muffin tins with vegetable oil cooking spray.

2 In a large bowl, sift together the flour, cornmeal, sugar, baking powder, baking soda, and salt. Mix well to combine.

3 In another bowl, combine the buttermilk, canola oil, and egg whites; whisk together with a fork.

4 Add the liquid ingredients to the dry ingredients and mix until just combined. Do not overmix, and don't worry if there are a few lumps.

5 Fold the blueberries gently into the batter. Divide the batter equally among the muffin cups. Bake for about 20 minutes, or until the muffins are golden and a toothpick inserted into the center comes out clean. Transfer the tin to a rack and cool for about 10 minutes. Turn the muffins out of the tin. Serve warm or at room temperature.

PER MUFFIN				
CALORIES	170	CARBOHYDRATES (G)	27	CARBOHYDRATE CHOICES: 2
FAT (G)	5	PROTEIN (G)	3	FOOD EXCHANGES PER SERVING: 2 STARCH,
CALORIES FROM FAT (%)	28	FIBER (G)	1	½ FAT
CHOLESTEROL (MG)	0	SODIUM (MG)	250	LOW-SODIUM DIETS: OMIT SALT.

FRENCH TOAST

MAKES 6 SLICES

The key to good French toast is dense, day-old bread. A slice of bread can vary greatly in size, making calories and carbohydrates subject to change—the rule of thumb is 80 calories per ounce of bread. Leave the bread out, unwrapped, overnight to dry it. Using liquid egg substitute for French toast adds the familiar yellow color without the cholesterol of egg yolks, but if you're a purist, just use plain egg whites and season with cinnamon. It's wonderful with Fresh Fruit Sauce.

½ cup liquid egg substitute or 4 large
   egg whites
2 tablespoons nonfat milk
6 slices whole wheat bread
½ teaspoon ground cinnamon

2 teaspoons powdered sugar
   (optional)
Fresh Fruit Sauce (page 126) or light
   or sugar-free syrup

1 In a wide, shallow bowl, whisk together the egg, egg whites, or egg substitute, and milk. Soak the bread in the mixture for 5 to 10 seconds, turning to coat each side of the bread evenly. Sprinkle the cinnamon evenly over the soaked bread.

2 Heat a large nonstick skillet over medium heat. Using tongs, cook the bread in two batches for about 3 minutes on each side, or until golden brown. Keep the first batch of French toast warm on a platter in a low-heat oven while you cook the second batch.

3 Just before serving, sift a little powdered sugar over the toasts. Accompany with Fresh Fruit Sauce.

PER 1-OUNCE SLICE (OROWHEAT BREAD)					
	BEFORE	**AFTER**			
CALORIES	120	115	CARBOHYDRATES (G)	18	**CARBOHYDRATE CHOICES:** 1
FAT (G)	3.5	3	PROTEIN (G)	6	**FOOD EXCHANGES PER SERVING:** 1 STARCH,
CALORIES FROM FAT (%)	24	23	FIBER (G)	2	1 VERY LEAN MEAT
CHOLESTEROL (MG)	70	0	SODIUM (MG)	210	**LOW-SODIUM DIETS:** IF ON A 500 OR 1000 MG
					SODIUM DIET, USE LOW-SODIUM OR
					SALT-FREE BREAD.

FRESH FRUIT SAUCE

This topping for French toast or pancakes is an easy and healthy alternative to syrup, but remember, with the new guidelines, you can take your pick. Just note the carbohydrate comparison: 1 tablespoon of real maple syrup has 13 grams of carbohydrates, or 52 grams per ¼ cup, while ¼ cup of this tangy fruit sauce has only 20 grams of carbohydrates. If you choose the fruit sauce, you also get added vitamin C and vitamin A.

¼ cup water
¼ cup raisins
1 ripe banana, peeled and sliced

1 seedless orange, peeled and
  quartered
Juice of 1 lemon

1 In a medium saucepan, combine the water and raisins. Bring the mixture to a boil, remove from the heat, and allow to cool for 10 minutes.

2 In a food processor or blender, combine the banana and orange; puree until smooth.

3 Add the raisin-water mixture and the lemon juice, and puree until almost smooth.

4 Serve as a topping for pancakes, French toast, or waffles. It's also great, heated slightly, over ice cream or frozen yogurt.

PER ¼-CUP SERVING					
CALORIES	80	CARBOHYDRATES (G)	20	CARBOHYDRATE CHOICES: 1	
FAT (G)	0	PROTEIN (G)	1	FOOD EXCHANGES PER SERVING: 1 FRUIT	
CALORIES FROM FAT (%)	0	FIBER (G)	2	LOW-SODIUM DIETS: EXCELLENT.	
CHOLESTEROL (MG)	0	SODIUM (MG)	0		

GRANDMOTHER GRIFFIN'S POPOVERS

MAKES 9 POPOVERS

This is one of the easiest, no-fail baked goods for adapting to fat-free. They're great for Sunday brunch. When making popovers, follow the two cardinal rules: Do not overbeat the batter, and always cook in a very hot oven. Serve with apple butter or preserves when they are puffed and hot out of the oven. Popovers are a little like a soufflé—they fall as they cool down.

Vegetable oil cooking spray
4 large egg whites
1 cup nonfat milk

1 cup all-purpose flour
½ teaspoon salt

1 With a rack on the bottom rung, preheat the oven to 425° F.

2 Thoroughly spray a 12-cup muffin tin or popover molds with vegetable oil cooking spray.

3 In a large bowl, beat the egg whites just until frothy and beat in the milk.

4 Sift the flour and salt into the egg whites, mixing just until the batter is smooth.

5 Fill the muffin cups about ¾ of the way to the top. Do not overfill. Too much batter in the cup will give a muffinlike texture. Place on the lower rack of the oven and after 15 minutes, reduce the heat to 350° F. Bake for 40 to 45 minutes, until very puffy and golden. Serve immediately.

PER POPOVER					
CALORIES	60	CARBOHYDRATES (G)	11	CARBOHYDRATE CHOICES: 1	
FAT (G)	LESS THAN .5	PROTEIN (G)	4	FOOD EXCHANGES PER SERVING: 1 STARCH	
CALORIES FROM FAT (%)	3	FIBER (G)	0	LOW-SODIUM DIETS: OMIT SALT IF ON A 500 OR	
CHOLESTEROL (MG)	0	SODIUM (MG)	140	1000 MG SODIUM DIET.	

SPINACH QUICHE

MAKES 8 SERVINGS

Although quiche is typically a high-fat dish, this one is not. By using egg substitute instead of whole eggs and flavoring the quiche with a good amount of spinach, mushrooms, and half the usual cheese, you have a great-tasting brunch dish or appetizer. The crust, made of bread crumbs with a touch of rosemary, is a perfect way to get a flavorful crispy exterior.

Crust
Vegetable oil cooking spray
1 cup seasoned bread crumbs
1 teaspoon dried rosemary,
  crumbled
2 tablespoons plus 2 teaspoons
  canola oil
½ cup grated Gruyère cheese

Filling
½ teaspoon canola oil
½ cup finely chopped onion
1 tablespoon finely chopped red bell
  pepper
½ cup chopped mushrooms
4 cups coarsely chopped spinach,
  leaves only (about ¼ pound)
¼ teaspoon salt
¼ teaspoon black pepper
¾ cup fat-free liquid egg substitute
1½ cups nonfat evaporated milk

1 For the crust: Lightly coat a 9-inch pie plate with the vegetable oil cooking spray. In a small bowl, combine the bread crumbs, rosemary, and canola oil, then press the mixture evenly across the base and up the sides of the pie plate. Spray lightly with vegetable oil spray, cover with waxed paper, and place a second pie plate over the waxed paper. Press down firmly to compact the crust. Remove the top pie plate and the wax paper, and sprinkle the crust with the grated cheese. Set aside.

2 Preheat the oven to 375°F.

3 For the filling: In a large nonstick skillet, heat the canola oil over medium-high heat. Sauté the onion, bell pepper, and mushrooms for 5 minutes, or until the onion and mushrooms begin to soften. Add the spinach, salt, and pepper, and sauté just until the spinach begins to wilt, about 3 minutes more. Spread the spinach mixture evenly over the cheese in the pie plate.

4 Whisk together the egg substitute and the evaporated milk, and pour the liquid gently over the spinach mixture. Bake for 45 minutes, or until a knife inserted in the center comes out clean. Set on a wire rack to cool for about 10 minutes. Serve warm, cut into wedges.

PER SERVING

	BEFORE	AFTER				
CALORIES	230	190	CARBOHYDRATES (G)	19	CARBOHYDRATE CHOICES: 1	
FAT (G)	14	7	PROTEIN (G)	12	FOOD EXCHANGES PER SERVING: 2 LEAN MEAT,	
CALORIES FROM FAT (%)	57	35	FIBER (G)	1	1 STARCH	
CHOLESTEROL (MG)	100	5	SODIUM (MG)	700	LOW-SODIUM DIETS: THIS RECIPE IS NOT SUITABLE	
					FOR LOW-SODIUM DIETS.	

EGGS WITH SPINACH IN A PITA POCKET

This dish is a great one to include in a weekend breakfast or brunch. Use your choice of egg substitute or all fresh whites. A combination of one or two whole eggs, and two to four egg whites also results in a significant fat and cholesterol savings over using four whole eggs.

8 ounces fat-free liquid egg substitute
   (equivalent to 4 eggs) or
   8 large fresh egg whites
2 tablespoons nonfat milk
1 teaspoon fresh lemon juice
6 leaves raw spinach, chopped, or
   2 tablespoons thawed frozen
   chopped spinach, squeezed dry
2 green onions (scallions), white and
   light green parts only, finely
   chopped

2 tablespoons finely chopped parsley
Freshly ground black pepper
1 tablespoon grated Parmesan, or to
   taste
Vegetable oil cooking spray
2 whole wheat pita breads
   (5-inch diameter)
Extra sprigs of parsley, for garnish

1 In a mixing bowl, combine the egg substitute, milk, lemon juice, spinach, green onions, parsley, pepper, and Parmesan. Whisk together until evenly blended.

2 Coat a nonstick skillet with vegetable oil cooking spray and heat it over medium heat. Add the egg mixture and cook, stirring occasionally, until the eggs are done to your liking.

3 While the eggs are cooking, warm the pita breads in a low oven or toaster. Cut each pita in half across the center and fill each of the four pockets with about ⅓ cup of the scrambled egg mixture. Serve immediately, garnished with sprigs of parsley.

PER SERVING					
CALORIES	120	CARBOHYDRATES (G)	15	CARBOHYDRATE CHOICES: 1	
FAT (G)	2.5	PROTEIN (G)	10	FOOD EXCHANGES PER SERVING: 1 LEAN MEAT,	
CALORIES FROM FAT (%)	22	FIBER (G)	2	1 STARCH	
CHOLESTEROL (MG)	0	SODIUM (MG)	260	LOW-SODIUM DIETS: OMIT PARMESAN.	

TROPICAL FRUIT SMOOTHIE

MAKES 2 SERVINGS

This smoothie can be varied according to the season and availability of fruit. Some nice combinations are strawberry and banana, and raspberry and banana. This can also be served as a topping for pancakes or French toast. Add additional juice or milk to make a thinner consistency. Using nonfat yogurt instead of whole, plain yogurt cuts down on the cholesterol and the number of calories that come from fat.

1 cup plain nonfat yogurt
1 ripe banana, peeled and cut into
   2-inch pieces
1 orange, peeled and quartered

½ ripe mango, skin and pit removed
   and cut into 1-inch chunks
Honey, to taste (optional)
2 sprigs of mint, for garnish

1 In a blender, combine the yogurt, banana, orange, mango, and honey, if using; cover tightly and blend until smooth.

2 Pour into tall glasses, garnish with a sprig of mint, and serve.

PER SERVING

	BEFORE	AFTER			
CALORIES	240	200	**CARBOHYDRATES** (G)	39	**CARBOHYDRATE CHOICES: 2½**
FAT (G)	4.5	1	PROTEIN (G)	6	FOOD EXCHANGES PER SERVING: 1 SKIM
CALORIES FROM FAT (%)	20	5	FIBER (G)	4	MILK, 2 FRUITS
CHOLESTEROL (MG)	15	LESS THAN 5	SODIUM (MG)	60	LOW-SODIUM DIETS: FINE. FRUITS ARE
					NATURALLY LOW IN SODIUM.

CHAPTER 13

APPETIZERS AND SMALL MEALS

I f you take insulin, your food plan may include two or three snacks in addition to your meals so that your blood glucose doesn't sink too low. A bedtime snack with some protein is good, since the protein will slowly convert to carbohydrates during the night, warding off early morning insulin reactions. However, those who control diabetes with diet alone or oral hypoglycemic agents probably do not need snacks because they will almost never have too much insulin in their bloodstream.

If you enjoy these recipes as appetizers before a meal, make sure you compensate by eating fewer carbohydrates in the main course. There's nothing wrong with having appetizers for dinner, as long as they are within your plan. Recipes like the toppings for bruschetta can be part of a light lunch or supper, as long as you make sure you have enough protein along with them, such as a piece of fish or chicken. I like it when a cocktail party turns into dinner, without formally being called dinner. The casual nature makes everyone more relaxed. These recipes make it fun and easy to have friends in your home for cocktails and hors d'oeuvres.

GRILLED PORTOBELLO MUSHROOMS

MAKES 4 SERVINGS

Look for grilled portobellos as a low-calorie side on restaurant menus. They're also easy to make at home. The portobello mushroom is so rich, it's like eating a tender piece of steak, but without the fat. This recipe was adapted from Hans Rockenwagner's Santa Monica restaurant.

½ cup balsamic vinegar
½ cup olive oil
2 shallots, finely chopped
4 cloves garlic, finely chopped
½ teaspoon freshly ground black
   pepper

¼ teaspoon red pepper flakes
3 large portobello mushrooms (about
   8 ounces each), stems discarded,
   brushed clean

1 In a bowl with a tight-fitting lid, combine the vinegar, olive oil, shallots, garlic, black pepper, and pepper flakes. Add the mushrooms, turn to coat them evenly, and weight them with a plate, if necessary, to keep them submerged in the marinade. Cover the bowl and marinate overnight, refrigerated.

2 Prepare an outdoor grill for medium-heat grilling or heat a well-seasoned ridged cast-iron griddle pan over medium heat. Remove the mushrooms from the marinade and pat them dry with paper towels. Grill the mushrooms for three to five minutes on each side, or until slightly charred. Cool and slice about ¼-inch thick and serve on a bruschetta, as a sandwich filling, or simply with a knife and fork.

PER SERVING					
CALORIES	120	CARBOHYDRATES (G)	11	CARBOHYDRATE CHOICES: 1	
FAT (G)	7	PROTEIN (G)	4	FOOD EXCHANGES PER SERVING: 2 VEGETABLE,	
CALORIES FROM FAT (%)	54	FIBER (G)	2	1½ MONO FAT	
CHOLESTEROL (MG)	0	SODIUM (MG)	10	LOW-SODIUM DIETS: EXCELLENT CHOICE— THIS IS A RARE RECIPE WITH ABSOLUTELY NO SODIUM!	

ARTICHOKES STUFFED WITH PROSCIUTTO, PARSLEY, AND MINT

MAKES 6 SERVINGS

The fat is kept low in this indulgent dish by using highly flavored Parmesan cheese and prosciutto in very small amounts, and by replacing most of the olive oil with chicken broth. The original recipe called for pancetta, or Italian bacon. I chose prosciutto instead because it is leaner than pancetta, but still has a distinctly traditional Italian smoky flavor. Italian meats are cured for long periods of time, up to a year or so, whereas American ham or bacon is smoked in a matter of hours. Either prosciutto or ham will work—just make sure you buy the lean version and trim all visible fat. This stuffing also would be great in a turkey or an artichoke.

This dish can be finished in an oven at 350° F., rather than on the stovetop, if you prefer. It will take about one hour, or until the bases of the artichokes are tender.

This festive treat is impressive and actually quite simple to prepare. The artichokes can be made a day in advance and cooked just before serving. Serve hot or at room temperature, as a side dish or a first course, depending on the menu.

2 cups bread crumbs, plain or
    seasoned
½ cup chopped parsley
¼ cup chopped fresh mint
3 cloves garlic, finely chopped
¼ cup freshly grated Parmesan
    cheese
4 thin slices (2 ounces) prosciutto, fat
    trimmed, finely chopped

2 tablespoons olive oil
1 (14½-ounce) can de-fatted chicken
    broth
6 medium artichokes, rinsed
2 lemons, halved
Salt and freshly ground black pepper,
    to taste

1 In a mixing bowl, combine the bread crumbs, parsley, mint, garlic, Parmesan, prosciutto, olive oil, and ½ of the chicken broth. Toss together until evenly mixed.

2 To prepare the artichokes, with a sharp, heavy knife slice off the top third of each artichoke, cutting down below the level of the pointed ends of the leaves. Trim the bottom stem so that it will sit flat in the bottom of the pan. With scissors, trim off the dark, coarse leaves around the base and the sharp tips of the outer leaves. Spread the leaves open from the center and scrape out the hairy chokes with a paring knife and a spoon. Rub lemons all over and inside of the artichokes to prevent browning.

3 Pack the stuffing firmly into the centers of each artichoke and tuck around the leaves. (This can be done a day in advance, and the artichokes wrapped tightly with plastic wrap and refrigerated.)

4 Place the artichokes upright in a large deep flameproof baking dish, and drizzle 1 tablespoon of chicken broth over the top of each artichoke; then add the remaining chicken broth. Add water so that the level is 1 inch above the bases of the artichokes. Tent the top of the dish loosely with aluminum foil, making sure the foil does not touch the artichokes. Bring to a simmer over medium-low heat. Simmer gently for about 45 minutes, or until the bases are tender. Serve immediately or cool to room temperature. Season with salt and pepper, if desired.

PER SERVING

	BEFORE	AFTER				
CALORIES	300	230	CARBOHYDRATES (G)	28	CARBOHYDRATE CHOICES: 2	
FAT (G)	15	9	PROTEIN (G)	12	FOOD EXCHANGES PER SERVING: 2 STARCH,	
CALORIES FROM FAT (%)	45	35	FIBER (G)	4	1½ FATS	
CHOLESTEROL (MG)	20	10	SODIUM (MG)	520	LOW-SODIUM DIETS: SUBSTITUTE TURKEY OR CHICKEN FOR HAM AND OMIT SALT.	

OYSTERS ON THE HALF SHELL WITH TEQUILA, HABANERO, LIME JUICE, AND CILANTRO

MAKES 2 TO 4 SERVINGS

These oysters are flavorful, but not too hot since such a small amount of the hot habaneros pepper is used, leaving just a slight chile burn in the back of the throat. Be very careful when handling habaneros, or wear gloves to avoid getting it on your fingers, and from there into your eyes. Remember, a little goes a long way. If habaneros are not available, substitute green serrano chiles and increase the quantity slightly.

12 live oysters in their shells, well scrubbed

¼ teaspoon minced, seeded habanero chile

1 teaspoon tequila

1 tablespoon fresh lime juice

1 tablespoon finely chopped fresh cilantro

Lime wedges, for garnish

Sprigs of cilantro, for garnish

1 Holding each oyster in a thick towel to protect the palm of your hand if the oyster knife should slip, open the oysters over a bowl, saving the oyster "liquor" or juice, and pouring it back over the oyster. Open the oysters and discard the rounded half of each shell and place the flat shells on a platter mounded with shaved ice (regular "crushed" ice is too coarse, but could be substituted).

2 In a small nonreactive bowl, combine the minced chile, tequila, and lime juice. Spoon about ½ teaspoon of the mixture over each oyster and scatter the chopped cilantro evenly over the tops. Garnish the edges of the platter with lime wedges and sprigs of cilantro. If desired, refrigerate for up to 30 minutes before serving.

Variation: Oysters can also be dressed with cocktail sauce, lemon juice and/or horseradish, or finely diced onion and pimento.

PER SERVING OF 3 OYSTERS					
CALORIES	60	CARBOHYDRATES (G)	4	CARBOHYDRATE CHOICES: 0	
FAT (G)	2	PROTEIN (G)	6	FOOD EXCHANGES PER SERVING: 1 LEAN MEAT	
CALORIES FROM FAT (%)	33	FIBER (G)	0	LOW-SODIUM DIETS: OYSTERS COME FROM SEA	
CHOLESTEROL (MG)	45	SODIUM (MG)	180	WATER AND NATURALLY CONTAIN SODIUM;	
				SO IF YOU'RE SEVERELY RESTRICTING SODIUM,	
				EAT THIS IN LIMITED QUANTITIES.	

MUSHROOMS MARINATED IN GARLIC SAUCE

MAKES 32 MUSHROOMS, OR 8 SERVINGS

I serve these mushrooms as part of my Spanish tapas menu, along with Seafood Paella for consistency (page 232). The red pepper flakes make them spicy hot, and you can rev it up or tone it down at your own discretion. This recipe also makes a nice low-calorie side dish for two alongside a sandwich, salad, or grilled meats.

2 teaspoons olive oil
6 cloves garlic, finely chopped
¼ teaspoon red pepper flakes
½ cup low-fat, low-sodium beef broth
1 pound small white mushrooms, brushed clean, trimmed, and halved

2 tablespoons dry sherry
1 tablespoon lemon juice
1 teaspoon paprika
½ teaspoon salt
½ teaspoon black pepper

1 In a heavy nonstick skillet, heat the oil over medium-low heat. Add the garlic and red pepper flakes and stir for one to two minutes, until the garlic has released its aroma and softened slightly. Do not allow it to burn.

2 Add the beef broth, increase the heat to medium-high, and bring to a simmer. Simmer until reduced by half.

3 Add the mushrooms and cook for 2 minutes, or until coated and slightly tender, shaking the pan occasionally to cook them evenly.

4 Reduce the heat again to low and add the sherry, lemon juice, paprika, salt, and pepper. Cook for 8 minutes, or until mushrooms are glossy, brown, and soft.

5 Allow the mushrooms to come to room temperature, then cover and refrigerate overnight so the flavors can marry. Bring to room temperature again before serving. These are best eaten the next day, but they will keep an extra day or two.

PER SERVING					
CALORIES	70	CARBOHYDRATES (G)	8	**CARBOHYDRATE CHOICES:** ½	
FAT (G)	3	PROTEIN (G)	3	**FOOD EXCHANGES PER SERVING:** 2 VEGETABLE,	
CALORIES FROM FAT (%)	38	FIBER (G)	2	½ FAT	
CHOLESTEROL (MG)	0	SODIUM (MG)	280	LOW-SODIUM DIETS: OMIT SALT.	

TWICE-BAKED STUFFED CLAMS

MAKES 20 HALF-SHELL STUFFED CLAMS

This is an updated version of Clams Casino, sans bacon and butter. I prefer the flavor of the small littleneck clams to the taste of the larger ocean clams. The smaller size also makes it easy for guests to eat this hors d'oeuvre right out of the shell without utensils. Stuff the clams and place on a bed of rock salt in a paella pan or a favorite ovenproof platter for last-minute reheating in the oven. If you prefer, this dish can be made with mussels in place of clams. Garnish with parsley and lemon wedges for a nice presentation.

10 fresh littleneck clams, such as Manila

1 tablespoon olive oil

½ small onion, finely chopped

2 cloves garlic, finely chopped

¼ red bell pepper, cored, seeded, and finely diced

10 medium shrimp, shelled, deveined, and finely chopped

½ cup unseasoned dry bread crumbs

1 tablespoon finely chopped parsley

1 teaspoon fresh lemon juice

¼ teaspoon cayenne (optional)

1 teaspoon paprika

Rock salt, for serving (optional)

1 Brush clams. Discard any clams that do not close when lightly tapped, or any that feel especially heavy (they are probably filled with sand). Place the clams in a sauté pan with ½ inch of simmering water. Turn on the heat and cover, checking until the clams open, about five minutes. Remove from the heat, drain, and let cool until they can be handled. Cut through the muscle at the hinge and scrape out the meat, being careful not to break the shells. Set shells aside and discard the juice. Finely chop the clams and set aside.

2 In a large cast-iron or nonstick skillet, heat the olive oil over medium-low heat. Sauté the onion, garlic, and bell pepper for about eight minutes, until very soft. Add the chopped clams and shrimp and cook gently, stirring occasionally, until just firm and opaque, about 4 minutes more, then remove from the heat. Do not overcook the shellfish.

3 Preheat the oven to 350°F. Stir the bread crumbs, parsley, lemon juice, cayenne, and paprika into the clam mixture and place about 1½ tablespoons of the filling into each half shell. Compact the filling with the palm of your hand into a mound and place the shells on a baking sheet. Bake for about 10 to 15 minutes, just to warm through (any longer would overcook the shellfish and make it tough).

4 Make a bed of rock salt on a platter, if desired. Transfer the clams to the platter and serve immediately.

PER SERVING OF 2 HALF-SHELL CLAMS					
CALORIES	50	CARBOHYDRATES (G)	5	CARBOHYDRATE CHOICES: 1/2	
FAT (G)	2.0	PROTEIN (G)	4	FOOD EXCHANGES PER SERVING: 1/2 STARCH	
CALORIES FROM FAT (%)	32	FIBER (G)	0	LOW-SODIUM DIETS: ACCEPTABLE	
CHOLESTEROL (MG)	13	SODIUM (MG)	60		

TURKEY POTSTICKERS

MAKES 40 DUMPLINGS

These potstickers or Chinese dumplings can be made with either round Gyoza wrappers or the 2½-inch square egg roll wrappers. They are available in the cold section of virtually every supermarket, or in Asian groceries. They make perfect ravioli wrappers as well. Once you get hooked on these, you'll never order the deep fried egg rolls at a Chinese restaurant again, especially after you check out how the two compare in the nutrition analysis opposite.

½ pound lean ground turkey
1 cup minced white cabbage
2 green onions (scallions), white and light green parts only, finely chopped
2 large egg whites, lightly beaten with ¼ teaspoon salt
2 teaspoons low-sodium soy sauce
1 teaspoon finely grated orange zest

½ teaspoon sesame oil
¼ teaspoon chile oil, or to taste
40 round Gyoza or wonton wrappers
Flour for dusting
2 teaspoons peanut oil
1 cup water
Rice vinegar, low-sodium soy sauce, or Ginger Marinade (page 212), for serving

1 In a large bowl, combine the turkey, cabbage, green onions, egg whites, soy sauce, orange zest, sesame oil, and chile oil. Toss together until evenly mixed.

2 Place 1 generous teaspoon of the filling in the center of one of the Gyoza wrappers and brush the edges sparingly with water. Bring the two opposing edges together to meet and press together firmly, forming a half-moon shape. Set on a large plate lightly dusted with flour and repeat with the remaining wrappers and the filling until you have 40 dumplings. If the dumplings are touching one another on the plate, they must be lightly dusted with flour to stop them from sticking together. Cover the dumplings with a kitchen towel.

3 Heat half of the peanut oil in a large nonstick skillet over medium heat. Add half the dumplings, or as many as will fit without crowding, to the pan and sauté until slightly browned, about two minutes on each side. Add ½ cup of the water to the skillet, cover and steam for about three minutes, until the wrappers are translucent. Transfer the dumplings to a serving platter and keep warm in a low oven while you wipe the pan dry with a paper towel and repeat the process with the remaining dumplings.

4 Serve the dumplings with rice vinegar, low-sodium soy sauce, or Ginger Marinade for dipping.

PER SERVING OF 5 DUMPLINGS

	BEFORE	AFTER
CALORIES	300	190
FAT (G)	8	2.5
CALORIES FROM FAT (%)	23	12
CHOLESTEROL (MG)	20	30

CARBOHYDRATES (G)	27
PROTEIN (G)	14
FIBER (G)	LESS THAN 1
SODIUM (MG)	370

CARBOHYDRATE CHOICES: 2

FOOD EXCHANGES PER SERVING: 1 VERY LEAN MEAT, 1 STARCH

LOW-SODIUM DIETS: OMIT SOY SAUCE, AND REPLACE WITH GINGER MARINADE OR VINEGAR.

SPINACH AND POTATO DUMPLINGS

MAKES APPROXIMATELY 40 DUMPLINGS

These flavorful dumplings can be served as an appetizer with rice vinegar or soy sauce mixed with chopped green onions for dipping. They are also a nice accompaniment to chicken. Wonton skins are an excellent and easier alternative to making your own dough, and can be found in most markets.

Dough

1 cup plus 2 tablespoons
    all-purpose flour, or half
    all-purpose and half whole wheat
    flour
½ teaspoon salt
1 large egg, lightly beaten
1 large egg white
1 tablespoon water

Filling

½ pound small red potatoes, peeled
    and cut into ¼-inch dice
1 tablespoon fennel seeds
1 teaspoon ground cumin
½ teaspoon turmeric

2 tablespoons vegetable oil
1 onion, coarsely chopped
1 small serrano or jalapeño chile,
    stemmed, seeded, and finely
    chopped
2-inch piece fresh ginger, peeled and
    finely grated
3 cloves garlic, finely chopped
½ pound fresh spinach, leaves only,
    well washed, drained, and
    chopped (about 4 cups packed)
Salt and pepper to taste
Rice vinegar or low-sodium soy
    sauce mixed with chopped green
    onions (scallions), for dipping

1 To make the dough: In a bowl, cut together the flour, salt, egg, egg white, and water with two knives or a pastry cutter until the mixture comes together into a rough mass, or pulse the mixture in a food processor. Turn out onto a lightly floured work surface and work the dough with the palm of your hand until it comes together into a ball. Cover with plastic wrap and let rest for 30 minutes while you make the filling. (If using wonton skins, skip this step.)

2 To make the filling: In a saucepan, simmer the potatoes in lightly salted water to cover until barely tender, about 15 minutes, then drain in a colander.

3 Heat a heavy skillet over medium heat. Dry-roast the fennel seeds, cumin, and turmeric for about 2 minutes, stirring occasionally, until fragrant and several shades darker (be careful not to burn the delicate spices). Add the oil, onion, chile,

ginger, and garlic, and cook, stirring occasionally until the onion is softened, about 4 minutes. Increase the heat to medium-high and add the potatoes and the spinach. Sauté, stirring, until the spinach is wilted but still bright green, about 2 minutes more. Season the filling with salt and pepper to taste, remove from the heat, and let cool.

4 To assemble the dumplings: (If using wonton skins, lay them out on the counter and proceed to step 5.) Divide the dough into halves. Sprinkle some flour on a work surface and roll out half the dough until it is as thin as possible, about ⅟₁₆ inch. Cut the dough into 2-inch squares.

5 Place about 2 teaspoons of filling in the center of each dough square or wonton skin. Wet the edges of the dough on one side and fold over so that the opposite edges meet, sealing in the filling and making a triangular dumpling, or, if using wonton skins, a half-moon dumpling. Make sure there is no air inside the dumplings, and press the edges together firmly to seal. Repeat with the second half of the dough.

6 Fill a large pan with lightly salted water about 4 to 5 inches deep. Bring to a gentle simmer. Cook the dumplings in batches to prevent overcrowding, for three to five minutes, until they rise to the surface and look slightly translucent.

7 Remove the dumplings with a slotted spoon and rest the spoon on paper towels briefly to remove excess water. Serve with rice vinegar or soy sauce with chopped green onions.

PER SERVING OF 4 DUMPLINGS					
CALORIES	110	CARBOHYDRATES (G)	16	CARBOHYDRATE CHOICES: 1	
FAT (G)	3.5	PROTEIN (G)	4	FOOD EXCHANGES PER SERVING: 1 STARCH,	
CALORIES FROM FAT (%)	29	FIBER (G)	3	½ FAT	
CHOLESTEROL (MG)	20	SODIUM (MG)	140	LOW-SODIUM DIETS: ACCEPTABLE. FOR DIPPING	
				SAUCE; USE RICE VINEGAR RATHER THAN SOY	
				SAUCE.	

SWEDISH MEATBALLS

MAKES ABOUT 32 MEATBALLS

Sound old-fashioned? Hardly! I serve these wonderful meatballs with Piedmontese Tomato Sauce and they are always eaten down to the last tasty morsel. These little meatballs make great appetizers; they're highly seasoned and low in fat. Protein tends to take the edge off hunger—50 calories of a high-protein food keeps hunger at bay longer than an equal caloric quantity of carbohydrates. Of course, if your blood sugar is low, have a cracker or other carbohydrate along with the protein. Remember, 60 percent of protein is converted to glucose in the bloodstream, so its effect on your blood glucose is delayed and less pronounced.

Whites of 2 large eggs
1 teaspoon dried rosemary, crumbled
1 teaspoon dried marjoram, crumbled
1 teaspoon dried basil, crumbled
½ teaspoon celery salt
1 to 2 Roasted Garlic cloves (see page 151, optional)
2 tablespoons ketchup

½ teaspoon Worcestershire sauce
1 pound lean ground beef (not exceeding 20% fat) or ground turkey
2 tablespoons fine dry bread crumbs
1 small onion, finely chopped
Piedmontese Tomato Sauce (page 234)

1 In a large, chilled mixing bowl, whisk together the egg whites, rosemary, marjoram, basil, celery salt, Roasted Garlic, if using, ketchup, and Worcestershire sauce.

2 Add the ground beef or turkey, bread crumbs, and onion, using your hands to quickly but thoroughly combine the mixture. Cover the bowl and refrigerate for one hour.

3 Form the mixture into ½-inch balls, using a small ice cream scoop, if desired. Place the meatballs on a baking sheet and again refrigerate for at least 30 minutes and up to 2 hours.

4 Preheat the oven to 350°F. Heat 1 teaspoon oil in a nonstick pan over high heat. Add the meatballs in batches, without crowding the pan, and sear till brown on all sides, about two to three minutes. Remove from pan and place in an ovenproof pan, ideally one that can also be used for serving.

5 Finish cooking in the oven about 10 minutes, and serve warm with the Piedmontese Tomato Sauce on the side with toothpicks for serving and dipping.

PER SERVING OF 4 MEATBALLS					
CALORIES	120	CARBOHYDRATES (G)	4	CARBOHYDRATE CHOICES: 0	
FAT (G)	5.5	PROTEIN (G)	13	FOOD EXCHANGES PER SERVING: 2 LEAN MEAT	
CALORIES FROM FAT (%)	42	FIBER (G)	0	LOW-SODIUM DIETS: OMIT SALT.	
CHOLESTEROL (MG)	20	SODIUM (MG)	115		

QUESADILLAS

MAKES 4 SERVINGS

A quesadilla is sort of a Mexican grilled cheese sandwich made with 2 tortillas instead of 2 slices of bread. By using part-skim mozzarella cheese and fat-free sour cream, we cut the fat significantly. Nonfat yogurt or low-fat sour cream can also be used. This dish presents an opportunity to be creative; anything left over can be thrown inside a quesadilla if it's cut small enough. Try the same tricks next time you make a grilled cheese sandwich.

4 large flour tortillas
1 ounce (about ⅓ cup) low-fat mozzarella cheese, grated or thinly sliced
1 medium zucchini, trimmed and coarsely grated

2 plum tomatoes, seeded and diced
2 tablespoons finely chopped cilantro
2 tablespoons bottled salsa or homemade pico de gallo (page 207)
1 tablespoon fat-free sour cream

1 Heat a large nonstick skillet over medium heat. Place one of the tortillas in the pan and immediately scatter half of the mozzarella evenly over it, leaving a ¼-inch border. Scatter half of the zucchini, tomato, and cilantro evenly on top of the cheese and immediately cover with another tortilla. Press down on the top.

2 Cook until the bottom is slightly golden and the cheese is beginning to melt, about 2 minutes. With a wide spatula, flip the quesadilla over and continue to cook, pressing down with the spatula to make sure the tortilla browns evenly, for about 1 minute more, until all the cheese is melted. Transfer to a platter in a warm oven and repeat with the remaining 2 tortillas and ingredients.

3 Using a pizza cutter or a large knife, cut each quesadilla into six wedges. Top each wedge with ½ teaspoon of salsa and a tiny dollop of sour cream and serve warm.

PER SERVING					
	BEFORE	AFTER			
CALORIES	200	190	CARBOHYDRATES (G) 31	CARBOHYDRATE CHOICES: 2	
FAT (G)	6	4.5	PROTEIN (G) 7	FOOD EXCHANGES PER SERVING: 2 STARCH,	
CALORIES FROM FAT (%)	28	21	FIBER (G) LESS THAN 1	½ FAT	
CHOLESTEROL (MG)	9	LESS THAN 5	SODIUM (MG) 460	LOW-SODIUM DIETS: USE A SALT-FREE	
				CHEESE, OR DECREASE CHEESE BY HALF AND	
				INCREASE VEGETABLES; TOP WITH SALT-FREE	
				SALSA OR TOMATO SLICES.	

FRUIT AND PROSCIUTTO WRAPS

MAKES 6 SERVINGS

This is a traditional Italian appetizer in which thin slices of prosciutto are wrapped around slices of melon, usually cantaloupe. The salty meat goes well with the sweet and juicy fruit, and in this version mango and papaya add an interesting twist to this classic. It makes an excellent appetizer during the warmer months. For a variation that's easy to serve as finger food, substitute bread sticks for the melon.

12 very thin slices prosciutto, fat around outside trimmed away, halved lengthwise

24 small wedges of melon, mango, papaya, or a combination
1 teaspoon finely chopped mint

Wrap each wedge of melon with a slice of prosciutto, winding it around several times. If desired, secure with a toothpick (this is not necessary, as the prosciutto will adhere to itself and will not unravel). Arrange four of the packages on each of six chilled plates, or place them on a large platter. If desired, at this point the "wraps" may be refrigerated for up to 3 hours, covered with plastic wrap. Serve chilled, sprinkled with the chopped mint.

PER SERVING					
CALORIES	60	CARBOHYDRATES (G)	6	CARBOHYDRATE CHOICES: 1/2 CHOICE	
FAT (G)	1.5	PROTEIN (G)	6	FOOD EXCHANGES PER SERVING: 1/2 FRUIT,	
CALORIES FROM FAT (%)	23	FIBER (G)	LESS THAN 1	1 VERY LEAN MEAT	
CHOLESTEROL (MG)	15	SODIUM (MG)	410	LOW-SODIUM DIETS: PROSCIUTTO PROVIDES A SIGNIFICANT AMOUNT OF SODIUM. PORTION SHOULD BE LIMITED TO 1 WRAP.	

BRUSCHETTA

MAKES 4 SERVINGS

Grilled bread with a savory topping—called bruschetta or crostini in Italian—is a great low-fat appetizer alternative that in my opinion is a welcome change from the traditional cheese and crackers. There is no end to the variety of toppings that can be used on bruschetta. Here are a few of my favorites, with very little fat and lots of flavor. For bruschetta toasts, use ½-inch-thick slices of country Italian bread. Crostini are generally cut thinner or from a small-diameter baguette. Depending on the topping, you may wish to rub the grilled bread with a cut garlic clove before topping it.

Olive oil cooking spray or
 ½ teaspoon olive oil
4 (½-inch) slices country Italian
 bread (about ½ ounce each)

Topping of your choice (recipes
 follow)

If using olive oil cooking spray: Heat a nonstick pan over medium heat. Spray the bread with a quick burst or two of olive oil cooking spray, directly on both sides of the bread. Pan-grill the bread for about 3 minutes per side until golden. Arrange the bruschetta on a platter and top as desired, then serve immediately.

If using olive oil: Heat the olive oil in a nonstick pan over medium heat. Roast the bread in the pan on both sides until golden, about 3 minutes per side. Arrange the bruschetta on a platter and top as desired. Serve immediately.

PER SERVING WITH TOPPING					
CALORIES	40	CARBOHYDRATES (G)	7	CARBOHYDRATE CHOICES: ½	
FAT (G)	1	PROTEIN (G)	1	FOOD EXCHANGES PER SERVING: ½ STARCH	
CALORIES FROM FAT (%)	22	FIBER (G)	0	LOW-SODIUM DIETS: IF ON A 500 OR 1000 MG	
CHOLESTEROL (MG)	0	SODIUM (MG)	82	SODIUM DIET, USE LOW-SODIUM BREAD.	

TOMATO AND BASIL TOPPING FOR BRUSCHETTA

MAKES 8 SERVINGS, ABOUT 2 CUPS

The simple combination of tomato, garlic, and balsamic vinegar with the best olive oil available makes this a deliciously popular standard on Italian menus. Called by various names, but always a favorite classic, it makes an irresistible appetizer or accompaniment to a bowl of soup at lunchtime.

6 plum tomatoes, seeded and cut into
    ¼-inch dice
2 to 3 cloves garlic, finely chopped
10 leaves fresh basil, finely slivered
1 tablespoon olive oil
¼ teaspoon salt
2 teaspoons balsamic vinegar
Freshly made Bruschetta
    (opposite)

Combine the tomatoes, garlic, basil, olive oil, salt, and vinegar in a glass bowl and toss together gently. Let sit at room temperature for about 30 minutes to allow flavors to marry. Place approximately one heaping tablespoon of the topping on each bruschetta.

PER 1-TEASPOON SERVING

CALORIES	30	CARBOHYDRATES (G)	3
FAT (G)	2	PROTEIN (G)	.5
CALORIES FROM FAT (%)	55	FIBER (G)	.5
CHOLESTEROL (MG)	0	SODIUM (MG)	70

PER 1-TEASPOON SERVING WITH 1 SLICE BRUSCHETTA

CALORIES	70	CARBOHYDRATES (G)	10	CARBOHYDRATE CHOICES: 0; ADD 1 CHOICE PER BRUSCHETTA
FAT (G)	3	PROTEIN (G)	2	
CALORIES FROM FAT (%)	36	FIBER (G)	1	FOOD EXCHANGES PER SERVING: 1 VEGETABLE; ADD ½ STARCH PER BRUSCHETTA
CHOLESTEROL (MG)	0	SODIUM (MG)	150	LOW-SODIUM DIETS: OMIT SALT.

ANCHOVY, GARLIC, AND PARSLEY TOPPING FOR BRUSCHETTA

MAKES 16 SERVINGS, ABOUT ¼ CUP

This recipe was passed on to me by a French friend, Chantal Calmo, whose grandmother, from the French Alps region, always kept this topping on hand for the fresh baguettes she made daily. The great thing about it, besides its taste, is that it can be made in advance and will store in the refrigerator for a week or two. Anchovies, by the way, are a source of omega-3 fatty acids, the kind that have been linked to lowering cholesterol in the blood, making this an excellent replacement for traditional cheese and crackers, which are high in saturated fat. If you don't want to make bruschetta, spread a teaspoon on fresh bread or crackers for an easy, tangy treat.

1 (2-ounce) tin anchovies packed
   in oil
2 to 3 cloves garlic, finely chopped
½ cup finely chopped parsley sprigs,
   loosely packed

1 tablespoon olive oil
Lemon slices, for garnish

1 Drain the anchovies, then rinse them under warm running water, removing most of the oil. Drain and pat them dry with paper towels.

2 In a blender or a mini-food processor, blend the anchovies, garlic, chopped parsley, and oil until smooth. Store in a tightly sealed container, preferably glass.

3 Serve garnished with lemon slices.

PER 1-TEASPOON SERVING

CALORIES	15	**CARBOHYDRATES (G)**	0
FAT (G)	1	PROTEIN (G)	1
CALORIES FROM FAT (%)	70	FIBER (G)	0
CHOLESTEROL (MG)	5	SODIUM (MG)	130

PER 1-TEASPOON SERVING WITH 1 SLICE BRUSCHETTA

CALORIES	60	**CARBOHYDRATES (G)**	7	**CARBOHYDRATE CHOICES:** 0; ADD ½ CHOICE PER BRUSCHETTA.
FAT (G)	2	PROTEIN (G)	2	**FOOD EXCHANGES PER SERVING:** 1 TEASPOON, FREE; ADD ½ STARCH PER BRUSCHETTA.
CALORIES FROM FAT (%)	34	FIBER (G)	1	
CHOLESTEROL (MG)	3	SODIUM (MG)	210	**LOW-SODIUM DIETS:** LIMIT PORTION TO 1 TEASPOON.

ROASTED WHOLE GARLIC BRUSCHETTA

MAKES 16 SERVINGS, ABOUT ¼ CUP

Garlic, simply roasted, makes a wonderful bruschetta topping. Try to find the freshest "new-crop" garlic that is firm and non-sprouting.

6 medium heads garlic
2 tablespoons olive oil
¼ teaspoon salt

Pepper, to taste
2 or 3 sprigs thyme

1 Preheat the oven to 275° F. Cut the top off the heads of garlic to expose the individual cloves. Arrange heads in baking dish just big enough to hold all. Drizzle the olive oil over, and sprinkle with salt and pepper. Tuck the thyme sprigs between the heads. Cover the dish with tin foil or a lid.

2 Bake the garlic for 1 to 1½ hours, depending on size of heads. Garlic should be very tender and sweet.

3 When garlic is done, serve whole heads with oil from the baking dish spooned over them, with bruschetta or crusty Italian bread. Squeeze the garlic on the bread and eat warm.

PER 1-TEASPOON SERVING				
CALORIES	15	CARBOHYDRATES (G)	0	
FAT (G)	1.5	PROTEIN (G)	0	
CALORIES FROM FAT (%)	52	FIBER (G)	0	
CHOLESTEROL (MG)	0	SODIUM (MG)	35	
PER 1-TEASPOON SERVING WITH 1 SLICE BRUSCHETTA				
CALORIES	70	CARBOHYDRATES (G)	7	CARBOHYDRATE CHOICES: 0; ADD 1 CHOICE
FAT (G)	3	PROTEIN (G)	2	PER BRUSCHETTA.
CALORIES FROM FAT (%)	34	FIBER (G)	0	FOOD EXCHANGES PER SERVING: FREE; ADD
CHOLESTEROL (MG)	0	SODIUM (MG)	120	½ STARCH PER BRUSCHETTA.
				LOW-SODIUM DIETS: OMIT SALT.

TAPENADE TOPPING FOR BRUSCHETTA

MAKES 24 SERVINGS, ABOUT 1 CUP

Tapenade is traditionally made with oil- or brine-cured black, or sometimes green, olives which have a much more pronounced flavor than the canned ripe black olives that many of us are familiar with. It is purely a matter of taste, and also the fact that oil-and-brine–cured olives must be pitted by hand, which is a time-consuming task but well worthwhile if you prefer more flavorful olives.

1¼ cups pitted ripe whole medium
    olives, drained
1 tablespoon olive oil
2 tablespoons pine nuts, toasted
1 large clove garlic

Freshly ground black pepper
    (optional)
1 roasted red bell pepper, homemade
    or jarred, peeled, seeded, and
    sliced into thin strips

1 In a food processor, combine the olives, olive oil, pine nuts, and garlic. Pulse several times to combine, scraping down the sides of the bowl. Do not process so long that it becomes a smooth paste; the tapenade should still have a little texture. Taste for seasoning and add a little pepper, if desired. (The tapenade may be covered and refrigerated for up to 1 week.)

2 Spread a tablespoon or so of the tapenade on each warm bruschetta. Top with two small strips of red pepper and serve.

PER 2-TEASPOON SERVING

CALORIES	50	CARBOHYDRATES (G)	2
FAT (G)	4.5	PROTEIN (G)	0
CALORIES FROM FAT (%)	83	FIBER (G)	0
CHOLESTEROL (MG)	0	SODIUM (MG)	230

PER 2-TEASPOON SERVING WITH 1 SLICE BRUSCHETTA

CALORIES	90	CARBOHYDRATES (G)	9
FAT (G)	6	PROTEIN (G)	2
CALORIES FROM FAT (%)	55	FIBER (G)	LESS THAN 1
CHOLESTEROL (MG)	0	SODIUM (MG)	310

CARBOHYDRATE CHOICES: 0; ADD 1 CHOICE
    PER BRUSCHETTA.
FOOD EXCHANGES PER SERVING: 1 FAT; ADD
    ½ STARCH PER BRUSCHETTA.
LOW-SODIUM DIETS: NOT ACCEPTABLE BECAUSE
    OLIVES, DUE TO THEIR CURING PROCESS, ARE
    HIGH IN SODIUM. TRY ANOTHER BRUSCHETTA
    TOPPING SUCH AS TOMATO OR GARLIC.

WHITE BEAN HUMMUS BRUSCHETTA TOPPING

MAKES 12 SERVINGS, ABOUT 1 1/2 CUPS

Hummus is a Middle Eastern dish that gets its characteristic flavor from tahini, a paste made from ground sesame seeds. Although tahini does contain fat, the amount used here is less than in the traditional recipe, and therefore makes for less than .5 gram of fat per tablespoon of hummus, so this recipe falls within the guidelines for a nonfat dish. (The original recipe calls for 3 tablespoons tahini and 1 tablespoon olive oil.) Hummus is nice served on bruschetta, pita bread, or crackers, accompanied by some diced tomato and finely shredded lettuce.

1 (16-ounce) can cannellini (white kidney beans), rinsed and drained
Juice of 1 lemon (about 3 tablespoons)
1 tablespoon tahini

1/2 teaspoon ground cumin
1/2 teaspoon paprika
1/4 teaspoon salt
2 cloves garlic, minced

1 In a food processor or blender, combine the cannellini, lemon juice, tahini, cumin, paprika, salt, and garlic and process until smooth, scraping down the sides of the bowl as necessary. Add a tablespoon or two of water if you prefer a thinner consistency.

2 Transfer to an airtight container, refrigerate, and use within 4 days.

PER 2-TABLESPOON SERVING			
CALORIES	40	CARBOHYDRATES (G)	6
FAT (G)	1	PROTEIN (G)	1
CALORIES FROM FAT (%)	20	FIBER (G)	1
CHOLESTEROL (MG)	0	SODIUM (MG)	120

PER 2-TABLESPOON SERVING WITH 1 BRUSCHETTA			
CALORIES	80	CARBOHYDRATES (G)	13
FAT (G)	2	PROTEIN (G)	3
CALORIES	21	FIBER (G)	2
CHOLESTEROL (MG)	0	SODIUM (MG)	210

CARBOHYDRATE CHOICES: 0; ADD 1 CHOICE PER BRUSCHETTA.
FOOD EXCHANGES PER SERVING: 1/2 STARCH; ADD 1/2 STARCH PER BRUSCHETTA.
LOW-SODIUM DIETS: OMIT SALT; INCREASE LEMON JUICE TO TASTE.

BRUSCHETTA WITH ROASTED RED PEPPER–EGGPLANT SPREAD

MAKES 20 SERVINGS, ABOUT 2½ CUPS

A serving of this sublime red pepper spread contains only 1 gram of monounsaturated fat.

1 medium eggplant, sliced ⅜ inch thick
1 tablespoon salt
6 cloves garlic, roasted and peeled (see page 151)
4 oil-packed anchovies, rinsed, patted dry, and chopped

1 (12-ounce) jar roasted red peppers, drained, or 3 fresh red peppers, roasted, seeded, and peeled (see Note)
2 tablespoons olive oil
Freshly ground black pepper

1 Preheat the oven to 350°F. Place the eggplant slices in a colander and sprinkle them evenly with the salt. Let sit in the sink for 20 minutes to extract the liquid. Rinse quickly with cold water and pat dry with paper towels. Place on a lightly oiled baking sheet and bake for 30 minutes, or until tender and golden. Remove peel.

2 In a food processor or blender, combine the peeled eggplant, garlic cloves, anchovies, red peppers, olive oil, and pepper. Puree until smooth. Taste for seasoning, adding salt if necessary, and additional pepper to taste.

Note: You can roast peppers either on a pan 2 inches from a broiler, turning when the skin becomes charred and blistered, or on a metal skewer over an open flame, rotating slowly until the skin blackens. Place the peppers in a bowl and cover, letting them steam until they cool enough to handle. Then peel the peppers and remove the core and seeds.

PER 2-TABLESPOON SERVING

CALORIES	25	CARBOHYDRATES (G)	3
FAT (G)	1.5	PROTEIN (G)	1
CALORIES FROM FAT (%)	50	FIBER (G)	1
CHOLESTEROL (MG)	0	SODIUM (MG)	350

PER 2-TABLESPOON SERVING WITH 1 SLICE BRUSCHETTA

CALORIES	70	CARBOHYDRATES (G)	10	CARBOHYDRATE CHOICES: 0; ADD 1 CHOICE PER BRUSCHETTA.
FAT (G)	2.5	PROTEIN (G)	2	FOOD EXCHANGES PER SERVING: 1 VEGETABLE;
CALORIES FROM FAT (%)	33	FIBER (G)	1	ADD ½ STARCH PER BRUSCHETTA.
CHOLESTEROL (MG)	0	SODIUM (MG)	430	LOW-SODIUM DIETS: REDUCE SALT BY HALF OR OMIT.

CUCUMBER-DILL YOGURT DIP

MAKES 1 CUP

This is a wonderful light dip for crudités, or for serving on the side with any Middle Eastern dish. It is best eaten the day it is made because it tends to separate and get a bit watery. Nonfat yogurt is used in place of regular yogurt to reduce the fat, but you can use low fat if you prefer.

1 European cucumber, grated on the
    largest hole of the grater
1 cup plain nonfat yogurt
½ teaspoon salt

¼ teaspoon white pepper
1 large clove garlic, finely chopped
1 tablespoon finely chopped fresh
    dill, or 2 teaspoons dried dill

1 In a kitchen towel, twist and squeeze the grated cucumber to rid it of as much excess water as possible.

2 Combine the cucumber, yogurt, salt, pepper, garlic, and dill in a nonreactive bowl, cover, and refrigerate for 30 minutes to allow the flavors to marry.

PER 2-TABLESPOON SERVING					
	BEFORE	AFTER			
CALORIES	25	25	CARBOHYDRATES (G)	4	CARBOHYDRATE CHOICES: 0.
FAT (G)	1	0	PROTEIN (G)	2	FOOD EXCHANGES PER SERVING: FREE
CALORIES FROM FAT (%)	36	4	FIBER (G)	0	LOW-SODIUM DIETS: OMIT SALT.
CHOLESTEROL (MG)	LESS THAN 5	0	SODIUM (MG)	160	

TEQUILA AND CILANTRO GRAVLAX

MAKES 8 SERVINGS

Traditionally from Sweden, gravlax—literally meaning cured salmon—is salmon fillets that have been cured in salt, sugar, black pepper, fresh dill, and sometimes vodka or gin. It is more delicate in taste than smoked salmon, and is so easy to make yourself, although it impresses guests like little else. Try this new southwestern twist using tequila and cilantro. Gravlax are ideal for a large party, because they can be started a week in advance. Use the leftovers for next day's sandwich, or toss it in with your Pasta Primavera (page 302). To start off a meal, serve with bruschetta or water crackers, and the Chopped Cucumber Salad (page 184).

1 cup firmly packed brown sugar
1 cup kosher salt
1 bunch fresh cilantro, stems removed
12 black peppercorns

1 pound salmon fillet, skin on
¼ cup tequila
Bruschetta or water biscuits, for
   serving

1 In a mixing bowl, combine the brown sugar and salt and mix together.

2 In a container just large enough to hold the salmon in a flat layer, spread half of the sugar/salt mixture in an even layer. Spread half of the cilantro leaves and 6 of the peppercorns evenly over the top.

3 Lay the salmon, flesh side down, over the cure. Cover with the remaining sugar/salt mixture, cilantro, and peppercorns. Drizzle the tequila evenly over the salmon.

4 Cover the container tightly with plastic wrap (if a firmer consistency is required, weight the fish with a board topped by several cans to compress the flesh as it cures). Refrigerate the fish for at least 2 and up to 3 days, turning it over every 8 hours. To test doneness, check flesh of fish at its thickest part. Flesh should look "cooked."

5 To serve, rinse the salmon under cold running water, removing the cure, and pat dry with paper towels. With a long, sharp knife, slice finely across the grain and serve with bruschetta or water biscuits. The salmon will keep, tightly wrapped, for three to four days in the refrigerator.

VARIATIONS: Gravlax can be made with many different combinations of ingredients. Substitute equal quantities of the following for the cilantro and tequila, keeping the proportion of sugar, salt, and peppercorns the same:

1 Traditional gravlax: ¼ cup vodka, gin, or aquavit; ½ cup chopped fresh dill

2 Japanese: ¼ cup sake; ½ cup chopped green onion and 2 tablespoons miso lees (miso lees is the leftover yeast from the process of making miso, available at Asian markets)

3 Thai: ¼ cup vermouth; ½ cup chopped lemongrass, ¼ cup fresh ginger root, and 1 chile, chopped

PER 2-OUNCE SERVING

CALORIES	65	CARBOHYDRATES (G)	0
FAT (G)	2	PROTEIN (G)	10
CALORIES FROM FAT (%)	50	FIBER (G)	0
CHOLESTEROL (MG)	13	SODIUM (MG)	445

PER 2-OUNCE SERVING WITH BRUSCHETTA

CALORIES	110	CARBOHYDRATES (G)	7
FAT (G)	3	PROTEIN (G)	11
CALORIES FROM FAT (%)	25	FIBER (G)	0
CHOLESTEROL (MG)	0	SODIUM (MG)	525

CARBOHYDRATE CHOICES: 0; ADD ½ CHOICE
  PER BRUSCHETTA.
FOOD EXCHANGES PER SERVING: 1 LEAN MEAT;
  ADD ½ STARCH PER BRUSCHETTA.
LOW-SODIUM DIETS: NOT APPROPRIATE FOR
  LOW-SODIUM DIET
NUTRITION BONUS: 2 OUNCES SALMON CONTAINS
  CONTAINS 670 MG OMEGA-3 FATTY ACIDS—
  THE KIND OF FAT THAT MAY HELP TO
  PREVENT HEART DISEASE.

CHAPTER 14

SOUPS

A French proverb says a good soup smiles as it simmers. It reminds us that eating is only half of the pleasure of soup. The other is the aroma that fills the kitchen as it cooks and its flavors develop. With the following soup recipes, you can enjoy the taste and know that you're eating light.

A pot of well-seasoned broth, stocked with vegetables, meats, or seafood, is a delicious way to get your vitamins, minerals, and fiber—essential to the person with diabetes. These homemade soups are designed to keep fat low, without compromising flavor or body. Take special note that soups vary widely in their carbohydrate contents. A puree of vegetable, like the Broccoli Soup, may not meet your carbohydrate requirement for a meal, so you may need to add a slice of bread or other starch. The White Bean Soup, on the other hand, may suffice as a meal in itself. Check the carbohydrate values against your own food plan and it will be easy to get it just right.

ARTICHOKE SOUP

MAKES ABOUT 4 SERVINGS

The unique texture and flavor of artichokes allow this soup to be creamy without the cream of the original recipe. The fat is reduced by de-fatting the beef stock and limiting the oil in the sauté. The soup is thickened by the artichoke and potato rather than cream, butter, or egg. Served as a first course or a light main course, this soup is a delicious gourmet pleaser. Try it in the late summer, when artichokes are in season. Off season, use frozen artichoke hearts.

8 ounces fresh or frozen and thawed artichoke hearts (about 2 cups), trimmed to the hearts
1 tablespoon olive oil
1 leek, white and light green part only, halved lengthwise, thoroughly rinsed, and thinly sliced
1 large potato, peeled and cut into ¾-inch dice

1 celery stalk, coarsely chopped
1 bay leaf
4 cups low-sodium, low-fat beef broth
1 teaspoon fresh lemon juice
Salt and freshly ground black pepper, to taste

1 Cut the artichoke hearts into thin wedges. In a large saucepan, heat the oil over medium heat. Add the artichokes, leek, potato, celery, and bay leaf. Sauté, stirring frequently, until the leek starts to wilt, 4 to 5 minutes.

2 Add the beef stock, cover the pan, and reduce the heat to low. Stirring occasionally, simmer until the potato and artichokes are tender, about 30 minutes.

3 Remove from the heat and discard the bay leaf. Let the soup cool for 5 minutes. Puree the soup in a food processor or blender in batches.

4 Add the lemon juice and salt and pepper to taste. Reheat gently before serving.

PER 1⅓-CUP SERVING					
	BEFORE	AFTER			
CALORIES	230	180	CARBOHYDRATES (G)	27	CARBOHYDRATE CHOICES: 2
FAT (G)	10	5	PROTEIN (G)	10	FOOD EXCHANGES PER SERVING: 2 STARCH,
CALORIES FROM FAT (%)	40	25	FIBER (G)	8	½ FAT
CHOLESTEROL (MG)	120	0	SODIUM (MG)	200	LOW-SODIUM DIETS: OMIT SALT; ADD MORE
					LEMON JUICE.

BORSCHT

My dear friend Susan, a borscht connoisseur who claims that this dish got her through the morning sickness stage of her pregnancy, explains that the seasoning of this naturally fat-free cold soup must be just the right combination of sugar and salt. She says that "sour salt" adds the magic touch. Sour salt is actually citric acid, a harmless ingredient found naturally in fruits and vegetables that can be found at the grocery store in the spice section. Since borscht is generally eaten cold, sugar substitute can easily replace the sugar if you prefer it. The amount of sugar is negligible, since a teaspoon contains only 4 grams of carbohydrate, and that's divided among 6 servings of soup.

3 pounds medium beets, scrubbed, 1 inch of the stem left on
6 cups water or vegetable broth
2 tablespoons red wine vinegar
1 teaspoon sugar
1 clove garlic, finely chopped

1 cup mushrooms, wiped clean and finely chopped
Juice of ½ lemon
Sour salt or salt and pepper, to taste
Spinach and Potato Dumplings (page 142; optional)

1 Place the beets in a large saucepan and cover them generously with cold water. Bring to a boil, partially cover the pan, and reduce the heat. Simmer the beets for 35 to 50 minutes, or until tender when pierced with the tip of a knife. Drain the beets and, when cool enough to handle, slip off the skins and cut the beets into fine matchsticks.

2 In a clean saucepan, combine the beets with the 6 cups water, vinegar, sugar, and garlic. Over low heat, simmer the mixture very gently, covered, for 30 minutes.

3 Add the mushrooms, lemon juice, and salt and pepper to taste. Heat just until warmed through and serve, accompanied by Mushroom Dumplings, if desired.

PER 1⅓-CUP SERVING					
CALORIES	110	CARBOHYDRATES (G)	25	CARBOHYDRATE CHOICES: 1½	
FAT (G)	0.5	PROTEIN (G)	4	FOOD EXCHANGES PER SERVING: 1 STARCH,	
CALORIES FROM FAT	0	FIBER (G)	7	1 VEGETABLE	
CHOLESTEROL (MG)	0	SODIUM (MG)	360	LOW-SODIUM DIETS: OMIT SALT.	

BROCCOLI SOUP

MAKES 6 (1-CUP) OR 4 (1½-CUP) SERVINGS

Once you have made this very simple dish, you're likely to add it to your list of staples that can be made quickly. If chicken stock is used, be sure to taste before adding additional salt—sometimes the salt in the broth is just enough. Whisk in a cup of nonfat yogurt or sour cream at the end for a creamier version. The "before" recipe is made with real cream, something you'll never miss in this lightened-up version. If you use water instead of broth, you'll be able to classify this soup as vegetarian.

1 medium onion, chopped
2 cloves garlic, minced
1 carrot, thinly sliced
1 medium potato, peeled and cut into
    1-inch slices
2 teaspoons mustard seed

¾ pound broccoli, trimmed
    and coarsely chopped (about
    3½ cups)
3 cups low-sodium chicken broth or
    water
Salt and pepper, to taste

1 In a heavy saucepan, place the onion, garlic, carrot, potato, mustard seed, broccoli, and chicken broth or water and simmer the mixture uncovered for 15 to 20 minutes or until broccoli is very tender.

2 In a food processor or blender, puree the soup in batches until smooth, transferring into another heavy saucepan. Return to heat and whisk in salt and pepper. Serve hot.

PER 1-CUP SERVING					
	BEFORE	AFTER			
CALORIES	150	70	CARBOHYDRATES (G)	12	CARBOHYDRATE CHOICES: 1
FAT (G)	10	1.5	PROTEIN (G)	4	FOOD EXCHANGES PER SERVING: 1 STARCH
CALORIES FROM FAT (%)	55	19	FIBER (G)	3	LOW-SODIUM DIETS: AVOID ADDING SALT.
CHOLESTEROL (MG)	25	LESS THAN 5	SODIUM (MG)	170	USE NO-SALT-ADDED CHICKEN STOCK, PREFERABLY HOMEMADE.

CAULIFLOWER SOUP WITH CURRY FLAVORS

MAKES 4 SERVINGS

This satisfying soup is good served hot or cold. Adjust the water or broth to make the soup as thick or thin as you like. Make sure you use low-sodium chicken broth, as five cups of regular broth will be very salty. If you wish to cut back on the sodium even more, you can substitute water for some of the chicken broth.

1 tablespoon olive oil
2 medium onions, coarsely chopped
1 teaspoon chopped fresh peeled ginger
4 cloves garlic, finely chopped
6 cups low-fat, low-sodium chicken broth
½ teaspoon ground cumin
1 teaspoon ground coriander
¼ teaspoon turmeric

Pinch of cayenne pepper
2 russet potatoes (about ½ pound), peeled and cut into ½-inch cubes
2 generous cups cauliflower florets (about ½ pound)
1 teaspoon salt
Freshly ground black pepper, to taste
2 tablespoons low-fat or nonfat yogurt
2 teaspoons finely chopped parsley

1 Heat the oil in a nonstick stockpot over medium-high heat, and sauté the onions, ginger, and garlic, stirring constantly for about 5 minutes, until the onions are golden. Do not allow the vegetables to turn dark brown. Add ½ cup of chicken broth, the cumin, coriander, turmeric, and cayenne. Stir for 1 minute more.

2 Add the potatoes, cauliflower, and remaining chicken broth to the onion mixture. Add the salt and pepper to taste, and stir. Bring the mixture to a simmer and cook, partially covered, for 10 minutes, or until the potatoes and cauliflower are tender.

3 In a blender, puree the soup, in batches if necessary, until smooth and return to the pot. Stir and serve in heated bowls, garnishing each bowl with one teaspoon yogurt and a sprinkle of parsley.

PER 1½-CUP SERVING					
CALORIES	160	CARBOHYDRATES (G)	22	CARBOHYDRATE CHOICES: 1½	
FAT (G)	7	PROTEIN (G)	8	FOOD EXCHANGES PER SERVING: 1½ STARCH,	
CALORIES FROM FAT (%)	34	FIBER (G)	4	1 FAT	
CHOLESTEROL (MG)	10	SODIUM (MG)	730	LOW-SODIUM DIETS: USE WATER OR HOMEMADE,	
				NO-SALT-ADDED BROTH.	

CARROT GINGER SOUP

MAKES 4 SERVINGS

It's the ginger in this recipe that gives it such a zingy flavor. I buy pickled ginger in the Japanese section of my grocery store—it's easier than chopping fresh ginger and it gives the soup a slightly more intense flavor.

1 tablespoon extra-virgin olive oil
2 pounds peeled carrots (very ripe and orange)
½ onion, diced
¼ cup peeled and diced ginger, fresh or pickled

1 leek, white part only, diced
5 cups low-fat, low-sodium chicken broth, or water, or combination
2 tablespoons nonfat yogurt and chopped chives for garnish (optional)

1 In a large, deep skillet, heat the olive oil over medium-low heat. Sauté the carrots, onion, ginger, and leek for about 10 minutes, stirring occasionally. The vegetables should not brown. When the onions, leek, and ginger are tender, add the chicken broth or water, which should be enough to just cover the vegetables. Bring the liquid up to a simmer.

2 Simmer the mixture for 30 to 40 minutes, until the carrots are tender all the way through. Remove from the heat and allow to cool for 15 minutes.

3 In a blender or food processor, puree the soup until smooth, in batches if necessary. Taste for seasoning (the soup will not need any pepper, as the ginger brings sufficient spiciness). Serve very hot, in warmed bowls.

4 As an optional garnish, place a dollop of nonfat yogurt on soup and sprinkle with chopped chives. For a more creative presentation, place the yogurt in a squeeze bottle or pastry bag with a small tip, and squeeze the yogurt onto the soup in decorative designs.

PER 1½-CUP SERVING

CALORIES	180	CARBOHYDRATES (G)	29
FAT (G)	6	PROTEIN (G)	7
CALORIES FROM FAT (%)	29	FIBER (G)	7
CHOLESTEROL (MG)	6	SODIUM (MG)	350

CARBOHYDRATE CHOICES: 2

FOOD EXCHANGES PER SERVING: 1 STARCH, 2 VEGETABLE, 1 FAT

LOW-SODIUM DIETS: SUBSTITUTE WATER FOR HALF OF THE CHICKEN BROTH. USE FRESH GINGER INSTEAD OF PICKLED AND INCREASE GINGER AND ONION.

CIOPPINO

Cioppino is the San Francisco version of bouillabaisse, the highly seasoned French fish stew made with several different kinds of fish. Cioppino is considered more Spanish because it uses nuts, chiles, garlic, and fennel rather than saffron to build flavor. Both versions are quick, light, filling, and flavorful. I recommend that you grind the almonds, fennel, and garlic in a spice grinder or coffee mill that is used solely for grinding spices. It's a handy tool to have around and well worth the investment of $20 or so. It's also great for grinding black peppercorns, which lose their flavor soon after they are cracked. If you don't have a spice grinder, try a mortar and pestle or a rolling pin.

If you're not familiar with them, ancho chiles are actually poblano chiles in their dried form. They are generally available in the ever-growing ethnic section of most supermarkets. Using these dried chiles to make a flavor paste adds an intense, earthy flavor—a good base for this rich-tasting soup.

1 pound mussels (optional)
2 tablespoons cornmeal (if using
    mussels)

Flavor Paste
2 dried pasilla pods, or ancho chiles,
    seeds removed
1 ounce ground almonds, lightly
    toasted
$\frac{1}{4}$ teaspoon fennel seeds, ground in a
    spice grinder
2 teaspoons anchovy paste
3 cloves garlic, crushed

12 medium tomatoes (about
    5 pounds)

1 tablespoon olive oil
1 medium onion, diced
2 green bell peppers, cored, seeded,
    and diced
2 red bell peppers, cored, seeded, and
    diced
1 (8-ounce) bottle clam juice
$\frac{1}{2}$ cup dry white wine
1 cup canned tomato puree
1 pound halibut, cut into 1-inch
    cubes
$\frac{1}{2}$ pound raw medium or large
    shrimp, peeled and deveined
$\frac{1}{2}$ teaspoon dried rosemary, crumbled
$\frac{1}{2}$ teaspoon dried thyme
Dash of cayenne pepper (optional)

1 If using mussels, clean and debeard them under cold running water. Discard any mussels that do not close when touched. Soak the mussels with cornmeal and enough cold water to cover in the refrigerator, for at least an hour, preferably overnight.

2 To prepare the flavor paste, place the dried pasilla or ancho chiles in a small bowl, cover with boiling water and allow to sit for 30 minutes. Drain well, reserving the soaking water. Transfer the chiles to a blender and puree, adding just enough of the soaking water to help the mixture move in the blender. Add the almonds, fennel, anchovy paste, and garlic. Blend until somewhat smooth and set aside. If not using a spice grinder, crush seeds and almonds under a rolling pin or chop finely with a knife.

3 Preheat the oven to 350° F. Core the tomatoes and place them in a large roasting pan. Roast uncovered in the oven until their skins are bursting, but they are still fairly firm, about 30 minutes. Remove from the oven and, when cool enough to handle, peel off and discard the skins. Roughly chop the tomato pulp and set aside.

4 Heat the oil in a large heavy saucepan or Dutch oven over medium-high heat. Sauté the onion and bell peppers until slightly soft, about five minutes. Deglaze the pan with the clam juice and add the wine, rosemary, thyme, and pepper, if using. Add the chopped tomatoes, flavor paste, and tomato puree. Stir thoroughly and adjust the heat so that the mixture simmers gently. Cover the pan and simmer the mixture for two hours.

5 About 15 minutes prior to serving, add the halibut and simmer for five minutes. Then add the shrimp and push them down to make sure they are submerged in the liquid. If using the mussels, place them on the top of the mixture and cover the pan. Simmer for 10 minutes more, and serve immediately with crusty bread, if you like.

PER 1½-CUP SERVING				
CALORIES	320	CARBOHYDRATES (G)	28	CARBOHYDRATE CHOICES: 2
FAT (G)	10	PROTEIN (G)	30	FOOD EXCHANGES PER SERVING: 3 LEAN MEAT,
CALORIES FROM FAT (%)	28	FIBER (G)	7	2 STARCH
CHOLESTEROL (MG)	85	SODIUM (MG)	330	LOW-SODIUM DIETS: OMIT ANCHOVY PASTE.

ROASTED CORN CHOWDER

MAKES 10 SERVINGS

Traditionally, chowder is loaded with fat. The secret to flavor without fat in this dish is roasting the corn. Although it takes a bit more time, it's worth the effort, and it allows the switch from cream to nonfat milk to go unnoticed. Use frozen corn only if you are in a real pinch, or if you have a craving for corn chowder in non-corn season. Since it takes time to cook this soup, I make a large batch and freeze half for future use.

6 ears corn, husks pulled back and silk removed, and husks pulled back up around the corn (tie at the top if the husks become very loose)

½ teaspoon olive oil

3 leeks, white part only, root end trimmed, cut halfway through lengthwise and well rinsed, then thinly sliced

2 cloves garlic, finely chopped

5 tablespoons all-purpose flour

8 cups low-fat, low-sodium chicken broth

1 teaspoon ground cumin

1 teaspoon ground coriander

2 teaspoons chili powder

¾ cups nonfat milk

½ teaspoon salt

⅛ teaspoon black pepper

Dash of Tabasco sauce

¼ cup finely chopped fresh cilantro

1 Place an ungreased baking sheet over medium–high heat on top of the stove. Place the corn on the hot baking sheet and roast, turning frequently with tongs as the corn blackens, until the kernels are tender, about 20 minutes. Set aside to cool. (If desired, the corn can also be roasted on an outdoor grill.)

2 When cool enough to handle, remove and discard the husks and cut the kernels off the cob over a large bowl to catch any juices.

3 In a large, heavy nonstick saucepan, heat the olive oil over medium–low heat. Sauté the leeks until slightly softened, about 3 minutes. Add the garlic and cook for 1 minute more.

4 In a small bowl, whisk the flour with ¼ cup of the chicken broth. Whisk in the cumin, coriander, and chili powder and add this mixture to the leeks. Stir with a wooden spoon until well blended and beginning to thicken, about 3 minutes.

5 Add the remaining chicken broth and all but ¼ cup of the corn and its liquid to the pan (set aside the ¼ cup for garnish). Stir to mix thoroughly, partially cover the pan and simmer for 10 to 15 minutes, stirring occasionally.

6 Puree the mixture, in batches if necessary, and return to the saucepan. Stir in the milk, salt, and pepper and heat through. Add the Tabasco sauce and the cilantro and serve in heated soup bowls, garnished with a few kernels of the remaining corn.

PER 1-CUP SERVING

	BEFORE	AFTER			
CALORIES	250	150	CARBOHYDRATES (G)	29	CARBOHYDRATE CHOICES: 2
FAT (G)	15	3	PROTEIN (G)	6	FOOD EXCHANGES PER SERVING: 2 STARCH
CALORIES FROM FAT (%)	50	15	FIBER (G)	4	LOW-SODIUM DIETS: THIS RECIPE IS ACCEPTABLE.
CHOLESTEROL (MG)	30	5	SODIUM (MG)	220	IF FOLLOWING 500 OR 1000 MG SODIUM
					DIET, OMIT SALT.

CORN AND TOMATILLO SOUP

MAKES 2 SERVINGS

Since I grew up in Iowa, corn was always a staple in my diet, and still is. I'm always looking for new recipes that include corn. This fabulous corn soup is made exotic by the addition of tart tomatillos, the small green Mexican tomatoes. Then a bit of fresh lime adds a citrus note that tops it all off. Make sure that you puree this soup well, until smooth and not grainy. It's creamy and indulgent without a drop of cream or milk. If you're serving more than two people, this recipe can be easily doubled.

2 teaspoons canola oil
½ white onion, coarsely chopped
¼ pound tomatillos (papery skins removed), washed and quartered
1½ cups frozen corn kernels, thawed
½ serrano or jalapeño chile, stemmed, seeded, and finely chopped

3 cups low-fat, low-sodium chicken stock
Salt and freshly ground black pepper, to taste
Juice of ½ lime

1 Heat the oil in a large saucepan over medium heat. Sauté the onion until softened, about five minutes.

2 Add the tomatillos, corn, and serrano chile and sauté for five minutes more, then add the chicken stock and raise the heat to high. Bring the mixture to a boil, then lower the heat and simmer gently, partially covered, for 45 minutes.

3 Transfer the soup to a blender or food processor and blend until smooth, scraping down the sides with a rubber spatula as needed. You may need to blend as long as 5 minutes in order to achieve the desired consistency. Return to the pan, add the salt, pepper, and lime juice, bring back just to a simmer, and serve immediately.

PER 1¼-CUP SERVING					
CALORIES	210	CARBOHYDRATES (G)	34	CARBOHYDRATE CHOICES: 2	
FAT (G)	8	PROTEIN (G)	9	FOOD EXCHANGES PER SERVING: 2 STARCH, 1 FAT	
CALORIES FROM FAT (%)	30	FIBER (G)	6	LOW-SODIUM DIETS: ACCEPTABLE.	
CHOLESTEROL (MG)	10	SODIUM (MG)	170		

CORN AND CHICKEN NOODLE SOUP

MAKES 6 SERVINGS

On a cold winter night, this old favorite, with the added color, texture, and flavor of the corn and red bell pepper, is a great, tasty comfort. A whole chicken with skin was used in the original recipe, whereas here I've called for boneless, skinless breasts. Serve with a warm spinach salad to make a light supper.

6 cups water
2 cups low-sodium chicken broth
2 boneless, skinless chicken breasts (about ½ pound), pounded to an even thickness
¼ teaspoon salt
¼ teaspoon freshly ground black pepper
1 medium onion, finely chopped

2 teaspoons finely chopped fresh rosemary, or 1 scant teaspoon dried rosemary, crumbled
¼ red bell pepper, cored, seeded, and diced
2 ounces linguine, broken into 2-inch lengths
1 cup corn kernels (about 2 ears corn, or use thawed frozen corn)

1 In a large, heavy skillet, heat the water and broth to boiling. Add the chicken breasts and salt and pepper and simmer for about 10 to 12 minutes, or until done through with no trace of pink remaining. Remove chicken, leaving the broth in the pan, and cut into 2-inch strips. Set aside.

2 Add the onion, rosemary, and bell pepper to the broth.

3 Partially cover the pan and simmer for about 15 minutes. Increase the heat to high and, when the liquid is beginning to boil, add the linguine and cook uncovered until the noodles are al dente, about 7 to 8 minutes. Add the corn and the chicken, simmer for 2 minutes more, and taste for seasoning. Serve immediately.

PER 1-CUP SERVING						
	BEFORE	AFTER				
CALORIES	210	130	CARBOHYDRATES (G)	15	CARBOHYDRATE CHOICES: 1	
FAT (G)	5	3.5	PROTEIN (G)	12	FOOD EXCHANGES PER SERVING: 1 STARCH,	
CALORIES FROM FAT (%)	25	24	FIBER (G)	2	1 LEAN MEAT	
CHOLESTEROL (MG)	75	25	SODIUM (MG)	180	LOW-SODIUM DIETS: OMIT SALT; INCREASE ROSEMARY.	

EASY CHICKEN SOUP FOR ONE

MAKES 1 SERVING

Made from the simplest of ingredients, which you probably have on hand, this recipe is perfect if you or someone in your home is feeling under the weather, or simply needs a little TLC at the end of a busy day. It's not only soothing, it's also one of the best recipes I've ever tasted, and the recipe can be multiplied as needed.

¼ cup orzo pasta or any favorite small noodle
1 can low-fat, low-sodium chicken broth

1 clove garlic, finely chopped
1 teaspoon lemon juice
Freshly ground black pepper, to taste

1 Place the orzo or other pasta in a saucepan of lightly salted boiling water and cook until al dente, 9 minutes for orzo or according to the package instructions. Drain well in a colander.

2 Place the chicken broth in the same saucepan and add the garlic. Bring to a simmer over medium heat and cook gently for five minutes.

3 Add the noodles to the broth. Add the lemon juice and black pepper and serve at once.

PER 1½-CUP SERVING					
CALORIES	150	CARBOHYDRATES (G)	23	**CARBOHYDRATE CHOICES:** 1½	
FAT (G)	4	PROTEIN (G)	9	**FOOD EXCHANGES PER SERVING:** 1½ STARCH,	
CALORIES FROM FAT (%)	22	FIBER (G)	2	½ **FAT**	
CHOLESTEROL (MG)	10	SODIUM (MG)	200	**LOW-SODIUM DIETS: THIS RECIPE IS ACCEPTABLE.**	
				IF ON 500 OR 1000 MG SODIUM, MAKE YOUR	
				OWN CHICKEN STOCK WITHOUT SALT.	
				INCREASE LEMON JUICE, GARLIC, AND BLACK	
				PEPPER TO TASTE.	

CREAMY CELERY SOUP

MAKES 2 CUPS

I created this dish one night when I came home and had only a head of celery and some chicken stock in my refrigerator. I combined the two and discovered this incredibly easy creamy-tasting soup that has no cream. It can be made for a simple dinner on a rainy night or it can be doubled and served as an elegant first course with a few croutons on top. Make a day ahead and reheat, if you like. Serve with homemade croutons or crusty bread and sliced herbed tomatoes.

2 teaspoons olive oil
½ medium onion, coarsely chopped
½ pound celery stalks, trimmed and
   roughly chopped

1 clove garlic, thinly sliced
3½ cups low-fat, low-sodium chicken
   broth
Salt and black pepper, to taste

1 Heat the oil in a large saucepan over medium heat. Sauté the onion, celery, and garlic until softened, approximately 7 minutes.

2 Add the chicken broth and bring to a boil. Reduce the heat and simmer gently, partially covered, for 45 minutes.

3 Transfer the soup to a blender or food processor and puree until smooth and velvety. Return to the pan, season with salt and pepper to taste, and bring back to a simmer before serving.

PER 1-CUP SERVING					
CALORIES	120	CARBOHYDRATES (G)	10	CARBOHYDRATE CHOICES: ½	
FAT (G)	8	PROTEIN (G)	7	FOOD EXCHANGES PER SERVING: 1 STARCH, 1 FAT	
CALORIES FROM FAT (%)	53	FIBER (G)	3	LOW-SODIUM DIETS: ACCEPTABLE AS AN ENTREE	
CHOLESTEROL (MG)	10	SODIUM (MG)	290	WITH OTHER LOW-SODIUM ACCOMPANIMENT,	
				LIKE A SALAD OR FRUIT. MOST REGULAR CANNED	
				SOUPS RUN AROUND 700 TO 1000 MG SODIUM	
				PER CUP.	

ONION SOUP GRATIN

MAKES 6 SERVINGS

Gratin *usually refers to dishes topped with cheese and butter, which often means dishes high in fat. This classic dish has been updated by cutting back on the cheese without eliminating it, and reducing the oil. The result is less than 5 grams of fat per serving rather than the usual 15 to 20 grams.*

1 tablespoon canola oil
1½ pounds yellow onions, very thinly sliced
1½ tablespoons all-purpose flour
6 cups water or chicken broth, or a combination
Salt and freshly ground black pepper

2 ounces baguette, very thinly sliced (6 thin slices) and toasted until golden
1 ounce (about ¼ cup) Gruyère or Swiss cheese, grated
1 ounce (about ¼ cup) nonfat mozzarella cheese, grated

1 In a large nonstick skillet or stockpot, heat the oil over low heat. Sauté the onions very slowly until soft and browned, stirring often. This may take up to 45 minutes.

2 Sprinkle over the flour and stir for 3 to 4 minutes, taking care not to scorch it. Add the water, and salt and pepper to taste. Stir the mixture thoroughly and bring it up to a simmer. Partially cover and cook for about 20 minutes more, until thickened.

3 Preheat the broiler. Ladle the soup into 6 ovenproof bowls and top each with a slice of the toasted bread. Scatter the bread slices evenly with the grated cheeses and place the bowls under the broiler for 2 or 3 minutes, until the cheese is bubbling and brown. Serve immediately.

PER 1-CUP SERVING					
	BEFORE	AFTER			
CALORIES	320	140	CARBOHYDRATES (G)	18	CARBOHYDRATE CHOICES: 1
FAT (G)	17	5	PROTEIN (G)	5	FOOD EXCHANGES PER SERVING: 1 STARCH, 1 FAT
CALORIES FROM FAT (%)	50	34	FIBER (G)	3	LOW-SODIUM DIETS: OMIT SALT; USE SALT-FREE
CHOLESTEROL (MG)	45	10	SODIUM (MG)	200	CHEESE IF ON 1000 MG SODIUM DIET OR LESS.

LENTIL SOUP WITH LAMB MEATBALLS

MAKES 10 SERVINGS

Lentils cook in about 20 minutes, so they are great for a same-day soup. You can also make them ahead of time, and reheat them on a winter night. Sausage, which often seasons traditional lentil soup recipes, is very successfully replaced with a combination of lemon, molasses, red wine vinegar, and basil. The lamb meatballs make a nice addition, bringing in the flavors of the Middle East.

1 medium onion, coarsely chopped
2 cloves garlic, finely chopped
3 carrots, coarsely chopped
3 cups lentils, rinsed and picked over
6 cups water
1 teaspoon salt
¼ teaspoon freshly ground black pepper
1 (14-ounce) can whole plum tomatoes in their juice

2 tablespoons red wine
Juice of 1 lemon
1½ tablespoons molasses, or firmly packed brown sugar
1 tablespoon red wine vinegar
2 tablespoons finely chopped fresh basil
1 recipe fully prepared Lamb Meatballs (optional; see page 277)

1 In a large saucepan, place the onion, garlic, carrots, lentils, water, salt, and pepper. Set pan over high heat and bring the mixture to a simmer. Cover the pan and reduce the heat so that the mixture simmers gently for 25 minutes.

2 Add the tomatoes, wine, lemon juice, molasses, and vinegar, and simmer for 15 minutes more, or until the lentils are very tender.

3 Transfer about one quarter of the mixture to a blender and blend until smooth, then return to the pan and mix together. Serve in hot soup bowls, sprinkled with chopped basil. Spoon three meatballs into each bowl, if desired.

PER 1-CUP SERVING

	BEFORE	AFTER				
CALORIES	340	230	CARBOHYDRATES (G)	40	CARBOHYDRATE CHOICES: 2½	
FAT (G)	10	1	PROTEIN (G)	17	FOOD EXCHANGES PER SERVING: 2½ STARCH,	
CALORIES FROM FAT (%)	26	3	FIBER (G)	9	1 VERY LEAN MEAT	
CHOLESTEROL (MG)	30	0	SODIUM (MG)	290	LOW-SODIUM DIETS: OMIT SALT.	

PER 1-CUP SERVING WITH 3 MEATBALLS

	BEFORE	AFTER				
CALORIES	430	340	CARBOHYDRATES (G)	49	CARBOHYDRATE CHOICES: 3	
FAT (G)	14	4.5	PROTEIN (G)	29	FOOD EXCHANGES PER SERVING: 3 STARCH,	
CALORIES FROM FAT (%)	29	11	FIBER (G)	9	3 VERY LEAN MEAT	
CHOLESTEROL (MG)	65	35	SODIUM (MG)	380	LOW-SODIUM DIETS: OMIT SALT.	

WHITE BEAN SOUP

MAKES 8 SERVINGS

I spent one New Year's in a small village in Mexico, where white beans are a New Year's Day tradition, eaten for good luck. My version has less oil and includes turkey ham instead of a ham hock. This easy, do-ahead recipe is for a large group of guests the day after *New Year's Eve.*

1 (8-ounce) package white beans or marrow beans, well rinsed and, if possible, soaked overnight in water to cover

1 tablespoon olive oil

3 medium onions, coarsely chopped

3 medium carrots, peeled and coarsely chopped

8 ounces sliced turkey ham, chopped

7 green onions, white and light green parts only, coarsely chopped

2 cups low-fat, low-sodium chicken broth

2 cups water

3 dashes Tabasco sauce, or to taste

2 tablespoons bottled barbecue sauce

½ cup dry red wine

Salt, to taste

Red, black, and white pepper to taste (see Note) *or* black or white pepper

1 If beans were soaked overnight, drain and rinse them thoroughly, then proceed to step 2. If beans were not soaked overnight, put them in a large saucepan, generously cover the beans with fresh water, and bring to a boil. Boil for 2 minutes, then remove from heat, cover, and let stand for 1 hour. Drain well in a colander.

2 Dry the pan and heat over medium heat. Add the oil and sauté the onions, carrots, and turkey ham, stirring frequently, for about 8 minutes, until the onions are translucent. Add the green onions and cook for 2 minutes more.

3 Stir in the chicken broth, water, drained beans, Tabasco sauce, barbecue sauce, and wine. Stir well and bring to a boil, reduce the heat, and cover the pan. Simmer for 45 to 50 minutes, until beans are tender. Add water or additional broth, if necessary. Add salt halfway through the cooking time. Stir in red, black, and white pepper and serve.

PER 1-CUP SERVING

	BEFORE	AFTER			
CALORIES	270	220	CARBOHYDRATES (G)	29	CARBOHYDRATE CHOICES: 2
FAT (G)	9	4	PROTEIN (G)	15	FOOD EXCHANGES PER SERVING: 1 LEAN MEAT,
CALORIES FROM FAT (%)	30	20	FIBER (G)	7	2 STARCH
CHOLESTEROL (MG)	20	15	SODIUM (MG)	360	LOW-SODIUM DIETS: SUBSTITUTE CHICKEN OR
					TURKEY FOR HAM AND OMIT SALT.

POTATO-GARLIC SOUP

MAKES 4 SERVINGS

This is a rich, warm, and satisfying soup, that's also surprisingly easy. This recipe is also an excellent base for many other tempting creations; for variation, you might want to add ½ cup of green peas or sliced mushrooms. The thickness can also be varied by adding more or less water, whichever you prefer. Whisk in 2 tablespoons of fat-free sour cream for a creamier version. Avoid cooking after adding sour cream to prevent curdling.

1 tablespoon olive oil
1 pound red potatoes, thinly sliced
10 large cloves garlic, chopped
2 cups water
2 cups low-sodium chicken broth

White pepper, to taste
2 tablespoons finely snipped chives

1 In a heavy saucepan, heat the oil over medium heat. Add the potatoes and the garlic and sauté, stirring occasionally, until the vegetables are pale golden, 3 to 4 minutes. Add the water and broth and bring to a boil. Reduce the heat and simmer the mixture for 20 minutes, uncovered, or until the potatoes are very soft.

2 In a blender or food processor, puree the soup, in batches if necessary, until smooth. Add white pepper to taste. Serve in warmed bowls, scattered with chives.

PER 1¹/₂-CUP SERVING					
CALORIES	130	CARBOHYDRATES (G)	18	CARBOHYDRATE CHOICES: 1	
FAT (G)	4.5	PROTEIN (G)	5	FOOD EXCHANGES PER SERVING: 1 STARCH,	
CALORIES FROM FAT (%)	31	FIBER (G)	2	1 FAT	
CHOLESTEROL (MG) LESS THAN 5		SODIUM (MG)	65	LOW-SODIUM DIETS: ACCEPTABLE	

CHAPTER 15

SALADS

O nly a few years ago, the whole idea of diet food meant traditional green salads with fat-free dressings. But salads have really grown up, achieving entree status even to those who once ate salads only as part of a restricted diet. The salads I've included here offer a vivid contrast of flavors and textures and are served with great-tasting low-fat or no-fat dressings, such as Cilantro Basil Dressing or Roasted Garlic Sour Cream.

Several of these salads work well as a main course—including Chinese Chicken Salad, Grilled Vegetable Salad, Tomato-Bread Salad, and Shrimp Salad with Cannelini Beans. They all provide fiber as well as flavor and crunch, with the dressing offering your taste buds the tangy experience essential to ultimate satisfaction after a meal.

Several of these salads include a variety of vegetables and make excellent side dishes with an entree. Next time you're looking for an alternative to a traditional green salad, check out Asparagus-Tomato Salad with Dijon Vinaigrette, Céleri Rémoulade, Orange and Red Onion Salad, or Jicama and Carrot Salad with Lime. The mixed green vegetables and salads detailed here will help you increase your intake of vegetables without a significant increase in fat. That's a primary objective for anyone trying to limit calories.

BASIC GREEN SALAD WITH VINAIGRETTE

For a variation, add half of a minced shallot and a bit of chopped basil, a teaspoon of anchovy paste or one minced anchovy, or ½ teaspoon Dijon mustard to the vinaigrette. Vary the greens according to the season. Or, add your own homemade croutons by tossing 1 cubed slice of whole wheat bread with 1 tablespoon olive oil and a crushed clove of garlic. Then toast the croutons in a 350° F oven for about eight minutes, until golden, stirring once or twice.

1 clove garlic, finely chopped
1 tablespoon balsamic vinegar
1 teaspoon fresh lemon juice
Sugar substitute equivalent to
      ¼ teaspoon sugar (optional;
      see Note)

¼ teaspoon salt
Pinch freshly ground black pepper
2 tablespoons olive oil, preferably
      extra-virgin
4 cups (4 ounces) salad greens,
      washed and dried

1 In a jar with a tight-fitting lid, combine the garlic, vinegar, lemon juice, sugar, salt, and pepper. Shake vigorously, then add the oil and shake again until the dressing is emulsified. If desired, refrigerate the dressing for up to 1 day.

2 In a chilled bowl, toss the salad greens with enough dressing just to coat, and serve immediately.

Note: Using regular sugar rather than sugar substitute increases carbohydrate content by less than ½ gram, an insignificant amount.

PER 2-CUP SERVING WITH 1 TABLESPOON DRESSING					
CALORIES	70	CARBOHYDRATES (G)	3	CARBOHYDRATE CHOICES: 0	
FAT (G)	7	PROTEIN (G)	0	FOOD EXCHANGES PER SERVING: 1 VEGETABLE,	
CALORIES FROM FAT (%)	83	FIBER (G)	0	1 FAT	
CHOLESTEROL (MG)	0	SODIUM (MG)	135	LOW-SODIUM DIETS: OMIT SALT.	

ORANGE AND RED ONION SALAD

MAKES 6 SERVINGS

This is a simple salad that adds a special "orange" touch to a meal. With two teaspoons of dressing per serving, you can limit the fat to 5 grams per serving, which is the same as 1 teaspoon of oil.

1 tablespoon rice vinegar
1 clove garlic, finely chopped
1 tablespoon frozen orange juice concentrate
2 teaspoons finely chopped parsley
½ teaspoon freshly ground black pepper

2 tablespoons olive oil, preferably extra-virgin
2 heads butter lettuce, washed, dried, and torn into bite-sized pieces
3 oranges, peeled and sectioned
1 small red onion, sliced paper-thin
2 teaspoons finely snipped chives

1 In a jar with a tight-fitting lid, combine the vinegar, garlic, frozen orange juice, parsley, and black pepper. Shake well.

2 Add the olive oil and shake again until the mixture is emulsified. In a chilled bowl, combine the lettuce, orange sections, and red onion. Toss together gently and add enough vinaigrette just to lightly coat the leaves. Serve immediately, sprinkled with the chives.

PER 1-CUP SERVING WITH 2 TEASPOONS VINAIGRETTE					
CALORIES	90	CARBOHYDRATES (G)	13	CARBOHYDRATE CHOICES: 1	
FAT (G)	5	PROTEIN (G)	2	FOOD EXCHANGES PER SERVING: 1 FRUIT, 1 FAT	
CALORIES FROM FAT (%)	43	FIBER (G)	2	LOW-SODIUM DIETS: EXCELLENT CHOICE	
CHOLESTEROL (MG)	0	SODIUM (MG)	0		

CÉLERI RÉMOULADE

MAKES 8 SERVINGS

If you've overlooked that big, woody, knobby-looking round vegetable known as celery root or celeriac, it's time to explore it. Its white insides have the flavor of celery with the texture of a turnip or jicama. Because it's so tough, it's hard to grate without a food processor. The fiber in this root vegetable contains a lot of cellulose, so it's very filling without too many calories. Céleri Rémoulade is usually bound together with a fattening mayonnaise-based mixture; here a vinaigrette-type dressing cuts down on the fat grams and allows the clean flavor of the celery root to shine.

1 celery root, peeled
2 tablespoons red wine vinegar
Salt
3 tablespoons Dijon-style mustard
½ cup low-fat, low-sodium chicken
    broth, boiling hot

2 tablespoons olive oil
2 tablespoons chopped, fresh parsley
Freshly ground pepper, to taste

1 Coarsely grate the celery root (you can use a food processor with the medium grating blade). It should yield about 4 cups.

2 Immediately toss the celery root with the vinegar and some salt in a large bowl. Let macerate for 5 minutes. Work quickly to prevent browning.

3 Place the mustard in a serving bowl. Whisk in the boiling chicken broth bit by bit, and then the oil, again a dab at a time, whisking until the dressing is well homogenized and almost creamy. Add the celery root and the parsley, tossing together until evenly coated with the dressing. Add pepper to taste. Serve at once or refrigerate for up to 1 day, covered.

PER ½-CUP SERVING						
	BEFORE	AFTER				
CALORIES	100	70	CARBOHYDRATES (G)	8	CARBOHYDRATE CHOICES: ½	
FAT (G)	7	4	PROTEIN (G)	2	FOOD EXCHANGES PER SERVING: 1 VEGETABLE,	
CALORIES FROM FAT (%)	70	50	FIBER (G)	5	1 FAT	
CHOLESTEROL (MG)	0	0	SODIUM (MG)	290	LOW-SODIUM DIETS: OMIT SALT.	

ASPARAGUS-TOMATO SALAD WITH DIJON VINAIGRETTE

MAKES 2 SERVINGS, EACH WITH ½ TABLESPOON DRESSING

The tablespoon of dressing ties the tomatoes and asparagus together for a nice alternative to tossed green salad. Aside from variety, you get the bonus of increased fiber and vitamins A and C.

1 teaspoon champagne or white wine vinegar
½ teaspoon Dijon-style mustard
Freshly ground black pepper, to taste
2 teaspoons canola oil

½ pound asparagus, bottom 2 inches peeled
2 ripe plum tomatoes, cored and thinly sliced
1 teaspoon finely snipped chives

1 In a jar with a tight-fitting lid, combine the vinegar, mustard, and pepper to taste. Shake well, then add the oil and shake again until completely emulsified. Refrigerate for up to 1 day before using. Shake again thoroughly just before serving.

2 Bring a large skillet of lightly salted water to boil and simmer the asparagus for about 4 minutes, or until crisp-tender. Drain immediately and cool under cold running water to keep green.

3 Arrange the asparagus and tomatoes on each plate and drizzle with a little of the vinaigrette. Scatter a few chives over the top and serve immediately.

PER SERVING					
CALORIES	80	CARBOHYDRATES (G)	8	CARBOHYDRATE CHOICES: ½	
FAT (G)	5	PROTEIN (G)	3	FOOD EXCHANGES PER SERVING: 2 VEGETABLE,	
CALORIES FROM FAT (%)	50	FIBER (G)	3	1 FAT	
CHOLESTEROL (MG)	0	SODIUM (MG)	40	LOW-SODIUM DIETS: EXCELLENT CHOICE	

TOMATO AND HERB SALAD

MAKES 4 SERVINGS

This dressing can also be used as a marinade for chicken or fish.

1 tablespoon finely chopped cilantro leaves

1 tablespoon finely chopped basil leaves

2 teaspoons fresh lemon juice

1 clove garlic, finely chopped

¼ teaspoon salt

¼ teaspoon black pepper

2 tablespoons olive oil

1 tablespoon rice vinegar

4 large plum tomatoes, ends trimmed and thinly sliced crosswise

1 In a jar with a tight-fitting lid, combine the cilantro, basil, lemon juice, garlic, salt, pepper, olive oil, and rice vinegar and shake until well blended. Set aside to let the flavors marry.

2 Arrange the tomato slices, overlapping, on four salad plates. Drizzle each serving with 2 teaspoons of dressing and sprinkle with extra black pepper to taste. Serve immediately.

PER SERVING WITH 2 TEASPOONS DRESSING					
CALORIES	75	CARBOHYDRATES (G)	4	CARBOHYDRATE CHOICES: 0	
FAT (G)	7	PROTEIN (G)	LESS THAN 1	FOOD EXCHANGES PER SERVING: 1 VEGETABLE,	
CALORIES FROM FAT (%)	79	FIBER (G)	LESS THAN 1	1 FAT	
CHOLESTEROL (MG)	0	SODIUM (MG)	140	LOW-SODIUM DIETS: OMIT SALT.	

TOMATO AND MOZZARELLA SALAD WITH BASIL

MAKES 4 SERVINGS

Tomato and basil are soul mates, and are a natural for a summer appetizer when tomatoes are in season. If you can find fresh mozzarella—which usually comes in a round shape, packed in water—you'll find the taste and texture far superior to regular dry-packed mozzarella. Look for the low-fat version, which is made with part skim milk and has about 5 grams of fat per ounce. This salad may be called insalata alla caprese *on Italian menus.*

1 pound very ripe tomatoes, sliced
  ¼ inch thick
4 ounces fresh buffalo mozzarella,
  sliced ⅛ inch thick
5 fresh basil leaves, torn into small
  pieces

1 tablespoon balsamic vinegar
1 teaspoon salt, or to taste
¼ teaspoon freshly ground black
  pepper

1 On individual plates or on a round or oval platter, layer the tomatoes alternately with the cheese. There will be about 4 slices of tomato for every 1 slice of cheese. Scatter the torn basil evenly over the top.

2 Drizzle the vinegar over the top and sprinkle with the salt and pepper.

3 Leave at room temperature, loosely covered, so that the flavors marry for at least an hour or so. Serve the same day.

PER SERVING						
CALORIES	110	CARBOHYDRATES (G)	7	CARBOHYDRATE CHOICES: ½
FAT (G)	5	PROTEIN (G)	9	FOOD EXCHANGES PER SERVING: 1 MEDIUM FAT
CALORIES FROM FAT (%)	42	FIBER (G)	5	MEAT, 1 VEGETABLE
CHOLESTEROL (MG)	15	SODIUM (MG)	427	LOW-SODIUM DIETS: OMIT SALT.

JAPANESE CUCUMBER SLICES

If European cucumbers are available, use them for this recipe. They are equal to about 2 regular cucumbers, and since they do not need to be peeled or seeded, you do not lose vitamins and nutrients by removing the skin.

1 large regular cucumber, peeled, halved lengthwise, and seeded (or 1 European cucumber, washed and halved)

1 teaspoon kosher salt

1 green onion (scallion), white and light green parts only, thinly sliced

½ cup rice vinegar

Freshly ground black pepper, to taste

1 teaspoon black sesame seeds

1 Cut the cucumber on the diagonal into ¼-inch slices. Lay the cucumber slices on a paper towel or in a colander and sprinkle each layer with the salt. Leave to drain for 30 minutes, then thoroughly blot the salt and liquid from the tops of the cucumbers.

2 In a small serving bowl, combine the cucumbers with the green onion and drizzle with the rice vinegar. Add black pepper to taste and refrigerate for 1 hour for the flavors to develop.

3 Just before serving, scatter the sesame seeds over the top.

PER SERVING WITH MARINADE					
CALORIES	35	CARBOHYDRATES (G)	7	CARBOHYDRATE CHOICES: ½	
FAT (G)	1	PROTEIN (G)	2	FOOD EXCHANGES PER SERVING: 1 VEGETABLE	
CALORIES FROM FAT (%)	21	FIBER (G)	2	LOW-SODIUM DIETS: MARINATE IN RICE	
CHOLESTEROL (MG)	0	SODIUM (MG)	540	VINEGAR ONLY, OMITTING THE SALT.	

CHOPPED CUCUMBER SALAD

MAKES 2 CUPS

A short marination in lemon, tomato, and caper juice heightens the flavor of this wonderful cucumber salad that can be used as part of a sandwich construction, such as bagels and lox, or as an accompaniment to grilled or poached fish. No fat at all is necessary in this delicious combination of ingredients.

1 European cucumber, seeded and diced, or 2 medium cucumbers, peeled, seeded, and diced

3 medium plum tomatoes, seeded and diced

1 tablespoon fresh lemon juice

2 tablespoons capers, rinsed and patted dry

Freshly ground black pepper, to taste

In a medium container with a tight-fitting cover, combine the diced cucumber, tomatoes, lemon juice, capers, and pepper and toss to mix. Cover and refrigerate for 30 minutes before serving.

PER ¼-CUP SERVING					
CALORIES	15	CARBOHYDRATES (G)	3	CARBOHYDRATE CHOICES: 0	
FAT (G)	0	PROTEIN (G)	1	FOOD EXCHANGES PER SERVING: FREE (IF A	
CALORIES FROM FAT (%)	10	FIBER (G)	1	LARGER PORTION IS EATEN, IT SHOULD BE	
CHOLESTEROL (MG)	0	SODIUM (MG)	85	COUNTED AS A VEGETABLE).	
				LOW-SODIUM DIETS: APPROPRIATE. IF ON A	
				500 OR 1000 MG SODIUM DIET, OMIT CAPERS.	

CUCUMBER-TOMATO SALAD WITH CREAMY DRESSING

MAKES 6 SERVINGS

This colorful recipe can be served as a salad or a side dish, and adds a festive touch to a buffet table. To eliminate the fat, I've used fat-free mayonnaise in the dressing, instead of regular.

2 tablespoons fat-free mayonnaise

1 tablespoon rice vinegar (see Note)

Sugar substitute equal to 1 teaspoon sugar (optional; see page 32)

1 teaspoon finely chopped cilantro or parsley

Tiny pinch cayenne pepper, or to taste

1 cucumber, peeled, seeded, and sliced ½ inch thick

2 ripe plum tomatoes, cored, seeded, and cut into ½-inch chunks

½ red bell pepper, cored, seeded, and cut into ½-inch squares

3 green onions (scallions), light and dark green parts only, thinly sliced (white parts reserved for another use)

Lime wedges, for serving

1 In a small bowl, whisk together the mayonnaise, vinegar, and sugar substitute with a fork until smooth. Stir in the cilantro and the cayenne. Cover and refrigerate for up to 1 day before using, if desired.

2 In a shallow serving bowl, gently toss together the cucumber, tomatoes, red pepper, and green onions. Drizzle over enough dressing just to coat the ingredients and toss together. Serve with lime wedges.

Note: Rice vinegar can be found in most supermarkets, often in the Asian foods section.

PER ½-CUP SERVING WITH DRESSING				
	BEFORE	**AFTER**		
CALORIES	60	30	CARBOHYDRATES (G) 6	CARBOHYDRATE CHOICES: ½
FAT (G)	4	0	PROTEIN (G) 1	FOOD EXCHANGES PER SERVING: 1 VEGETABLE
CALORIES FROM FAT (%)	50	7	FIBER (G) 2	LOW-SODIUM DIETS: ACCEPTABLE
CHOLESTEROL (MG) LESS THAN 5		0	SODIUM (MG) 45	

JICAMA AND CARROT SALAD WITH LIME

MAKES 6 SERVINGS

In Mexico, jicama is usually eaten raw with a little lime juice, and maybe some salt or pow-dered chile. I took this simple and flavorful root vegetable and spiced it up with carrots for color and a little olive oil for a more refined dressing. This salad is a great accompaniment to the Fish Taco with Cabbage (page 312). While jicama is generally harvested in the fall in Mexico, many larger markets carry it year-round.

2 tablespoons olive oil
2 tablespoons fresh lime juice
¼ teaspoon salt
¼ jalapeño chile, stem, ribs, and seeds
   removed, minced

1 medium jicama (about ¾ pound),
   peeled and cut into ⅛-by-1½-
   inch matchsticks
2 carrots, peeled and coarsely grated

1 In a small bowl, whisk together the olive oil, lime juice, and salt until smooth. Stir in the minced chile.

2 In a salad bowl, toss the jicama and the carrots together, then drizzle the dressing over and toss again just until all the ingredients are evenly coated.

PER ¾-CUP SERVING					
CALORIES	75	CARBOHYDRATES (G)	8	CARBOHYDRATE CHOICES: ½	
FAT (G)	4.5	PROTEIN (G)	1	FOOD EXCHANGES PER SERVING: 1 VEGETABLE,	
CALORIES FROM FAT (%)	55	FIBER (G)	3	1 FAT	
CHOLESTEROL (MG)	0	SODIUM (MG)	80	LOW-SODIUM DIETS: OMIT SALT.	

SNOW PEA, YELLOW PEPPER, AND MUSHROOM SALAD

MAKES 6 SERVINGS, WITH ABOUT 2½ TABLESPOONS DRESSING

This sweet, sesame-tinged dressing makes this salad go well with Japanese Glazed Salmon (page 221). Sesame oil has a strong flavor so I use it in very small amounts, in combination with unflavored canola oil. Store it in the refrigerator to keep it from getting rancid. It will become solid, so just let it sit out at room temperature before using and it will liquefy.

1 tablespoon white wine vinegar
Sugar substitute equivalent to 1 tablespoon sugar (see Note)
½ teaspoon finely minced fresh peeled ginger
1 small clove garlic, finely chopped
¼ teaspoon light soy sauce
⅛ teaspoon freshly ground black pepper

1 teaspoon sesame oil
1 tablespoon vegetable oil
½ pound snow peas, trimmed
1 large yellow bell pepper, cored, seeded, and cut into ¼-inch strips
½ pound white mushrooms, brushed clean and thinly sliced

1 In a jar with a tight-fitting lid, combine the vinegar, sugar, ginger, garlic, soy sauce, and pepper. Shake well, then add the sesame and vegetable oils and shake again until well emulsified. Refrigerate, if desired, for up to 2 days before using. Shake again immediately before serving.

2 In a saucepan of lightly salted boiling water, blanch the snow peas for 1 minute. Immediately drain, and run them under cold water to stop the cooking process and preserve the color. Drain and pat dry with paper towels.

3 In a serving bowl, combine the peas, yellow pepper, and mushrooms. Toss together gently, then drizzle with just enough dressing to lightly coat the ingredients.

Note: Using regular sugar rather than sugar substitute increases carbohydrate content by less than 2 grams, an insignificant amount.

PER ¾-CUP SERVING WITH 1½ TEASPOONS DRESSING					
CALORIES	60	CARBOHYDRATES (G)	7	CARBOHYDRATE CHOICES: ½	
FAT (G)	3.5	PROTEIN (G)	2	FOOD EXCHANGES PER SERVING: 1 VEGETABLE,	
CALORIES FROM FAT (%)	47	FIBER (G)	2	1 FAT	
CHOLESTEROL (MG)	0	SODIUM (MG)	10	LOW-SODIUM DIETS: EXCELLENT CHOICE	

CHOPPED BELGIAN ENDIVE SALAD

MAKES 4 SERVINGS

This salad is too sophisticated to be this easy!

2 medium Belgian endives, root ends
    trimmed (about 10 ounces)
2 tablespoons All-Purpose Dressing
    (page 206)

Salt and pepper, to taste
1 tablespoon diced canned pimientos

1 Cut out the cores of the endives in a rounded cone from the base. Slice the endives crosswise into ¼-inch slices.

2 Toss the endives with just enough of the dressing to coat lightly. Check the dressing for seasoning and add more salt and pepper, if desired.

3 Mound the salad onto chilled plates and garnish with the chopped pimientos.

PER ½-CUP SERVING WITH 1½ TEASPOONS DRESSING			
CALORIES	20	CARBOHYDRATES (G)	4
FAT (G)	LESS THAN .5	PROTEIN (G)	1
CALORIES FROM FAT (%)	10	FIBER (G)	2
CHOLESTEROL (MG)	0	SODIUM (MG)	85

CARBOHYDRATE CHOICES: 0
FOOD EXCHANGES PER SERVING: 1 VEGETABLE
LOW-SODIUM DIETS: ACCEPTABLE

WARM SPINACH SALAD

MAKES 4 SERVINGS

I prefer spinach salads to be simple and served warm, so the spinach is slightly wilted. I like to heat the dressing, which takes care of wilting the spinach slightly when it is poured. This version of spinach salad bypasses the bacon and hard-boiled egg of the standard spinach salad, but you'll never miss them, especially when you review the fat and cholesterol savings. The high vitamin A content naturally present in spinach makes this a particularly nutritious, as well as tasty, salad choice.

Dressing
1 teaspoon balsamic vinegar
½ teaspoon fresh lemon juice
⅛ teaspoon salt
1 clove garlic, finely chopped
Sugar substitute equivalent to ¼
    teaspoon sugar (see Note)
2 tablespoons canola oil

Salad
1 bunch fresh spinach, leaves only,
    washed and well dried
4 green onions (scallions), white and
    light green parts only, thinly
    sliced
½ pound mushrooms, wiped clean
    and sliced
Freshly ground black pepper

1 To make the dressing, in a small microwave-safe bowl, blend the vinegar, lemon juice, salt, garlic, and sweetener. Add the oil in a thin stream, blending all the time, until the dressing is emulsified.

2 In a salad bowl, combine the spinach, green onions, and mushrooms, and toss together gently.

3 Just before serving, heat the dressing in a microwave for 10 to 20 seconds. Drizzle the dressing over the salad and toss together immediately to slightly wilt the greens. Top with freshly ground pepper to taste and serve.

Note: Using regular sugar rather than sugar substitute increases carbohydrate content by less than ½ gram, an insignificant amount.

PER 1-CUP SERVING						
	BEFORE	**AFTER**				
CALORIES	170	90	**CARBOHYDRATES (G)**	5	**CARBOHYDRATE CHOICES:** ½	
FAT (G)	15	7	PROTEIN (G)	2	**FOOD EXCHANGES PER SERVING:** 1 VEGETABLE,	
CALORIES FROM FAT (%)	80	70	FIBER (G)	2	1 FAT	
CHOLESTEROL (MG)	60	0	SODIUM (MG)	230	LOW-SODIUM DIETS: OMIT SALT.	

STRAWBERRY SPINACH SALAD

MAKES 4 TO 5 SERVINGS

This dish is quick, easy, and flavorful, and a lot of the fat and calories are eliminated by reducing the oil and sugar that go into the dressing. Make sure fresh strawberries are used, as frozen strawberries tend to be less firm and flavorful. Also, dry the washed spinach well to prevent watering down the flavor of the dressing.

2 teaspoons olive oil

2 tablespoons red wine vinegar

¼ teaspoon paprika

¼ teaspoon Worcestershire sauce

1 teaspoon minced shallots

¼ teaspoon Dijon mustard

½ teaspoon sugar

1 cup strawberries, stemmed and quartered

1 bunch (about ½ pound) raw spinach, washed, stemmed, and chopped

1 tablespoon sesame seeds, toasted

1 In a small bowl, mix together the oil, vinegar, paprika, Worcestershire sauce, shallots, mustard, and sugar until well blended. Set aside.

2 Combine strawberries with the spinach in a large salad bowl. Toss with the dressing and sesame seeds and serve immediately.

PER 1-CUP SERVING					
CALORIES	110	CARBOHYDRATES (G)	9	CARBOHYDRATE CHOICES: ½	
FAT (G)	8	PROTEIN (G)	2	FOOD EXCHANGES PER SERVING: 2 FATS,	
CALORIES FROM FAT (%)	62	FIBER (G)	2	1 VEGETABLE	
CHOLESTEROL (MG)	0	SODIUM (MG)	55	LOW-SODIUM DIETS: ACCEPTABLE. OMIT WORCESTERSHIRE SAUCE IF ON 500 OR 1000 MG SODIUM RESTRICTION.	

SESAME-GINGER SLAW

MAKES 5 SERVINGS

I discovered this dish at a potluck Sunday brunch given by a friend of mine, and was delighted when the woman who brought it, Denise Wingate, agreed to send me the recipe. It combines two regional cuisines, blending an all-American favorite—coleslaw—with the Asian ingredients sesame and ginger, creating a sweet and spicy version of a favorite side dish. For a shortcut, buy the premixed shredded cabbage with carrot. Look for pickled ginger in the sushi section of the supermarket.

Sugar substitute equivalent to 1 tablespoon sugar (see Note)
½ cup rice vinegar
1 tablespoon sesame oil

4 cups shredded green cabbage
2 carrots, peeled and shredded
¼ cup pickled ginger, chopped

1 In a small bowl, whisk together the sugar and vinegar until the sugar dissolves. Whisk in the sesame oil and set aside.

2 In a large bowl, preferably with a tight-fitting lid, combine the cabbage, carrots, and ginger. Toss together gently, then add just enough dressing to lightly coat all the ingredients. Toss to mix and, if desired, cover and refrigerate for up to 5 days. Toss again and taste for seasoning just before serving.

Note: Using regular sugar rather than sugar substitute increases carbohydrate content by 2 grams, an insignificant amount.

PER 1-CUP SERVING WITH DRESSING					
CALORIES	50	CARBOHYDRATES (G)	7	CARBOHYDRATE CHOICES: ½	
FAT (G)	3	PROTEIN (G)	1	FOOD EXCHANGES PER SERVING: 1 VEGETABLE,	
CALORIES FROM FAT (%)	46	FIBER (G)	2	½ FAT	
CHOLESTEROL (MG)	0	SODIUM (MG)	20	LOW-SODIUM DIETS: EXCELLENT CHOICE	

COLESLAW WITH APPLES

MAKES 7 SERVINGS

This is a crunchy, light salad, without the heavy dressing traditionally mixed into coleslaw. The key to this delicious side dish is firm, fresh, sweet red apples. If you use regular sugar instead of sugar substitute, you will have an additional 2 grams of carbohydrate per serving.

1½ tablespoons lemon juice
Sugar substitute equivalent to
    2 teaspoons sugar
1 tablespoon red wine vinegar
1 tablespoon cider vinegar
1 teaspoon canola oil
¼ teaspoon salt
½ teaspoon celery seeds
¼ teaspoon freshly ground black
    pepper

2 large red Delicious apples, cored
    and cut into ½-inch dice
¼ medium head green cabbage,
    cored and shredded
¼ medium head red cabbage, cored
    and shredded
½ small red onion, finely chopped

1 In a small bowl, whisk the lemon juice, sugar, vinegars, oil, salt, celery seeds, and pepper together until the sugar dissolves.

2 In a large bowl, preferably with a tight-fitting lid, combine the apples, green and red cabbage, and onion. Toss together gently, then add the dressing. Toss to mix and, if desired, cover and refrigerate for up to 5 days.

PER 1-CUP SERVING	BEFORE	AFTER			
CALORIES	130	70	CARBOHYDRATES (G)	15	CARBOHYDRATE CHOICES: 1
FAT (G)	10	1	PROTEIN (G)	1	FOOD EXCHANGES PER SERVING: ½ FRUIT,
CALORIES FROM FAT (%)	70	13	FIBER (G)	3	2 VEGETABLE
CHOLESTEROL (MG)	5	0	SODIUM (MG)	85	LOW-SODIUM DIETS: OMIT SALT.

WALDORF SALAD WITH FENNEL

MAKES 5 SERVINGS

The original Waldorf salad never featured fennel or fennel seeds, also known as anise and aniseed, but I think they add a nice flavor to the dish. I also reduced the amount of walnuts that the original recipe calls for, and substituted fat-free mayonnaise to reduce fat and calories while maintaining taste.

1 tart green apple, peeled, cored, and cut into ½-inch chunks

1 red Delicious apple, peeled, cored, and cut into ½-inch chunks

1 medium bulb fennel, cored and cut into ½-inch dice

1 rib celery, cut into ½-inch dice

¼ cup red seedless grapes, halved

2 tablespoons coarsely chopped and toasted walnuts

2 teaspoons fresh lemon juice

2 tablespoons fat-free mayonnaise

1 tablespoon fat-free sour cream

Pinch of salt

Pinch of white pepper

¼ teaspoon fennel seeds, crushed

1 In a large bowl, combine the apples, fennel, celery, grapes, walnuts, and lemon juice. Toss together gently.

2 In a small bowl, whisk together the mayonnaise, sour cream, salt, white pepper, and fennel seeds. Stir the dressing into the apple mixture until well combined. Taste for seasoning and chill for at least 1 hour and up to 3 hours before serving. Check seasoning again before serving.

PER 1-CUP SERVING	BEFORE	AFTER				
CALORIES	155	80	CARBOHYDRATES (G)	16	CARBOHYDRATE CHOICES: 1	
FAT (G)	11	2	PROTEIN (G)	1	FOOD EXCHANGES PER SERVING: 1 FRUIT	
CALORIES FROM FAT (%)	59	23	FIBER (G)	3	LOW-SODIUM DIETS: ACCEPTABLE	
CHOLESTEROL (MG)	5	0	SODIUM (MG)	130		

YELLOW AND GREEN BEAN VINAIGRETTE

MAKES 4 SERVINGS

If you were raised on home-grown garden-fresh green beans like I was, you'll love this gussied-up version of a childhood favorite. The oil can be omitted if you prefer to make it fat-free, but I think this is a good place to spend your fat grams.

½ pound green beans, washed and trimmed (about 2 cups)
½ pound yellow beans, washed and trimmed (about 2 cups)
1 tablespoon rice vinegar
2 teaspoons Dijon-style mustard

½ teaspoon salt
¼ teaspoon freshly ground black pepper
1 tablespoon olive oil
2 teaspoons chopped fresh dill
1 cup halved cherry tomatoes

1 Bring a generous amount of lightly salted water to a boil in a medium saucepan. Blanch both of the beans together for 4 minutes, then drain and immediately run under cold running water to stop the cooking and preserve the color. Shake dry.

2 In a small bowl, whisk together the vinegar, mustard, salt, and pepper. Whisk in the oil, then stir in the dill.

3 Toss the beans with the vinaigrette and serve garnished with cherry tomatoes.

PER 1-CUP SERVING					
CALORIES	140	CARBOHYDRATES (G)	21	CARBOHYDRATE CHOICES: 1½	
FAT (G)	4.5	PROTEIN (G)	7	FOOD EXCHANGES PER SERVING: 1½ STARCH	
CALORIES FROM FAT (%)	27	FIBER (G)	3	(OR 4 VEGETABLE) AND 1 FAT	
CHOLESTEROL (MG)	0	SODIUM (MG)	370	LOW-SODIUM DIETS: OMIT SALT AND DECREASE	
				MUSTARD TO 1 TEASPOON.	

ORANGE AND RADISH SALAD

MAKES 4 SERVINGS

Middle Eastern dishes often call for orange flower water, a flavoring ingredient that is almost like perfume and adds a wonderful, authentic touch (see the Appendix for a mail-order source). If you don't have it, be assured that the radishes and orange sections make a great combination all by themselves!

1 bunch small red radishes, washed
    and trimmed
Sugar substitute equivalent to
    1 tablespoon sugar (see Note)
1 tablespoon fresh lemon juice
2 teaspoons orange flower water
    (optional)

Pinch of salt
2 large navel oranges
1 small red onion, sliced paper-thin
    and separated into rings
1 teaspoon finely chopped fresh mint

1 Grate the radishes on the largest hole of a cheese grater or in a food processor fitted with the large grating blade. Press them in a sieve to remove their excess liquid. In a large glass bowl, combine the radishes with the sugar, lemon juice, orange flower water, if using, and salt. Toss to mix, cover, and refrigerate for at least 1½ hours and up to 3 hours.

2 Using a small, sharp knife, cut away the orange peel, removing all the bitter white pith with it. Holding the oranges over a bowl to catch the juices, slice down along both sides of each membrane to release the sections. Put them in the bowl with the juices and refrigerate until serving time, up to 3 hours.

3 Just before serving, add the orange sections, with their juice, to the radishes and toss gently to mix. Place a mound of the salad mixture in the center of each plate and jumble some of the red onion rings around the edges. Sprinkle a little mint over the top and serve at once.

Note: Using regular sugar rather than sugar substitute increases carbohydrate content by 3 grams, an insignificant amount.

PER ½-CUP SERVING					
CALORIES	70	CARBOHYDRATES (G)	13	CARBOHYDRATE CHOICES: 1	
FAT (G)	LESS THAN .5	PROTEIN (G)	1	FOOD EXCHANGES PER SERVING: 1 FRUIT	
CALORIES FROM FAT (%)	6	FIBER (G)	2	LOW-SODIUM DIETS: OMIT SALT.	
CHOLESTEROL (MG)	0	SODIUM (MG)	150		

GRILLED VEGETABLE SALAD

MAKES 2 TO 4 SERVINGS

So many of my clients raved about the grilled vegetable salad at the Ivy, a renowned restaurant in Los Angeles, that I had to include a low-fat version of it here. If using your outside barbecue, you will need a rack with very small holes for grilling; otherwise, the vegetables will fall through into the fire.

8 spears asparagus
1 medium zucchini, in ½-inch dice
½ cup coarsely shredded red cabbage
4 ounces raw medium shrimp, peeled and deveined
2½ teaspoons olive oil
1 ear fresh corn, husked

Salt and freshly ground black pepper, to taste
2 tablespoons fresh lemon juice
3 fresh basil leaves, slivered
2 cups torn romaine lettuce
1 medium tomato, seeded and diced
2 tablespoons rice vinegar (optional)

1 Discard the woody ends from the asparagus and peel the lowest 2 inches with a vegetable peeler. Cut into 1-inch lengths. Place the asparagus, zucchini, red cabbage, and shrimp in a bowl and toss with 2 teaspoons of the olive oil.

2 Preheat an outdoor grill or ridged cast-iron stovetop griddle for medium-heat grilling. Rub ½ teaspoon of the olive oil on the corn and grill for 8 to 10 minutes, turning frequently. Remove from the fire and set aside to cool. If using an outdoor barbecue, place a rack with smaller holes on top of the grill to preheat.

3 While the corn is cooling, grill the vegetable-shrimp mixture for about 8 minutes, turning occasionally to cook everything evenly, until tender and slightly charred. When done, coarsely chop the shrimp, then recombine with the vegetables.

4 Cut the kernels from the corn and combine with the grilled vegetable-shrimp mixture. Add salt and pepper, lemon juice, and basil; toss gently but thoroughly.

5 In a separate bowl, toss the romaine and tomato together. Place a bed of the romaine mixture on each of the plates and top evenly with the grilled vegetables. Serve with rice vinegar, if desired. Serve at room temperature.

PER 3-CUP SERVING					
CALORIES	220	CARBOHYDRATES	25	CARBOHYDRATE CHOICES: 1½	
FAT (G)	7	PROTEIN (G)	17	FOOD EXCHANGES PER SERVING: 2 VERY LEAN	
CALORIES FROM FAT (%)	28	FIBER (G)	6	MEAT, 1 STARCH, 2 VEGETABLE, ½ FAT	
CHOLESTEROL (MG)	85	SODIUM (MG)	100	LOW-SODIUM DIETS: EXCELLENT CHOICE	

TOMATO-BREAD SALAD

MAKES 2 TO 4 SERVINGS

This Tuscan-style bread salad, known as panzanella, *makes good use of old bread softened with tomatoes and very good olive oil. This is a recipe to remember during the summer when fresh tomatoes are at their peak—the juicier the tomatoes, the less oil needed. It's great as an entree salad for a warm-weather lunch.*

3 large ripe tomatoes, chopped
½ red onion, minced
1 clove garlic, finely minced
¼ cup fresh basil leaves, washed, well dried, and finely chopped
1½ teaspoons extra-virgin olive oil

2 tablespoons red wine vinegar
Kosher salt to taste
Freshly ground black pepper, to taste
¼ loaf stale crusty Italian-style bread, or French bread (about 2½ ounces)

1 Combine the tomatoes, onion, garlic, and basil in a large bowl suitable for serving the salad. Add the olive oil, 1 tablespoon of the vinegar, salt, and pepper.

2 Cut the bread into ½-inch cubes. In a small bowl, mix 1 tablespoon water with remaining 1 tablespoon vinegar. Sprinkle the water-vinegar mixture on the bread and let sit for 5 to 10 minutes, giving bread time to soak up mixture. Add the bread to the tomato mixture and toss to combine well. Serve immediately.

PER 1½-CUP SERVING					
CALORIES	180	CARBOHYDRATES (G)	31	CARBOHYDRATE CHOICES: 2	
FAT (G)	5	PROTEIN (G)	5	FOOD EXCHANGES PER SERVING: 1 STARCH,	
CALORIES FROM FAT (%)	25	FIBER (G)	3	3 VEGETABLE, ½ FAT	
CHOLESTEROL (MG)	0	SODIUM (MG)	350	LOW-SODIUM DIETS: OMIT OR DECREASE SALT	
				AND INCREASE GARLIC AND BASIL.	

SHRIMP SALAD WITH CANNELLINI BEANS

MAKES 8 SERVINGS

One of my favorite sources for new recipe ideas is restaurants. This one came from Leonard Schwartz, executive chef at Maple Drive, Dudley Moore's restaurant in Beverly Hills. The tender beans, with the sweet shrimp dressed so subtly, create a memorable blend of flavors and textures. And so nutritious! In the old days, we called beans and other complex carbohydrates "meat or protein extenders." A prudent homemaker on a budget could cut the cost of her meal by adding beans, rice, or pasta to chicken, beef, or fish. These days, we know that this practice not only lowers cost but also raises the nutritive value—less fat and cholesterol, and more fiber, vitamins, and minerals than the shrimp salad you find at most delis.

Salad
1½ cups small arugula leaves, rinsed, dried, and coarsely chopped
1½ cups coarsely chopped radicchio (about 1 medium head)
½ small sweet onion, such as Maui or Vidalia, coarsely chopped
4 ripe plum tomatoes, seeded and diced
½ pound cooked medium or large peeled shrimp, diced to the size of cannellini beans

1½ cups cooked cannellini beans or 1 (10-ounce) can, drained and rinsed

Vinaigrette
2 tablespoons fresh lemon juice
¼ cup extra-virgin olive oil
1 clove garlic, finely chopped
Salt and freshly ground black pepper, to taste

1 To make the salad, in a salad bowl, combine the arugula, radicchio, onion, and tomatoes. Toss together thoroughly. If desired, refrigerate for up to 1 hour, covered.

2 To make the vinaigrette, in a small bowl, whisk the lemon juice with the oil, garlic, and salt and pepper to taste. Just before serving, add the shrimp, beans, and vinaigrette to the vegetables and toss gently just to mix. Season with more black pepper to taste and serve.

PER 1-CUP SERVING						
	BEFORE	AFTER				
CALORIES	220	110	CARBOHYDRATES (G)	4	CARBOHYDRATE CHOICES: 0	
FAT (G)		16	7	PROTEIN (G)	7	FOOD EXCHANGES PER SERVING: ½ STARCH,
CALORIES FROM FAT (%)	65	57	FIBER (G)	1	1 LEAN MEAT	
CHOLESTEROL (MG)	65	55	SODIUM (MG)	135	LOW-SODIUM DIETS: THIS RECIPE IS FINE.	

BABY SHRIMP SALAD WITH DILL

MAKES 8 SERVINGS

If you like shrimp, you'll love this dish, where fat-free sour cream and mayonnaise have been substituted for regular. You can't beat the combination of sweet, plump shrimp, cool cucumbers, and dill. The dish is also very attractive to the eye, and is great for a buffet or a light afternoon luncheon. It is best made and eaten the same day.

¼ cup fat-free sour cream
¼ cup fat-free or low-fat mayonnaise
1 teaspoon whole-grain mustard
2 teaspoons finely chopped fresh dill, or 1 teaspoon dried
1 teaspoon fresh lemon juice
Salt and black pepper, to taste
1 pound cooked baby, popcorn, or Florida rock shrimp, peeled and deveined

½ European cucumber, washed, halved lengthwise, and cut into ¼-inch dice, or 1 regular cucumber, peeled, seeded, and cut into ¼-inch dice (about 2 cups)
Sprigs of fresh dill, for garnish (optional)

1 In a large bowl, whisk together the sour cream, mayonnaise, mustard, dill, and lemon juice. Thin the dressing with a little water (about 4 tablespoons) to obtain a nice coating consistency, and season it to taste with salt and pepper.

2 Fold the shrimp and half the diced cucumber into the dressing and mound the salad onto a chilled serving platter. Scatter the remaining diced cucumber over the top of the salad and garnish with sprigs of dill, if desired. Serve immediately.

PER ½-CUP SERVING					
	BEFORE	AFTER			
CALORIES	130	70	CARBOHYDRATES (G)	3	CARBOHYDRATE CHOICES: 0
FAT (G)	8	.5	PROTEIN (G)	13	FOOD EXCHANGES PER SERVING: 2 VERY
CALORIES FROM FAT (%)	56	9	FIBER (G)	0	LEAN MEAT, 1 VEGETABLE
CHOLESTEROL (MG)	120	110	SODIUM (MG)	230	LOW-SODIUM DIETS: OMIT SALT AND INCREASE
					DILL, LEMON JUICE, AND BLACK PEPPER.

CHINESE CHICKEN SALAD

MAKES 4 SERVINGS

My friend Hillary Jaye came up with this version of Chinese chicken salad, and it is sure to become a regular in your repertoire. She took the standard lettuce, chicken, and dressing formula and spruced it up with fresh mint, cilantro, and lots of ginger. The result is an infinitely more flavorful and healthy salad than many you encounter at restaurants. Reserve a little undressed salad for your lunch the next day, and add the dressing when you're ready to eat—this will keep the salad fresh and crunchy. Note that the longer you allow the dressing to mellow, the more it becomes infused with the ginger, and the tastier it gets.

Dressing
½ cup seasoned rice vinegar
   (see Note)
Sugar substitute equivalent to
   1 teaspoon sugar
½ teaspoon olive oil
½ teaspoon sesame oil
½ teaspoon low-sodium soy sauce
2 teaspoons finely minced fresh
   peeled ginger

Salad
1 tablespoon low-sodium soy sauce
1 tablespoon sesame oil
4 boneless, skinless chicken breasts,
   about 1 pound
Freshly ground black pepper
½ pound mixed baby greens or
   chopped lettuce, such as romaine,
   butter, or salad bowl
¼ pound bean sprouts
½ cup packed chopped fresh cilantro
½ cup packed chopped fresh mint
   leaves
1 medium red bell pepper, cored,
   seeded, and cut into ½-inch dice
Sesame seeds for garnish

1 To make the dressing, combine the rice vinegar, sugar substitute, olive oil, sesame oil, soy sauce, and ginger in a small bowl, mix well, and set aside at room temperature while preparing the salad.

2 Preheat the oven to 350° F. In a square baking dish (approximately 8 inches square), combine the soy sauce and sesame oil. Add the chicken breasts and turn to coat all sides evenly. Season with pepper and bake, uncovered, for 25 to 30 minutes, turning once after 20 minutes, until the breasts are firm, golden and cooked through. Remove the pan from the oven, drain any liquid that may have accumulated and, when cool enough to handle, cut the breasts into 1-inch dice and set aside.

3 While the chicken is baking, combine the mixed greens, bean sprouts, cilantro, mint, and bell pepper in a large salad bowl. When the chicken is diced, add it to the lettuce mixture along with the dressing and toss to coat all ingredients well. Sprinkle with the sesame seeds and serve.

Note: Seasoned rice vinegar is available at most supermarkets, often in the Asian foods section.

PER 2¹/₂-CUP SERVING					
CALORIES	220	CARBOHYDRATES (G)	13	CARBOHYDRATE CHOICES: 1	
FAT (G)	4.5	PROTEIN (G)	32	FOOD EXCHANGES PER SERVING: 4 VERY LEAN	
CALORIES FROM FAT (%)	18	FIBER (G)	6	MEAT, 3 VEGETABLE	
CHOLESTEROL (MG)	65	SODIUM (MG)	280	LOW-SODIUM DIETS: REDUCE OR ELIMINATE	
				SOY SAUCE.	

CURRIED CHICKEN SALAD

MAKES 4 SERVINGS

This chicken salad's exotic Indian flair emerges just by adding curry to the dressing. The apple, orange, and celery add crunch and flavor. Serve on a bed of salad greens or as an entree salad, or make ahead for a buffet. It keeps well in the refrigerator for a day or two, and turns a brown-bag lunch into a gourmet treat. Even those who aren't crazy about curry will love this dish.

Dressing
¼ cup fat-free sour cream
¼ cup fat-free mayonnaise
1 tablespoon whole-grain mustard
½ teaspoon good-quality curry powder, such as Madras
1 teaspoon fresh lemon juice
Salt and freshly ground black pepper, to taste

Salad
4 cooked boneless, skinless chicken breasts, about 1 pound, cut into ½-inch dice (approximately half the meat from a 3-pound poached chicken, see page 259)
1 rib celery, cut into ¼-inch dice
¼ onion, chopped
1 small apple, peeled, cored, and diced
1 tablespoon finely chopped fresh cilantro
½ cup mandarin orange segments, halved crosswise
2 tablespoons shredded coconut

1 In a large bowl, whisk together the sour cream, mayonnaise, mustard, curry, and lemon juice. If desired, thin with water to a nice coating consistency, and whisk in salt and pepper to taste.

2 Fold the diced chicken, celery, onion, apple, cilantro, and orange segments into the dressing until mixed. Taste for seasoning.

3 Mound the salad on a chilled platter and garnish with a sprinkle of coconut. Serve immediately, or cover and refrigerate for up to 2 hours.

PER 1-CUP SERVING				
CALORIES	210	CARBOHYDRATES (G)	16	CARBOHYDRATE CHOICES: 1
FAT (G)	3	PROTEIN (G)	28	FOOD EXCHANGES PER SERVING: 4 VERY LEAN
CALORIES FROM FAT (%)	13	FIBER (G)	1	MEAT, 1 FRUIT
CHOLESTEROL (MG)	65	SODIUM (MG)	300	LOW-SODIUM DIETS: NOT ACCEPTABLE FOR
				THOSE ON A 500 OR 1000 MG SODIUM DIET

MOM'S POTATO SALAD REVISITED

MAKES 10 SERVINGS

This is the one potato salad that purists dream of—tangy dressing and just a bit of crunch. Fat-free mayonnaise and sour cream help essentially to eliminate the fat of a traditional potato salad. Serve this dressing over your favorite coleslaw mix, too. To make a chicken salad, simply substitute the same weight of cooked, cubed chicken for the potatoes.

The dressing should just coat and flavor the ingredients in the salad. Feel free to improvise by changing the ratios or adding other ingredients such as chopped cornichons, pickles, olives, or herbs.

3½ pounds red-skinned potatoes, peeled and cut into ¾-inch pieces
2 tablespoons white wine vinegar
½ cup fat-free sour cream
½ cup fat-free mayonnaise
1 tablespoon whole-grain mustard
1 tablespoon Dijon mustard
2 teaspoons fresh lemon juice

Sugar substitute equivalent to 1 teaspoon sugar
Salt and black pepper, to taste
½ cup finely chopped onion
¼ cup finely chopped red onion
½ cup coarsely chopped celery
⅓ cup finely chopped Italian parsley

1 In a large saucepan of lightly salted boiling water, cook the potatoes just until tender, about 12 minutes. Drain well and transfer the potatoes to a large bowl. Drizzle the vinegar over the hot potatoes, toss gently, and cool to room temperature.

2 In a medium bowl, whisk together the sour cream, mayonnaise, mustards, lemon juice, and sugar substitute. Whisk in salt and pepper to taste.

3 Add the onions, celery, and parsley to the potato mixture and toss gently just to mix. Add the dressing and gently mix the salad until all the ingredients are well coated with the dressing, but not so much that the potatoes start to break up. Cover and refrigerate for up to 1 day before serving, if desired.

PER 1-CUP SERVING					
CALORIES	170	CARBOHYDRATES (G)	38	CARBOHYDRATE CHOICES: 2½	
FAT (G)	.5	PROTEIN (G)	4	FOOD EXCHANGES PER SERVING: 2 STARCH,	
CALORIES FROM FAT (%)	3	FIBER (G)	4	1 VEGETABLE	
CHOLESTEROL (MG)	0	SODIUM (MG)	190	LOW-SODIUM DIETS: OMIT SALT, DECREASE	
				MUSTARD BY HALF, AND INCREASE LEMON	
				JUICE AND ONION.	

WARM POTATO-LEEK SALAD

MAKES 4 SERVINGS

This is a modern potato salad, simply gourmet, with great flavor and very little of the fat in a traditional potato salad. I serve this with Ahi tuna steaks with black pepper and coriander crust (page 222).

1 pound red potatoes, peeled and cut into ½-inch dice

1 tablespoon extra-virgin olive oil

1 large leek, white part only, well washed and cut into ¼-inch dice

Salt and freshly ground black pepper, to taste

¼ cup rice vinegar

Sugar substitute equivalent to 1 tablespoon sugar

1 In a large saucepan, cover the potatoes with cold water and add a little salt. Bring to a boil, reduce the heat, and simmer until the potatoes are tender but not mushy, about 10 minutes. Drain immediately and set aside.

2 Meanwhile, in a large cast-iron or nonstick skillet, heat the olive oil over medium-low heat. Sauté the leeks until softened, 5 to 10 minutes. Season with salt and black pepper to taste and add the vinegar and sugar substitute. Increase the heat to medium and deglaze the pan, stirring and scraping all the flavorful bits into the liquid. Cook, stirring, until most of the liquid has evaporated, then add the potatoes and stir them in gently, taking care not to break them up into a mush. Serve warm or at room temperature.

PER ¾-CUP SERVING					
CALORIES	120	CARBOHYDRATES (G)	18	CARBOHYDRATE CHOICES: 1	
FAT (G)	3.5	PROTEIN (G)	3	FOOD EXCHANGES PER SERVING: 1 STARCH,	
CALORIES FROM FAT (%)	27	FIBER (G)	3	1 FAT	
CHOLESTEROL (MG)	0	SODIUM (MG)	10	LOW-SODIUM DIETS: EXCELLENT CHOICE	

CHAPTER 16

SALAD DRESSINGS, SAUCES, AND MARINADES

Salad dressings are big business these days, and everyone is trying to sell you fat-free, calorie-free, everything-free dressing. Unfortunately, many of these products are also flavor-free. Once you sample the selection of dressings and sauces detailed here, you'll never go back to store-bought. These creamy dressings, light vinaigrettes, ultrafresh sauces, and condiments are all fabulous.

Fresh ingredients are one of the secrets to making great salad dressings. For example, lemon and lime juices should always be freshly squeezed. If you're in a pinch, bottled will do, but it won't be quite as citrusy. And fresh herbs are always preferable to dried, although of course when the fresh version is not available, dry herbs are an option. If using a dried herb, it is a good idea to warm it in one of the recipe liquids, such as vinegar, in order to release its flavor, and then let the mixture cool before proceeding with the dressing recipe. Or you might try substituting another fresh herb, such as parsley. Many of the salad dressings call for black pepper, which is always at its best when freshly ground.

ALL-PURPOSE DRESSING

MAKES ½ CUP, OR 8 SERVINGS

This dressing is virtually fat-free and very versatile. It is nice drizzled on roasted chicken or baked ham, spread on bread for sandwiches, or as a slightly more tangy dressing for potato salad. You can play with the ratios to fit your taste, or toss in other ingredients such as chopped cornichons, pickles, olives, or fresh herbs. The purpose of the dressing is to lightly coat, not smother, salads of all kinds.

¼ cup fat-free sour cream
¼ cup fat-free mayonnaise
1 tablespoon whole-grain mustard

1 teaspoon fresh lemon juice
Salt and freshly ground black pepper,
   to taste

In a bowl, whisk together the sour cream, mayonnaise, mustard, lemon juice, salt, and pepper. Taste for seasoning, cover, and refrigerate until needed up to a week or so.

PER TABLESPOON					
CALORIES	15	CARBOHYDRATES (G)	3	CARBOHYDRATE CHOICES: 0	
FAT (G)	LESS THAN .5	PROTEIN (G)	1	FOOD EXCHANGES PER SERVING: FREE	
CALORIES FROM FAT (%)	11	FIBER (G)	0	LOW-SODIUM DIETS: OMIT SALT. LIMIT PORTION	
CHOLESTEROL (MG)	0	SODIUM (MG)	170	TO 1 TEASPOON.	

ALL-PURPOSE PICO DE GALLO

MAKES 1½ CUPS

This fresh salsa is a delicious condiment to serve with rice, beans, or burritos filled with seasoned meat. Actually, since it's naturally low in calories and fat-free, you may think of it as a side dish rather than a condiment! This salsa can be embellished in countless ways. To make a saucier salsa, add a teaspoon of tomato paste whisked together with 1 teaspoon of the adobo sauce from canned chipotle chiles en adobo, *available at Hispanic markets. Other options: add a clove of finely chopped garlic; an orange, peeled and cut into ½-inch dice; ¼ cup peeled and chopped jicama; or 1 teaspoon chili powder.*

½ pound plum tomatoes, peeled,
   seeded, and cut into ½-inch dice
½ small yellow onion, cut into
   ½-inch dice
2 teaspoons fresh lemon juice
¼ serrano or jalapeño chile,
   stemmed, seeded, and minced

2 tablespoons finely chopped fresh
   cilantro
Salt and freshly ground black pepper,
   to taste

In a medium bowl or container, combine the tomatoes, onion, lemon juice, chile, cilantro, salt, and pepper and toss together until evenly mixed. Let the salsa rest at room temperature for 30 minutes before serving. This pico de gallo is best on the day that it's made, but it can be covered and refrigerated for up to 2 days, if desired.

PER ¼-CUP SERVING					
CALORIES	10	CARBOHYDRATES (G)	3	CARBOHYDRATE CHOICES: 0	
FAT (G)	0	PROTEIN (G)	0	FOOD EXCHANGES PER SERVING: FREE	
CALORIES FROM FAT (%)	10	FIBER (G)	LESS THAN 1	LOW-SODIUM DIETS: EXCELLENT CONDIMENT	
CHOLESTEROL (MG)	0	SODIUM (MG)	95		

CAESAR SALAD DRESSING

MAKES 1 CUP, OR 16 SERVINGS

At Manhattan's deluxe Reebok Sports Club/NY, their delicious Caesar dressing is thickened by a mild garlic puree instead of egg yolk, cutting the fat from over 6 grams per tablespoon down to 3.5 grams. It will keep in the refrigerator for up to a week. Let it return to room temperature before tossing your salad.

½ cup low-fat, low-sodium chicken broth

¼ cup Blanched Garlic Puree (recipe follows)

2 anchovy fillets, rinsed well and patted dry, then minced, or 1 teaspoon anchovy paste

1 medium shallot, finely chopped

1 tablespoon Dijon-style mustard

2 tablespoons fresh lemon juice

2 tablespoons white wine vinegar

¼ cup extra-virgin olive oil

¼ teaspoon freshly ground pepper, or to taste

In a small bowl or a mini food processor, combine the chicken broth, garlic puree, anchovies, shallot, mustard, lemon juice, and vinegar and whisk or pulse until well blended. Gradually add the olive oil in a thin stream, whisking or pureeing until the dressing is smooth and emulsified. Add pepper and taste for seasoning.

BLANCHED GARLIC PUREE (makes ¼ cup)

Although oven-roasted garlic is used in many of my recipes, I prefer blanched garlic in this one because it adds a milder flavor.

1 large head of garlic, cloves separated and peeled

In a small saucepan, cover the garlic cloves with cold water. Place the pan over medium-high heat and bring to a boil. After only a few seconds drain the garlic in a sieve, then return to the pan. Again cover with cold water, and bring to a boil. Repeat the process twice more, for a total of four blanchings. The garlic should be very soft. Transfer to a bowl and mash with a fork until smooth.

PER TABLESPOON	BEFORE	AFTER				
CALORIES	100	35	CARBOHYDRATES (G)	1	CARBOHYDRATE CHOICES: 0	
FAT (G)	10	3.5	PROTEIN (G)	0	FOOD EXCHANGES PER SERVING: 1 FAT	
CALORIES FROM FAT (%)	90	80	FIBER (G)	0	LOW-SODIUM DIETS: OMIT ANCHOVIES.	
CHOLESTEROL (MG)	15	0	SODIUM (MG)	75		

COCKTAIL SAUCE

MAKES 2 1/3 CUPS, OR ABOUT 37 SERVINGS

Use this as a sauce with any seafood dish, especially chilled poached shrimp and oysters.

2 cups ketchup

2 tablespoons horseradish

2 teaspoons fresh lemon juice

1 tablespoon Worcestershire sauce

5 drops Tabasco sauce

1/4 teaspoon lemon pepper

In a bowl, combine the ketchup, horseradish, lemon juice, Worcestershire and Tabasco sauces, and lemon pepper and mix together well. Place in a clean jar, cover tightly, and refrigerate for up to 1 week.

PER TABLESPOON					
CALORIES	15	CARBOHYDRATES (G)	4	CARBOHYDRATE CHOICES: 0	
FAT (G)	0	PROTEIN (G)	0	FOOD EXCHANGES PER SERVING: FREE	
CALORIES FROM FAT (%)	0	FIBER (G)	0	LOW-SODIUM DIETS: NOT SUITABLE FOR VERY	
CHOLESTEROL (MG)	0	SODIUM (MG)	170	LOW SODIUM DIETS. USE 1 TEASPOON	
				INSTEAD OF 1 TABLESPOON FOR MODERATELY	
				LOW SODIUM DIETS.	

CHIPOTLE MAYONNAISE OR SOUR CREAM

MAKES 1¹/₂ CUPS, OR ABOUT 24 1-TABLESPOON SERVINGS)

A spread of this smoky-flavored mayonnaise tastes great on any sandwich, but I find it goes particularly well with chicken. It has the creamy consistency but lacks the fat of regular mayonnaise and sour cream. Once you've opened the can of adobos, use the rest in a pot of black or pinto beans (page 323), salsa (page 207), or Roasted, Diced Potatoes with Chipotle (page 358).

1 cup fat-free sour cream	¹/₄ teaspoon onion powder
¹/₂ cup fat-free mayonnaise	¹/₄ teaspoon garlic powder
1 teaspoon adobo sauce (sauce from canned *chipotles chiles en adobo*)	Dash mild chili powder
	Dash paprika
2 teaspoons fresh lemon juice	

1 In a large bowl, combine the sour cream, mayonnaise, adobo sauce, lemon juice, onion powder, garlic powder, chili powder, and paprika and mix together thoroughly.

2 Cover tightly and keep refrigerated until ready to use, not longer than 3 days. Stir or shake well before using.

PER TABLESPOON						
	BEFORE	**AFTER**				
CALORIES	45	15	CARBOHYDRATES (G)	3	CARBOHYDRATE CHOICES: 0	
FAT (G)	3.5	0	PROTEIN (G)	1	FOOD EXCHANGES PER SERVING: FREE. IF	
CALORIES FROM FAT (%)	80	0	FIBER (G)	0	PORTION IS 2 TABLESPOONS, 1 VEGETABLE	
CHOLESTEROL (MG)	0	0	SODIUM (MG)	40	LOW-SODIUM DIETS: APPROPRIATE	

CILANTRO BASIL DRESSING

MAKES ¼ CUP

Use cold as a marinade or hot as a sauce with chicken or sea bass, or other white fish.

1 tablespoon chopped fresh cilantro,
    leaves only
1 tablespoon loosely packed chopped
    fresh basil leaves
2 teaspoons fresh lemon juice
1 clove garlic, finely chopped

¼ teaspoon salt
¼ teaspoon freshly ground black
    pepper
2 tablespoons olive oil
1 tablespoon rice vinegar

In a jar with a tight-fitting lid, combine all ingredients and shake until well blended.
Cover tightly and refrigerate until needed, up to 3 days.

PER 2 TEASPOONS					
CALORIES	45	CARBOHYDRATES (G)	0	CARBOHYDRATE CHOICES: 0	
FAT (G)	4.5	PROTEIN (G)	0	FOOD EXCHANGES PER SERVING: 1 FAT	
CALORIES FROM FAT (%)	95	FIBER (G)	0	LOW-SODIUM DIETS: OMIT SALT.	
CHOLESTEROL (MG)	0	SODIUM (MG)	90		

GINGER MARINADE

I originally created this recipe to use as a dip for homemade egg rolls, but it turned out to be quite versatile. Use it as a salad dressing with greens or shredded Asian-style vegetables, or use it as a marinade for fish or chicken. You can find the Asian ingredients such as oyster sauce at most large supermarkets or at specialty Asian groceries. For mail-order information, see the Appendix.

¼ cup rice wine or dry sherry
2 tablespoons oyster sauce
2 teaspoons sesame oil
2 tablespoons finely chopped peeled
    fresh ginger

2 cloves garlic, finely chopped
2 green onions (scallions), white and
    light green parts only, thinly
    sliced

In a small container, combine the rice wine, oyster sauce, sesame oil, ginger, garlic, and green onions and whisk to blend. Keep refrigerated for a week or so.

PER TABLESPOON					
CALORIES	25	CARBOHYDRATES (G)	2	CARBOHYDRATE CHOICES: 0	
FAT (G)	1	PROTEIN (G)	LESS THAN 1	FOOD EXCHANGES PER SERVING: FREE	
CALORIES FROM FAT (%)	38	FIBER (G)	0	LOW-SODIUM DIETS: DECREASE OYSTER SAUCE	
CHOLESTEROL (MG)	0	SODIUM (MG)	170	TO 1 TEASPOON.	

PUREED RED PEPPER DRESSING

MAKES 1½ CUPS, OR 24 SERVINGS

Try this simple combination of ingredients to dress salads, to stir into soups, or to top ratatouille or grilled or roasted fish or chicken.

2 red bell peppers, roasted, peeled,
   cored, and seeded (see page 154)
   or bottled roasted red peppers
   (about 1 cup)
1 large clove garlic, finely chopped

½ cup fat-free sour cream
¼ teaspoon salt
Freshly ground white or black
   pepper, to taste

1 In a blender, combine the roasted peppers with the garlic and puree until very smooth, scraping down the sides of the container as necessary.

2 Transfer the puree to a bowl and fold in sour cream until well blended.

3 Season to taste with salt and pepper and chill well before serving. Taste again for seasoning just before serving. Store in the refrigerator for up to a week.

PER TABLESPOON					
CALORIES	8	CARBOHYDRATES (G)	1	CARBOHYDRATE CHOICES: 0	
FAT (G)	LESS THAN .5	PROTEIN (G)	0	FOOD EXCHANGES PER SERVING: FREE	
CALORIES FROM FAT (%)	5	FIBER (G)	0	LOW-SODIUM DIETS: OMIT SALT.	
CHOLESTEROL (MG)	0	SODIUM (MG)	50		

ROASTED GARLIC SOUR CREAM

MAKES ½ CUP

This is excellent as an "aioli"- or mayonnaise-type dressing for steamed asparagus and artichokes.

2 tablespoons roasted garlic puree
   (approximately 6 large cloves)

½ cup fat-free sour cream
Salt and black pepper, to taste

1 Roast the garlic as directed on page 151. Mash the softened pulp with the back of a fork until smooth.

2 Fold in sour cream until well mixed. Season to taste with salt and pepper.

3 Chill well before serving. Keeps well refrigerated up to 3 days.

PER TABLESPOON					
CALORIES	20	CARBOHYDRATES (G)	3	CARBOHYDRATE CHOICES: 0	
FAT (G)	0	PROTEIN (G)	1	FOOD EXCHANGES PER SERVING: FREE	
CALORIES FROM FAT (%)	1	FIBER (G)	0	LOW-SODIUM DIETS: ACCEPTABLE	
CHOLESTEROL (MG)	0	SODIUM (MG)	10		

PINEAPPLE SALSA

MAKES 2 CUPS

Salsa is a great low-fat way to accent so many foods, and this one goes particularly well with roast pork (page 272) or any grilled fish or poultry. Substitute diced papaya for the pineapple, if desired, and add some diced jicama for a nice crunch.

½ small pineapple, peeled, cored, and cut into ½-inch cubes (2 cups)

¼ red bell pepper, cored, seeded, and cut into ¼-inch dice

¼ green bell pepper, cored, seeded, and cut into ¼-inch dice

½ small red onion, finely diced

½ serrano chile or jalapeño, stemmed, seeded, and minced

1 tablespoon finely chopped fresh cilantro

1 tablespoon finely chopped fresh mint

Juice of 1 lime

2 teaspoons rice vinegar

⅛ teaspoon salt

Pinch of red pepper flakes, or to taste

1 In a large nonreactive bowl, combine the pineapple, red and green peppers, onion, chile, cilantro, and mint. Toss together.

2 Add the lime juice, vinegar, salt, and red pepper flakes. Toss until evenly combined, cover, and refrigerate for 30 minutes to allow the flavors to marry. As with all salsas, it will last for up to 3 days but is best consumed on the day it is made.

PER ¼ CUP					
CALORIES	30	CARBOHYDRATES (G)	7	CARBOHYDRATE CHOICES: ½	
FAT (G)	0	PROTEIN (G)	LESS THAN 1	FOOD EXCHANGES PER SERVING: ½ FRUIT	
CALORIES FROM FAT (%)	7	FIBER (G)	1	LOW-SODIUM DIETS: EXCELLENT CHOICE	
CHOLESTEROL (MG)	0	SODIUM (MG)	40		

CRANBERRY SAUCE

MAKES 2½ CUPS, OR 20 SERVINGS

For years, I've served my mother's tasty but somewhat ordinary cranberry sauce with my turkey at Thanksgiving. Now that I've discovered this one, I'm starting a new tradition! If you prefer to save your carbohydrate calories for other dishes in your meal, 2½ tablespoons of Equal can be substituted for the 1 cup of sugar. For a complete chart of sugar substitutes to replace sugar, see page 35.

1 cup sugar (see Note)	1 (12-ounce) bag cranberries
½ cup raspberry vinegar	1 cinnamon stick
¼ cup water	Grated zest of 1 orange

1 In a medium saucepan, combine the sugar, vinegar, and water. Over low heat, stir the mixture until the sugar dissolves, then increase the heat and bring to a boil.

2 Add the cranberries and cinnamon stick and reduce the heat to medium. Simmer for 10 minutes, stirring frequently, until all the cranberries burst and the sauce has thickened. Stir in the orange zest and remove pan from the heat. Remove the cinnamon stick before serving, and serve warm, cold, or at room temperature.

Note: If made with sugar substitute: 2 tablespoons provides only 1 gram of carbohydrate, saving 1 carbohydrate choice.

PER 2 TABLESPOONS MADE WITH REGULAR SUGAR					
CALORIES	45	CARBOHYDRATES (G)	13	CARBOHYDRATE CHOICES: 1 IF MADE WITH	
FAT (G)	0	PROTEIN (G)	0	SUGAR, 0 IF MADE WITHOUT	
CALORIES FROM FAT (%)	0	FIBER (G)	0	FOOD EXCHANGES PER SERVING: 1 CARBOHY-	
CHOLESTEROL (MG)	0	SODIUM (MG)	0	DRATE IF MADE WITH SUGAR; FREE IF MADE	

WITH NON-CALORIC SUGAR SUBSTITUTE
LOW-SODIUM DIETS: THIS RECIPE IS FINE.
FRUITS ARE NATURALLY SODIUM-FREE.

CHAPTER 17

FISH

Even good cooks are often intimidated by the thought of cooking fish and seafood. People think that fish is difficult to prepare and so they only order it in a restaurant, where often it is battered and fried.

As you'll see in this chapter, there are plenty of far more tasty and easy ways to prepare fish and seafood, and a few bites of Garlic Shrimp, Grilled Crab Burgers, or Pan-Roasted Snapper with Mushrooms and Two Peppers will be enough to convince you. Fish is naturally low in fat and is very adaptable to different cooking methods, and quick to prepare as well.

In fact, its hard to ruin fish, provided you follow three important rules. First, use absolutely fresh fish: firm to the touch, fresh smelling, and with clear eyes. Second, avoid overcooking fish, as excessive heat will make it very dry. Generally, fish should be cooked about 10 minutes per inch thick. Frozen fish requires twice the cooking time, and can end up being overcooked on the outside while still cold on the inside; it's best to thaw it in the refrigerator and cook it immediately. Finally, use unsaturated fat during cooking.

Fish is an excellent source of protein with very little saturated fat. And the omega-3 fatty acids abundant in fish help protect your heart and blood vessels. I recommend eating fish at least three times a week.

POACHED SALMON WITH TOMATO-LEMON SAUCE

MAKES 4 SERVINGS

Poaching fish in this variety of vegetables is a great way to add flavor to the fish and end up with a colorful, flavorful bed of vegetables on which to serve the pink salmon. Although I like to use a sauvignon blanc for the wine in the poaching liquid, you can also use extra-dry vermouth—unlike wine, it will not go bad upon opening the bottle. For a truly grand presentation, top with the Tomato-Lemon Sauce and serve with small red boiled potatoes on a bed of Sautéed Cucumbers (page 333).

1 leek, white part only, well washed and thinly sliced

1 medium carrot, peeled and cut into very thin strips, about 1 to 2 inches by ⅛ to 1/16 inch (julienned)

1 rib celery, cut into fine julienne

2 bay leaves

10 whole black peppercorns

5 sprigs thyme

½ lemon, thinly sliced

1 pound salmon fillet

½ teaspoon salt

½ teaspoon white pepper

2 cups dry white wine, such as sauvignon blanc

4 cups water

Tomato-Lemon Sauce (opposite)

1 In a large flameproof casserole, sprinkle about half each of the leek, carrot, celery, bay leaves, peppercorns, thyme, and lemon. Season the salmon fillet with salt and pepper and place it on top. Strew the remaining vegetables on top of the fish. Drizzle the wine and water around the edges (the liquid should just cover the fish).

2 Cover the dish and, over medium-low heat, bring the liquid just up to a bare simmer. Reduce the heat to very low and keep just below the simmering point for 15 minutes (do not allow the liquid to boil, and keep checking to make sure it stays just at a tremble). Remove from the heat and rest, covered, for 5 minutes. Transfer the fish to a platter, cover, and set aside while you make the sauce. Strain the vegetables and reserve the vegetables and the poaching liquid separately (discard the lemon, bay leaves, thyme sprigs, and peppercorns).

3 Just before the sauce is finished, reheat the salmon and vegetables in a low oven, covered with foil so the fish does not dry out. Serve with the sauce passed on the side.

TOMATO-LEMON SAUCE (makes about 1 cup)

1 tablespoon extra-virgin olive oil
1 medium leek, white part only, well
    washed and finely chopped
1 clove garlic
1 tablespoon balsamic vinegar

3 cups reserved strained fish-poaching
    liquid
1 cup tomato sauce
2 tablespoons fresh lemon juice

1 In a large heavy sauté pan, heat the olive oil over medium-low heat. Sauté the leek and garlic for 4 to 5 minutes, until softened. Add the balsamic vinegar and simmer, stirring, for 1 to 2 minutes, or until almost all of the liquid has evaporated.

2 Add the poaching liquid and tomato sauce and bring the mixture to a boil. Reduce the heat so the mixture is simmering, and cook for about 30 minutes. Transfer to a blender and puree until smooth.

3 Add the lemon juice and taste for seasoning.

PER 4-OUNCE FILLET WITH ½ CUP VEGETABLES AND ¼ CUP TOMATO-LEMON SAUCE					
CALORIES	260	CARBOHYDRATES (G)	17	CARBOHYDRATE CHOICES: 1	
FAT (G)	9	PROTEIN (G)	26	FOOD EXCHANGES PER SERVING: 3 LEAN MEAT,	
CALORIES FROM FAT (%)	31	FIBER (G)	4	3 VEGETABLE	
CHOLESTEROL (MG)	60	SODIUM (MG)	690	LOW-SODIUM DIETS: OMIT SALT; USE LOW-SODIUM TOMATO SAUCE.	

SALMON SCALLOPS WITH SORREL

MAKES 4 SERVINGS

In this classic French dish I used nonfat milk instead of cream, then thickened it with corn-starch and added a touch of nonfat sour cream. Sorrel is an herb common in French cooking but not always available here. If you can't find it, use sage. Any leftover sauce makes a great condiment for grilled turkey or crab burgers.

4 salmon fillets, 6 ounces each, about
 ⅜ inch thick
1 cup bottled clam juice or chicken
 stock
½ cup dry white wine or vermouth
1 shallot, finely chopped
1 teaspoon cornstarch

½ cup nonfat milk
1 tablespoon nonfat sour cream
10 to 12 large fresh sorrel leaves, cut
 into ¼-inch strips
Salt and freshly ground black pepper,
 to taste

1 Place each salmon fillet between 2 sheets of plastic wrap and, using the side of a large chef's knife, pound gently to flatten them slightly to an even thickness.

2 In a small nonreactive saucepan, combine the clam juice, white wine, and shallot. Over medium-high heat, reduce the mixture, stirring occasionally, until almost all the liquid has evaporated and the shallot is very tender.

3 Mix cornstarch with the milk. Then add the milk-cornstarch mixture to the shallots and bring the mixture back up to a simmer. Reduce for 5 to 8 minutes, until the sauce thickens slightly. Add the sour cream and sorrel and stir for 30 seconds, then remove the pan from the heat. Add the salt and pepper to taste.

4 Heat a large nonstick skillet. Season one side of each salmon scallop with salt and pepper. Sauté the scallops, seasoned side down, for 1 minute, then flip to the other side and cook for 1 minute more so the salmon is barely cooked, not dry.

5 Blot the salmon scallops with a paper towel. Serve with the sauce.

PER 6-OUNCE FILLET WITH ¼ CUP SAUCE					
	BEFORE	**AFTER**			
CALORIES	395	295	CARBOHYDRATES (G)	6	CARBOHYDRATE CHOICES: ½
FAT (G)	23	11	PROTEIN (G)	36	FOOD EXCHANGES PER SERVING: 5 LEAN MEAT,
CALORIES FROM FAT (%)	56	34	FIBER (G)	1	1 VEGETABLE
CHOLESTEROL (MG)	130	95	SODIUM (MG)	490	LOW-SODIUM DIETS: OMIT SALT.

JAPANESE GLAZED SALMON

MAKES 6 SERVINGS

This marinade works well with any firm fish or chicken, either whole or diced in ¾-inch cubes and skewered. I reduced the oil from the original recipe to lower the fat. Slice some zucchini lengthwise, baste it with the same marinade, and grill until tender. For a traditional Japanese meal, serve with Seasoned Sticky Rice (page 342).

For the garnish, toast the sesame seeds in a dry nonstick skillet over medium heat, shaking the pan frequently until golden. Take care that they do not burn—it only takes a minute or so. Black sesame seeds make for a particularly nice contrast, and they are available at Asian markets and some supermarkets.

¾ cup low-sodium soy sauce
1 teaspoon cornstarch
1 teaspoon canola oil
2 teaspoons minced peeled fresh ginger
2 cloves garlic, finely chopped

1 green onion (scallion), white and light green part only, finely chopped
1½ pounds salmon steaks, ¾ inch thick, in 6 portions
2 teaspoons regular or black sesame seeds, toasted

1 In a small saucepan, whisk the soy sauce and the cornstarch together until smooth. Stir in the oil, ginger, garlic, and green onion and bring the mixture to a boil over medium-high heat, stirring. Cook until thickened, then set aside to cool.

2 Place the salmon in a large shallow baking dish and coat both sides of each steak with the cooled marinade. Cover with plastic wrap and refrigerate for 1 hour.

3 Preheat a ridged griddle pan or grill to medium-high heat. When the pan or grill is hot, grill the steaks for 3 to 4 minutes, then turn and cook 3 to 4 minutes more. Baste with the sauce twice during the cooking time. Garnish with the toasted sesame seeds before serving.

PER 4-OUNCE FILLET WITH 2 TABLESPOONS MARINADE					
	BEFORE	AFTER			
CALORIES	170	150	CARBOHYDRATES (G)	2	CARBOHYDRATE CHOICES: 0
FAT (G)		7	5	PROTEIN (G)	24	FOOD EXCHANGES PER SERVING: 3 LEAN MEAT
CALORIES FROM FAT (%)	40	30	FIBER (G)	0	LOW-SODIUM DIETS: LIMIT THE AMOUNT OF
CHOLESTEROL (MG)	60	60	SODIUM (MG)	450	MARINADE TO 1 TABLESPOON PER SERVING

CARBOHYDRATE CHOICES: 0
FOOD EXCHANGES PER SERVING: 3 LEAN MEAT
LOW-SODIUM DIETS: LIMIT THE AMOUNT OF
   MARINADE TO 1 TABLESPOON PER SERVING
   OF SALMON PORTION TO REDUCE SODIUM
   TO 265 MG.

CORIANDER-PEPPER CRUSTED AHI TUNA STEAKS WITH MIXED GREENS

SERVES 6

This dish sounds exotic and complicated, but it's really fairly simple. I like to garnish each serving with a few sesame seeds (black ones are more dramatic if you can find them in an Asian market) and several thin slices of Asian fruits, such as mandarin oranges, star fruits, or Asian pears. Do not overcook the tuna. It is best served rare to medium-rare.

Vinaigrette
- ¼ cup fresh lemon juice
- 2 tablespoons chopped peeled fresh ginger
- 1 clove garlic, finely chopped
- ¼ cup low-sodium soy sauce
- ¼ cup low-fat, low-sodium chicken broth
- 2 teaspoons canola oil (or olive oil)

- 1 teaspoon whole black peppercorns
- 2 tablespoons whole coriander seeds
- 2 teaspoons salt
- 2 teaspoons mild olive oil
- 6 small tuna steaks, 1½ inches thick (3 to 4 ounces each)
- 6 cups baby greens or torn mixed greens, washed and dried (a combination of any of the following: butter, red leaf, lamb's lettuce, radicchio, endive, curly endive, arugula)

1 To make the vinaigrette: In a blender, combine the lemon juice, ginger, garlic, soy sauce, chicken broth, and canola oil and puree until frothy and smooth. Set aside for up to 24 hours, refrigerated, before using. Puree again or shake vigorously in a jar just before serving, to re-emulsify.

2 To make the crust for the tuna, combine the peppercorns and coriander seeds in a spice mill, or a coffee grinder reserved only for spices, or a mortar and pestle. Coarsely grind the spices (do not grind finely). On a plate, combine the ground spices with the salt. Rub both sides of each steak with a little of the olive oil and press the pepper crust mixture firmly onto the tops and bottoms of each.

3 Preheat the oven to 350° F and place a baking sheet lined with parchment paper, or sprayed with vegetable oil cooking spray, in oven to heat up.

4 Heat a large skillet or sauté pan over high heat. Add 1 tablespoon of the olive oil to the hot pan and sear the fish, in two batches, for 2 to 3 minutes per side, until golden brown. The pan must be very hot in order to give the fish a nice, brown color. Remove from pan with a slotted spatula and transfer the fish as they are done to the baking sheet in the hot oven. Finish cooking for 3 to 4 minutes, until the fish reaches the desired doneness (when the tuna is firm, it is done through, but many people prefer tuna served pink in the center, when it will still "give" a little when pushed gently with a finger).

5 Toss the mixed greens with enough of the vinaigrette to just coat the leaves, and mound some greens on each plate. Top the greens with the Ahi steak and serve immediately.

PER 4-OUNCE STEAK WITH MIXED GREENS AND 2 TEASPOONS VINAIGRETTE					
CALORIES	220	CARBOHYDRATES (G)	9	CARBOHYDRATE CHOICES: 1/2	
FAT (G)	9	PROTEIN (G)	27	FOOD EXCHANGES PER SERVING: 4 VERY LEAN	
CALORIES FROM FAT (%)	36	FIBER (G)	3	MEAT, 2 VEGETABLE, 1 FAT	
CHOLESTEROL (MG)	40	SODIUM (MG)	1100	LOW-SODIUM DIETS: OMIT SALT FROM THE CRUST.	

PAN-ROASTED SNAPPER WITH MUSHROOMS AND TWO PEPPERS

MAKES 4 SERVINGS

I like to pan-roast fish in a nonstick pan with a single teaspoon of oil. Throwing in a few vegetables adds even more moisture, so there's no need for extra fat. Glaze the fish with balsamic vinegar just before it's finished cooking, if you like. This method is much healthier than the older version of fried fish, where fish is breaded or battered and fried in ¼ cup or more of oil.

1 teaspoon canola oil
1 shallot, finely chopped
16 small white mushrooms, brushed clean and thinly sliced
1 red bell pepper, cored, seeded, and cut into ¼-inch dice
1 yellow bell pepper, cored, seeded, and cut into ¼-inch dice

1 pound red snapper or orange roughy fillets, divided into 4 portions
Salt and freshly ground black pepper, to taste
1 tablespoon balsamic vinegar

1 In a large nonstick skillet, heat the oil over medium heat. Add the shallot and sauté, stirring occasionally, for 5 minutes or until softened. Add the mushrooms and both the peppers and sauté for 5 to 7 minutes, stirring and regulating the heat so that the vegetables are softened and slightly golden but not scorched. Transfer the vegetables to a bowl and set aside, covered.

2 Season the fish to taste with salt and black pepper. Using the same pan, increase the heat to medium–high. When it is hot, sauté the snapper for about 2 minutes, then turn to the other side and cook for 2 minutes more. Add the balsamic vinegar to the pan and swirl until the fish are lightly coated, then transfer to warm dinner plates and top each one with an equal amount of the vegetable mixture.

PER 4-OUNCE FILLET WITH ⅓ CUP VEGETABLES						
	BEFORE	AFTER			
CALORIES	180	170	CARBOHYDRATES (G)	10	CARBOHYDRATE CHOICES: ½
FAT (G)	5	3	PROTEIN (G)	26	FOOD EXCHANGES PER SERVING: 3 VERY LEAN
CALORIES FROM FAT (%)	25	15	FIBER (G)	2	MEAT, 2 VEGETABLE
CHOLESTEROL (MG)	50	40	SODIUM (MG)	210	LOW-SODIUM DIETS: OMIT SALT.

SWORDFISH STEAKS WITH LEMON, CAPERS, AND CRACKED PEPPER

MAKES 4 SERVINGS

Baking foods in wrapped packages is a great method for low-fat cooking, and has enabled me to eliminate the butter used in the original recipe. Parchment paper is used instead of aluminum foil because it doesn't react with lemon juice, wine, or vinegar. The cooking time for fish in general is 10 minutes per inch of thickness, no matter what the cooking method.

4 (15-inch) squares parchment paper
2 teaspoons olive oil
4 (4-ounce) swordfish steaks, rinsed
    and patted dry
Salt and coarsely cracked black
    pepper, to taste

4 very thin slices of lemon
1 tablespoon capers, rinsed, drained,
    and chopped
1 tablespoon finely chopped parsley

1 Preheat the oven to 425°F. Fold each sheet of parchment paper in half. Cut to make a heart shape: starting about 3 inches down from the top of the fold, first cut upwards in a large rounded circle to form the tops of the heart, and then downward and gradually inward to finish just at the bottom of the fold to form the pointed bottom of the heart. Repeat with the remaining sheets of parchment.

2 Unfold each heart to reveal the center fold line. Brush one side of each heart with ½ teaspoon olive oil and place a swordfish steak on the top. Season to taste with salt and cracked pepper. Top each steak with a slice of lemon and divide the capers evenly on the steaks. Scatter a little parsley over the tops.

3 Fold the other half of the parchment paper over, then fold and crimp the edges together to seal the packet, forming four half-heart-shaped packets. Place the packets on a large baking sheet and cook for about 10 minutes, or 15 if the steaks are more than 1 inch thick. Serve the packets immediately and let each diner open their own, releasing the aroma and steam.

PER SERVING						
	BEFORE	AFTER				
CALORIES	190	160	CARBOHYDRATES (G)	LESS THAN 1	CARBOHYDRATE CHOICES: 0	
FAT (G)	10	7	PROTEIN (G)	23	FOOD EXCHANGES PER SERVING:	
CALORIES FROM FAT (%)	50	40	FIBER (G)	LESS THAN 1	3 LEAN MEAT	
CHOLESTEROL (MG)	60	45	SODIUM (MG)	370	LOW-SODIUM DIETS: OMIT SALT.	

GRILLED FISH WITH PICO DE GALLO

MAKES 6 SERVINGS

Pico de gallo is the salsa often served with Mexican tortilla chips, but it is also wonderful with any white fish, such as halibut or swordfish. You may also want to try it with chicken.

Salsa
½ pound ripe plum tomatoes, seeded and coarsely chopped
⅓ cup finely chopped white onion
2 teaspoons fresh lemon juice
¼ serrano or jalapeño chile, stemmed, seeded, and minced
2 tablespoons, packed, finely chopped fresh cilantro
Salt and freshly ground black pepper, to taste

1½ pounds lean, dense whitefish (such as halibut or swordfish), in 6 equal portions
1 teaspoon mild olive oil
2 tablespoons fresh lemon juice
Lemon slices and paprika, for garnish

1 Preheat a covered outdoor grill for medium-heat cooking.

2 While the grill is preheating, make the salsa. Combine the tomatoes, onion, lemon juice, chile, cilantro, and salt and pepper in a bowl, and set aside to allow the flavors to marry.

3 Place a fish rack, if available, on the grill to heat up. Season each piece of fish by first rubbing with a little oil, then sprinkling with salt and pepper to taste. Grill the fish for approximately 4 minutes on each side, depending on the thickness (always allow about 10 minutes of cooking time per 1-inch thickness of fish, no matter what the cooking method). When the fish is firm and opaque, remove from heat and transfer to warm plates. Sprinkle a little fresh lemon juice on each, garnish the plates with slices of lemon and a sprinkling of paprika. Top the fish with a generous spoonful of the salsa and serve at once.

PER 4-OUNCE SERVING WITH ¼ CUP SALSA					
CALORIES	180	CARBOHYDRATES (G)	3	CARBOHYDRATE CHOICES: 0	
FAT (G)	4	PROTEIN (G)	30	FOOD EXCHANGES PER SERVING: 4 VERY LEAN	
CALORIES FROM FAT (%)	22	FIBER (G)	LESS THAN 1	MEAT, 1 VEGETABLE	
CHOLESTEROL (MG)	45	SODIUM (MG)	125	LOW-SODIUM DIETS: ACCEPTABLE	

GARLIC SHRIMP

MAKES 4 SERVINGS

A good shrimp dish is always a treat, and this simple combination of flavor-enhancing ingredients makes these superb. If you choose to serve these garlicky shrimp hot, basmati rice is a wonderful accompaniment.

The dark line on the back of the shrimp is the intestinal vein which may be left in on smaller shrimp. If you prefer to remove it, simply cut with a knife over the vein, and gently pull it out with the knife or your fingers, rinsing the shrimp under water. Be sure to keep the shrimp on ice during the process, and if you are doing more than a pound of shrimp, rotate them in and out of your refrigerator, in order to maintain their quality.

1 teaspoon olive oil
30 medium shrimp (about 1 pound), peeled and deveined
1 to 2 cloves garlic, finely chopped
Finely chopped zest of ½ lemon
2 tablespoons lemon juice
1 teaspoon soy sauce

Salt and freshly ground black pepper, to taste
2 tablespoons finely chopped parsley
½ teaspoon finely chopped fresh dill, or ¼ teaspoon dried dill, crumbled

1 In a large nonstick or cast-iron skillet, heat the olive oil over medium–high heat. Add the shrimp, garlic, and lemon zest, and tossing occasionally, cook for 2 to 3 minutes, until the shrimp are firm and pink. Do not let the garlic burn. Add a teaspoon or two of water, if needed, to prevent garlic from burning.

2 Remove the pan from the heat and immediately add the lemon juice, soy sauce, salt and pepper to taste, parsley, and dill. Serve immediately, at room temperature, or refrigerate up to 12 hours and serve chilled.

PER 4-OUNCE SERVING (7 OR 8 SHRIMP)					
CALORIES	140	CARBOHYDRATES (G)	3	CARBOHYDRATE CHOICES: 0	
FAT (G)	3	PROTEIN (G)	23	FOOD EXCHANGES PER SERVING: 4 VERY LEAN	
CALORIES FROM FAT (%)	21	FIBER (G)	0	MEAT	
CHOLESTEROL (MG)	175	SODIUM (MG)	210	LOW-SODIUM DIETS: OMIT SOY SAUCE.	

ROCK SHRIMP WITH SNOW PEAS

MAKES 4 SERVINGS

Nothing beats the combination of shrimp and garlic, and this recipe improves on a good thing by adding crisp snow peas and fluffy rice. I prefer to peel the shrimp all the way to the tail, pinch the shell where it meets the tail, and leave the tail on the shrimp. I reduced the oil by half to decrease the fat in this fresh-tasting dish.

1 pound snow peas, trimmed and
  strings removed
1 teaspoon canola oil
2 cloves garlic, finely chopped
1 large shallot, finely chopped
16 medium raw rock or regular
  shrimp, peeled and deveined if
  necessary

2 tablespoons white wine
1 tablespoon finely chopped parsley
Salt and freshly ground black pepper,
  to taste
1 teaspoon pre-sifted flour (such as
  Wondra)
4 cups cooked white rice, hot

1 Bring a generous amount of lightly salted water to a boil. Throw in the snow peas and blanch for 1 minute, then immediately drain and rinse under cold running water to stop the cooking process and preserve the bright green color. Shake the peas dry and set aside.

2 In a medium nonstick skillet, heat the oil over medium-low heat. Sauté the garlic and shallot, stirring occasionally for about 3 minutes, until slightly wilted. Increase the heat to medium-high and add the shrimp. Cook for 1 minute, then add the white wine, parsley, and salt and pepper to taste. Bring the wine to a simmer, stirring, and sprinkle the pre-sifted flour over the top. Simmer the mixture, stirring, for 1 minute more, until slightly thickened.

3 Serve the rice on warmed dinner plates and top with an equal amount of the snow peas. Spoon the shrimp mixture over the top and serve immediately.

PER SERVING (4 SHRIMP, ½ CUP SNOW PEAS, 1 CUP RICE)					
	BEFORE	AFTER			
CALORIES	330	320	CARBOHYDRATES (G) 59	CARBOHYDRATE CHOICES: 4	
FAT (G)	4.5	3	PROTEIN (G) 12	FOOD EXCHANGES PER SERVING: 1 VERY LEAN	
CALORIES FROM FAT (%)	12	9	FIBER (G) 7	MEAT, 3½ STARCH, 1 VEGETABLE	
CHOLESTEROL (MG)	35	35	SODIUM (MG) 250	LOW-SODIUM DIETS: OMIT SALT.	

SPANISH-STYLE SHRIMP

MAKES 4 SERVINGS

Serve over rice, noodles, or any other starch, such as polenta. This dish is really good over toasted country bread, and could also make a first course for 6 people, served solo. Olive oil along with wine and lemon juice helps to keep the fat low.

2 teaspoons olive oil
4 large cloves garlic, finely chopped
¼ teaspoon red pepper flakes
1 red bell pepper, cored, seeded, and cut into ¼-inch strips
16 medium shrimp (about 1 pound), peeled and deveined but with tails still attached

Salt, to taste
1 tablespoon fresh lemon juice
2 tablespoons dry white wine, sherry, or vermouth
2 tablespoons finely chopped parsley
Wedges of lemon, for serving

1 In a large heavy skillet, heat the olive oil over medium-low heat. Add the garlic, red pepper flakes, and red bell pepper and cook, stirring occasionally, until the bell pepper is softened, about 10 minutes. Add a tablespoon of water or wine if more liquid is needed to prevent burning.

2 Increase the heat to high, and when the pan is very hot, add the shrimp and season with salt to taste. Stir the shrimp for 1 minute, then add the lemon juice and white wine. Continue stirring and tossing for 2 to 3 minutes more, until the shrimp are pink.

3 Serve immediately, sprinkled with parsley and accompanied by wedges of lemon.

PER SERVING (4 SHRIMP WITH 2 TABLESPOONS SAUCE)					
CALORIES	70	CARBOHYDRATES (G)	5	CARBOHYDRATE CHOICES: 0	
FAT (G)	3.5	PROTEIN (G)	6	FOOD EXCHANGES PER SERVING: 1 LEAN MEAT,	
CALORIES FROM FAT (%)	41	FIBER (G)	1	1 VEGETABLE	
CHOLESTEROL (MG)	35	SODIUM (MG)	240	LOW-SODIUM DIETS: OMIT SALT.	

SHRIMP CEVICHE

MAKES 4 SERVINGS

Typically, ceviche is made with raw fish and/or seafood that is "cooked" or pickled by an acid marinade. I prefer to make it with shrimp that are pre-cooked. It's safer and easier, reducing the time needed to prepare this tasty recipe to mere minutes. Simply chop up the shrimp and throw these few ingredients together. Because avocados are high in fat, they're used as a condiment rather than a main ingredient (the fat in avocados is mostly monounsaturated, the best kind of fat there is). Serve this dish on salad greens to make a delightful first course or entree salad for a summer evening.

1 pound medium shrimp, cooked and cut into ¼-inch dice
1 pound plum tomatoes, peeled, seeded, and cut into ¼-inch dice
¼ cup chopped cilantro
⅛ teaspoon salt

⅛ teaspoon freshly ground black pepper
1 clove garlic, finely chopped
1 tablespoon fresh lemon juice
¼ avocado, peeled, pitted, and cut into ¼-inch dice

1 In a large nonreactive bowl, combine the shrimp, tomatoes, cilantro, salt, pepper, garlic, and lemon juice. Toss together gently until combined but do not overmix.

2 Just before serving, fold in the avocado. Chill. This is best if eaten the same day.

PER ¾-CUP SERVING					
CALORIES	170	CARBOHYDRATES (G)	8	CARBOHYDRATE CHOICES: ½	
FAT (G)	4	PROTEIN (G)	24	FOOD EXCHANGES PER SERVING: 4 VERY	
CALORIES FROM FAT (%)	25	FIBER (G)	2	LEAN MEAT, 1 VEGETABLE	
CHOLESTEROL (MG)	170	SODIUM (MG)	250	LOW-SODIUM DIETS: OMIT SALT; ADD MORE	
				LEMON JUICE, GARLIC, AND BLACK PEPPER	
				AS YOU LIKE.	

SANTA FE SHRIMP SKEWERS

MAKES 4 SERVINGS

Peel pearl onions easily by blanching for 1 minute in boiling water. Serve with Garlicky Seasoned Rice (page 338). My original recipe for these spicy shrimp skewers called for twice the oil, but with so many seasonings the fat was easy to cut.

4 (10-inch) wooden skewers
¾ cup fresh lemon juice
2 tablespoons olive oil
1 tablespoon finely chopped red onion
2 cloves garlic, finely chopped
½ serrano or jalapeño chile, cored, seeded, and minced
1 teaspoon ground cumin
1 tablespoon finely chopped fresh cilantro

½ teaspoon salt
12 large shrimp, peeled and deveined

12 large green onions (scallions), root ends trimmed and dark green part discarded
12 firm medium white mushrooms
2 medium red bell peppers, cored, seeded, and cut into 2-inch squares

1 Soak the skewers in water for at least 1 hour. In a shallow bowl, combine the lemon juice, olive oil, red onion, garlic, chile, cumin, cilantro, and salt. Stir the mixture to combine, then add the shrimp and turn so they are all evenly covered. Cover the bowl and marinate the shrimp, refrigerated, for 1 hour.

2 Cut the green onions into 1½-inch lengths. Drain the shrimp, reserving the marinade, and drain the skewers. Thread equal amounts of all the ingredients onto the skewers, alternating shrimp, green onions, mushrooms, and red peppers and leaving 2 inches at the top of each skewer free for turning. Be gentle when threading the mushrooms onto the skewers, otherwise they may split.

3 Preheat a grill or broiler to medium-high heat. Grill or broil the skewers for about 3 minutes on each side, or until pink, basting once halfway through with the reserved marinade.

PER SKEWER	BEFORE	AFTER			
CALORIES	100	90	CARBOHYDRATES (G)	13	CARBOHYDRATE CHOICES: 1
FAT (G)	3	2	PROTEIN (G)	8	FOOD EXCHANGES PER SERVING: 1 STARCH,
CALORIES FROM FAT (%)	26	18	FIBER (G)	4	1 VERY LEAN MEAT
CHOLESTEROL (MG)	30	30	SODIUM (MG)	50	LOW-SODIUM DIETS: ACCEPTABLE

SEAFOOD PAELLA

MAKES 8 SERVINGS

Almost anything can be added to a paella—customize it to suit your own likes. Substitute or add chicken, sausage, rabbit, or ham, adjusting the cooking time and pre-cooking items accordingly. Remember that meats, especially those with skin, will increase the fat content per serving. You can also make it more elaborate by adding diced sautéed red and green bell peppers, and tomatoes. This is an impressive dish for entertaining.

1 tablespoon olive oil
1¼ cups long-grain white rice
1 (14½-ounce) can low-fat, low-sodium chicken broth
2 cups bottled clam juice
¼ teaspoon saffron threads, soaked for 10 minutes in 1 tablespoon warm water
1 cup Piedmontese Tomato Sauce (see page 234)
1 pound sea bass or halibut, cut into 1-inch chunks

1 pound medium shrimp, peeled and deveined
¾ pound live mussels, scrubbed and debearded (see page 240)
1 cup frozen French-cut string beans, thoroughly thawed
¼ cup frozen petite peas, thoroughly thawed
2 tablespoons finely chopped parsley
2 lemons, cut into wedges

1 Preheat the oven to 350°F. In a large, wide sauté pan with an ovenproof handle, heat the oil over medium-high heat. Add the rice and sauté, stirring frequently, for about 4 minutes or until it has just begun to turn golden. Stir in the broth and the clam juice (to prevent spattering, remove the pan from the heat for a moment and allow to cool slightly before adding the liquid). Add the saffron. Stir in the Piedmontese Tomato Sauce and bring the mixture to a simmer. Cover and place in the oven for 20 to 25 minutes. Before removing, check the rice; it should be still wet and the individual kernels firm and slightly undercooked.

2 Add the sea bass to the pan, burying it slightly in the rice, then place the shrimp and the mussels decoratively over the top. Cover and return the pan to the oven for 5 to 10 minutes more, until the sea bass is cooked through, the shrimp are pink, and the mussels have opened.

3 Scatter the beans and peas evenly over the top and return the pan to the oven, covered, for 2 minutes more to warm the vegetables through. Do not leave in the oven for too long at this point or the fish will overcook and the vegetables will lose their color. Scatter the parsley over the top.

4 Bring the pan to the table and set it on a heat-proof trivet. Serve at the table, accompanied by lemon wedges.

PER ¾ CUP RICE MIXTURE AND 5 OUNCES SEAFOOD

CALORIES	300	CARBOHYDRATES (G)	29		
FAT (G)	6	PROTEIN (G)	32		
CALORIES FROM FAT (%)	20	FIBER (G)	2		
CHOLESTEROL (MG)	120	SODIUM (MG)	540		

CARBOHYDRATE CHOICES: 2

FOOD EXCHANGES PER SERVING: 2 STARCH, 4 VERY LEAN MEAT

LOW-SODIUM DIETS: OMIT SALT, USE LOW-SODIUM CLAM JUICE OR SUBSTITUTE LOW-SODIUM CHICKEN BROTH, AND MAKE PIED-MONTESE TOMATO SAUCE WITHOUT SALT. ADD GARLIC AND WHITE OR BLACK PEPPER AS DESIRED.

PIEDMONTESE TOMATO SAUCE

MAKES ABOUT 4 CUPS

This recipe comes from the northwestern mountainous region of Italy. Although it's a large recipe, I recommend making the full quantity and using it for the Seafood Paella (see page 232), as a sauce for hot pasta, and as a condiment for Grilled Turkey Burgers (see page 306). The sauce can be stored, covered and refrigerated, for several days, or frozen for up to six months.

2 tablespoons olive oil
½ large onion, diced
1 clove garlic, finely chopped
1 large green bell pepper, cored, seeded, and diced
2 tablespoons dry vermouth or white wine

1 (28-ounce) can crushed tomatoes in juice, drained and juice reserved
1 cup canned tomato puree
1 tablespoon salt
1 tablespoon sugar
1 teaspoon ground white pepper

1 In a large heavy saucepan, heat the olive oil over medium-low heat. Add the onion and sauté for 10 to 12 minutes, stirring occasionally, until soft and transparent but not browned. Add the garlic and cook for 2 minutes, then add the green pepper, vermouth, and the juice from the crushed tomatoes.

2 Increase the heat to medium-high and bring the mixture to a simmer. Simmer, uncovered, until reduced by half, stirring frequently to keep it from sticking. Stir in the tomato puree, the crushed tomatoes, salt, sugar, and pepper. Reduce the heat to medium-low, partially cover the pan, and continue to simmer gently, stirring occasionally, for 30 minutes more, until sauce is thickened and chunky. Serve over pasta or meatballs.

PER ¼-CUP SERVING					
CALORIES	50	CARBOHYDRATES (G)	7	CARBOHYDRATE CHOICES: ½	
FAT (G)	2	PROTEIN (G)	1	FOOD EXCHANGES PER SERVING: 2 VEGETABLE	
CALORIES FROM FAT (%)	35	FIBER (G)	1	LOW-SODIUM DIETS: OMIT SALT; USE LOW-	
CHOLESTEROL (MG)	0	SODIUM (MG)	510	SODIUM TOMATO PRODUCTS.	

SUMMER SCALLOPS AND TOMATOES IN WHITE WINE

MAKES 4 SERVINGS

Fresh scallops make this an exceptional dish, but since it's highly seasoned, with a prevalent tomato flavor, this is a good place to use frozen scallops. Serve with cooked rice or cooked linguine.

2 teaspoons olive oil
1 pound large fresh sea scallops,
    rinsed and patted dry
Salt and freshly ground black pepper,
    to taste
¼ cup dry white wine

2 ripe plum tomatoes, peeled, seeded,
    and cut into ¼-inch dice
1 tablespoon finely chopped fresh
    basil
1 tablespoon finely chopped Italian
    parsley

1 In a large nonstick skillet, heat the olive oil over medium-high heat. Season the scallops to taste with salt and pepper. When the pan is very hot, sear the scallops for 30 seconds on each side.

2 Add the wine and the tomatoes to the pan and simmer rapidly for about 1 minute more, swirling the pan. Remove from the heat, add the basil and parsley, and stir to mix. Serve over hot rice or linguine, if desired, spooning the juices over the top.

PER 4-OUNCE SERVING					
CALORIES	140	CARBOHYDRATES (G)	4	CARBOHYDRATE CHOICES: 0	
FAT (G)	3	PROTEIN (G)	19	FOOD EXCHANGES PER SERVING: 3 VERY LEAN	
CALORIES FROM FAT (%)	21	FIBER (G)	0	MEAT, 1 VEGETABLE	
CHOLESTEROL (MG)	37	SODIUM (MG)	320	LOW-SODIUM DIETS: OMIT SALT.	

GRILLED CRAB BURGERS

MAKES 4 BURGERS

This crab burger is a light and flavorful alternative to the backyard burger. Compare this burger made with sweet delicate crabmeat, at only 1½ grams of fat, to the leanest of all-beef burgers at 12 grams of fat. Serve open-faced on crusty bread smeared with the punchy Dijon mayonnaise, and garnished with sliced tomatoes.

Dijon Mayonnaise
1½ tablespoons Dijon-style mustard
2½ tablespoons fat-free mayonnaise

Crab Burgers
6 ounces fresh lump crabmeat or 1 (6-ounce) can, drained and picked through
1 cup fresh white bread crumbs
5 green onions (scallions), white and light green parts only, finely chopped

¼ red bell pepper, cored, seeded, and finely diced
1 teaspoon dried marjoram, crumbled
Salt and freshly ground black pepper, to taste
½ cup liquid egg substitute or 4 egg whites
Vegetable oil cooking spray
2 large ripe plum tomatoes, thinly sliced, for garnish

1 For the Dijon mayonnaise, combine mustard and mayonnaise in a small bowl, whisk together, and set aside.

2 In a large bowl, combine the crabmeat, bread crumbs, green onions, and red pepper. Add the marjoram and salt and pepper to taste. Toss the mixture loosely together, but do not compact.

3 Mix in the egg substitute or egg whites, again keeping the mixture loose and making sure it is all evenly moistened. Gently form the mixture into four 2½-inch-diameter patties and place them on a plate. Cover the plate tightly with plastic wrap and refrigerate for at least 1 and up to 3 hours.

4 Spray a grill or broiler rack with vegetable oil cooking spray and preheat it to medium-high heat. Grill or broil the burgers until golden brown, about 4 minutes per side. Serve with the Dijon mayonnaise and sliced tomatoes.

PER 3-OUNCE BURGER WITH 1 TABLESPOON DIJON MAYONNAISE AND

1/2 PLUM TOMATO (BREAD NOT INCLUDED)

CALORIES	130	CARBOHYDRATES (G)	11	CARBOHYDRATE CHOICES: 1	
FAT (G)	2.5	PROTEIN (G)	15	FOOD EXCHANGES PER SERVING: 2 VERY LEAN	
CALORIES FROM FAT (%)	19	FIBER (G)	1	MEAT, 1 STARCH	
CHOLESTEROL (MG)	35	SODIUM (MG)	620	LOW-SODIUM DIETS: USE FRESH CRAB AND BOIL	

WITHOUT SALT. IF USING CANNED CRAB,
THOROUGHLY RINSE WITH WATER THROUGH
A COLANDER AT LEAST 2 OR 3 TIMES.

PER TABLESPOON DIJON MAYONNAISE

CALORIES	15	CARBOHYDRATES (G)	2	CARBOHYDRATE CHOICES: 0	
FAT (G)	0	PROTEIN (G)	0	FOOD EXCHANGES PER SERVING: FREE	
CALORIES FROM FAT (%)	0	FIBER (G)	0	LOW-SODIUM DIETS: DILUTE THE MAYONNAISE	
CHOLESTEROL (MG)	0	SODIUM (MG)	200	WITH WINE OR WATER BY HALF.	

SEAFOOD ENCHILADAS

MAKES 12 ENCHILADAS

This dish can also be made with chicken. Die-hard Mexican cooks make their enchiladas with lard and real cheddar cheese, but I've gone for the low-fat alternatives. Corn tortillas have less than 1 gram of fat, while flour tortillas generally have 1½ or 2 grams. The serrano chile is the small green one that is hotter than jalapeño, so if you prefer less heat, use the jalapeño.

½ medium white onion, thinly sliced
1 pound boneless flaky white fish
    (snapper, sea bass, etc.)
2 teaspoons fresh lemon juice
½ cup low-fat, low-sodium chicken
    broth
½ teaspoon salt
¼ teaspoon freshly ground black
    pepper

Verde Sauce (makes 6 cups)
1 pound tomatillos, husked and
    washed
2 cloves garlic, halved
1 serrano or jalapeño chile, stemmed,
    seeded, and halved

1 small onion, coarsely chopped
6 sprigs fresh cilantro
2 cups low-fat, low-sodium chicken
    broth
⅓ cup buttermilk
1 tablespoon vegetable oil

12 corn tortillas

Garnishes
Finely chopped red onion
Chopped fresh cilantro
½ cup fat-free sour cream, thinned
    with ¼ cup nonfat milk

1 Preheat the oven to 350°F. To cook the fish: place a large sheet of heavy-duty aluminum foil on a baking sheet. Scatter the sliced onion in the center of the foil and place the fish over the top. Crimp and fold up the sides of the foil so that it forms a container, and drizzle the lemon juice and chicken broth over the fish. Season with salt and pepper and fold the foil together firmly at the top to seal the package. Bake the fish for 20 to 25 minutes, or until firm, flaky, and opaque.

2 Remove from oven and open the foil package at the top. Allow the fish to cool slightly while you prepare the sauce. (Or, prepare the fish ahead of time: when cool, rewrap and place it in the refrigerator.) Reserve the liquid and the onion for the sauce.

3 To make the Verde Sauce: In a saucepan of boiling water, blanch the tomatillos for 2 minutes. Drain and set aside to cool.

4 In a medium nonstick skillet, roast the garlic, serrano chile, and onion over medium-low heat until golden. (See page 196 for how to roast vegetables.)

5 In a blender, combine the roasted chile mixture, the cilantro, chicken broth, and buttermilk. Add the reserved fish-cooking liquid and onion. Blend to a smooth puree. Add the cooled tomatillos and blend again briefly, leaving a little texture.

6 Heat a large heavy sauté pan and add the oil. Add all the sauce and cook, stirring frequently, for 10 minutes, until dark and thick. If the sauce gets too thick, thin it with a little water or chicken broth.

7 In a bowl, combine the fish and about ¼ cup of the Verde Sauce (just enough to flavor the fish, but not be too saucy). Break the fish up into large chunks.

8 In a large dry skillet, toast the corn tortillas for about 5 seconds on each side, until warm and pliable. As they are done, transfer them to a towel-lined dish or basket and fold the towel over the top. This will keep the tortillas warm and moist.

9 Preheat the oven to 350° F. Spread a thin layer of sauce in the base of an 8 × 11-inch baking dish. Spoon about 2 tablespoons of the filling in the center of a tortilla, roll it up, and place in the baking dish, seam side down. Continue until you have used all the tortillas. Cover the dish with foil and place in the oven for 15 minutes, then add a thin layer of sauce over the top, cover again, and return to the oven for 10 minutes more.

10 Serve in the baking dish at the table with the garnishes on the side. Or, if desired, serve 2 enchiladas per plate, drizzled with a little extra sauce and garnished with chopped onion, cilantro, and sour cream.

PER 2 ENCHILADAS

	BEFORE	AFTER			
CALORIES	585	270	CARBOHYDRATES (G)	30	CARBOHYDRATE CHOICES: 2
FAT (G)	22	8	PROTEIN (G)	20	FOOD EXCHANGES PER SERVING: 3 VERY LEAN
CALORIES FROM FAT (%)	35	27	FIBER (G)	3	MEAT, 2 STARCH
CHOLESTEROL (MG)	115	55	SODIUM (MG)	310	LOW-SODIUM DIETS: OMIT SALT.

MUSSELS OVER CHOPPED COUNTRY BREAD

MAKES 4 SERVINGS

Although this is an extremely easy dish to make, it looks very impressive, with the mussels in their shells. Mussels have a wonderful flavor on their own, and when cooked in wine, their taste infuses into the wine to make a delicious broth, my favorite part of this dish. Vary the recipe by serving with linguine or other pasta instead of bread if you like. They make a great light supper, served in a bowl or on the half shell, topped with the cooking broth. Soaking the mussels in cornmeal and water overnight before cooking is an old trick to make the mussels spit out any sand, so there is no grit in your mussels.

Shopping tip: Medium-sized mussels are about 1 ounce each, or 16 mussels in a pound; large mussels are closer to 2 ounces each, or 8 mussels in a pound.

2 pounds live mussels in shells
¼ cup coarse cornmeal
1 (14½-ounce) can low-fat, low-sodium chicken broth
5 cloves garlic, finely chopped
½ cup dry vermouth or dry white wine
1 teaspoon chopped fresh thyme leaves or ½ teaspoon dried thyme, crumbled
1 teaspoon chopped fresh tarragon leaves or ½ teaspoon dried tarragon, crumbled
¼ teaspoon saffron threads, soaked for 10 minutes in 1 tablespoon warm water

¼ teaspoon salt
⅛ teaspoon freshly ground black pepper
Cayenne pepper or red pepper flakes to taste (optional)
6 large plum tomatoes, peeled, seeded, and diced
6 generous slices of good rustic country bread (1 ounce each), cut into ¾-inch chunks
1½ lemons, cut into wedges
1 tablespoon finely chopped parsley

1 Under cold running water, scrub the mussels clean and pull away the tough beards. Discard any mussels that do not close when agitated. Place the mussels in a large bowl and cover them generously with cold water. Stir in the cornmeal and leave them to soak for 2 to 8 hours in the refrigerator.

2 In a large sauté pan, combine the chicken broth, garlic, and vermouth and bring to a boil. If using dried herbs, add them now (if using fresh, add just before serving). Add the saffron, and salt and pepper to taste. If desired, add cayenne or red pepper flakes to taste.

3 Add the tomatoes and simmer the mixture uncovered until it has reduced by about half, approximately 20 minutes.

4 Drain mussels and rinse off all the cornmeal. Add them to the pan and immediately cover. Cook for 5 to 7 minutes, holding the top firmly and shaking the pan every few minutes to distribute the mussels and make sure they cook evenly. The mussels should all open; if after 10 minutes some mussels have not opened, discard them. If using fresh thyme and tarragon, stir them into the broth now.

5 Place the bread in large deep soup bowls and ladle the mussels and broth over the top. Squeeze a wedge of lemon over the top and sprinkle with a little chopped parsley.

PER 6-OUNCE EDIBLE PORTION OF MUSSELS WITH SAUCE (WITHOUT BREAD)

CALORIES	140	CARBOHYDRATES (G)	11	CARBOHYDRATE CHOICES: 1	
FAT (G)	4	PROTEIN (G)	16	FOOD EXCHANGES PER SERVING: 3 VERY	
CALORIES FROM FAT (%)	24	FIBER (G)	1	LEAN MEAT, 1 STARCH	
CHOLESTEROL (MG)	35	SODIUM (MG)	520	LOW-SODIUM DIETS: THIS RECIPE IS NOT	
				APPROPRIATE FOR 500 AND 1000 MG	
				SODIUM RESTRICTIONS; FOR OTHER	
				DIETS, OMIT SALT.	

PER 6-OUNCE EDIBLE PORTION OF MUSSELS WITH SAUCE (WITH BREAD)

CALORIES	220	CARBOHYDRATES (G)	25	CARBOHYDRATE CHOICES: 2	
FAT (G)	4	PROTEIN (G)	18	FOOD EXCHANGES PER SERVING: ADD	
CALORIES FROM FAT (%)	19	FIBER (G)	2	1 STARCH	
CHOLESTEROL (MG)	35	SODIUM (MG)	660	LOW-SODIUM DIETS: THIS RECIPE IS NOT	
				APPROPRIATE FOR 500 OR 1000 MG	
				SODIUM RESTRICTIONS; FOR OTHER	
				DIETS, OMIT SALT.	

CHAPTER 18

POULTRY

Preparing dishes with chicken or turkey has many advantages. If you're entertaining, you'll find chicken to be more universally accepted than red meat, which many people don't eat, and than fish, to which some people may be allergic. Many of the recipes here are classic chicken recipes that I've adapted for today's tastes and nutritional objectives without compromising flavor. With the transformation in cooking that's occurred during the last decade, many classic dishes have fallen out of popularity, not for taste, but for their high fat content coming from butter, cream, or cheese. Now that they're "new and improved," you can go back to enjoying your favorite recipes like Chicken Chasseur, Chicken Marsala, Chicken Piccata, and even Chicken Pot Pie. You'll also find that many of the recipes may be cooked in advance, including Chicken Tandoori served with Banana Chutney, Teriyaki Chicken with Grilled Pineapple and Green Onions, and Rosemary Chicken. These recipes augment the delicate flavor of chicken with aromatic spices and herbs.

Be careful not to overcook those recipes calling for the white meat of the poultry chicken or turkey. Since the white meat does not contain a great deal of fat, overcooking results in a dry dish. If you're looking for some new ideas to add variety to your chicken dishes while keeping fats low, you'll find them here.

CHICKEN MARSALA

MAKES 4 SERVINGS

The sweet flavor of marsala wine gives this classic dish its name. This updated version replaces butter with olive oil and chicken broth, for a significant fat savings.

4 skinless, boneless chicken breasts, about 1 pound
¼ cup nonfat milk
¼ cup all-purpose flour
Salt and pepper, to taste

1 tablespoon olive oil
¾ cup Marsala wine
¼ cup low-fat, low-sodium chicken broth

1 Place the chicken between two sheets of waxed paper, one at a time, and pound with a rolling pin or mallet to a thickness of about ¼ inch. Place the milk in a shallow bowl and the flour on a plate. Season the chicken with salt and pepper, then dredge first in the milk, then in the flour, shaking off any excess.

2 Heat the oil in a large nonstick pan over medium-high heat, and sauté chicken breasts until golden brown on both sides, about 4 minutes per side. Remove breasts and drain on paper towels, blotting away any excess oil, then transfer to a plate and tent with foil to keep warm.

3 Deglaze the pan with the wine, stirring with a wooden spoon to incorporate all the juices, then add chicken broth and simmer until the sauce is reduced by half.

4 To serve, spoon chicken breasts with sauce and serve immediately.

PER 4-OUNCE BREAST WITH SAUCE					
	BEFORE	AFTER			
CALORIES	290	220	CARBOHYDRATES (G)	8	CARBOHYDRATE CHOICES: ½
FAT (G)	14	5	PROTEIN (G)	28	FOOD EXCHANGES PER SERVING: 4 VERY LEAN
CALORIES FROM FAT (%)	42	21	FIBER (G)	0	MEAT, ½ STARCH
CHOLESTEROL (MG)	100	65	SODIUM (MG)	85	LOW-SODIUM DIETS: ACCEPTABLE

CHICKEN CHASSEUR (HUNTER'S CHICKEN)

MAKES 4 SERVINGS

This is the perfect chicken dish—it is easy, flavorful, low in fat, and makes a great presentation. It's excellent served with rice or roasted potatoes.

4 boneless, skinless chicken breasts, about 1 pound
Salt and freshly ground black pepper, to taste
¼ cup nonfat milk
¼ cup all-purpose flour
1 tablespoon canola oil
½ cup sliced mushrooms
1 tablespoon finely chopped white onion

½ cup vermouth or dry white wine
1 tablespoon Madeira or cooking sherry
1 cup low-fat, low-sodium chicken broth, or more as needed
½ medium tomato or 1 plum tomato, seeded and finely chopped
1 teaspoon fresh chopped rosemary, or ½ teaspoon dried

1 Season chicken with salt and pepper. Place the milk in a wide shallow bowl and the flour on a plate. Dredge the chicken first in the milk, then in the flour, shaking off any excess.

2 Heat the oil in a large, nonstick pan over medium heat. Sauté chicken breasts until golden brown on both sides, about 4 minutes per side. Transfer the chicken with a fork to a plate and set aside.

3 In the same pan, sauté the mushrooms and onion until soft, about 2 to 3 minutes. (If the pan becomes too dry, add a teaspoon or two of the chicken broth). Deglaze the pan with the vermouth and Madeira, stirring with a wooden spoon to incorporate all the juices in the pan. Add the chicken broth and the tomato, and bring the mixture to a boil.

4 Return the chicken to the pan, reduce the heat, and cover. Simmer gently for 5 to 10 minutes, or until the chicken is fully cooked. If necessary, add a little more chicken broth.

5 Remove the chicken to a warm serving platter or plates, increase the heat to high, add the rosemary and salt and pepper to taste, and reduce the sauce by about one third, about 3 minutes. Spoon the sauce over the chicken and serve immediately.

PER 4-OUNCE BREAST WITH SAUCE					
CALORIES	220	CARBOHYDRATES (G)	9	CARBOHYDRATE CHOICES: 1	
FAT (G)	6	PROTEIN (G)	29	FOOD EXCHANGES PER SERVING: 4 VERY LEAN	
CALORIES FROM FAT (%)	25	FIBER (G)	LESS THAN 1	MEAT, 1 STARCH	
CHOLESTEROL (MG)	65	SODIUM (MG)	120	LOW-SODIUM DIETS: ACCEPTABLE	

CHICKEN IN PHYLLO POCKETS

MAKES 10 PACKETS

This Moroccan dish brings a wonderful surprise of flavors in a neatly wrapped package made with phyllo dough. These delicious packets are wonderful served on salad greens as a first course, followed by Lentil Soup with Lamb Meatballs (page 173).

The secret to success when you're using fragile phyllo dough is to always remove the package from the freezer and put it in the refrigerator to thaw overnight, then remove it from the refrigerator and bring to room temperature before using. Unwrap it just before using and lay it out flat, covered with a slightly damp dishtowel to prevent it from drying out.

Filling
2 teaspoons canola oil
4 boneless, skinless chicken breasts, about 1 pound, trimmed and cut into ½-inch dice
Salt and freshly ground pepper, to taste
¾ cup low-fat, low-sodium chicken broth, divided
½ cup coarsely chopped onions
¼ teaspoon ground ginger
¼ teaspoon ground cumin
¼ teaspoon cayenne pepper
¼ teaspoon turmeric

¼ teaspoon ground cinnamon
Pinch of saffron
10 sheets phyllo dough (14 by 17 inches), thawed according to package instructions
Vegetable oil cooking spray

Topping
1 teaspoon ground cinnamon
1 tablespoon sugar
1 tablespoon blanched, ground almonds
1 large egg white

1 In a heavy nonstick skillet, heat the oil over medium-high heat. Season the chicken with salt and pepper to taste and sauté until golden, about 4 minutes on each side. Transfer the chicken to a bowl. Deglaze the pan with ¼ cup of the chicken broth.

2 Simmer until reduced by half and add the onions. Sauté for 4 to 5 minutes, until softened; add the ginger, cumin, cayenne, turmeric, cinnamon, and saffron and sauté for 1 minute more, stirring occasionally.

3 Return the chicken to the pan and add the remaining ½ cup of chicken broth. Bring the liquid to a simmer, reduce the heat and cook, covered, for 15 minutes, or until the chicken is cooked through. Add a tablespoon or two of water if neces-

sary. Remove from the heat and cool to room temperature (at this point, the filling could be refrigerated for up to 1 day before assembling).

4 Preheat oven to 350°F and line a 12 × 18-inch sheet pan with parchment paper. For the topping, combine the cinnamon, sugar, and almonds in a small bowl.

5 Spray each of the phyllo sheets with vegetable oil cooking spray and fold in half lengthwise. Spray again, then fold in half crosswise. Spray once more. Each phyllo dough sheet will be one-quarter its original size.

6 Place 2 tablespoons of the filling in the center of each folded sheet and fold all 4 corners into the center, overlapping them slightly. Brush with the egg white. Sprinkle the cinnamon mixture on top. Make 4 slits in each envelope to allow steam to escape during cooking.

7 Place on parchment-lined sheet pan and bake until slightly golden brown and hot in the center, about 15 minutes.

8 Cool and serve at room temperature as a stand-alone appetizer or on greens as a salad.

PER 2-PACKAGE SERVING					
CALORIES	200	CARBOHYDRATES (G)	13	CARBOHYDRATE CHOICES: 1	
FAT (G)	5	PROTEIN (G)	25	FOOD EXCHANGES PER SERVING: 3 VERY LEAN	
CALORIES FROM FAT (%)	24	FIBER (G)	1	MEAT, 1 STARCH	
CHOLESTEROL (MG)	55	SODIUM (MG)	270	LOW-SODIUM DIETS: OMIT SALT; SUBSTITUTE	
				WATER FOR HALF OR ALL OF THE CHICKEN	
				BROTH.	

CHICKEN PICCATA

MAKES 4 SERVINGS

My friend Susan Gerson is a busy attorney and doesn't like to cook. She affectionately calls this dish her "lover" meal, since she cooks it only when she is trying to impress someone special. The chicken is pan-fried in a small amount of oil and then the sauce is made with the tasty drippings. The complete lover meal is served with rice pilaf and steamed seasoned broccoli.

4 skinless, boneless chicken breasts, about 1 pound
¼ cup nonfat milk
¼ cup all-purpose flour
Salt and freshly ground black pepper, to taste
1 tablespoon olive oil
2 tablespoons dry white wine or vermouth

¼ cup low-fat, low-sodium chicken broth
2 tablespoons fresh lemon juice
2 tablespoons capers, rinsed and drained
Lemon wedges, for garnish

1 One at a time, place the chicken breasts between two sheets of waxed paper and pound with a rolling pin or mallet to about ¼-inch thickness. Place the milk in a small shallow bowl and the flour on a plate. Season the chicken with salt and pepper to taste, then dredge first in the milk, then in the flour, shaking off any excess.

2 Heat the oil in a large, nonstick pan over medium-high heat, and sauté the chicken breasts until golden brown, about 4 minutes per side. Drain briefly on paper towels to remove any excess oil. Transfer to a warm plate and tent with foil.

3 Increase the heat to high and deglaze the pan with the wine, stirring with a wooden spoon to incorporate all the juices. Add the chicken broth, bring to a simmer, and cook until the sauce is reduced by half, about 2 minutes.

4 Add the lemon juice and capers, bring back to a boil and remove from the heat. When ready to serve, spoon a little sauce over each of the chicken breasts and garnish with wedges of lemon.

PER 4-OUNCE BREAST WITH SAUCE					
CALORIES	190	CARBOHYDRATES (G)	7	CARBOHYDRATE CHOICES: ½	
FAT (G)	5	PROTEIN (G)	28	FOOD EXCHANGES PER SERVING: 4 VERY LEAN	
CALORIES FROM FAT (%)	25	FIBER (G)	0	MEAT, ½ STARCH	
CHOLESTEROL (MG)	65	SODIUM (MG)	250	LOW-SODIUM DIETS: OMIT SALT AND CAPERS.	

GRILLED CHICKEN BREASTS WITH BEER AND LIME

MAKES 4 SERVINGS

Here's an oil-free marinade that adds no extra calories but lots of flavor. Using skinless chicken breasts instead of regular also helps keep the fat to a minimum. To simplify this easy recipe even further, marinate the chicken in fresh lime juice only, without the seasonings. When grilling skinless chicken, take extra care not to overcook or the meat will be dry.

½ cup dark Mexican beer, such as
    Negro Modelo
Juice of 1 lime
2 cloves garlic, finely chopped
1 teaspoon dried oregano, crumbled

1 teaspoon chili powder
Freshly ground black pepper, to taste
4 boneless, skinless chicken breasts,
    about 1 pound
Thin wedges of lime, for serving

1 In a nonreactive bowl large enough to hold the chicken, combine the beer, lime juice, garlic, oregano, chili powder, and black pepper to taste. Place the chicken breasts in the marinade and turn to coat them evenly. Cover and marinate at room temperature for 1 hour, or for up to 6 hours in the refrigerator (the longer the better).

2 When ready to cook, let the chicken breasts come to room temperature for 20 minutes in the marinade. Preheat a grill or ridged cast–iron griddle pan to medium-high heat. Remove the chicken breasts from the marinade and pat them with paper towels to absorb the excess marinade (discard the marinade).

3 Grill the breasts for about 8 minutes on each side, depending on their size, or until they are done through with no trace of pink remaining. Do not overcook, or they will be dry. Let the chicken rest for 4 minutes, then cut each single breast into 4 thick slices and serve with wedges of lime.

PER 4-OUNCE BREAST WITH MARINADE					
	BEFORE	AFTER			
CALORIES	270	150	CARBOHYDRATES (G)	3	CARBOHYDRATE CHOICES: 0
FAT (G)	14	1.5	PROTEIN (G)	27	FOOD EXCHANGES PER SERVING: 4 VERY LEAN
CALORIES FROM FAT (%)	48	10	FIBER (G)	0	MEAT
CHOLESTEROL (MG)	93	65	SODIUM (MG)	80	LOW-SODIUM DIETS: ACCEPTABLE

ROSEMARY CHICKEN

MAKES 4 SERVINGS

This recipe is a staple of mine, for weeknights when I come home late and want a simple, hot home-cooked meal.

1 teaspoon olive oil
2 large cloves garlic, halved
   lengthwise
2 sprigs fresh or dried rosemary
4 boneless, skinless chicken breasts
   (about 1 pound)

⅔ cup dry white wine
Salt and freshly ground pepper, to
   taste

1 In a large nonstick skillet, heat the olive oil over low heat. Sauté the garlic and rosemary, stirring frequently, until golden and aromatic, about 3 minutes. Add a small amount of water, if needed. Do not allow the garlic to burn.

2 When the oil is nicely infused, remove the garlic and rosemary and set them aside. Increase the heat to medium-high and add the chicken pieces. Sauté the chicken, turning with tongs until golden on both sides, about 5 to 8 minutes in all. Regulate the heat so that the chicken browns but does not burn.

3 Chop the garlic and rosemary leaves and return them to the pan. Add the white wine and salt and pepper to taste. Reduce the heat to very low and simmer, covered, for about 8 to 10 minutes, until the chicken is done through with no trace of pink remaining.

4 If the juices need to be thickened, remove the chicken and set aside, loosely covered. Continue cooking the juices uncovered for 5 minutes more. Serve the chicken with the cooking juices immediately.

PER 4-OUNCE SERVING					
CALORIES	140	CARBOHYDRATES (G)	1	CARBOHYDRATE CHOICES: 0	
FAT (G)	2.5	PROTEIN (G)	26	FOOD EXCHANGES PER SERVING: 4 VERY LEAN	
CALORIES FROM FAT (%)	14	FIBER (G)	0	MEAT	
CHOLESTEROL (MG)	65	SODIUM (MG)	210	LOW-SODIUM DIETS: OMIT SALT.	

CHICKEN TANDOORI

MAKES 4 SERVINGS

Traditionally, tandoori is colored with beet juice, but many restaurants get the bright red color via food coloring. If you'd like the red color, add 2 to 3 drops of red food coloring to the yogurt mixture. I serve this dish with Easy Banana Chutney (page 253) and Saffron-Scented Basmati Rice (page 339).

1 small onion, coarsely chopped
2 tablespoons coarsely chopped
    peeled fresh ginger
3 cloves garlic, coarsely chopped
3 serrano chiles, stemmed, seeded,
    and ribs removed, or ¼ teaspoon
    cayenne pepper

1 teaspoon ground cumin
½ teaspoon paprika
2 tablespoons fresh lime juice
1 cup nonfat yogurt
4 boneless, skinless chicken breasts,
    about 1 pound

1 In a food processor, combine the onion, ginger, garlic, chiles, cumin, paprika, and lime juice. Pulse to a fine puree, scraping down the sides of the bowl.

2 In a medium nonreactive baking dish, combine the spice paste with the yogurt and blend together well. Add the chicken breasts and turn to coat each one evenly with the marinade. Cover the dish and marinate the chicken, refrigerated, for 24 hours.

3 Prepare a grill or broiler for medium–high heat grilling. Remove the chicken from the refrigerator 20 minutes before you plan to grill, to allow it to come to room temperature.

4 Grill or broil the chicken breasts for 10 to 12 minutes on each side, basting occasionally with the marinade. When the chicken is done through with no trace of pink remaining, transfer to heated plates and serve at once.

PER 4-OUNCE BREAST					
CALORIES	150	CARBOHYDRATES (G)	4	CARBOHYDRATE CHOICES: 0	
FAT (G)	1.5	PROTEIN (G)	28	FOOD EXCHANGES PER SERVING: 4 VERY LEAN	
CALORIES FROM FAT (%)	10	FIBER (G)	0	MEAT	
CHOLESTEROL (MG)	65	SODIUM (MG)	90	LOW-SODIUM DIETS: ACCEPTABLE	

TERIYAKI CHICKEN WITH GRILLED PINEAPPLE AND GREEN ONIONS

MAKES 4 SERVINGS

You will need eight skewers for this dish. If you use bamboo ones, soak them in water for at least an hour or two. You can substitute 1-inch cubes of Ahi tuna for the chicken, if desired. Serve this dish with rice.

Marinade
2 teaspoons finely chopped peeled
  fresh ginger
1 clove garlic, finely chopped
1/3 cup soy sauce
1/4 cup pineapple juice
1 tablespoon sake or sweet rice
  wine or Mirin

4 boneless, skinless chicken breasts
  (about 1 pound), cut into 1-inch
  chunks
1 ripe pineapple, peeled, cored, eyes
  removed, and cut into 1-inch chunks
8 green onions (scallions), roots and
  very dark green ends trimmed
Pickled ginger, for garnish (optional)
Black sesame seeds, for garnish (optional)

1 To make the marinade: in a large, shallow bowl, combine the ginger, garlic, soy sauce, pineapple juice, and sake and whisk together. Add the chicken, pineapple, and green onions and turn to coat all items evenly. Marinate, refrigerated, for 1 hour.

2 Thread the chicken onto the skewers. Discard the marinade. Thread the pineapple onto separate skewers.

3 Prepare an outdoor grill or a broiler for medium-high-heat grilling. Grill or broil the chicken skewers for 5 minutes on each side, or until done through with no trace of pink remaining. Meanwhile, grill or broil the pineapple skewers for 3 to 4 minutes, turning occasionally, until golden brown and slightly charred.

4 Grill the green onions for about 2 minutes, then serve the chicken skewers with the pineapple skewers and 2 green onions per person. Garnish the plates with remaining pineapple, pickled ginger, and black sesame seeds, if desired.

PER 2 SKEWERS					
CALORIES	200	CARBOHYDRATES (G)	18	CARBOHYDRATE CHOICES: 1	
FAT (G)	2	PROTEIN (G)	27	FOOD EXCHANGES PER SERVING: 4 VERY LEAN	
CALORIES FROM FAT (%)	9	FIBER (G)	2	MEAT, 1 FRUIT	
CHOLESTEROL (MG)	66	SODIUM (MG)	135	LOW-SODIUM DIETS: LIMIT TERIYAKI MARINADE	
				TO 1 TEASPOON PER SERVING.	

EASY BANANA CHUTNEY

MAKES ABOUT 1 CUP

Serve this unusual fruit condiment with Chicken Tandoori (page 251). Tamarind paste is made from the sticky pods of the tamarind tree and is often the base for colas. The paste can be found at most Middle Eastern or Southeast Asian grocery stores. It has a distinctly mellow flavor, and is a perfect foil for the tart and sweet citrus flavors in this chutney.

1 tablespoon fresh lemon juice
1 teaspoon tamarind paste (available at Asian markets; optional)
1 tablespoon mango chutney, preferably Major Grey's

1 ripe yellow banana, peeled and quarter cut (cut in half lengthwise twice), then sliced crosswise in ¼-inch slices
1 tablespoon currants

1 In a medium glass or ceramic bowl, whisk together the lemon juice and tamarind paste, if using, until the paste has dissolved. Mix in the chutney.

2 Fold the bananas and currants into the mixture, taking care not to crush the bananas to a mush. Serve immediately, or cover and refrigerate for up to 24 hours.

PER 2-TABLESPOON SERVING					
CALORIES	20	CARBOHYDRATES (G)	5	CARBOHYDRATE CHOICES: 0	
FAT (G)	0	PROTEIN (G)	0	FOOD EXCHANGES PER SERVING: ½ FRUIT	
CALORIES FROM FAT (%)	3	FIBER (G)	0	LOW-SODIUM DIETS: ACCEPTABLE	
CHOLESTEROL (MG)	0	SODIUM (MG)	5		

CHILI-RUBBED BARBECUE CHICKEN

MAKES 10 SERVINGS

The dry rub is one of my favorite low-fat, high-flavor cooking tricks. It takes the place of the more common liquid marinade, but is made with spices and no fat or oil. Note the savings in fat between the "before" and "after" recipes, and the only difference is using skinless chicken in the "after." Try it first as described here, with chicken, then again with fish, pork, or beef. This festive Southwestern-inspired rub can turn any seafood or meat into a crowd-pleasing entree, and it couldn't be easier to toss together from ingredients that you can keep on hand in the pantry.

Chili Rub
¾ cup chili powder (about
    3½ ounces)
3 tablespoons firmly packed brown
    sugar
2 teaspoons cayenne pepper

10 skinless, boneless chicken breasts,
    about 4 ounces each

Barbecue "Mop"
1 cup bottled fat-free hickory
    barbecue sauce
½ cup ketchup
¼ cup orange juice
2 teaspoons low-sodium soy sauce
1 teaspoon Tabasco sauce

1 To make the chili rub, combine the chili powder, brown sugar, and cayenne pepper in a bowl and toss together.

2 Arrange the chicken breasts in a single layer on a large baking sheet (or two if necessary). Sprinkle chili rub generously on both sides of the chicken and rub it lightly into the flesh. Cover with plastic wrap and let stand at room temperature for 1 hour.

3 To make the "Mop": In a medium nonreactive bowl, stir together the barbecue sauce, ketchup, orange juice, soy sauce, and Tabasco sauce. Place half the "mop" in a saucepan and set aside.

4 Preheat a barbecue, grill, or broiler to medium-high heat. If using an outdoor grill: When the coals are covered with fine gray ash, brush the chicken generously with the "mop" from the bowl and place on the grill rack away from the direct heat. Cover the barbecue and cook the chicken until it is done through with no trace of pink remaining. This will take about 20 minutes, turning every 5 minutes and re-covering the grill. If using a broiler: Place pan of chicken breasts under broiler, turning every 5 minutes, until done through.

5 While the chicken is cooking, heat the reserved "mop" in the saucepan over medium-low heat, stirring occasionally, until heated through. Serve the chicken hot, and pass the warm sauce in a separate bowl on the side.

PER 4-OUNCE BREAST WITH 1 TABLESPOON BARBECUE SAUCE AND 1/2 TEASPOON DRY RUB

	BEFORE	AFTER			
CALORIES	270	150	CARBOHYDRATES (G)	5	CARBOHYDRATE CHOICES: 0
FAT (G)	14	2	PROTEIN (G)	28	FOOD EXCHANGES PER SERVING: 4 VERY LEAN
CALORIES FROM FAT (%)	45	10	FIBER (G)	0.4	MEAT, 1 VEGETABLE
CHOLESTEROL (MG)	95	70	SODIUM (MG)	220	LOW-SODIUM DIETS: USE LOW-SODIUM SOY SAUCE.

GRILLED CHICKEN FAJITAS

MAKES 6 SERVINGS

This is a great dinner for entertaining. Much of the work can be done in advance; just remember to marinate the chicken overnight. The presentation of chicken and vegetables is very attractive. Serve with Garlicky Seasoned Rice (page 338) and Chipotle Black Beans (page 323) or Refried Pinto Beans (page 322).

Chicken
2 tablespoons chili powder, preferably
    New Mexico
1 teaspoon salt
2 teaspoons olive oil
2 tablespoons white vinegar
6 boneless, skinless chicken breasts
    (about 1½ pounds)

Vegetables
1 tablespoon canola oil
1 pound medium white onions
    (about 3), halved lengthwise and
    cut into ¼-inch strips
½ pound green bell pepper (about
    2), cored, seeded, and cut into
    ¼-inch strips
½ pound red bell pepper (about 2),
    cored, seeded, and cut into
    ¼-inch strips
Salt and freshly ground black pepper
1 tablespoon Worcestershire sauce
Six to twelve 8-inch flour tortillas

1 In a large shallow baking dish, mix together the chili powder, salt, olive oil, and vinegar. Add the chicken breasts and turn to coat them evenly. Cover the dish, refrigerate, and marinate overnight.

2 In a large cast-iron or heavy nonstick skillet, heat the oil over medium heat. Mix the vegetables in a large bowl, and sauté them in three batches, using 1 teaspoon of oil per batch, stirring occasionally, for about 6 minutes. (This will ensure that they sauté to a nice golden brown, which they would not if overcrowded in the pan.) Add a teaspoon or two of water as needed to keep vegetables from burning. As the vegetables are done, transfer them to a flameproof roasting pan and toss together. Season to taste with salt and pepper. (If desired, the vegetables can be prepared ahead of time to this point and refrigerated.) Just before serving, heat the pan again and add all the vegetables. Stir together just until heated through and add the Worcestershire sauce.

3 When ready to serve, remove the chicken from the refrigerator and allow it to come to room temperature while you prepare a barbecue or grill for high-heat cooking. Pat off the excess marinade with paper towels and grill the chicken directly over the heat for 3 to 5 minutes on each side. Move to the edge of the grill to finish cooking until done through with no trace of pink remaining. Let the chicken rest for 5 minutes, loosely covered with aluminum foil, and slice crosswise on the diagonal. While the chicken is resting, warm the vegetables. Arrange the chicken and vegetables on a large serving platter and serve with warm tortillas.

PER 4-OUNCE BREAST WITH 1 CUP VEGETABLES AND 1 TORTILLA

CALORIES	350	CARBOHYDRATES (G)	37	CARBOHYDRATE CHOICES: 2½	
FAT (G)	8	PROTEIN (G)	31	FOOD EXCHANGES PER SERVING: 4 VERY LEAN	
CALORIES FROM FAT (%)	22	FIBER (G)	4	MEAT, 2½ STARCH	
CHOLESTEROL (MG)	65	SODIUM (MG)	750	LOW-SODIUM DIETS: OMIT OR DECREASE	

LOW-SODIUM DIETS: OMIT OR DECREASE WORCESTERSHIRE SAUCE. USE RICE VINEGAR OR LIME JUICE TO SAUTÉ FAJITA VEGETABLES. OMIT OR DECREASE SALT IN CHICKEN MARINADE.

EASY ROAST CHICKEN

MAKES 4 TO 5 SERVINGS

My husband likes to roast a chicken at least one night a week, usually on Sunday. Here's his secret to a delicious and easy dinner. The chicken is stuffed and cooked breast side down to keep the meat moist. It's amazing how many calories and how much fat you can cut, simply by using skinless white meat instead of skinless dark.

2 medium onions, quartered
1 lemon, quartered
5 whole cloves garlic, peeled
1 sprig fresh rosemary
One 4- to 5-pound chicken, rinsed and patted dry, with the skin left on, giblets discarded

1 tablespoon olive oil
Salt and freshly ground black pepper, to taste

1 Preheat the oven to 450°F.

2 Place the onions, lemon, garlic, and rosemary inside the cavity of the chicken. Rub the outside of the chicken with the olive oil and season generously all over with salt and pepper. Truss the bird, if desired, for more even cooking.

3 Place the chicken breast side down on a roasting rack in a roasting pan. Roast for 15 minutes, until it has begun to brown. Reduce the heat to 350°F, baste, and cook for 30 minutes, then turn the bird breast side up and roast for 1 to 1¼ hours more, or until the thigh meat reaches 170°F and the juices from the leg run clear with no trace of pink remaining. Baste with its juices every 20 minutes or so.

4 Remove from the oven and tent the roasting pan very loosely with aluminum foil. Let the chicken rest for 15 to 20 minutes before carving (discard the flavoring ingredients from the cavity before serving).

PER 4-OUNCE SERVING OF WHITE MEAT				
	BEFORE	AFTER		
CALORIES	240	180	CARBOHYDRATES (G) 0	CARBOHYDRATE CHOICES: 0
FAT (G)	12	5	PROTEIN (G) 35	FOOD EXCHANGES PER SERVING LIGHT
CALORIES FROM FAT (%)	49	25	FIBER (G) 0	MEAT CHICKEN: 4 VERY LEAN MEAT
CHOLESTEROL (MG)	110	100	SODIUM (MG) 85	LOW-SODIUM DIETS: EXCELLENT CHOICE.
				UNPROCESSED CHICKEN IS NATURALLY
				LOW IN SODIUM.

CHICKEN POT ROAST WITH VEGETABLES

MAKES 4 SERVINGS

This one-pot dish is great for guests, since it can be prepared in advance. Just make sure you time it so that it comes out of the oven about the time your guests are ready to eat.

2 teaspoons olive oil
1 medium onion, coarsely chopped
4 carrots, peeled, halved lengthwise, and cut into ½-inch chunks
4 sprigs fresh rosemary, or 1 teaspoon dried rosemary, crumbled
5 cloves garlic, halved
1 (3-pound) chicken, rinsed with cold water and patted dry

¼ cup dry white wine or vermouth
¼ cup low-fat, low-sodium chicken broth
1 bay leaf
4 medium red or white rose or other waxy potatoes, scrubbed and halved

1 Preheat the oven to 350° F. In a large cast-iron and enamel casserole with a lid, heat the olive oil over medium heat. Add the onion and cook, stirring frequently, for about 5 minutes or until slightly softened. Add the carrots, rosemary, and garlic and cook for 4 minutes more, stirring occasionally. Take care that the vegetables do not burn. Add a tablespoon or two of water, broth, or wine if the pan is too hot.

2 Place the chicken, breast side down, in the pan on top of the vegetables and pour the wine and broth over the top. Throw in the bay leaf and arrange the potatoes around and over the chicken. Cover the pan and bake for 35 minutes, then turn the chicken over, adding up to ½ cup water if the pan seems very dry. Cook for about 45 minutes more, or until the juices from the thigh run clear. Serve the chicken with all of the vegetables and the juices, discarding the bay leaf and the rosemary sprigs.

PER 4-OUNCE SERVING OF CHICKEN WITH 1 CARROT AND 1 POTATO					
CALORIES	340	CARBOHYDRATES (G)	28	CARBOHYDRATE CHOICES: 2	
FAT (G)	7	PROTEIN (G)	40	FOOD EXCHANGES PER SERVING: 4 LEAN MEAT,	
CALORIES FROM FAT (%)	18	FIBER (G)	5	2 STARCH	
CHOLESTEROL (MG)	97	SODIUM (MG)	120	LOW-SODIUM DIETS: ACCEPTABLE	

CHICKEN POT PIE

MAKES 4 TO 6 SERVINGS

This is a standard chicken pot pie, except for the fact that it has only a top crust. We removed the bottom crust and found the pie to be just as tasty and satisfying without the extra calories. There are a few steps to this recipe, but they're all simple, and the result is definitely worth it!

Piecrust
1 cup all-purpose flour
¼ teaspoon salt
1 tablespoon cornstarch
3 tablespoons canola oil
4 tablespoons ice water

Filling
1 large russet potato (about
    ¾ pound), peeled and diced
1 tablespoon olive oil
4 boneless, skinless chicken breasts
    (about 1 pound), chopped into
    ¾-inch chunks
1 carrot, peeled and cut into
    ½-inch dice

1 celery stalk, peeled and cut into
    ½-inch dice
½ white onion, finely chopped
1 clove garlic, finely chopped
1½ cups low-fat, low-sodium chicken
    broth
2 tablespoons cornstarch dissolved in
    2 tablespoons water
¼ teaspoon salt
¼ teaspoon freshly ground black
    pepper
½ cup frozen petite peas, thawed
1 tablespoon freshly chopped parsley

1 To make the pie crust: Combine flour, salt, and cornstarch in a bowl. Drizzle with the canola oil and mix gently with a fork until the oil is absorbed and the mixture is mealy. Drizzle just enough water over the flour mixture, mixing to make the dough soft and workable without crumbling. Form the dough into a ball, and place between two large pieces of waxed paper. With a rolling pin, roll the dough into a large 13-inch-diameter circle, then place the dough, with the waxed paper, into the refrigerator to chill while preparing the filling.

2 Preheat oven to 350° F.

3 Bring to a boil enough water to cover the potatoes. Add the potato, and parboil for 5 minutes. Drain and set aside.

4 Heat the oil in a large, nonstick pan over medium-low heat. Add the chicken, potato, carrot, celery, onion, and garlic, cover, and sweat the mixture for approximately 10 minutes, being careful not to brown the chicken. Increase the heat, add the chicken broth, and bring to a boil.

5 Whisk in the cornstarch and water mixture a little at a time until the sauce is slightly thickened, being careful not to add too much. Season with salt and pepper.

6 Remove the mixture from the heat, and allow to cool for 5 minutes. Add the peas and the parsley, mix to combine, then pour the mixture into a 9-inch pie dish. Cover with the pie dough, seal the edges, and cut 2 or 3 slits in the top to vent.

7 Bake until the crust is golden brown and the pie mixture is hot, about 40 to 45 minutes (see Note).

Note: Crust may not brown sufficiently at this temperature. If you prefer a browner crust, place the pie under a broiler just long enough to brown the crust to your liking. It will not take long, so be careful and watch the pie so it doesn't burn.

PER SLICE (⅙ OF THE PIE)					
CALORIES	330	CARBOHYDRATES (G)	35	CARBOHYDRATE CHOICES: 2	
FAT (G)	11	PROTEIN (G)	23	FOOD EXCHANGES PER SERVING: 3 VERY LEAN	
CALORIES FROM FAT (%)	30	FIBER (G)	3	MEAT, 2 STARCH, 1 VEGETABLE, 1 FAT	
CHOLESTEROL (MG)	45	SODIUM (MG)	280	LOW-SODIUM DIETS: ACCEPTABLE	

CUBAN PICADILLO

MAKES 4 SERVINGS

This recipe came to me from a Cuban friend, Lou. His aunt Maria makes it with ground pork. Here we've substituted lean ground turkey. Use capers as a variation instead of Spanish olives if you like. Serve it in tortillas or with a side of rice. It's a great dish to include at a make-your-own-taco buffet.

1 cooked potato, cut into
    ½-inch cubes
1 teaspoon canola oil
1 small red onion, cut into
    ¼-inch dice
2 cloves garlic, finely chopped
1 green bell pepper, cored, seeded,
    and cut into ¼-inch dice
1 red bell pepper, cored, seeded, and
    cut into ¼-inch dice
1 pound lean ground turkey
½ teaspoon salt

Freshly ground black pepper, to taste
1 teaspoon finely chopped fresh
    thyme or ½ teaspoon dried
    thyme, crumbled
1 tablespoon chopped brine-cured
    green olives
2 tablespoons raisins
4 flour tortillas, warmed
2 plum tomatoes, seeded and cut into
    ¼-inch dice
¼ cup finely chopped Italian parsley

1 In a small saucepan, boil potato cubes until tender, about 10 minutes. Drain.

2 In a large nonstick skillet, heat the oil over medium–low heat. Sauté the onion, garlic, and the green and red peppers for about 10 minutes, stirring occasionally, until softened.

3 Preheat the oven to 300° F. Increase the heat to medium-high and add the turkey, salt, pepper to taste, and the thyme to the pan with the vegetables. Break up the turkey with a spoon and cook, stirring occasionally, until the turkey is just golden and done through with no trace of pink remaining. Do not overcook, or the dish will be dry.

4 Tip the pan to the side and spoon off any accumulated fat. Reduce the heat again and add the olives, raisins, and potato. Cook for 1 or 2 minutes, stirring occasionally without breaking up the potato, until the filling is warm through.

5 Spoon some of the filling onto one side of each of the warm tortillas and roll them up snugly. Place in a baking dish just large enough to hold all the rolled tortillas. Scatter the tomatoes and parsley over the top and warm in the oven for 10 minutes. Serve immediately.

PER 1-CUP SERVING (ABOUT 5 OUNCES) WITH ONE 8-INCH TORTILLA

	BEFORE	AFTER			
CALORIES	510	330	CARBOHYDRATES (G)	32	CARBOHYDRATE CHOICES: 2
FAT (G)	27	5	PROTEIN (G)	39	FOOD EXCHANGES PER SERVING: 5 VERY LEAN
CALORIES FROM FAT (%)	48	14	FIBER (G)	2	MEAT, 1 STARCH, 1 VEGETABLE
CHOLESTEROL (MG)	105	95	SODIUM (MG)	540	LOW-SODIUM DIETS: OMIT OLIVES AND SALT.

TURKEY LOAF

MAKES 8 SERVINGS

If your ground turkey is made from turkey breast without skin, there will be very little fat in it, especially when compared to meatloaf made with ground beef and eggs. You may still want to invest in special pans with holes in the bottom so the fat drains off as it cooks. Bake a couple of sweet potatoes to go alongside your turkey loaf, and enjoy with a green salad.

1½ pounds ground turkey
1 cup finely crushed soda cracker
 crumbs
½ cup chopped celery leaves
¼ cup finely chopped onion
¼ cup finely chopped parsley
1 carrot, peeled and coarsely chopped
1 cup bottled chili sauce or ketchup,
 divided
¼ cup dry white wine or chicken
 broth

1 tablespoon red wine vinegar
3 large egg whites
2 teaspoons finely chopped fresh
 thyme, or 1 teaspoon dried
 thyme, crumbled
½ teaspoon salt
¼ teaspoon freshly ground black
 pepper
Dash of Tabasco sauce, or to taste

1 Preheat the oven to 350°F. In a large mixing bowl, combine the turkey, cracker crumbs, celery leaves, onion, parsley, carrot, ½ cup chili sauce, white wine, vinegar, egg whites, thyme, salt, pepper, and Tabasco sauce. With your hands, squeeze and blend the mixture until it is evenly mixed.

2 Mold the mixture into a loaf shape and place it into a 9 × 5-inch baking dish. Spoon the remaining ½ cup of chili sauce evenly over the top and bake for about 1 hour, or until the internal temperature reaches 160°F. Let the loaf stand for 15 minutes, then slice into 8 pieces and serve.

PER 3½-OUNCE SERVING

	BEFORE	AFTER				
CALORIES	430	220	CARBOHYDRATES (G)	16	CARBOHYDRATE CHOICES: 2	
FAT (G)	21	4	PROTEIN (G)	29	FOOD EXCHANGES PER SERVING: 3 LEAN MEAT,	
CALORIES FROM FAT (%)	45	17	FIBER (G)	1	1 STARCH	
CHOLESTEROL (MG)	145	60	SODIUM (MG)	560	LOW-SODIUM DIETS: SUBSTITUTE ½ CUP TOMATO	

LOW-SODIUM DIETS: SUBSTITUTE ½ CUP TOMATO PASTE PLUS ½ CUP WATER FOR CHILI SAUCE OR KETCHUP. USE UNSALTED CRACKERS TO MAKE CRUMBS.

GROUND TURKEY WITH GINGER, HOISIN, AND GREEN ONIONS

MAKES 4 SERVINGS

The idea for this recipe came to me while leafing through a Chinese cookbook and studying a recipe for moo shu lamb and Chinese pancakes. This version uses ground turkey, which contains half the fat, and has no oil. If you choose to serve it with rice, you may wish to wrap it with a lettuce leaf, Vietnamese-style, instead of tortillas, to keep carbohydrates in check.

2 tablespoons orange juice
1 tablespoon cornstarch
1 pound ground turkey
2 tablespoons finely chopped peeled
    fresh ginger
1 tablespoon finely chopped fresh
    garlic
1 tablespoon minced orange zest

1 small bunch green onions
    (scallions), white and light green
    parts only, finely chopped
¼ cup hoisin sauce (available at Asian
    markets and in the Asian section
    of some supermarkets)
4 butter lettuce leaves or warmed
    tortillas, for serving

1 In a small bowl, whisk together the orange juice and cornstarch and set aside.

2 In a large nonstick skillet, sauté the turkey over high heat, breaking up the meat with a spoon and stirring, until cooked through with no trace of pink remaining, about 3 minutes. Remove the turkey from skillet and set aside.

3 Add the ginger, garlic, and orange zest to the same skillet and stir-fry for 2 minutes, then add the green onions and stir-fry for 1 minute more.

4 Add the hoisin sauce and return the turkey to skillet. Stir to combine, then stir in the orange juice-cornstarch mixture and stir until thickened, about 1 minute.

5 Spoon the mixture into lettuce leaves or tortillas, roll them up, and serve immediately.

PER 4-OUNCE SERVING IN LETTUCE LEAF					
CALORIES	240	CARBOHYDRATES (G)	12	CARBOHYDRATE CHOICES: 1	
FAT (G)	5	PROTEIN (G)	35	FOOD EXCHANGES PER SERVING: 3 LEAN MEAT,	
CALORIES FROM FAT (%)	20	FIBER (G)	1	1 CARBOHYDRATE	
CHOLESTEROL (MG)	80	SODIUM (MG)	320	LOW-SODIUM DIETS: NOT ACCEPTABLE FOR	
				LOW-SODIUM DIETS	

ROAST TURKEY, ITALIAN-STYLE

MAKES 15 SERVINGS

Since the size of turkey breasts varies, and there is shrinkage during cooking, the number of servings is approximate. Cooking time is 20 to 25 minutes per pound. If desired, cool the turkey breast to room temperature after cooking, then refrigerate and use for sandwiches. Note the fat and calories you cut when you remove the skin.

1 boneless, skinless turkey breast, about 4 pounds
3 cloves garlic
Juice of 1 lemon
2 teaspoons fresh oregano, or 1 teaspoon dried oregano, crumbled
½ teaspoon red pepper flakes, or to taste

½ teaspoon salt
¼ teaspoon freshly ground black pepper
1 medium onion, cut into ¼-inch thick slices and separated into rings
3 thin slices prosciutto, visible fat removed

1 With a small, sharp knife, make shallow slits all over the breast and insert slivers of garlic into them. In a small bowl, combine the lemon juice, oregano, red pepper flakes, salt, and pepper. Rub this paste into the surface of the turkey and refrigerate for at least 1 hour, preferably 3 or 4. Remove the turkey and allow it to come to room temperature for about 20 minutes before cooking.

2 Preheat the oven to 425°F. In a roasting pan, spread the onion rings in a flat mound approximately the same size as the turkey breast. Place the breast over the onion and drape the prosciutto evenly over the top. Roast for 15 minutes, then reduce the temperature to 350°F, cover, and continue cooking for about 1 to 1½ hours (20 to 25 minutes per pound), or until the juices run clear and the internal temperature is 170°F. Take care not to overcook the breast or it will be dry. Allow to rest for five minutes, then carve into thin slices for serving.

PER 4-OUNCE SERVING						
	BEFORE	AFTER				
CALORIES	190	150	CARBOHYDRATES (G)	0	CARBOHYDRATE CHOICES: 0	
FAT (G)	8	3	PROTEIN (G)	30	FOOD EXCHANGES PER SERVING: 4 VERY LEAN	
CALORIES FROM FAT (%)	38	18	FIBER (G)	0	MEAT	
CHOLESTEROL (MG)	75	70	SODIUM (MG)	65	LOW-SODIUM DIETS: ACCEPTABLE	

CHAPTER 19

LEAN MEATS

T hings have changed with red meat. In the previous decade, it received a bad rap for its high saturated-fat content, and nearly every client who came into my office proudly reported eating little or no red meat. But now we know that if you select a lean cut of meat and prepare it properly, it's easy to fit into a low-fat diet, and it's a great source of protein, iron, zinc, and B vitamins. Meats have become leaner as farmers raise leaner animals and butchers trim away more fat. Here you'll find lean, tender, and flavorful Country-Seared Pepper Steak, lean cuts of pork marinated, stewed with port, prunes, and apricots, or roasted with garlic, and for lamb lovers, the delicious Lamb Meatballs that make great appetizers or additions to lentil soup. And the lamb brochettes are perfect for the barbecue. I've kept each entree below 14 grams of fat—the amount you'd get in a "diet dinner"—but with oh so much flavor!

GRILLED TERIYAKI FLANK STEAK

MAKES 4 SERVINGS

Be sure not to overcook flank steak beyond medium-rare, or it will be tough. Make sure portions are kept at 3 to 4 ounces, about the size of a deck of cards, in order to have an entree that fits into a low-fat diet. Any leftovers will make great sandwiches, between 2 slices of bread or wrapped in a tortilla.

1 cup pineapple juice (preferably fresh)
½ cup light soy sauce
2 cloves garlic, finely chopped
1 tablespoon grated peeled fresh ginger

1 tablespoon powdered mustard
1 teaspoon coarsely cracked black pepper
1 pound flank steak, well trimmed

1 In a rectangular, nonreactive baking dish, combine the pineapple juice, soy sauce, garlic, ginger, mustard, and black pepper, and whisk together until evenly blended.

2 Add the flank steak and turn to coat both sides. Marinate for 2 hours at room temperature or overnight, covered, in the refrigerator, turning the steak over every few hours.

3 When you are ready to grill the steak, remove it from the refrigerator and bring to room temperature, if necessary. Preheat a grill or broiler to medium–high heat and pat the steak dry with paper towels to remove the excess marinade. Grill or broil the steak for about 5 minutes on each side for medium-rare, then allow to rest, loosely covered with foil, for 5 minutes. Discard the marinade. Thinly slice on the diagonal for serving.

PER 4-OUNCE SERVING					
CALORIES	240	CARBOHYDRATES (G)	0	CARBOHYDRATE CHOICES: 0	
FAT (G)	12	PROTEIN (G)	31	FOOD EXCHANGES PER SERVING: 4 LEAN MEAT	
CALORIES FROM FAT (%)	46	FIBER (G)	0	LOW-SODIUM DIETS: ACCEPTABLE	
CHOLESTEROL (MG)	90	SODIUM (MG)	94		

COUNTRY-SEARED PEPPER STEAK

MAKES 4 SERVINGS

For a very easy and rich-tasting fat-free gravy, try this combination of ingredients. It tenderizes a lean cut of meat and turns it into a delicious treat.

½ teaspoon coarsely ground black pepper

4 (4-ounce) boneless round steaks, about 1 inch thick, excess fat trimmed

Kosher salt

4 cloves garlic, finely chopped

1 cup dry red wine

1 cup low-fat, low-sodium beef broth

2 tablespoons whole-grain Dijon mustard

3 tablespoons finely chopped fresh parsley

1 Rub pepper into both sides of each steak and let rest at room temperature for 15 minutes before preheating the skillet.

2 Heat a large, heavy cast–iron or nonstick skillet over medium-high heat. When it is very hot, add the steaks and cook to the desired doneness, about 3½ minutes per side for medium-rare. Add water a teaspoon at a time to keep the steaks from burning. When the steaks are done, transfer them to a platter and season both sides with salt. Tent loosely with foil to keep warm while you make the sauce.

3 Add the garlic to the skillet and sauté for 30 seconds, stirring. Stir in the wine and the broth. Bring the liquid to a boil, scraping the bottom and sides of the pan to release all the flavorful bits into the sauce. Simmer the sauce for about 10 minutes, until slightly thickened, then stir in the mustard. Return the steaks to the pan and let them warm through in the sauce, about 1 minute more.

4 Serve the steaks immediately on warmed plates, with some of the sauce poured over each, and a little parsley sprinkled over the top.

PER SERVING WITH 2 TABLESPOONS SAUCE					
CALORIES	220	CARBOHYDRATES (G)	3	CARBOHYDRATE CHOICES: 0	
FAT (G)	7	PROTEIN (G)	34	FOOD EXCHANGES PER SERVING: 4 LEAN MEAT	
CALORIES FROM FAT (%)	28	FIBER (G)	0	LOW-SODIUM DIETS: ENJOY THE STEAK WITH-	
CHOLESTEROL (MG)	80	SODIUM (MG)	270	OUT ADDING EXTRA SAUCE AT THE TABLE.	

MARINATED PORK CHOPS

MAKES 4 SERVINGS

This soy-ginger marinade creates an Asian barbecue flavor without any added fat. It is also well suited to chicken or beef. Marinating the pork overnight provides lots of flavor and keeps this lean meat tender.

1 tablespoon low-sodium soy sauce
¼ cup ketchup
¼ cup sherry
1 tablespoon fresh ginger, peeled and finely chopped

1 clove garlic, finely chopped
½ teaspoon freshly ground black pepper
4 boneless pork loin cutlets (about 4 ounces each)

1 In a large rectangular baking dish, mix together the soy sauce, ketchup, sherry, ginger, garlic, and pepper.

2 Place the cutlets in the marinade and turn to coat all sides evenly. Cover and marinate in the refrigerator, at least 12 and up to 24 hours, turning and brushing the cutlets with the marinade occasionally.

3 Preheat the oven to 325° F. Drain the cutlets and pat them dry with paper towels, reserving the marinade. Place the cutlets on a rack over a large roasting pan containing about 2 inches of water. Place the remaining marinade in a small saucepan and bring to a simmer. Simmer for 3 minutes and remove from the heat. Baste the cutlets with the marinade and bake in the hot oven for 45 minutes, basting every 10 to 15 minutes with more of the marinade. Cutlets are done when they feel fairly firm to the touch, are still juicy, and are a faint pink when you cut into the flesh near the center.

PER CHOP WITH APPROXIMATELY 1 TO 2 TABLESPOONS MARINADE					
CALORIES	180	CARBOHYDRATES (G)	3	CARBOHYDRATE CHOICES: 1	
FAT (G)	6	PROTEIN (G)	25	FOOD EXCHANGES PER SERVING: 3 LEAN MEAT	
CALORIES FROM FAT (%)	32	FIBER (G)	0	LOW-SODIUM DIETS: NOT ACCEPTABLE FOR	
CHOLESTEROL (MG)	72	SODIUM (MG)	230	500 OR 1000 MG SODIUM DIETS	

PORK TENDERLOINS WITH PORT SAUCE, PRUNES, AND APRICOTS

MAKES 4 SERVINGS

Look for a market where you can get lean pork cutlets with minimal marbling. The fabulous sauce tenderizes the pork and adds a rich, fruity flavor with a hint of port that can't be beat. This is just right for an autumn or winter Sunday-night dinner.

4 center-cut, boneless tenderloin
    pork cutlets (about ½ inch thick,
    4 ounces each), trimmed
1 tablespoon canola oil
1 medium onion, sliced
2¼ cups canned low-salt beef broth

1 cup port or red wine
½ cup pitted prunes
¼ cup dried apricots
1 teaspoon fresh lemon juice
¼ teaspoon grated lemon zest

1 Heat oil in a heavy, nonstick ovenproof pan over high heat. Add the pork cutlets, searing them until brown, about 3 minutes per side, adding a small amount of water or broth, if necessary. Transfer to paper towels; drain. Deglaze the pan with ¼ cup broth or water, scraping the bottom of the pan with a wooden spoon. Add sliced onion to pan and sauté until soft and light brown, about 5 minutes.

2 Place pork cutlets over onion. Add remaining broth (if any was used) and the wine. Bring to a simmer. Reduce heat, and add prunes, apricots, lemon juice, and lemon zest. Cover; simmer until pork is very tender, about 30 minutes.

3 Using a slotted spoon, transfer the pork to a serving platter. Using same spoon, arrange onion, prunes, and apricots around pork. Tent with foil. Boil cooking liquid until thickened slightly, stirring occasionally, 10 to 15 minutes. Spoon over the pork and serve immediately.

PER CUTLET WITH 1 PRUNE, 1 APRICOT, AND 2 TABLESPOONS SAUCE					
CALORIES	390	CARBOHYDRATES (G)	31	CARBOHYDRATE CHOICES: 2	
FAT (G)	12	PROTEIN (G)	39	FOOD EXCHANGES PER SERVING: 5 LEAN	
CALORIES FROM FAT (%)	27	FIBER (G)	5	MEAT, 2 FRUIT	
CHOLESTEROL (MG)	105	SODIUM (MG)	120	LOW-SODIUM DIETS: EXCELLENT CHOICE	

ROAST LOIN OF PORK WITH GARLIC

MAKES 8 TO 12 SERVINGS

I consider this dish to be one of the all-time best. Because I was born and raised on an Iowa hog farm, I must admit I'm a bit biased toward pork. But pork has changed over the years, and lean cuts now really do deserve to be called the "other white meat." Now that consumers demand leaner meats, farmers raise leaner pigs, and sell them before they get too fat. According to my dad, processors pay farmers a bonus for lean hogs.

This is my favorite way to cook a pork roast. Just make sure you select a lean one at the market. The loin refers to the "tenderloin," which is part of the pig's back, running all the way from the shoulder to the hind legs. You can buy it either with the bone in or bone removed. The boneless roast is my favorite for an elegant dish suitable for special guests. Seasoning the roast with the garlic and rosemary a day or two in advance makes for an even better flavor.

1 (4-pound) boneless center-cut
    rolled and tied double pork loin
    roast (see Note)
5 garlic cloves, slivered
2 to 3 sprigs fresh rosemary leaves,
    removed from sprigs

Kosher salt
Black pepper, to taste
About ¾ cup dry white wine, or
    water (optional)

1 Remove pork roast from refrigerator an hour or so before cooking. Remove any fat that may remain on the exterior of the meat.

2 Preheat the oven to 450°F.

3 With a small, sharp knife, make tiny slits all over the meat and insert the garlic slivers and rosemary. Sprinkle the roast with kosher salt and freshly cracked black pepper. Place it on a rack in a roasting pan (the rack allows all the fat to drip off of the meat so the meat doesn't cook in it).

4 Roast the meat for 10 to 15 minutes, until just beginning to brown. Reduce the heat to 325°F and roast for about 30 minutes per pound, or until the internal temperature is 140°F (for a 4-pound roast, it should take about 2 hours total).

5 Remove the roast from the oven and let it rest, loosely tented with aluminum foil, for 10 to 15 minutes before carving (this allows the juices to gelatinize slightly, keeping more flavor and moisture in the meat).

6 Once roast is removed, set the roasting pan over a medium flame, and deglaze with wine or water, scraping up all the accumulated drippings. Reduce for 5 minutes, stirring occasionally, then remove from the heat and pour into a gravy separator or glass bowl. Once fat has sufficiently separated to the top, skim or pour it off, return the gravy to a small saucepan, season to taste, and heat through.

7 With a sharp carving knife, cut the meat into neat, thin slices and serve at once, with gravy on the side.

Note: 2-pound roast = 6 servings; 3-pound roast = 9 servings

PER 4-OUNCE SERVING					
CALORIES	270	CARBOHYDRATES (G)	0	CARBOHYDRATE CHOICES: 0	
FAT (G)	14	PROTEIN (G)	33	FOOD EXCHANGES PER SERVING: 5 LEAN MEAT	
CALORIES FROM FAT (%)	47	FIBER (G)	0	LOW-SODIUM DIETS: THIS RECIPE IS FINE.	
CHOLESTEROL (MG)	110	SODIUM (MG)	70	UNPROCESSED PORK IS NATURALLY LOW IN SODIUM.	

OSSO BUCCO (VEAL SHANKS)

MAKES 4 SERVINGS

These shanks are lean pieces of veal, braised in a flavorful liquid until fork-tender. I have also made this with veal loin, when the loin in the meat case appeared leaner than the shank. I serve it with risotto or pasta. Try the Risotto with Tomato and Basil (page 350).

4 veal shanks or lean veal loin chops
    (about 1 pound)
Salt and pepper, to taste
1 teaspoon olive oil
1 carrot, peeled and diced
¾ cup diced onion
4 garlic cloves, minced
2 teaspoons anchovy paste
½ cup brandy
½ cup cream sherry
1 (14½-ounce) can beef broth, or
    more as needed
3 cups peeled chopped tomatoes, or
    1 (28-ounce) can peeled, chopped
    tomatoes

Bouquet garni (1 bay leaf, 4 black
    peppercorns, two 2-inch zests
    each of orange and lemon, a sprig
    of fresh thyme; all wrapped in
    cheesecloth, and tied together
    with string; see Note, page 279)
2 tablespoons cornstarch dissolved in
    2 tablespoons water
1 tablespoon chopped parsley, for
    garnish

1 Preheat oven to 325° F.

2 Season the veal with salt and pepper to taste.

3 Heat the oil in a large, heavy saucepan or Dutch oven over medium-high heat. Brown the meat on both sides, about 4 minutes per side. Remove and drain the meat on paper towels.

4 Add the carrot, onion, and garlic and cook until the onion is beginning to brown, about 5 minutes. Add a little beef broth if the pan becomes too dry.

5 Add the anchovy paste, then deglaze with the brandy, stirring with a wooden spoon to incorporate all the juices. Add the sherry, beef broth, and tomatoes. Bring to boil and skim off any foam that collects on top of the liquid.

6 Return the meat to the pan, add the bouquet garni, cover the pan, and place in the oven for approximately 1 hour, until the meat is fork-tender. If necessary, add more beef broth (the sauce should not quite cover the meat).

7 Remove the meat from the pan. Discard the bouquet garni and adjust the seasoning. Whisk the cornstarch mixture into the sauce a little at a time, over high heat, until the desired consistency is reached—it should be the consistency of heavy cream. Spoon the sauce over the meat, sprinkle with parsley, and serve immediately.

PER SHANK WITH SAUCE					
CALORIES	310	CARBOHYDRATES (G)	17	CARBOHYDRATE CHOICES: 1	
FAT (G)	10	PROTEIN (G)	34	FOOD EXCHANGES PER SERVING: 5 LEAN MEAT,	
CALORIES FROM FAT (%)	31	FIBER (G)	3	1 STARCH, 2 VEGETABLE	
CHOLESTEROL (MG)	120	SODIUM (MG)	240	LOW-SODIUM DIETS: OMIT ANCHOVY PASTE.	

VEAL SALTIMBOCCA

MAKES 4 SERVINGS

Although this dish is traditionally made with veal, it can also be made with a chicken breast cutlet. This recipe comes from Rome and is a very elegant dish for two. The combination of veal, prosciutto, and sage is wonderful. Serve with Polenta with Hot Pepper (page 352). A simple risotto and vegetable ragout are also satisfying accompaniments.

4 veal cutlets (approximately 4
    ounces each), cut in half
Freshly ground black pepper, to taste
4 slices of prosciutto, halved crosswise

8 fresh sage leaves
1 tablespoon olive oil
½ cup vermouth or dry white wine

1 Place veal cutlets in plastic wrap and, one by one, pound with a meat pounder or rolling pin to ¼-inch even thickness. Season the veal with pepper to taste. Place a slice of prosciutto and a sage leaf on top of each veal half and fasten with a toothpick. To do this, pierce the sage and prosciutto in one end, then continue piercing into the veal, then bring the toothpick out of the veal and back into the prosciutto and sage, as if you were sewing with a needle.

2 Heat the oil in a large, nonstick skillet over medium-high heat. Sauté the veal on both sides, finishing with the prosciutto and sage leaf on top, about 3 minutes per side. (If too much liquid accumulates in the pan while veal is cooking, spoon it out and reserve for the sauce.)

3 Remove the cutlets and tent with foil to keep warm. Deglaze the pan with the vermouth and any reserved juices, and cook until the liquid is reduced and slightly syrupy, about 4 minutes.

4 Remove the toothpicks and serve the veal with the prosciutto and sage side up, spooning the pan juices evenly over each portion.

PER SERVING					
CALORIES	300	CARBOHYDRATES (G)	4	CARBOHYDRATE CHOICES: 0	
FAT (G)	12	PROTEIN (G)	33	FOOD EXCHANGES PER SERVING: 5 LEAN	
CALORIES FROM FAT (%)	37	FIBER (G)	2	MEAT, 1 VEGETABLE	
CHOLESTEROL (MG)	125	SODIUM (MG)	320	LOW-SODIUM DIETS: OMIT PROSCIUTTO.	

LAMB MEATBALLS

MAKES APPROXIMATELY 30 MEATBALLS

I serve these fabulous meatballs in lentil soup (page 173), but they also stand on their own as a highly seasoned appetizer or sandwich filling. If you can find lean ground lamb, use it. I buy lean lamb, trim all the fat, and put it in the food processor using a flat steel blade. A few pulses, and you have all lean ground lamb. It's the best!

¾ pound lean ground lamb
½ cup fine bread crumbs
½ cup finely chopped onion
⅓ cup currants
2 large egg whites
4 garlic cloves, chopped
2 tablespoons chopped fresh cilantro

¼ teaspoon chile pepper flakes
   (optional)
Salt and black pepper, to taste
2 teaspoons olive oil
½ cup low-sodium, low-fat chicken
   broth

1 In a large bowl, combine the lamb, crumbs, onion, currants, egg whites, garlic, cilantro, chile pepper flakes (if using), and salt and pepper; mix well with hands. Form into about 30 small meatballs, about ½ ounce or ¾ inch each.

2 In a large nonstick pan, heat olive oil over medium-high heat. Place the meatballs in the pan and sauté until brown on all sides, about 10 minutes. Then add chicken broth, reduce heat to low, and cook the meatballs, covered, another 15 minutes or until cooked through.

PER 5-MEATBALL SERVING					
CALORIES	210	CARBOHYDRATES (G)	14	CARBOHYDRATE CHOICES: 1	
FAT (G)	8	PROTEIN (G)	20	FOOD EXCHANGES PER SERVING: 3 LEAN MEAT,	
CALORIES FROM FAT (%)	34	FIBER (G)	1	1 STARCH	
CHOLESTEROL (MG)	55	SODIUM (MG)	240	LOW-SODIUM DIETS: ACCEPTABLE	

NAVARIN D'AGNEAU (LAMB STEW)

MAKES 8 SERVINGS

This was inspired by my friend Anne Albertine from a class she took at Le Cordon Bleu in London. Make this recipe around Easter when spring lambs are available. Though a simple stew, it can be dressed up by surrounding the platter with cooked spring vegetables. You can substitute beef for the lamb, if you desire.

2 pounds lamb loin, well trimmed and cut into ½-inch cubes (about 1½ pounds meat)
Salt and black pepper, to taste
1 tablespoon olive oil
1 small onion, minced
4 cloves garlic, minced
¾ cup white wine
¼ cup tomato paste
1 (14½-ounce) can beef broth

1 bouquet garni (1 bay leaf, 2 sprigs of thyme, 4 black peppercorns; see Note)
8 small red potatoes, scrubbed and quartered (about 1 pound)
4 carrots, peeled and cut into 1-inch pieces
3 tomatoes, peeled and quartered
1 tablespoon chopped fresh parsley

1 Season lamb chunks with salt and pepper.

2 In a large Dutch oven, heat the oil over medium-high heat and brown the meat in batches. Remove meat from the pot and drain in a colander to remove excess fat.

3 Drain all but a tablespoon of liquid from Dutch oven, then add the onion and sauté for 5 minutes, until onion is soft and slightly golden. Add garlic and sauté for another 3 minutes.

4 Bring the heat up to medium and deglaze the pan with the wine, stirring with a wooden spoon to incorporate all the juices. Add tomato paste and cook for 5 minutes more, stirring.

5 Preheat the oven to 350°F. Return the meat to the Dutch oven, along with the beef broth, bouquet garni, potatoes, and carrots and bring to a boil. Cover and place in the preheated oven. Bake, covered, for 45 minutes to an hour, or until meat is tender. Fifteen minutes before the meat is ready, add the quartered tomatoes. When the meat is tender, remove from the oven. Discard the bouquet garni. Season

with salt and pepper to taste. If needed, adjust sauce consistency with a cornstarch slurry or, if too thick, thin with some beef broth. To make a slurry, mix a teaspoon or two of cornstarch with a tablespoon or two of cold water or milk. Add a bit of hot liquid to temper it, then add it slowly to hot dish. Serve stew sprinkled with parsley.

Note: Bouquet garni is the French term for a bouquet of herbs. It is a combination of herbs and vegetables placed in a cheesecloth bag and used to flavor stocks and other savory preparations. It typically includes fresh thyme, parsley stems, a celery stalk, and a bay leaf, but you can use any combination of fresh herbs depending on the recipe or desired result. Simply assemble the herbs and place them in the center of a piece of cheesecloth. Bring together the edges of the cloth and tie the bundle with string or butcher's twine, leaving a long tail of string to tie the bouquet to the stockpot handle. Taste your dish, and when you determine that the bouquet garni has contributed adequate flavor, remove it from the preparation and discard it.

PER 1-CUP SERVING					
CALORIES	360	CARBOHYDRATES (G)	16	CARBOHYDRATE CHOICES: 1	
FAT (G)	14	PROTEIN (G)	38	FOOD EXCHANGES PER SERVING: 5 LEAN MEAT,	
CALORIES FROM FAT (%)	36	FIBER (G)	3	1 STARCH	
CHOLESTEROL (MG)	110	SODIUM (MG)	200	LOW-SODIUM DIETS: ACCEPTABLE	

LAMB AND VEGETABLE BROCHETTES

MAKES 4 SERVINGS

An easy way to peel pearl onions is to drop them into boiling water for 1 minute, then refresh under cold water. The skin will then slide off easily. This recipe can be used as a guideline; feel free to substitute chicken, turkey, or even lean beef for the lamb, and add any other suitable vegetables. Be gentle when threading the mushrooms onto the skewers; they split easily. Serve the brochettes with cooked white rice, rice pilaf, or orzo.

Marinade
¼ cup fresh lemon juice
¼ cup dry white wine
¼ cup olive oil, preferably extra-virgin
2 medium shallots, finely chopped
2 cloves garlic, finely chopped
1 tablespoon finely chopped fresh rosemary, or 2 teaspoons dried rosemary, crumbled
2 teaspoons fennel seed, crushed
1 teaspoon coarsely cracked black pepper

Brochettes
1 pound lean boneless lamb chop, cut into 1-inch cubes (see Note)
12 pearl onions, peeled
12 small white mushrooms, wiped clean
12 cherry tomatoes
1 red or green bell pepper, cored, seeded, and cut into 2-inch squares
Lemon wedges, for garnish
1 tablespoon finely chopped parsley, for garnish

1 In a large nonreactive bowl, combine the lemon juice, wine, olive oil, shallots, garlic, rosemary, fennel seed, and black pepper. Whisk to combine, and add the cubed lamb. Toss so that each piece of lamb is evenly coated with the marinade, cover the bowl, and refrigerate for at least 2 hours, or preferably overnight.

2 Soak four 8-inch bamboo skewers for at least 2 hours in water to cover (this will stop them from burning when you grill the brochettes). Drain the lamb, reserving the marinade, and pat the cubes lightly with paper towels to absorb the excess marinade.

3 Thread the skewers, alternating lamb, onions, mushrooms, tomatoes, and pepper squares, and making sure each skewer has 3 of each ingredient. Leave a 2-inch space at the end of the skewer to help turn them during cooking.

4 Preheat a grill or broiler to high heat. Grill or broil the skewers for 2 to 3 minutes on each of all four sides for medium-rare meat, basting occasionally with the reserved marinade. Place a wedge of lemon on each plate and sprinkle the brochettes with chopped parsley just before serving.

Note: Selecting a leaner cut of lamb can significantly reduce fat content.

PER BROCHETTE					
CALORIES	270	CARBOHYDRATES (G)	10	CARBOHYDRATE CHOICES: 1/2	
FAT (G)	10	PROTEIN (G)	34	FOOD EXCHANGES PER SERVING: 4 LEAN MEAT,	
CALORIES FROM FAT (%)	35	FIBER (G)	2	2 VEGETABLE	
CHOLESTEROL (MG)	100	SODIUM (MG)	190	LOW-SODIUM DIETS: ACCEPTABLE	

TEXAS-STYLE CHILI

MAKES 10 SERVINGS

What makes this chili truly Texan is the fact that it's made with all beef and no beans. Be fore-warned: it's very hot, which is how I like it! For a milder version, decrease the amount of chili powder. Any combination of Spanish, Mexican, or California chili is fine; this combination just happens to be my favorite. This traditional chili is best when made at least a day in advance, refrigerated, and reheated. If desired, serve with plain white rice or Chipotle Black Beans (page 323). (See the Appendix for a mail-order source for the chiles.)

3 whole dried California chiles, stemmed and seeded

1 whole dried New Mexico chile, stemmed and seeded

1 tablespoon vegetable oil

3 pounds beef round or lean sirloin, cut into 1-inch cubes

1 medium onion, finely chopped

2 teaspoons finely chopped garlic

3 tablespoons California chili powder

1 tablespoon New Mexico chili powder

2 tablespoons ground cumin

1 cup canned tomato sauce

1 (14½-ounce) can low-fat, low-sodium beef broth

1 (14½-ounce) can low-fat, low-sodium chicken broth

1 teaspoon brown sugar

1 teaspoon Tabasco sauce

Juice of 1 lime

Salt and freshly ground black pepper, to taste

Fat-free sour cream, chopped green onions (scallions), and chopped cilantro, for serving

1 In a small bowl, cover the California and New Mexico chiles with boiling water and allow to sit for 30 minutes. Drain well, reserving some of the soaking water. Transfer the chiles to a blender and puree, adding just enough of the soaking water to help the mixture move in the blender.

2 In a large covered casserole, preferably cast-iron, heat the oil over medium-high heat. Brown the meat in several batches, without crowding, so that it browns efficiently instead of poaching. Be sure to brown all sides evenly, until golden but not cooked through. With a slotted spoon, transfer the meat to a plate as it is done, and set aside.

3 Add the onion and the garlic to the casserole and reduce the heat to medium. Sauté, stirring occasionally, for 4 to 5 minutes, or until almost translucent.

4 Add the chili powders and the cumin, stirring to mix in well. Sauté for 1 minute, taking care not to let the spices burn. Return the beef to the pan and stir to coat with the spice mixture. Add the chile puree, tomato sauce, and beef and chicken broths, and bring the mixture to a boil. Reduce the heat, partially cover the pan, and simmer for 2 hours, stirring occasionally. Add water if it gets too thick or starts to burn. The beef should be very tender and the chili mixture slightly thickened.

5 Add the brown sugar, Tabasco, lime juice, salt, and pepper to the chili, stir to mix well, and taste for seasoning.

6 Serve with bowls of sour cream, chopped green onions, and chopped cilantro so guests can garnish their chili as desired.

PER ³/₄-CUP SERVING					
CALORIES	310	CARBOHYDRATES (G)	9	CARBOHYDRATE CHOICES: ½	
FAT (G)	11	PROTEIN (G)	43	FOOD EXCHANGES PER SERVING: 5 LEAN MEAT,	
CALORIES FROM FAT (%)	32	FIBER (G)	3	2 VEGETABLE	
CHOLESTEROL (MG)	95	SODIUM (MG)	310	LOW-SODIUM DIETS: SUBSTITUTE WATER FOR	
				LOW-SODIUM BROTHS AND OMIT TABASCO	
				SAUCE.	

WEINERSAFT GULYASS

MAKES 5 CUPS

My friend Jonah Hadary's parents, Janice and Joel, found this recipe in a cookbook while browsing bookstore shelves when they were college students. Unable to afford the luxury of cookbooks, they copied it from the book and went home and made it, over and over again. It's a warm and hearty stew for a cold night, and is just as wonderful made with chicken or lamb.

2 teaspoons dried marjoram
2 teaspoons finely chopped
    lemon zest
1 teaspoon caraway seeds
1 clove garlic, finely chopped
1½ teaspoons salt
1 tablespoon olive oil
2 pounds onions (about 6 medium),
    coarsely chopped

2 tablespoons Hungarian paprika
1 tablespoon tomato paste
1 pound lean rib eye steak, cubed
2 tablespoons all-purpose flour
2 cups hot water, or more as needed
1 recipe Saffron-Scented Basmati
    Rice (page 339)

1 In a mortar and pestle (or a blender or mini food processor), crush together the marjoram, lemon zest, caraway seeds, garlic, and salt.

2 Preheat the oven to 325°F. In a large, covered casserole, preferably cast-iron, heat the olive oil over medium-low heat. Add the crushed seasonings and the onions, and cook for about 5 minutes, until limp and transparent but not browned. Add the paprika, stir to mix in well, and cook for 1 minute. Stir in the tomato paste.

3 Reduce the heat to low and add the meat. Stir together until the meat is coated with the mixture and has lost its pinkness. Sprinkle the flour evenly over the top and stir until absorbed. Do not let the flour scorch. Add 1 to 2 cups hot water, just enough to cover the bottom of the casserole. Bring the liquid to a simmer, cover the pan, and bake in the oven for 1½ to 2 hours, or until the meat is tender. Check the pan occasionally to see if more liquid is needed, and add ½ cup more hot water as needed, just to keep the mixture moistened. Serve hot with basmati rice.

PER 1-CUP SERVING WITH ⅔ CUP RICE

CALORIES	400	CARBOHYDRATES (G)	47	CARBOHYDRATE CHOICES: 3	
FAT (G)	12	PROTEIN (G)	27	FOOD EXCHANGES PER SERVING: 3 STARCH,	
CALORIES FROM FAT (%)	27	FIBER (G)	4	3 LEAN MEAT	
CHOLESTEROL (MG)	60	SODIUM (MG)	500	LOW-SODIUM DIETS: OMIT SALT.	

CHAPTER 20

PASTA AND PIZZA

T he rise and fall of pasta is an interesting page in food history. When we first learned that we should limit fat and emphasize carbohydrates in the 1980s, many of us got carried away with pasta, considering it a "safe, healthy, good for you" food. And it is, but watch those portions! Once your eye is trained at home to recognize the quantity that suits you, ask for the same amount in a restaurant. From the punchy Penne Pasta with Puttanesca Sauce to the Lemon Pesto Spaghettini, these recipes are just the thing when it's pasta you're hungry for.

If it's pizza, try these versions. Pizza may well be America's favorite food, especially with those under 18. Keep it healthy, make it gourmet, and enjoy this hand-held treat. Make your own crust at home with this tried-and-true recipe or pick up a fresh or frozen crust at an Italian grocery or your favorite pizza restaurant, and get creative with the toppings.

PISSALADIÈRE (PROVENÇAL ONION TART)

MAKES 6 SLICES

My friend Annie Sabroux makes this classic French dish which originated in Nice. It's basically a pizza of onion and anchovies. The onions are cooked slowly in order to bring out their sweetness. Because of the brininess of the anchovy and olives, additional salt is not needed. Anchovy paste is simpler, so I use it here, but use 1 anchovy for each teaspoon of paste if you wish to have a more traditional version. For another shortcut, buy frozen pizza dough at Italian groceries and keep it in the freezer.

1 tablespoon olive oil
4 pounds onions, thinly sliced (about 3 cups)
½ cup dry sherry
5 teaspoons anchovy paste or 5 whole anchovies, rinsed and drained
1 teaspoon finely chopped fresh thyme, or ½ teaspoon dried, crumbled (optional)

Salt and freshly ground pepper, to taste
Vegetable oil cooking spray
Cornmeal or flour for dusting
8 ounces homemade or frozen pizza or bread dough, thawed to room temperature
10 brine-cured black olives such as Kalamata, pitted and halved

1 Heat a large heavy skillet over low heat and add the olive oil. Sauté the onions very slowly, allowing them to brown. Once they are beginning to brown, add the sherry a tablespoon or two at a time, as liquid is needed, each time stirring to scrape up the glaze formed at the bottom of the pan. It may take about 40 minutes until the onions are very soft and caramelized to a golden brown. Add the anchovy paste (if using), thyme, and salt and pepper to taste. Mix well. Cook for 5 minutes more and remove from the heat.

2 Preheat the oven to 400°F. Lightly oil a 14-inch round pie plate or a baking sheet and dust with cornmeal or flour. Roll out the pizza dough to a 14-inch circle, letting it rest for a few minutes covered with a kitchen towel if it seems to resist stretching out to the right size.

3 Ease the dough into the pie plate or transfer it to the baking sheet (it's fine if the edges are uneven). Spread the onion mixture over the dough, leaving a ½-inch border around the edges. If using whole anchovies, cut each one in half, lay them in a crisscross pattern over the onions and press an olive half in the middle of each diamond.

4 Bake for 25 minutes or until the edges of the dough are golden and the topping is bubbling. Cut into 6 wedges and serve immediately.

PER SLICE					
CALORIES	290	CARBOHYDRATES (G)	51	CARBOHYDRATE CHOICES: 3½	
FAT (G)	5	PROTEIN (G)	10	FOOD EXCHANGES PER SERVING: 3½ STARCH	
CALORIES FROM FAT (%)	15	FIBER (G)	7	LOW-SODIUM DIETS: OMIT SODIUM, AND ADD	
CHOLESTEROL (MG)	7	SODIUM (MG)	640	ROSEMARY, BASIL, OR MORE THYME.	

PIZZA CRUST

MAKES 2 PIZZA CRUSTS

If you'd like to make your own pizza crust, here is an easy recipe. You can also find ready-made crusts in the supermarket refrigerator case. This recipe makes 2 crusts, so freeze one to use later.

1¼ cups warm water	2 cups all-purpose white flour
2 teaspoons active dry yeast	½ teaspoon salt
½ teaspoon sugar	Vegetable oil cooking spray
1 cup whole wheat flour	Flour or cornmeal for dusting

1 Combine the water, yeast, and sugar in a bowl and let stand until foamy, about 5 to 10 minutes.

2 In a very large bowl, mix the flours and salt, then stir in the yeast mixture. Turn the mixture onto a lightly floured surface, and knead for 10 to 15 minutes, or place in a food processor with the metal blade and process for 1 minute. If using a food processor, place the flours and salt in the work bowl fitted with the metal blade, and with the motor running, pour the warm-water yeast mixture slowly through the feed tube. (You can also use an upright mixer with a dough hook.) The dough should form a rough ball on the central stem after about 20 seconds. If it has not, remove the cover and sprinkle 1 tablespoon water over, then process again. After it has formed a ball, process for 1 minute more, then turn out onto a lightly floured surface and knead briefly to form a round, smooth ball.

3 For the first rise, place the dough in a very large, lightly oiled bowl, cover tightly with plastic wrap, and let rise until not quite fully doubled, 45 minutes to 1 hour.

4 To shape the dough with a rolling pin, knead the dough briefly on a lightly floured surface to expel the air bubbles, 1 to 2 minutes. Roll into a ball and then flatten into a thick disk. With a rolling pin, roll out the dough ¼ to ⅜ inch thick, leaving a 1-inch rim. Place the dough in a 12 × 16-inch pan sprayed with vegetable oil cooking spray and dusted with flour or cornmeal.

5 To shape by hand, push the dough out from the center of a lightly floured surface, working around the circle and pushing to within an inch of the edge. When the dough is a bit more than ½ inch thick, place it over your fists and start moving them gently away from each other, stretching the dough between them. Move your

fists back to center, turn the dough a bit (you might even make it jump a bit in the air to accomplish this), and then move your fists apart again, being careful not to tear the fine dough in the middle. When it is almost the size you want, place it in the pan that has been sprinkled with flour or cornmeal. Finish shaping the dough with your fingers.

6 Cover the dough with a towel and let rise for no longer than 30 minutes. The dough should be puffy and softly risen.

7 Preheat the oven 30 minutes to 400°F. Top with selected toppings and bake large pizza 25 to 30 minutes and smaller ones 15 to 25 minutes. The pizza is done when the crust is golden brown and crisp and the cheese, if used, is melted and bubbling.

PER SLICE (¹/₆ OF PIZZA CRUST)					
CALORIES	110	CARBOHYDRATES (G)	23	CARBOHYDRATE CHOICES: 1¹/₂	
FAT (G)	LESS THAN 1	PROTEIN (G)	4	FOOD EXCHANGES PER SERVING: 1¹/₂ STARCH	
CALORIES FROM FAT (%)	0	FIBER (G)	2	LOW-SODIUM DIETS: OMIT SALT IF FOLLOWING	
CHOLESTEROL (MG)	0	SODIUM (MG)	90	500 OR 1000 MG SODIUM DIET.	

PIZZA MARGARITA (TOMATO, GARLIC, AND BASIL)

MAKES 6 PIZZA SLICES

Most of my clients tell me they eat pizza once every week or two, even more frequently if they have a family with teenagers. I like pizza myself, and have gotten into the habit of picking up an uncooked ball of pizza dough on my way home, where I let the spirit of Italian baking take over, using whatever combination of vegetables, cheese, and seasonings strikes my imagination (and also happens to be in my refrigerator). By making my own pizza, I eliminate at least half the fat of a regular pizza, because I use less oil and less cheese, or even omit the cheese altogether. You can find ready-made pizza crust in the supermarket refrigerator case. Also, some Italian delis and pizzerias sell frozen pizza dough, which is great. Just make sure you allow enough time to thaw it at room temperature; it can't be hurried. This is an easy and classic recipe that you'll find in virtually every restaurant in Italy that offers pizza. I prefer it without the cheese. Simple recipes are often the best, and I think this one is pretty great.

Vegetable oil cooking spray
Cornmeal or flour for dusting
8 ounces frozen pizza or bread dough, thawed to room temperature

1 tablespoon olive oil
4 to 5 medium plum tomatoes, thinly sliced
4 cloves garlic, finely chopped
10 leaves fresh basil, finely chopped

1 Preheat the oven to 400° F. Spray a large baking sheet with vegetable oil cooking spray, and dust with cornmeal or flour. Roll out the dough into a large circle or rectangle that will fit on the baking sheet, letting it rest for a few minutes covered with a kitchen towel if it seems to resist stretching out to the right size.

2 Brush the top of the dough with the olive oil, arrange tomato slices over the olive oil, then top with garlic and basil. Bake larger pizzas for 25 to 30 minutes and smaller ones 15 to 25 minutes, or until the crust is golden and crisp.

3 Remove pizza from the oven, divide into 6 equal slices and serve immediately.

PER SLICE				
CALORIES	146	CARBOHYDRATES (G)	26	CARBOHYDRATE CHOICES: 2
FAT (G)	3	PROTEIN (G)	4	FOOD EXCHANGES PER SERVING: 1½ STARCH,
CALORIES FROM FAT (%)	17	FIBER (G)	3	1 VEGETABLE
CHOLESTEROL (MG)	0	SODIUM (MG)	185	LOW-SODIUM DIETS: ACCEPTABLE

PIZZA WITH ROASTED RED PEPPER, CHICKEN SAUSAGE, AND CILANTRO

MAKES 6 PIZZA SLICES

The flavors in this pizza—tangy tomato sauce with mellow roasted red peppers, chicken sausage, cilantro, and red onion—hint of a tasty Mexican dish, and make for an excellent presentation as well.

Vegetable oil cooking spray
Cornmeal or flour for dusting
8 ounces frozen pizza or bread
    dough, thawed to room
    temperature
½ cup Zesty Marinara Sauce
    (page 298)
2 medium red bell peppers, roasted
    (see page 154), peeled, cored, and
    cut into 2-inch strips

Two 2-ounce pre-cooked chicken
    sausage links, cut into
    ½-inch slices
½ cup, packed, chopped fresh cilantro
¼ cup finely chopped red onion

1 Preheat the oven to 400° F. Spray a large baking sheet with vegetable oil cooking spray, and dust with cornmeal or flour. Roll out the dough into a large circle or rectangle that will fit on the baking sheet, letting it rest for a few minutes covered with a kitchen towel if it seems to resist stretching out to the right size.

2 Spread the marinara sauce evenly over the crust, leaving a ½-inch border around the edges. Arrange pepper strips and chicken sausage over the sauce, then sprinkle with cilantro and red onion. Bake in preheated oven—larger pizzas for 25 to 30 minutes and smaller ones 15 to 25 minutes, or until the crust is golden and crisp.

3 Remove pizza from the oven, divide into 6 equal slices and serve immediately.

PER SLICE				
CALORIES	176	CARBOHYDRATES (G)	28	**CARBOHYDRATE CHOICES: 2**
FAT (G)	4	PROTEIN (G)	8	**FOOD EXCHANGES PER SERVING: 2 STARCH,**
CALORIES FROM FAT (%)	20	FIBER (G)	3	**1 LEAN MEAT**
CHOLESTEROL (MG)	13	SODIUM (MG)	420	**LOW-SODIUM DIETS: THIS RECIPE IS NOT**
				SUITABLE. TRY THE PIZZA MARGARITA
				(OPPOSITE).

BARBECUED CHICKEN PIZZA

MAKES 6 SLICES

The most popular pizza at one of the most popular pizza chains, California Pizza Kitchen, is the barbecued chicken pizza. Making it at home is even better, because you can tailor the ingredients to your liking and know you're getting a low-fat pie. Bottled barbecue sauces are often fat-free, but check the label to make sure. Kraft honey-hickory barbecue sauce is my favorite.

1 teaspoon olive oil
1 leek, white and light-green parts only, halved lengthwise and thoroughly washed, chopped
1 red onion, chopped
1 clove garlic, minced
Salt and freshly ground black pepper, to taste
1 tablespoon plus ¼ cup water
¾ pound boneless, skinless chicken breasts, cut into 2-inch slices

½ cup hickory barbecue sauce, divided
Vegetable oil cooking spray
Cornmeal and flour as needed
One 8-ounce ball pizza dough, at room temperature (see crust options, page 288)
2 tablespoons fresh cilantro, leaves only, finely chopped
½ cup grated Parmesan cheese

1 Preheat the oven to 450°F.

2 In a medium nonstick skillet, heat 1 teaspoon olive oil over medium heat. Sauté the leek, red onion, and garlic, stirring occasionally, for 3 minutes. Season with salt and pepper to taste and add 1 tablespoon of the water. Stir and scrape the bottom of the pan to incorporate the glaze and continue cooking for a minute or two, until the onion is wilted. Transfer the mixture to a bowl and return the pan to the heat.

3 Increase the heat to medium-high and deglaze with the remaining ¼ cup of water. Reduce by half and add the chicken to the pan. Sauté until both sides are slightly browned, turning occasionally. Stir in ¼ cup of the barbecue sauce and continue cooking, regulating the heat so the mixture does not scorch, until the chicken is cooked through with no trace of pink remaining, about 5 minutes. Remove from the heat.

4 Spray a baking sheet generously with vegetable oil spray and dust it lightly with cornmeal. On a lightly floured surface, roll out the pizza dough to a large circle about 12 inches in diameter, or rectangle that will fit on the baking sheet. Transfer the dough to the baking sheet and spread the remaining ¼ cup barbecue sauce evenly over the dough, leaving a ½-inch border. Top evenly with the leek mixture and then the chicken strips. Finally, sprinkle the cilantro and cheese on top. Bake for 20 to 25 minutes, or until the top is bubbling and the crust is golden brown.

PER SLICE					
CALORIES	320	CARBOHYDRATES (G)	32	CARBOHYDRATE CHOICES: 2	
FAT (G)	8	PROTEIN (G)	29	FOOD EXCHANGES PER SERVING: 2 STARCH,	
CALORIES FROM FAT (%)	24	FIBER (G)	3	2 VERY LEAN MEAT	
CHOLESTEROL (MG)	45	SODIUM (MG)	740	LOW-SODIUM DIETS: NOT ACCEPTABLE FOR	
				LOW-SODIUM DIETS	

LEMON PESTO SPAGHETTINI

MAKES 4 SERVINGS

This is a lighter version of the traditional pesto, but what it lacks in fat, it makes up for in flavor. The combination of fresh lemon and herbs with the pine nuts makes for a fresh, clean taste, and only a little is needed for a serving of pasta. With the Basic Green Salad (page 177), you've got an easy and fabulous meal.

8 ounces dried linguine
⅔ cup packed stemmed fresh parsley
1 ounce pine nuts (about 2
    tablespoons)
1 tablespoon ground dried marjoram

1 tablespoon grated lemon peel
1 tablespoon fresh lemon juice
3 tablespoons olive oil
Salt and fresh ground black pepper,
    to taste

1 Bring a large pot of water to a boil. Add the linguine and cook until just done, about 8 minutes.

2 While the pasta is cooking, blend the parsley, pine nuts, marjoram, lemon peel, and lemon juice in a blender or food processor until almost smooth. With the machine running, gradually add ¼ cup oil and process until smooth. If pesto is dry, mix in more oil by spoonfuls. Season to taste with salt and pepper.

3 Divide the pasta among 4 plates, and drizzle 2 tablespoons of the pesto over each serving. Serve immediately.

PER SERVING					
CALORIES	330	CARBOHYDRATES (G)	42	CARBOHYDRATE CHOICES: 3	
FAT (G)	15	PROTEIN (G)	9	FOOD EXCHANGES PER SERVING: 3 STARCH,	
CALORIES FROM FAT (%)	40	FIBER (G)	3	2 FAT	
CHOLESTEROL (MG)	0	SODIUM (MG)	5	LOW-SODIUM DIETS: ACCEPTABLE	

SPAGHETTINI POMODORO

MAKES 4 SERVINGS

This dish is on almost every menu in good Italian restaurants, and I often order an appetizer portion of it as my main course, as restaurant entrees are usually oversized and consequently have substantial calorie and carbohydrate counts.

1 tablespoon olive oil
3 medium shallots, finely chopped
Salt
8 ounces dried spaghettini or
    cappellini
3 ripe plum tomatoes, seeded and cut
    into ¼-inch dice

2 tablespoons capers, rinsed, drained,
    and patted dry
2 tablespoons finely chopped fresh
    basil or parsley, or 2 teaspoons
    dried
Freshly ground black pepper, to taste
1 tablespoon grated Parmesan cheese

1 In a large nonstick skillet, heat the olive oil over medium-low heat. Add the shallots and cook, stirring frequently, for about 5 minutes or until softened.

2 Bring a generous quantity of water to the boil in a large saucepan and add ½ teaspoon salt. Cook the pasta until al dente, according to the package directions.

3 While the pasta is cooking, add the tomatoes to the pan with the shallots and cook for about 3 minutes, until they have just started to break down. Add the capers and the basil or parsley and stir to combine. Taste for seasoning and add salt and pepper.

4 Drain the pasta thoroughly and serve 1 cup per person on heated dinner plates. Spoon the sauce over the top and sprinkle each serving with a little Parmesan.

PER 1½-CUP SERVING					
CALORIES	260	CARBOHYDRATES (G)	45	CARBOHYDRATE CHOICES: 3	
FAT (G)	5	PROTEIN (G)	8	FOOD EXCHANGES PER SERVING: 2½ STARCH,	
CALORIES FROM FAT (%)	17	FIBER (G)	3	1 VEGETABLE, ½ FAT	
CHOLESTEROL (MG)	0	SODIUM (MG)	200	LOW-SODIUM DIETS: ACCEPTABLE	

PENNE PASTA WITH PUTTANESCA SAUCE

MAKES 4 SERVINGS

I learned to make this southern Italian sauce from my friend Ann Albertine. It's rich and heavy with an intense fragrance. In fact, it's so flavorful, you don't need a large serving. If desired, you could garnish the dish with chopped fresh tomatoes, in addition to the basil. To prevent scorching when cooking thick sauces for a long time, always use heavy saucepans. Another solution is to use a large double boiler, or even better, bring the sauce to a boil on the top of the stove in an ovenproof pan, cover, and place in an oven preheated to 325° F, stirring occasionally. This temperature will sustain a low simmer and even cooking.

Sauce
1 tablespoon extra-virgin olive oil
1 medium onion, finely chopped
2 medium cloves garlic, finely chopped
½ teaspoon red pepper flakes, or to taste
1 tablespoon anchovy paste
2 tablespoons dry vermouth
1 tablespoon capers, rinsed and drained
¼ cup Kalamata or other oil-cured black olives, pitted (see Note) and chopped

½ (28-ounce) can crushed tomatoes, with their juice
2 tablespoons tomato paste
1 cup tomato sauce
Freshly ground black pepper, to taste
8 ounces dried penne pasta
1 tablespoon salt, for cooking the pasta
10 leaves fresh basil, cut into a chiffonade (see Note), for garnish

1 In a large nonreactive saucepan, heat the olive oil over medium heat. Sauté the onion for 4 to 5 minutes, until softened, then add the garlic and red pepper flakes and sauté for 2 minutes more. Stir in the anchovy paste, vermouth, capers, and olives and stir for 1 minute, then add the crushed tomatoes with their juice, tomato paste, and tomato sauce. Stir to mix thoroughly and bring the mixture to a boil. Reduce the heat to very low and simmer the sauce, partially covered, for 30 minutes. Add a little water if the sauce becomes too thick, and stir frequently to prevent it from scorching. Taste for seasoning and add black pepper to taste (you will probably not need to add salt to this dish, since the olives, capers, and anchovy paste are fairly salty on their own).

2 Just before you are ready to serve, bring a very generous amount of water to a rolling boil in a large saucepan and add the salt. Add the pasta and stir frequently for the first few minutes to prevent sticking. Simmer until al dente, according to package directions, reducing the heat a little if the water threatens to boil over. Drain well.

3 Immediately place the pasta in heated shallow bowls and ladle some sauce over the top. Garnish with the basil chiffonade and serve immediately.

Note: To pit olives, place an olive on the cutting board and press down on it with your thumb or the side of a large knife until the flesh separates from the pit. Leafy vegetables or herbs cut into fine shreds are called chiffonade and are often used as a garnish. To make chiffonade, stack 5 or 6 leaves of basil (or mint) together, roll them up into a cigar shape, and then slice them thinly, crosswise. Since basil will darken on contact with metal, it is best to do this just before serving.

PER 1-CUP SERVING WITH ¾ CUP SAUCE					
CALORIES	400	CARBOHYDRATES (G)	60	CARBOHYDRATE CHOICES: 4	
FAT (G)	11	PROTEIN (G)	11	FOOD EXCHANGES PER SERVING: 4 STARCH,	
CALORIES FROM FAT (%)	26	FIBER (G)	7	1½ FAT	
CHOLESTEROL (MG)	2.5	SODIUM (MG)	1050	LOW-SODIUM DIETS: NOT ACCEPTABLE	

ZESTY MARINARA SAUCE

This recipe is for those who like their pasta to pack a punch. For a smoother sauce, you may want to blend the finished sauce a final time in a food processor before serving. This is a great base for pizza as well. Note that this recipe takes 1½ hours to prepare, though it doesn't require close monitoring for a good portion of the cooking time.

1½ cups low-fat, low-sodium chicken broth
2 medium cloves garlic, sliced
½ carrot, peeled and grated
1 tablespoon olive oil
1 onion, finely chopped
Pinch of red pepper flakes
½ cup dry vermouth
1 (14-ounce) can crushed tomatoes, with their juice

2 tablespoons finely chopped fresh oregano, or 1 tablespoon dried oregano, crumbled
Salt and freshly ground black pepper, to taste
Sugar substitute or sugar to taste (optional)

1 In a food processor or blender, combine the chicken broth, garlic, and carrot and blend until smooth. Set aside.

2 In a large, heavy, nonreactive saucepan, heat the olive oil over medium heat. Add the onion and sauté until softened and almost translucent, about 5 minutes. Add the red pepper flakes and stir for 1 minute more.

3 Stir in the vermouth and bring up to a simmer. Let reduce, uncovered, for 5 minutes. Add the chicken broth–garlic mixture, the crushed tomatoes with their juice, and the oregano; bring to a boil. Reduce the heat until the mixture is simmering and partially cover the pan. Regulate the heat so that the liquid continues to simmer, and cook for 45 to 60 minutes, until the sauce has reduced and thickened.

4 Stir in the salt and pepper to taste. If sauce is too acidic, add a pinch of sugar. Serve over pasta or freeze in small containers for future use.

PER ½-CUP SERVING					
CALORIES	110	CARBOHYDRATES (G)	15	CARBOHYDRATE CHOICES: 1	
FAT (G)	3	PROTEIN (G)	4	FOOD EXCHANGES PER SERVING: 1 STARCH,	
CALORIES FROM FAT (%)	26	FIBER (G)	3	½ FAT	
CHOLESTEROL (MG)	LESS THAN 1	SODIUM (MG)	240	LOW-SODIUM DIETS: ACCEPTABLE	

LINGUINE WITH SHRIMP AND BROCCOLI

MAKES 4 SERVINGS

Shrimp, albeit high in cholesterol, is very low in fat, and therefore has a relatively lower effect on blood cholesterol. In this recipe the pasta and broccoli share center stage, so you can control your shrimp portion. Eating a food from the cabbage family at least three times a week is thought to aid in cancer prevention; you'll find the broccoli in this dish a great way to reach your goal.

2 cups broccoli florets
2 teaspoons olive oil
1 shallot, finely chopped
3 cloves garlic, finely chopped
¾ pound medium shrimp, shelled and deveined
½ cup dry white wine

½ cup low-fat, low-sodium chicken broth
Salt
8 ounces dried linguine
¼ cup finely chopped Italian parsley
Freshly ground black pepper, to taste

1 In a steamer over simmering water, cook the broccoli, uncovered, for 7 minutes, until tender but still bright green. Remove the steamer from the pan and set aside.

2 Bring a generous amount of water to a boil in a large saucepan for the pasta. Meanwhile, in a large nonstick skillet, heat the olive oil over medium-low heat. Add the shallot and stir occasionally for about 3 minutes or until softened. Add the garlic and cook for about 1 minute, until it has released its aroma. Increase the heat to medium-high and add the shrimp. Cook for about 2 minutes, tossing until pink.

3 Transfer the shrimp to a plate with a slotted spoon and add the wine and the chicken broth to the pan. Simmer the mixture for about 5 minutes, until slightly reduced. Meanwhile, add ½ teaspoon of salt to the boiling pasta-cooking water and cook the pasta until al dente, according to the package instructions.

4 Reduce the heat under the sauce; return the shrimp to the pan and add the broccoli and parsley. Stir together for a minute or two, just until heated through. Season with salt and pepper. Thoroughly drain the pasta and add it to the pan with the sauce. Toss the pasta until well coated; serve on heated dinner plates.

PER 1-CUP SERVING OF PASTA WITH ½ CUP BROCCOLI AND 3 TO 4 SHRIMP					
CALORIES	310	CARBOHYDRATES (G)	37	CARBOHYDRATE CHOICES: 2½	
FAT (G)	5	PROTEIN (G)	25	FOOD EXCHANGES PER SERVING: 2 STARCH,	
CALORIES FROM FAT (%)	16	FIBER (G)	3	3 VERY LEAN MEAT, 1 VEGETABLE	
CHOLESTEROL (MG)	130	SODIUM (MG)	260	LOW-SODIUM DIETS: OMIT SALT.	

LINGUINE WITH CLAM SAUCE

MAKES 6 SERVINGS

This dish is typically made with lots of butter or olive oil, but it's certainly not missed in this version, which relies on the clams, garlic, and red pepper flakes for a great flavor. Adjust the amount of red pepper flakes to your liking.

4 pounds littleneck clams, cleaned, or
    1 (6½-ounce) can clams
½ teaspoon salt
1 pound dried linguine
1 tablespoon olive oil
3 cloves garlic, finely chopped

½ teaspoon red pepper flakes
½ cup dry white wine
½ cup bottled clam juice
Freshly ground black pepper, to taste
¼ cup finely chopped parsley
6 lemon wedges, for serving

1 If you are using fresh clams, steam them in a large stockpot with an inch or so of water over medium heat until they open, then strain and reserve the juices and pull the meat from the shells. Coarsely chop the meat, combine the meat and juices in a bowl, and set aside. If using canned clams, chop the meat and combine with all the juices in a bowl.

2 Bring a generous amount of water to a boil in the same large stockpot and add the salt. Cook the linguine until al dente, according to the package instructions.

3 While the pasta is cooking, in a large heavy skillet, heat the olive oil over medium-low heat. Add the garlic and the red pepper flakes and stir for about 1 minute, until the garlic releases its aroma. Add the white wine and clam juice and increase the heat to medium-high. Simmer for 3 minutes, then add the clams with their juices, and the parsley. Add the pepper to taste and allow to return to a simmer.

4 Drain the pasta. Serve a generous ¾ cup of pasta per person on heated dinner plates. Spoon the sauce over and serve with lemon wedges.

PER 1½-CUP SERVING OF PASTA WITH SAUCE					
CALORIES	270	CARBOHYDRATES (G)	44	CARBOHYDRATE CHOICES: 3	
FAT (G)	4.5	PROTEIN (G)	12	FOOD EXCHANGES PER SERVING: 3 STARCH,	
CALORIES FROM FAT (%)	15	FIBER (G)	2	1 LEAN MEAT	
CHOLESTEROL (MG)	10	SODIUM (MG)	370	LOW-SODIUM DIETS: OMIT SALT AND USE LOW-SODIUM CLAM JUICE. IF YOU CAN'T FIND IT, SUBSTITUTE LOW-SODIUM CHICKEN BROTH. IF USING CANNED CLAMS, DRAIN AND RINSE BEFORE USING.	

BAKED STUFFED SHELLS WITH SPINACH-HERB FILLING

MAKES APPROXIMATELY 14 SHELLS

This delicious casserole can be made easily a day or two in advance, making it ideal for dinner parties. For a shortcut, buy bottled marinara sauce and doctor it up with a bit of wine and/or Italian seasonings. The aroma of this dish will turn your kitchen into an Italian cucina.

1 (8-ounce) box manicotti shells (about 14 shells)
1 (15-ounce) container low-fat ricotta cheese
Whites of 2 large eggs
1 cup drained thawed frozen spinach, or 2 cups fresh
1 cup grated peeled carrot
1 small onion, finely chopped

1 tablespoon chopped fresh basil, or 1 teaspoon dried
1 tablespoon minced fresh thyme, or 1 teaspoon dried
3 cups Zesty Marinara Sauce (page 298)
½ cup part-skim (or fat-free) mozzarella cheese

1 Preheat the oven to 350° F. Bring a large saucepan bring of water to a boil and cook the shells for 3 minutes. Drain, rinse with cold water, and put them in a bowl of room-temperature water. Set aside.

2 In a bowl, combine the ricotta with the egg whites, spinach, carrot, onion, basil, and thyme. Mix together well.

3 In a 9 × 14-inch baking dish, place about ½ cup of the marinara sauce, enough to cover the bottom. Drain the manicotti shells. Stuff each shell with the filling and place in the baking dish. Spoon over the remaining sauce. Cover with foil and bake for 45 to 50 minutes, until the shells are fully cooked and the sauce is bubbling.

4 Ten minutes before the dish is done, remove the pan from oven and uncover, sprinkle evenly with the mozzarella and return to oven for 10 minutes more, until the cheese is melted and slightly golden. Let rest for 5 minutes before serving.

PER 2 SHELLS					
CALORIES	320	CARBOHYDRATES (G)	41	CARBOHYDRATE CHOICES: 3	
FAT (G)	10	PROTEIN (G)	18	FOOD EXCHANGES PER SERVING: 3 STARCH,	
CALORIES FROM FAT (%)	28	FIBER (G)	4	1 MEDIUM-FAT MEAT	
CHOLESTEROL (MG)	25	SODIUM (MG)	540	LOW-SODIUM DIETS: USE REDUCED-SODIUM CHEESE	
				AND SALT-FREE MARINARA SAUCE. NOT ACCEPTABLE	
				FOR 500 TO 1000 MG SODIUM DIETS.	

PASTA PRIMAVERA WITH CHICKEN, MUSHROOMS, PEPPERS, AND BROCCOLI

MAKES 6 SERVINGS

A classic pasta primavera consists of slightly undercooked, or al dente, vegetables in a light cream sauce. Here I've substituted chicken broth for the cream, and thickened it with cornstarch instead of making a cream-based sauce. By "diluting" the pasta with vegetables, I've reduced the total carbohydrate and calorie content. That's because vegetables are 25 to 50 calories per cup and pasta is closer to 200 calories per cup. For added flavor, substitute shiitake mushrooms for the white mushrooms.

3 cups broccoli florets
2 teaspoons olive oil
1 small onion, chopped
1 clove garlic, diced
2 skinless, boneless chicken breasts, about 4 ounces each
2 cups whole small white mushrooms
¼ cup dry white wine

1 cup low-fat, low-sodium chicken broth, whisked together with 1 tablespoon cornstarch
8 ounces dried vermicelli pasta
½ cup Parmesan cheese
¼ cup chopped fresh basil
1 small red bell pepper, cored, seeded, and diced

1 In a steamer basket set over simmering water, steam the broccoli florets until crisp-tender and still bright green, about 8 minutes. Remove the steamer from the pan and rinse briefly under cold running water to stop the cooking. Shake dry and set aside.

2 Heat a large nonstick skillet over medium-high heat and add the olive oil. Sauté the onion for 3 to 4 minutes, stirring frequently, until the onion is softened and slightly golden. Add the garlic and cook for about 30 seconds more, until the aroma of the garlic is released. Add the chicken breasts and the mushrooms to the pan and sauté until chicken breasts are done through with no trace of pink remaining, 5 to 6 minutes on each side.

3 With a slotted spoon, transfer the chicken and mushrooms to a plate and keep warm, covered with aluminum foil. Add the wine to the pan and deglaze, stirring up all the browned and flavorful bits from the bottom and sides of the pan.

4 Add the chicken broth/cornstarch mixture to the pan and bring to a boil, stirring occasionally. Reduce the heat and simmer the sauce, stirring constantly, until thickened, about 3 to 5 minutes.

5 Meanwhile, bring a large saucepan full of lightly salted water to a boil. Cook the vermicelli until tender, 8 to 10 minutes or according to package directions. Drain well. Slice the chicken breasts across the grain into ½-inch strips and return to the pan with the sauce just long enough to heat through.

6 Add the pasta and broccoli to the chicken mixture. Toss and heat. Add Parmesan, and fresh basil and combine thoroughly. Transfer to a large heated serving bowl and garnish with the diced red bell pepper. Serve immediately.

PER 1-CUP SERVING						
	BEFORE	AFTER				
CALORIES	380	260	CARBOHYDRATES (G)	31	CARBOHYDRATE CHOICES: 2	
FAT (G)	4.5	6	PROTEIN (G)	20	FOOD EXCHANGES PER SERVING: 2 STARCH,	
CALORIES FROM FAT (%)	45	21	FIBER (G)	5	2 LEAN MEAT	
CHOLESTEROL (MG)	65	30	SODIUM (MG)	270	LOW-SODIUM DIETS: THIS RECIPE IS EXCELLENT.	

COLD SESAME NOODLES

MAKES 4 SERVINGS

This recipe came from my friend Eileen from Hong Kong, who keeps this Asian-influenced dish on hand in the refrigerator for her teenaged boys to snack on after school. She also serves it as an accompaniment to her steamed fish dinners. It is very quick and simple to make, and can be served hot or cold. The fat is reduced by replacing some of the oil with chicken broth.

8 ounces dried linguine
1 tablespoon sesame oil
2 tablespoons low-sodium soy sauce
1 tablespoon red wine vinegar
¼ cup low-fat, low-sodium chicken broth
Sugar substitute equivalent to 2¼ teaspoons sugar (see Note)
½ teaspoon red pepper flakes

1 tablespoon finely chopped fresh cilantro
1 red bell pepper, cored, seeded, and diced
4 green onions (scallions), white and light green parts only, thinly sliced
Additional chopped cilantro, for garnish

1 In a large saucepan of lightly salted boiling water, cook the noodles until tender but still firm to the bite. Drain well, rinse under cold running water to cool, and again drain well. If serving hot, rinse with hot water. Transfer to a serving bowl and set aside.

2 In a blender or food processor, combine the sesame oil, soy sauce, vinegar, chicken broth, sugar, red pepper flakes, and cilantro. Puree until well combined, then add to the noodles and toss together gently.

3 Add the red pepper and green onions and toss again. Serve chilled or at room temperature, sprinkled with chopped cilantro.

Note: Using real sugar instead of sugar substitute increases the carbohydrate level by 2 grams, an insignificant amount.

PER 1-CUP SERVING					
CALORIES	240	CARBOHYDRATES (G)	43	CARBOHYDRATE CHOICES: 3	
FAT (G)	4.5	PROTEIN (G)	8	FOOD EXCHANGES PER SERVING: 3 STARCH	
CALORIES FROM FAT (%)	17	FIBER (G)	3	LOW-SODIUM DIETS: DECREASE SOY SAUCE	
CHOLESTEROL (MG)	0	SODIUM (MG)	260	BY HALF.	

CHAPTER 21

SANDWICHES AND TORTILLA STUFFERS

A sandwich served with salad or fruit makes an ideal lunch or light dinner. However, when ordered out, they can vary tremendously in fat and calorie content. Nowhere is it more true that America's portion sizes are on the rise than with this bread-meat construction. Still, by design, sandwiches provide a perfect fix for good blood glucose control, as long as the bread, protein filling, and condiments are there in the right proportion.

I've done some tinkering in the kitchen to come up with some great-tasting sandwich combinations that fit into a day's diet, and you'll find some new ideas here to add variety to your repertoire. Leaner versions of old favorites include Chicken Salad and Tuna Salad. The cucumber salad served with bagel and lox will become a staple. If it's vegetarian you want, try the Avocado, Pimiento, and Swiss Cheese, Zucchini and Tomato, Two-Bean Burrito, or the Grilled Portobello Burger. And for a special occasion, the Tea Sandwiches are a wonderful treat. The possibilities are endless and these recipes will give you a good jumping-off point.

GRILLED TURKEY BURGERS

MAKES 4 BURGERS

I created these tasty burgers when I was throwing a Sunday afternoon Superbowl party, and they were a big hit. Because poultry burgers have a tendency to fall apart during cooking, it is best to form them into thick patties and cook them in a dry nonstick pan, adding water as necessary to keep them from burning. If you want to grill them, use a grill rack with round holes.

1 pound extra-lean ground turkey
¼ small red onion, finely chopped
1 clove garlic, finely chopped
2 tablespoons finely chopped red bell pepper
1 tablespoon capers, rinsed, drained, and chopped
½ teaspoon salt
¼ teaspoon freshly ground black pepper

Small pinch cayenne pepper, or to taste
4 poppy-seed Kaiser rolls, or rolls of your choice, split
1 tablespoon Dijon-style mustard
2 cups chopped firm lettuce, such as iceberg
2 large, ripe plum tomatoes, sliced

1 In a bowl, combine the ground turkey, red onion, garlic, red pepper, capers, salt, black pepper, and cayenne. Toss together with your hands until thoroughly combined, then form into 4 equal balls.

2 Heat a large nonstick skillet over medium-high heat. Cook the burgers, using a plastic spatula to turn them, for about 8 to10 minutes on each side, or until no trace of pink remains in the center. While the burgers are cooking, toast the Kaiser rolls until golden.

3 Spread each roll thinly with the mustard and place each burger on a bun. Top with lettuce, tomato slices, and the top of the bun and serve immediately.

PER SERVING				
CALORIES	310	CARBOHYDRATES (G)	39	CARBOHYDRATE CHOICES: 2½
FAT (G)	7	PROTEIN (G)	23	FOOD EXCHANGES PER SERVING: 2½ STARCH,
CALORIES FROM FAT (%)	15	FIBER (G)	3	2 LEAN MEAT
CHOLESTEROL (MG)	97	SODIUM (MG)	850	LOW-SODIUM DIETS: OMIT SALT AND CAPERS,
				DECREASE MUSTARD, INCREASE CAYENNE
				PEPPER, AND ADD GARLIC.

GRILLED PORTOBELLO BURGERS

MAKES 4 SANDWICHES

The rich, nutty flavor, made even more intense by barbecuing, and the dense texture of the portobello mushroom make it ideal for an all-vegetable sandwich. This is a deceptively "meaty" sandwich, and best right off the grill.

1 tablespoon extra-virgin olive oil
¼ cup low-fat, low-sodium chicken broth
1 tablespoon finely chopped garlic
Salt and freshly ground black pepper, to taste
2 medium portobello mushrooms, wiped clean and stems trimmed

1 red bell pepper, cored, seeded, and quartered
1 red onion, sliced ¼ inch thick
4 hamburger buns, split
¼ cup Roasted Garlic Sour Cream (page 214)
1 medium tomato, sliced

1 Whisk together the olive oil, chicken broth, garlic, and salt and pepper to taste. With a sharp knife, score the tops of the mushrooms in a shallow crisscross pattern.

2 Either prepare an outdoor grill for indirect-heat cooking, or preheat the oven to 500° F. Brush the mushrooms, red pepper pieces, and onion with the oil mixture and place them on the grill away from the direct heat, or in a roasting pan in the oven. Grill the vegetables, basting and turning them often, about 3 minutes for the onion, 5 to 6 minutes for the mushrooms, and 8 minutes for the red bell pepper, until softened and slightly charred on the edges. If baking, double the cooking times for each. Be careful they do not burn or dry out.

3 While the vegetables are grilling, toast the buns over the direct heat, cut side down, until golden. Spread both cut sides with Roasted Garlic Sour Cream. Slice the mushrooms into thin strips and layer an equal quantity of the grilled mushrooms, pepper, and onion on the bottom side of each bun. Top with two slices of tomato and the other half of the bun, and serve.

PER SANDWICH					
CALORIES	220	CARBOHYDRATES (G)	35	CARBOHYDRATE CHOICES: 2	
FAT (G)	6	PROTEIN (G)	7	FOOD EXCHANGES PER SERVING: 2 STARCH,	
CALORIES FROM FAT (%)	26	FIBER (G)	4	1 VEGETABLE, 1 FAT	
CHOLESTEROL (MG)	0	SODIUM (MG)	370	LOW-SODIUM DIETS: OMIT SALT.	

CHICKEN SALAD SANDWICH

MAKES 4 SANDWICHES

This is a flavorful and versatile version of the chicken salad sandwich—flavorful in that it boasts crunchy vegetables and tangy dressing, and versatile in that it can be altered to suit individual tastes quite easily. You can substitute canned tuna for the chicken, or use barbecue sauce instead of mustard for a smokier flavor. This can be made one day in advance.

Dressing (see Note)
¼ cup fat-free sour cream
¼ cup fat-free mayonnaise
1½ teaspoons whole-grain mustard
1½ teaspoons Dijon mustard
1 teaspoon fresh lemon juice
Sugar substitute equivalent to
    ½ teaspoon sugar (see Note)
Salt and black pepper, to taste

4 boneless, skinless chicken breasts,
    about 1 pound, poached and
    cubed
¼ cup finely chopped white onion
¼ cup finely chopped red onion
¼ cup coarsely chopped celery
3 tablespoons finely chopped parsley
8 slices whole wheat bread
4 whole lettuce leaves, such as
    romaine or butter

1 To make the dressing: In a medium bowl, whisk together the sour cream, mayonnaise, both mustards, lemon juice, sugar, and salt and black pepper to taste.

2 In a large bowl, combine the chicken with the white and red onion, celery, and parsley. Add the dressing and mix until all the ingredients are well coated.

3 Set out the bread and divide the salad evenly between 4 slices. Top with lettuce leaf and another bread slice. Serve immediately.

Note: Using regular sugar rather than sugar substitute increases carbohydrate content by less than ½ gram, an insignificant amount. All-Purpose Dressing (½ cup, page 206) may be used in place of this Dressing.

PER SANDWICH					
CALORIES	340	CARBOHYDRATES (G)	40	CARBOHYDRATE CHOICES: 2½	
FAT (G)	5	PROTEIN (G)	35	FOOD EXCHANGES PER SERVING: 4 LEAN MEAT,	
CALORIES FROM FAT (%)	13	FIBER (G)	5	2½ STARCH	
CHOLESTEROL (MG)	65	SODIUM (MG)	660	LOW-SODIUM DIETS: OMIT MUSTARD.	
				THOSE ON 500 OR 1000 MG SODIUM DIETS	
				SHOULD USE LOW-SODIUM BREAD.	

BAGEL WITH CREAM CHEESE, SALMON, AND CUCUMBER SALAD

MAKES 4 BAGEL SANDWICHES

This is a gourmet twist on the standard lox and bagels, and is an excellent brunch item. Furthermore, if you replace the bagels with thinly sliced bread toasts with the crusts cut off, you have a wonderful addition to your appetizer tray or tea sandwich selection.

4 bagels, halved
6 ounces fat-free cream cheese
8 ounces sliced smoked salmon

1 cup Chopped Cucumber Salad
(page 184)
Lemon wedges, for serving (optional)

1 Preheat the oven to 350°F or heat a broiler or toaster oven. Toast the bagels until golden (if done in batches, keep them warm in a napkin-lined basket).

2 Spread a thin layer of cream cheese on the cut sides of each bagel half, using ¾ ounce cream cheese for each bagel. Arrange 1 slice of salmon on each halved bagel. Mound ¼ cup of cucumber salad on each and serve at once. Accompany each with a wedge of lemon.

PER SANDWICH						
CALORIES	160	CARBOHYDRATES (G)	23	CARBOHYDRATE CHOICES: 1½		
FAT (G)	2	PROTEIN (G)	13	FOOD EXCHANGES PER SERVING: 1 STARCH,		
CALORIES FROM FAT (%)	10	FIBER (G)	2	1 LEAN MEAT, 1 VEGETABLE		
CHOLESTEROL (MG)	10	SODIUM (MG)	590	LOW-SODIUM DIETS: SUBSTITUTE FRESH COOKED		
				SALMON, TURKEY, OR CHICKEN.		

TUNA SALAD SANDWICH

MAKES 2 SANDWICHES

You may be thinking, who needs a recipe for tuna sandwiches? But I have modified these old standby recipes to save on fat and calories without scrimping on flavor and nutritional quality. The carrots, celery, onion, and capers add texture (crunch), flavor (onion-celery-caper), and color (orange).

1 (6½-ounce) can water-packed tuna, well drained
2 tablespoons fat-free mayonnaise or All-Purpose Dressing (page 206)
¼ cup finely chopped celery
1 green onion (scallion), white and light green parts only, finely chopped
1 tablespoon capers, rinsed, patted dry, and finely chopped
¼ cup finely chopped peeled carrots
Freshly ground black pepper, to taste
1 plum tomato, sliced
¼ cup (or about 6) loosely packed baby lettuce leaves
4 slices whole wheat bread

1 In a mixing bowl, combine the tuna and mayonnaise. Mix with a fork until the tuna is flaked and evenly blended with the mayonnaise.

2 Add the celery, green onion, capers, carrots, and pepper and mix together.

3 Spread an equal amount of the salad onto 2 slices of the bread. Top with the sliced tomato and lettuce leaves, then cover with the remaining slices of bread.

4 Press the sandwich down gently with the palm of your hand and cut in half on the diagonal. Serve at once.

PER SANDWICH					
	BEFORE	AFTER			
CALORIES	430	340	CARBOHYDRATES (G)	41	CARBOHYDRATE CHOICES: 3
FAT (G)	17	6	PROTEIN (G)	33	FOOD EXCHANGES PER SERVING: 3 STARCH,
CALORIES FROM FAT (%)	34	14	FIBER (G)	7	3 VERY LEAN MEAT
CHOLESTEROL (MG)	45	40	SODIUM (MG)	1010	LOW-SODIUM DIETS: OMIT CAPERS; USE
					"NO-SALT-ADDED" TUNA.

CHICKEN TACO

This recipe is basically a guideline for using leftover chicken. I cut calories, fat, and cholesterol by using light meat instead of dark, nonfat sour cream, and no cheddar cheese. Enjoy one or two of these for lunch, depending on your carbohydrate allowance. It also works great with leftover fish—just add shredded cabbage and a squeeze of lemon. With lean beef, add lime juice and Chipotle Mayonnaise (page 210) in place of tomato, salsa, and sour cream.

1 corn tortilla
1 cooked chicken breast, skin and bones removed, shredded, about 4 ounces
1 plum tomato, seeded and diced
⅛ avocado

1 green onion (scallion), white and light green parts only, finely chopped
2 tablespoons salsa
2 tablespoons nonfat sour cream
2 teaspoons finely chopped cilantro

1 In a dry nonstick skillet, heat the tortilla for about 30 to 45 seconds, or 15 to 20 seconds in a microwave, just until warm and pliable.

2 Mound the chicken, tomato, avocado, green onion, salsa, sour cream, and cilantro in the center and roll up into a cylinder, keeping the filling inside. Serve immediately.

PER TACO						
	BEFORE	AFTER				
CALORIES	550	270	CARBOHYDRATES (G)	24	CARBOHYDRATE CHOICES: 1½	
FAT (G)	33	6	PROTEIN (G)	31	FOOD EXCHANGES PER SERVING: 1½ STARCH,	
CALORIES FROM FAT (%)	50	20	FIBER (G)	4	4 VERY LEAN MEAT	
CHOLESTEROL (MG)	160	65	SODIUM (MG)	260	LOW-SODIUM DIETS: CHOOSE SALSA WITHOUT SALT.	

FISH TACO WITH CABBAGE

MAKES 4 SERVINGS

Most fish tacos purchased at Mexican restaurants are breaded and deep-fried, and consequently much higher in fat than these. If you have some leftover fish from last night's dinner, this is a perfect dish—just proceed to step 2.

1 tablespoon fresh lemon juice
¼ teaspoon chili powder
1 cup low-fat, low-sodium chicken broth
½ pound firm white fish fillets, such as snapper or sea bass
1 cup water, or as needed
Salt and freshly ground black pepper
4 soft corn tortillas

Garnishes
1 cup finely shredded white cabbage
Juice of 1 lime
4 tablespoons bottled salsa
2 tablespoons finely chopped fresh cilantro or parsley
2 tablespoons nonfat yogurt or nonfat sour cream

1 In a medium saucepan, combine the lemon juice, chili powder, chicken broth, and the fish fillets. Add enough water so that the fish is covered by ½ inch of liquid. Over medium-high heat, bring the liquid to a simmer, partially cover the pan, and cook the fish, regulating the heat so the liquid just barely simmers. Depending on the thickness of the fish, it should take between 8 to 10 minutes to cook. When the fish is flaky, remove from the pan with a spatula and drain. Season with a little salt and pepper.

2 Warm the corn tortillas, wrapped in aluminum foil, in a low oven. Flake the fish with a fork, and assemble all the garnishes. Place a tortilla on each warmed dinner plate. Place an equal quantity of flaked fish and cabbage on each one and squeeze a little lime juice over the top. Top with some salsa, cilantro, and a small dollop of yogurt, fold or roll the tacos, and serve immediately. Alternately, you may pass the garnishes and let each diner fix his or her own taco.

PER TACO	BEFORE	AFTER			
CALORIES	230	130	CARBOHYDRATES (G)	13	CARBOHYDRATE CHOICES: 1
FAT (G)	11	2	PROTEIN (G)	14	FOOD EXCHANGES PER SERVING: 1 STARCH,
CALORIES FROM FAT (%)	43	13	FIBER (G)	1	1 LEAN MEAT
CHOLESTEROL (MG)	50	20	SODIUM (MG)	240	LOW-SODIUM DIETS: OMIT SALT; USE SALT-FREE
					SALSA OR FRESH SLICED TOMATOES.

TWO-BEAN BURRITO

MAKES 1 BURRITO

Tortillas vary in size and in fat content. Choose those that are made without lard, and count each ounce as a bread exchange. If you are not using a microwave, heat the beans in a small saucepan until just bubbling and warm the tortillas in a nonstick skillet before assembling.

1 flour tortilla
1½ ounces (¼ cup) canned pinto
    beans or Refried Pinto Beans
    (page 322)
1½ ounces (¼ cup) canned black
    beans or Chipotle Black Beans
    (page 323)
1 plum tomato, seeded and diced

1 tablespoon chopped red onion
1 tablespoon shredded iceberg lettuce
1 tablespoon grated low-fat cheese
1 tablespoon nonfat sour cream
1 tablespoon salsa
1 teaspoon finely chopped fresh
    cilantro

1 Place the tortilla on a work surface and combine the beans in the center. Top the beans with the tomato, onion, lettuce, cheese, sour cream, salsa, and cilantro.

2 Roll the tortilla into a cylinder shape and wrap snugly with plastic wrap. Microwave on high for 1 to 2 minutes until warm, and serve.

PER BURRITO					
CALORIES	240	CARBOHYDRATES (G)	39	CARBOHYDRATE CHOICES: 3	
FAT (G)	4.5	PROTEIN (G)	11	FOOD EXCHANGES PER SERVING: 2½ STARCH,	
CALORIES FROM FAT (%)	16	FIBER (G)	6	1 LEAN MEAT	
CHOLESTEROL (MG) LESS THAN 5		SODIUM (MG)	700	LOW-SODIUM DIETS: OMIT SALT; USE HOMEMADE	
				SALSA WITHOUT SALT.	

AVOCADO, PIMIENTO, AND SWISS CHEESE SANDWICH

MAKES 1 SANDWICH

Just a small slice of avocado adds the flavor and texture avocado lovers love, with only 4 to 5 grams of fat, which, by the way, is mostly monounsaturated, the kind that's in olive oil. Along with all the other vegetables, it makes a hearty and delicious sandwich.

2 slices whole wheat bread

1 teaspoon Dijon-style mustard

1/8 ripe avocado, peeled and thinly sliced

1 ounce reduced-fat Swiss cheese, thinly sliced

2-inch square bottled pimiento, patted dry and cut into strips

1 very thin slice red onion, or to taste

3 very thin slices green bell pepper

1-inch length peeled and seeded cucumber, thinly sliced

1 teaspoon finely chopped fresh basil, cilantro, or mint

1 Lay both slices of the bread on the work surface and spread each one with the mustard.

2 Layer the ingredients on one slice of bread in the order given, first the avocado, then the cheese, pimiento, onion, green pepper, and cucumber; then sprinkle with the herbs and top with the remaining slice of bread. Press down gently on the top of the sandwich with the palm of your hand to compact, then slice in half on the diagonal and serve.

PER SANDWICH				
CALORIES	280	CARBOHYDRATES (G)	42	CARBOHYDRATE CHOICES: 3
FAT (G)	7	PROTEIN (G)	15	FOOD EXCHANGES PER SERVING: 3 STARCH,
CALORIES FROM FAT (%)	25	FIBER (G)	7	2 LEAN MEAT
CHOLESTEROL (MG)	0	SODIUM (MG)	875	LOW-SODIUM DIETS: SUBSTITUTE ROASTED
				RED BELL PEPPER FOR PIMIENTO; OMIT
				MUSTARD OR USE LOW-SODIUM TYPE.
				FOR 500 TO 1000 MG SODIUM DIET, USE
				LOW-SODIUM CHEESE.

WARM ZUCCHINI, TOMATO, AND CHEESE SANDWICHES

MAKES 4 SANDWICHES

This colorful recipe has "star" quality, as it was part of the healthy holiday buffets menu I prepared on a TV cooking segment. Since a loaf of French bread can vary from 8 ounces to 1 pound, make sure you count your carbohydrates based on the actual weight of your serving of bread.

1 teaspoon olive oil
1 medium onion, coarsely chopped
1 clove garlic, finely chopped
2 cups diced zucchini
1 green bell pepper, cored, seeded, and coarsely chopped
1 red bell pepper, cored, seeded, and coarsely chopped

3 ounces smoked mozzarella cheese, cut into ½-inch dice (½ cup)
2 tablespoons chopped fresh basil
1 long loaf French or sourdough bread (about 14 ounces), halved lengthwise

1 Preheat the oven to 425°F. In a large nonstick skillet, heat the olive oil over medium heat. Add the onion and sauté, stirring occasionally, for about 5 minutes or until softened. Add the garlic, cook for 1 minute, then add the zucchini and the green and red bell peppers.

2 Sauté the vegetables together, stirring, until they are all tender, about 8 minutes more. Remove the pan from the heat and stir in the mozzarella and the basil. Let sit for 3 minutes, to allow the mozzarella to soften.

3 Pack the filling onto the lower layer of bread and top firmly with the top half of the loaf. Wrap the loaf snugly in aluminum foil and bake for 15 minutes. Cool for 10 minutes, then unwrap and slice into 4 sections for serving.

PER SANDWICH					
CALORIES	370	CARBOHYDRATES (G)	57	**CARBOHYDRATE CHOICES: 4**	
FAT (G)	8	PROTEIN (G)	15	FOOD EXCHANGES PER SERVING: 3 STARCH,	
CALORIES FROM FAT (%)	20	FIBER (G)	5	2 VEGETABLE, 1 MEDIUM-FAT MEAT	
CHOLESTEROL (MG)	10	SODIUM (MG)	680	LOW-SODIUM DIETS: USE A LOW-SODIUM	
				CHEESE, OR DECREASE OR OMIT CHEESE. IF	
				ON A 500 OR 1000 MG SODIUM DIET, USE	
				LOW-SODIUM BREAD, AS 3 OUNCES OF	
				REGULAR BREAD CONTRIBUTES AROUND	
				500 MG SODIUM.	

TEA SANDWICHES

MAKES 50 SANDWICHES

These recipes are intended to serve as a guide in making tea sandwiches. There are infinitesimal variations, but these are a few of the standards, and they can be built upon in any manner suitable. These are great for cocktail parties or "high tea" with some close friends. Note that these recipes can be made in smaller batches by halving them.

WATERCRESS, TOMATO, AND CREAM CHEESE (makes about ½ cup spread, enough for 10 sandwiches)

1 bunch watercress leaves and tender stems, washed and finely chopped
½ cup fat free whipped cream cheese
Salt and freshly ground black pepper, to taste

20 Bread Squares (recipe opposite)
2 medium plum tomatoes, thinly sliced (5 slices per tomato)

Combine the watercress, cream cheese, and salt and pepper in a medium bowl. When ready to serve, spread a tablespoon of the watercress mixture on each of ten bread squares. Top with a tomato slice and a second bread square and serve immediately.

CUCUMBER AND DILL (makes 20 open-faced sandwiches)

2 teaspoons chopped fresh dill or 1 teaspoon dried, or to taste
3 tablespoons fat-free mayonnaise
20 Bread Squares (recipe opposite)

1 medium cucumber, peeled, halved, seeded, and very thinly sliced
Kosher salt and chives, for garnish

Combine the dill and mayonnaise in a small bowl, then spread a ½ teaspoon of the dill-mayonnaise mixture on each of 20 bread squares. Top each bread square with 4 half slices of cucumber, then sprinkle with a few grains of kosher salt and garnish with chives. Serve immediately.

CRAB SALAD (makes 20 open-faced sandwiches)

½ pound crabmeat, picked over well
¼ cup fat-free mayonnaise
2 tablespoons finely chopped Italian parsley, plus extra for garnish, if desired
1 tablespoon finely chopped chives
1 teaspoon fresh lemon juice

1 teaspoon Worcestershire sauce
¼ cup finely minced red onion
Black pepper to taste
¼ ripe avocado, peeled and finely chopped
20 Bread Squares (recipe follows), toasted

Combine the crabmeat, mayonnaise, parsley, chives, lemon juice, Worcestershire sauce, onion, and pepper and mix well. Carefully fold in the avocado. Spread 1 tablespoon of the crab mixture on each of 20 toasted bread squares. Sprinkle with extra chopped Italian parsley for garnish. Serve immediately.

BREAD SQUARES (makes 56 small squares)

14 large square slices of bread (wheat, pumpernickel, or sourdough)

Remove crusts and cut into 4 equal quarters. (If you prefer rounds, simply use a round cookie cutter, a cup, or a lid, and cut out circles from each piece of bread.) If desired, toast lightly just before assembling the sandwiches.

PER WATERCRESS, TOMATO, AND CREAM CHEESE SANDWICH

CALORIES	45	CARBOHYDRATES (G)	8	CARBOHYDRATE CHOICES: ½	
FAT (G)	LESS THAN .5	PROTEIN (G)	2	FOOD EXCHANGES PER SERVING: ½ STARCH	
CALORIES FROM FAT (%)	9	FIBER (G)	LESS THAN 1	LOW-SODIUM DIETS: OMIT SALT.	
CHOLESTEROL (MG)	0	SODIUM (MG)	105		

PER CUCUMBER AND DILL SANDWICH

CALORIES	30	CARBOHYDRATES (G)	5	CARBOHYDRATE CHOICES: 0	
FAT (G)	LESS THAN .5	PROTEIN (G)	LESS THAN 1	FOOD EXCHANGES PER SERVING: ½ STARCH	
CALORIES FROM FAT (%)	9	FIBER (G)	0	LOW-SODIUM DIETS: OMIT SALT.	
CHOLESTEROL (MG)	0	SODIUM (MG)	75		

PER CRAB SALAD SANDWICH

CALORIES	35	CARBOHYDRATES (G)	4	CARBOHYDRATE CHOICES: 0	
FAT (G)	.5	PROTEIN (G)	3	FOOD EXCHANGES PER SERVING: ½ STARCH	
CALORIES FROM FAT (%)	18	FIBER (G)	0	LOW-SODIUM DIETS: OMIT SALT.	
CHOLESTEROL (MG)	10	SODIUM (MG)	105		

CHAPTER 22

MAIN DISHES WITH BEANS

No doubt about it, beans are a healthful addition to any diet, particularly those who are moving toward a vegetarian style of eating. The high-fiber, low-fat bean is high in carbohydrates and contains a respectable amount of protein. Beans can help limit protein. Just be aware that plant sources of protein are high in carbohydrates. For example, ½ cup beans, lentils, or red beans = 21 grams carbohydrates. The higher carbohydrate nature of a vegetarian diet may cause problems with high blood sugar if portions are large. The added fiber will offset this somewhat.

By using "good for you" ingredients in place of high-fat ones, I've trimmed the fat but not the flavor from two Mexican standards. "Refried" Pinto beans are fried in a small amount of oil rather than large amounts of lard, and the remaining liquid comes from buttermilk, adding a tangy flavor. Black beans are seasoned with chipotle chili instead of ham or sausage. For a new twist on a bean salad, try the Marinated White Bean Salad. It's always a hit at dinner parties, even among those who didn't think they liked bean salad.

SUCCOTASH

MAKES 4 TO 5 SERVINGS

I love this dish because it's so versatile. You can work with whatever vegetables and herbs you have on hand, including frozen vegetables. I serve it with fish or as a main dish, always reserving a bit to pack in my next day's lunch. I'm a big fan of making enough to have leftovers!

1 teaspoon olive oil
1 small onion, chopped
1 clove garlic, minced
1 red or green bell pepper, cored,
   seeded, and minced
Pinch of salt
Pinch of black pepper

1 cup frozen corn, thawed
1 cup lima beans or finely shredded
   green beans
2 ounces okra, fresh or frozen and
   defrosted, trimmed and cut up
2/3 cup water

1 Heat oil in a heavy saucepan. Add onion, garlic, bell pepper, salt, and pepper and sauté until tender, about 5 minutes. Add a little water if needed to prevent sticking.

2 Add the corn, lima beans or green beans, okra, and water and simmer, covered, until tender, about 8 minutes. Remove lid and continue to simmer until liquid has evaporated, about 2 to 3 minutes.

PER 1/2-CUP SERVING					
CALORIES	75	CARBOHYDRATES (G)	15	CARBOHYDRATE CHOICES: 1	
FAT (G)	1	PROTEIN (G)	3	FOOD EXCHANGES PER SERVING: 1 STARCH	
CALORIES FROM FAT (%)	12	FIBER (G)	3	LOW-SODIUM DIETS: EXCELLENT CHOICE	
CHOLESTEROL (MG)	0	SODIUM (MG)	95		

MARINATED WHITE BEAN SALAD

MAKES 12 SERVINGS

Beans are a perfect solution to the American diet dilemma of getting enough protein without excess fat. They're especially good for diabetic diets because they provide complex carbohydrates with no fat. This is a great lunch choice—just adjust the serving size according to your carbohydrate or starch exchange goal. This salad keeps for several days and the flavor improves over time. I like to make this in large batches and pack it in my lunch throughout the week, but the recipe can be easily cut in half.

½ pound white beans (navy or lima), rinsed and soaked overnight in water to cover
Salt
1 tablespoon olive oil
1 cup finely chopped white onions
½ red bell pepper, cored, seeded, and diced (about ½ cup)

½ cup currants, soaked for 10 minutes in hot water and drained
½ cup white wine vinegar
1½ tablespoons fresh thyme leaves, chopped, or 3½ teaspoons dried thyme, crumbled
Freshly ground black pepper, to taste

1 Drain the beans and place them in a large heavy saucepan. Add enough fresh water to cover the beans by about 2 inches. Bring to a simmer, cover the pan, and cook for 30 minutes. Add 2 tablespoons salt and cook for about 1 hour more, until tender but not mushy. Drain and set aside.

2 In a large, heavy nonstick skillet, heat the olive oil over medium heat. Add the onions and sauté for about 5 minutes until softened. Add the red pepper and sauté, stirring, for 2 minutes more.

3 Gently stir in the currants, drained beans, vinegar, and thyme, and remove from the heat. Let the mixture come to room temperature, then cover and refrigerate overnight for the flavors to develop. Bring back to room temperature, taste for seasoning, add salt and pepper to taste, and serve.

PER ½-CUP SERVING					
CALORIES	120	CARBOHYDRATES (G)	22	CARBOHYDRATE CHOICES: 1½	
FAT (G)	1.5	PROTEIN (G)	6	FOOD EXCHANGES PER SERVING: 1½ STARCH	
CALORIES FROM FAT (%)	11	FIBER (G)	6	LOW-SODIUM DIETS: DECREASE SALT BY HALF IN	
CHOLESTEROL (MG)	0	SODIUM (MG)	400	COOKING AND MAKE SURE TO DRAIN AND	
				RINSE BEANS. SALT IN THE DRESSING CAN	
				ALSO BE OMITTED; JUST INCREASE THE THYME	
				AND ADD A SQUEEZE OF FRESH LEMON.	

LENTIL SALAD WITH GOAT CHEESE AND SUN-DRIED TOMATOES

MAKES 6 SERVINGS

I prefer the French green lentils in salads because they are a bit more delicate than the regular brown ones, but either will work fine.

1 cup (8 ounces) French green lentils
2½ tablespoons olive oil, divided
1 medium onion, finely chopped
1 medium carrot, peeled and finely chopped
1 rib celery, finely chopped
3 cups water
Bouquet garni (see Note)
Salt, to taste

1 tablespoon red wine vinegar
4 large dry-packed sun-dried tomatoes, soaked for 20 minutes in warm water
½ cup diced red onion
½ teaspoon coarsely cracked black pepper
1½ ounces mild goat cheese
2 tablespoons finely chopped parsley

1 Rinse the lentils well under cold running water and pick over for grit and stones. In a large flameproof casserole, heat 1 tablespoon of the oil over medium heat. Add the onion, carrot, and celery and sauté for 4 to 5 minutes, stirring occasionally until just golden. Add the lentils, water, bouquet garni, and ½ teaspoon salt. Regulate the heat so the liquid is simmering, partially cover the pan, and cook for 20 to 25 minutes, until the lentils are tender but not falling apart. Drain in a colander and shake gently to remove excess liquid. Discard the bouquet garni.

2 In a large bowl, combine the drained lentils with the remaining 1½ tablespoons olive oil and the vinegar. Toss together gently. Squeeze the sun-dried tomatoes dry, chop them, and add to the bowl. Toss in the red onion, cracked pepper, and crumbled goat cheese. Let cool to room temperature and taste for seasoning. Mix in the parsley.

Note: Tie the following ingredients together in a square of doubled cheesecloth: 2 sprigs parsley, 1 sprig fresh thyme, and 1 bay leaf. (See also page 279.)

PER 1-CUP SERVING					
CALORIES	210	CARBOHYDRATES (G)	24	CARBOHYDRATE CHOICES: 1½	
FAT (G)	8	PROTEIN (G)	11	FOOD EXCHANGES PER SERVING: 1 STARCH,	
CALORIES FROM FAT (%)	35	FIBER (G)	6	1 LEAN MEAT, 1 VEGETABLE, 1 FAT	
CHOLESTEROL (MG)	5	SODIUM (MG)	55	LOW-SODIUM DIETS: ACCEPTABLE	

REFRIED PINTO BEANS

MAKES 12 SERVINGS

Most refried beans are liquefied by using generous amounts of lard, but here I use buttermilk to add not only liquid but the sour cream flavor I like in my burritos. A small amount of oil is used to carry the garlic flavor. If you don't intend to serve the entire batch at one meal, refry only the amount of beans you will use and adjust the amounts of buttermilk, oil, and garlic accordingly. This will prevent them from drying out when they're reheated.

1 pound pinto beans, rinsed and soaked overnight in water to cover

1 quart water

½ white onion, coarsely chopped

5 cloves garlic, finely chopped

1 serrano or jalapeño chile, stemmed, seeded, and minced

Salt

1 tablespoon olive oil

½ cup buttermilk

Freshly ground black pepper, to taste

1 Drain the beans. In a large saucepan, combine the beans with the water, onion, about ⅔ of the garlic, and the chile. Bring to a boil over medium-high heat. Reduce the heat, cover the pan and simmer gently for 45 minutes, then stir in 1 teaspoon salt. Simmer the beans for 45 minutes to 1 hour or more, until they are very tender and starting to fall apart. Skim the foam from the top of the water occasionally, and add water if needed to keep the beans covered. Drain the beans, reserving the cooking liquid. Refrigerate until ready to refry.

2 To refry the beans, heat a large nonstick sauté pan and add the olive oil and remaining garlic. Add ½ cup of the cooked beans and mash with a potato masher, adding some of the cooking liquid. Continue adding the beans ½ cup at a time, adding cooking liquid and mashing. Stir constantly and keep the beans just wet enough to bubble. Keep adding beans, mashing and adding liquid, until all the beans are mashed and slightly dry. Stir in the buttermilk, season to taste with salt and pepper, and serve hot.

PER ¼-CUP SERVING	BEFORE	AFTER			
CALORIES	100	70	CARBOHYDRATES (G)	11	CARBOHYDRATE CHOICES: 1
FAT (G)	4.5	1.5	PROTEIN (G)	4	FOOD EXCHANGES PER SERVING: 1 STARCH
CALORIES FROM FAT (%)	40	20	FIBER (G)	4	LOW-SODIUM DIETS: BEANS ARE NATURALLY
CHOLESTEROL (MG)	5	0	SODIUM (MG)	240	LOW IN SODIUM. OMIT OR DECREASE SALT
					OR USE FAT-FREE SOUR CREAM INSTEAD OF
					BUTTERMILK.

CHIPOTLE BLACK BEANS

MAKES 12 SERVINGS

Chipotle chiles are the smoked and dried version of the jalapeño chile. The canned chipotle chile en adobo *is quite easy to find, and can be substituted for the dried chile if desired, but many Latin American markets now carry the superior dried variety. For a mail-order source of this smoky-flavored chile, check the Appendix. It is worth searching out. The wonderful smoky flavor of the chile is a great substitution for the usual ham bone or pork fat that might otherwise be used to flavor the beans, and you can serve these beans to vegetarians, which is nice. Serve as a side dish with Fajitas (page 256) or rolled in a tortilla.*

1 pound black beans, well rinsed and soaked overnight in water to cover

4 cups water

1 tablespoon olive oil

1 dried chipotle chile, stemmed, seeded, and minced

½ cinnamon stick, or ¼ teaspoon dried cinnamon

½ white onion, stuck with 1 clove

2 cloves garlic, chopped

1 tablespoon salt

1 Drain the beans. In a large heavy saucepan, combine the beans with the water, olive oil, chipotle chile, cinnamon stick, clove-studded onion, and garlic. Stir to mix evenly and bring to a boil over medium-high heat. Cover the pan, reduce the heat to low and simmer gently for 45 minutes.

2 Stir in the salt and continue simmering the beans for 45 minutes to 1 hour more, until tender but not falling apart. Skim off the foamlike residue often, and add water if necessary to keep the beans covered.

PER ¼-CUP SERVING					
CALORIES	65	CARBOHYDRATES (G)	10	CARBOHYDRATE CHOICES: ½	
FAT (G)	3.5	PROTEIN (G)	3	FOOD EXCHANGES PER SERVING: ½ STARCH,	
CALORIES FROM FAT (%)	19	FIBER (G)	3	½ FAT	
CHOLESTEROL (MG)	0	SODIUM (MG)	540	LOW-SODIUM DIETS: OMIT SALT OR DECREASE TO 1 TEASPOON.	

CHAPTER 23

SMALL DISHES FEATURING VEGETABLES

I first came across "Small Dishes" on the Grange Hall menu in
New York City's Greenwich Village. The owner, Jay Savulich, says
they were so popular, he has increased their presence on his
menu. His innovative ways with vegetables prove that given the proper
motivation, vegetables can do almost anything. Eat your vegetables! No
problem here. Next time you think of vegetables, don't just relegate them
to the side of the plate; two or three can become an entree.

Vegetables are a part of the secret to the "eat more, weigh less" theory.
They are low in calories because they consist mainly of water and
nondigestable carbohydrate. This chapter covers a range of my favorites,
from Grilled Vegetable Towers to Ratatouille to dishes as radically simple
as Stir-Fried Spinach with Ginger and Garlic or Sautéed Cucumbers.
The uncomplicated recipe for Spaghetti Squash with Gremolata illus-
trates how a simple combination of seasonings—garlic, parsley, and lemon
zest—gives a single vegetable a chance to shine with big flavors.

SPAGHETTI SQUASH WITH GREMOLATA

MAKES 4 SERVINGS

Gremolata is a traditional Italian garnish made of simple ingredients—parsley, lemon zest, garlic, and black pepper—and can be used for meats as well as vegetables. It also happens to pack a big wallop of flavor and no fat. Spaghetti squash is definitely a fun food. When you cook it and cut it open, the inside comes out in pastalike strands, with a lovely flavor that makes a heavy sauce unnecessary.

I've added a bit of olive oil here because it adds a nice touch, and the dish still has less than 4 grams of fat per serving, but you can omit the oil if you want to skip the refrying step, and lower the fat in your meal even further.

1 small spaghetti squash, halved lengthwise and seeded (about 2 pounds)
1 tablespoon olive oil
2 small cloves garlic, finely chopped
2 tablespoons finely chopped parsley

2 teaspoons finely chopped lemon zest
Salt, to taste
Coarsely ground black pepper, to taste

1 In a large saucepan fitted with a steamer rack, steam the squash for about 20 minutes, or until tender. Set aside until cool enough to handle.

2 In a nonstick pan, heat the olive oil over medium heat. Add the garlic and sauté for 2 minutes.

3 Using a fork, scoop out the spaghettilike squash into a medium bowl, then drain off any excess water in the bowl. Transfer the squash to the nonstick pan and sauté for 5 minutes, or until slightly brown.

4 Remove the squash from the heat, add the parsley, lemon zest, and salt and pepper to taste, toss, and serve immediately.

PER 1-CUP SERVING					
CALORIES	100	CARBOHYDRATES (G)	16	CARBOHYDRATE CHOICES: 1	
FAT (G)	4	PROTEIN (G)	2	FOOD EXCHANGES PER SERVING: 1 STARCH, ½ FAT	
CALORIES FROM FAT (%)	34	FIBER (G)	3	LOW-SODIUM DIETS: OMIT SALT.	
CHOLESTEROL (MG)	0	SODIUM (MG)	180		

SPAGHETTI SQUASH WITH TOMATO SAUCE

MAKES 4 SERVINGS

When my pasta-loving clients are having difficulty losing weight, I suggest they substitute this dish for their usual plate of noodles, cutting the calories in half.

1 small spaghetti squash, halved and
    seeded (about 2 pounds)
2 teaspoons olive oil
1 medium shallot, finely chopped
3 plum tomatoes, peeled, seeded, and
    diced

½ teaspoon salt
¼ teaspoon freshly ground black
    pepper
1 tablespoon finely chopped parsley
1 tablespoon freshly grated Parmesan
    cheese

1 In a large saucepan fitted with a steamer, steam the squash over simmering water for about 20 minutes, until tender. With a fork, scoop out the spaghettilike flesh onto a warmed platter.

2 Meanwhile, in a medium nonstick skillet, heat the olive oil over medium heat. Add the shallot and sauté, stirring occasionally, for 3 to 4 minutes, until softened. Add the tomatoes and cook for 5 minutes, until they have begun to break down and be slightly saucy. Stir in the salt and pepper and remove from the heat.

3 Spoon the sauce over the squash and sprinkle the parsley and Parmesan over the top. Serve immediately.

PER 1-CUP SERVING				
CALORIES	110	CARBOHYDRATES (G)	18	CARBOHYDRATE CHOICES: 1
FAT (G)	3.5	PROTEIN (G)	3	FOOD EXCHANGES PER SERVING: 1 STARCH, ½ FAT
CALORIES FROM FAT (%)	28	FIBER (G)	4	LOW-SODIUM DIETS: OMIT SALT AND DECREASE
CHOLESTEROL (MG)	0	SODIUM (MG)	340	PARMESAN CHEESE TO A SPRINKLE.

STIR-FRIED SPINACH WITH GINGER AND GARLIC

MAKES 2 SERVINGS

Spinach is high in folic acid, now known to prevent birth defects as well as perhaps prevent heart disease. Try to include spinach greens in your salad at least once a week; more if you're pregnant!

1 teaspoon canola oil
1 teaspoon minced peeled fresh ginger
1 clove garlic, finely chopped
1 tablespoon low-fat chicken or vegetable broth, or water

1 (10-ounce) bag fresh spinach or 2 small bunches (about 1¼ pounds), leaves only, well washed
¼ teaspoon salt
¼ teaspoon freshly ground black pepper

1 In a large heavy skillet, heat the oil over medium-high heat until very hot but not smoking. Throw in the ginger and garlic, followed by the chicken broth, and stir-fry just until fragrant, 10 to 15 seconds.

2 Immediately add the spinach and stir-fry until wilted, about 1 minute. Season with the salt and pepper and serve immediately.

PER ³/₄-CUP SERVING					
CALORIES	90	CARBOHYDRATES (G)	11	CARBOHYDRATE CHOICES: 1	
FAT (G)	3.5	PROTEIN (G)	8	FOOD EXCHANGES PER SERVING: 2 VEGEGETABLE,	
CALORIES FROM FAT (%)	30	FIBER (G)	8	1 FAT	
CHOLESTEROL (MG)	0	SODIUM (MG)	500	LOW-SODIUM DIETS: OMIT SALT.	

GRILLED ASPARAGUS

MAKES 4 SERVINGS

This recipe is a nice alternative to the usual fat-filled hollandaise sauce or butter that often accompanies asparagus. The marinade has a tangy, rich flavor that suits the asparagus very well, and with a squeeze of lemon, these spears are nearly perfect. Keep in mind that cooking time will vary depending on the size of the spears (larger spears will take longer, while smaller spears may only take a few minutes). Peeling the skin off of the bottom 2 inches of each spear removes the tough skin and makes for an attractive presentation.

20 medium asparagus, bottom ends snapped off and bottom 2 inches peeled with a vegetable peeler, if desired
2 cloves garlic, finely chopped
1 tablespoon extra-virgin olive oil
1 tablespoon reduced-sodium soy sauce
Freshly ground black pepper, to taste
2 tablespoons low-sodium chicken broth
Wedges of lemon, for serving

1 Whisk together the garlic, olive oil, soy sauce, chicken broth, and pepper to taste.

2 Heat a nonstick pan over high heat. Place the asparagus spears and the marinade in the pan, sautéing and turning the spears until they are tender and dark green, and marinade is mostly evaporated, about 14 minutes, depending on the thickness of the asparagus. Place on a serving platter with wedges of lemon and serve immediately.

PER SERVING				
CALORIES	50	CARBOHYDRATES (G)	4	CARBOHYDRATE CHOICES: 0
FAT (G)	3.5	PROTEIN (G)	2	FOOD EXCHANGES PER SERVING: 1 VEGETABLE,
CALORIES FROM FAT (%)	56	FIBER (G)	2	½ FAT
CHOLESTEROL (MG)	0	SODIUM (MG)	260	LOW-SODIUM DIETS: SERVE ASPARAGUS WITH A SLOTTED SPOON TO AVOID ADDITIONAL MARINADE IN YOUR PORTION, OR OMIT SOY SAUCE.

GRILLED EGGPLANT WITH SPICY SOY MARINADE

MAKES 4 SERVINGS

This marinade was originally developed for eggplant, and I often use it just for that purpose, but it also tastes great on a variety of other vegetables.

Marinade (makes about 1 cup)
2 tablespoons Tabasco sauce
2 tablespoons low-sodium soy sauce
¼ cup sherry or vermouth
½ cup red wine vinegar
2 tablespoons sesame oil

1 tablespoon sugar (or sugar substitute; see Note)
2 cloves garlic, finely chopped

1 large eggplant, cut into ½-inch rounds (about 12 slices)

1 In a jar with a tight-fitting lid, combine the Tabasco sauce, soy sauce, sherry, red wine vinegar, sesame oil, sugar, and garlic and shake vigorously to blend.

2 Place the eggplant in a large bowl and toss with marinade mixture. Marinate for at least 1 hour at room temperature and up to 4 hours, covered and refrigerated.

3 Preheat an outdoor grill or a ridged cast-iron stovetop griddle for medium-heat grilling. Grill the eggplant, for about 4 minutes per side, until tender, turning occasionally to make sure they mark evenly and do not burn.

4 Arrange the eggplant on a platter, and serve warm or at room temperature.

Note: This recipe was calculated with regular sugar instead of sugar substitute because it was cooked. If sugar substitute were used, it would have 1 less gram of carbohydrate, an insignificant amount.

PER 3 SLICES EGGPLANT WITH 1 TABLESPOON MARINADE					
CALORIES	60	CARBOHYDRATES (G)	8	CARBOHYDRATE CHOICES: 1	
FAT (G)	2	PROTEIN (G)	1	FOOD EXCHANGES PER SERVING: 2 VEGETABLE	
CALORIES FROM FAT (%)	29	FIBER (G)	3	LOW-SODIUM DIETS: REDUCE OR OMIT SOY	
CHOLESTEROL (MG)	0	SODIUM (MG)	80	SAUCE AND/OR TABASCO SAUCE.	

GRILLED VEGETABLE TOWERS

MAKES 10 TOWERS, SERVING 5

The lasagnalike layering of the grilled vegetables, ricotta cheese, and marinara is truly the merging of food and architecture, best served plated as either an appetizer or side dish. Creating these "structures" requires some effort, but it's really fun and the flavor and the visual impact of the towers are wonderful.

1 zucchini, ends trimmed and sliced into ¼-inch rounds
1 yellow squash, ends trimmed and sliced into ¼-inch rounds
1 Japanese eggplant, ends trimmed and sliced into ¼-inch rounds
1½ teaspoons olive oil
Coarse sea salt and freshly ground black pepper, to taste

¼ cup low-fat ricotta cheese
2 tablespoons fresh basil chiffonade (page 297)
¼ cup Zesty Marinara Sauce (page 298), or bottled tomato sauce
1 small tomato, seeded and diced

1 In a large bowl, combine the zucchini, squash, and eggplant with the olive oil and coarse salt and pepper to taste. Prepare an outdoor grill or ridged cast-iron stove-top griddle for medium-heat grilling.

2 Grill the vegetables, turning occasionally with tongs so that they mark evenly, until they are slightly charred on both sides. Eggplant, zucchini, and squash should take approximately 2 minutes per side. Set aside to cool just to room temperature.

3 In a small bowl, stir together the ricotta, 1 tablespoon of the basil, and salt and pepper to taste. To assemble the towers, stack the vegetables, with 3 pieces in each layer, alternating them, and sandwiching 1 teaspoon of the ricotta mixture between each layer, until they are 3 or 4 layers tall.

4 Drizzle a little of the marinara sauce around the edge of each plate and dot the sauce with a few diced tomatoes and basil chiffonade. Serve at room temperature.

PER SERVING					
CALORIES	60	CARBOHYDRATES (G)	5	CARBOHYDRATE CHOICES: 0	
FAT (G)	3	PROTEIN (G)	3	FOOD EXCHANGES PER SERVING:	
CALORIES FROM FAT (%)	45	FIBER (G)	2	1 VEGETABLE, ½ FAT	
CHOLESTEROL (MG)	LESS THAN 5	SODIUM (MG)	75	LOW-SODIUM DIETS: ACCEPTABLE	

SIMPLE SUMMER STIR-FRY

MAKES 4 SERVINGS

So many of my clients are tired of eating their plain steamed vegetables, so tired that they report omitting them altogether and just eating a salad instead. Make the effort to keep vegetables interesting and varied. A small amount of oil goes a very long way to make this dish taste great.

½ cup fine green beans, ends trimmed

1 tablespoon olive oil

1 medium carrot, peeled, quartered lengthwise, and cut into ¼-inch matchsticks

1 clove garlic, finely chopped (optional)

1 medium zucchini, quartered lengthwise and cut into ¼-inch matchsticks

1 yellow zucchini, quartered lengthwise and cut into ¼-inch matchsticks

2 teaspoons fresh lemon juice

Salt and freshly ground black pepper, to taste

2 tablespoons finely chopped fresh basil

1 In a small saucepan of lightly salted boiling water, blanch the green beans for 4 minutes, then refresh under cold running water to stop the cooking and preserve the color. Drain on paper towels.

2 In a large heavy skillet or a well-seasoned wok, heat the olive oil over high heat. Add the carrot and toss for 1 minute. Add the garlic and toss for 30 seconds more, until it has released its aroma. Add the green and yellow zucchini and the blanched beans and toss for 3 or 4 minutes more, until all the vegetables are crisp-tender. Remove the pan from the heat and add the lemon juice, salt and pepper to taste, and the basil. Toss until mixed and serve immediately.

PER 1-CUP SERVING					
CALORIES	50	CARBOHYDRATES (G)	5	CARBOHYDRATE CHOICES: 0	
FAT (G)	3.5	PROTEIN (G)	1	FOOD EXCHANGES PER SERVING: 1 VEGETABLE,	
CALORIES FROM FAT (%)	55	FIBER (G)	2	½ FAT	
CHOLESTEROL (MG)	0	SODIUM (MG)	10	LOW-SODIUM DIETS: ACCEPTABLE	

COLCANNON (MASHED POTATOES WITH CABBAGE)

MAKES 6 SERVINGS

This dish is traditional at Halloween in Ireland. Leftovers may be fried and served again. In England, the refried Colcannon is referred to as bubble and squeak. In Scotland, the dish often appears with carrots and turnips. In the border areas between England and Scotland, the dish is called Rumbledethumps. Refry leftovers in a nonstick pan with just a teaspoon or two of oil.

6 large red or white rose potatoes, peeled and quartered
4 cups (7 to 8 ounces) thinly sliced white or green cabbage
1 tablespoon olive oil
1 medium leek, white and 2 inches of light green part, well washed and thinly sliced, or 6 green onions, white and 2 inches of green part, thinly sliced

1 cup hot nonfat milk
½ cup fat-free sour cream
½ teaspoon salt
Freshly ground black pepper, to taste
¼ teaspoon freshly ground nutmeg (optional)

1 In a large steamer set over simmering water, steam the potatoes, covered, for 20 minutes. Add the cabbage and steam covered for 10 minutes more or until tender. Set the cabbage aside and remove the steamer and water from the saucepan. Return the potatoes to the empty pan and set aside. Some cabbage will stick to the potatoes.

2 In a large skillet, heat the oil over medium-low heat. Cook the leeks, stirring occasionally, for 6 to 8 minutes, until softened. Add the cabbage and cook for about 4 minutes more, until all the vegetables are very limp. Meanwhile, add the milk and sour cream to the pan with the potatoes and mash them until smooth. Add the salt, pepper, and nutmeg and taste for seasoning.

3 Add the mashed potato mixture to the pan with the cabbage and stir until evenly mixed and warmed through, about 3 minutes. Serve immediately.

PER 1-CUP SERVING					
CALORIES	150	CARBOHYDRATES (G)	27	CARBOHYDRATE CHOICES: 2	
FAT (G)	2.5	PROTEIN (G)	6	FOOD EXCHANGES PER SERVING: 2 STARCH	
CALORIES FROM FAT (%)	14	FIBER (G)	4	LOW-SODIUM DIETS: OMIT SALT; INCREASE	
CHOLESTEROL (MG)	5	SODIUM (MG)	240	BLACK PEPPER AND NUTMEG.	

SAUTÉED CUCUMBERS

MAKES 4 SERVINGS

Cooked cucumber is rarely seen in American kitchens, but often seen in French cuisine. Cucumber makes a nice, delicate accompaniment for fish or chicken. If you are serving this dish alongside a poached fish entree, substitute some of the poaching liquid for the chicken stock.

2 medium cucumbers, peeled, or 1
    European cucumber, washed
¼ teaspoon salt
¼ cup low-fat, low-sodium chicken
    or vegetable broth

2 teaspoons finely chopped fresh dill,
    or snipped chives, or 1 teaspoon
    dried dill

1 Halve the cucumber(s) lengthwise and scrape out the seeds with the edge of a spoon. Slice diagonally about ¼ inch thick.

2 Heat a nonstick skillet over medium heat. Dry-sauté the cucumber and salt for 2 minutes until their aroma is released. Add the stock, increase the heat to high, and simmer, stirring occasionally, until the liquid has almost completely evaporated, about 5 minutes. Cucumbers should be slightly translucent and soft. Stir in the dill and serve immediately.

PER ½-CUP SERVING					
CALORIES	21	CARBOHYDRATES (G)	4	CARBOHYDRATE CHOICES: 0	
FAT (G)	LESS THAN .5	PROTEIN (G)	1	FOOD EXCHANGES PER SERVING: 1 VEGETABLE	
CALORIES FROM FAT (%)	12	FIBER (G)	1	LOW-SODIUM DIETS: OMIT SALT.	
CHOLESTEROL (MG)	0	SODIUM (MG)	140		

RATATOUILLE

MAKES 4 SERVINGS

This is one popular vegetarian item that is a big hit with non-vegetarians. Typically, this dish is very high in fat, with vegetables simmered in lots of olive oil. I use a very good-quality extra-virgin olive oil, and then limit it to 1 tablespoon, so you get plenty of flavor, but only a fraction of the fat. Serve as an entree or side dish—hot, room temperature, or cold. It will keep refrigerated for several days.

1 tablespoon olive oil
3 green bell peppers (about ¾ pound), cored, seeded, ribs removed, and thinly sliced
1 medium eggplant (about 1 pound), ends trimmed and thinly sliced
3 medium zucchini (about 1 pound), ends trimmed and thinly sliced

2 medium yellow onions, coarsely chopped
4 cloves garlic, finely chopped
2 pounds ripe plum tomatoes (about 6), peeled, seeded, and chopped
Salt and freshly ground black pepper, to taste

1 In a large, deep nonstick skillet, heat the olive oil over medium-low heat and sauté the green peppers for 10 minutes. Then add the eggplant and the zucchini and sauté them all together for 10 minutes or until tender and all the liquid has evaporated. With a slotted spoon, transfer to a plate.

2 In the same pan, sauté the onions over low heat for 10 to 12 minutes, until they are very soft and translucent. Add the garlic and cook for 1 minute more, then add eggplant, zucchini, peppers, tomatoes, and salt and pepper to taste. Continue to cook the mixture very slowly, stirring frequently, until it is almost the consistency of marmalade, about 20 minutes. Serve immediately, or cool to room temperature.

PER 1-CUP SERVING					
	BEFORE	AFTER			
CALORIES	190	170	CARBOHYDRATES (G) 32	CARBOHYDRATE CHOICES: 2	
FAT (G)	16	5	PROTEIN (G) 6	FOOD EXCHANGES PER SERVING: 6 VEGETABLE	
CALORIES FROM FAT (%)	80	22	FIBER (G) 9	(OR 2 STARCHES), 1 FAT	
CHOLESTEROL (MG)	5	0	SODIUM (MG) 300	LOW-SODIUM DIETS: OMIT SALT IF ON 500	
				OR 1000 MG SODIUM DIET.	

BRUSSELS SPROUTS WITH CHESTNUTS

MAKES 4 SERVINGS

This is a great fall or winter holiday dish. I serve it on Christmas garnished with slices of roasted red bell pepper. Added bonus: Brussels sprouts are part of the cruciferous family that may help prevent cancer. Fresh chestnuts are generally most available around Christmastime. If you can't find fresh, frozen are the next best choice, followed by canned.

1 pound small, bright green Brussels sprouts, cleaned and trimmed (about 16 large or 32 small)
Salt and freshly ground black pepper
4 ounces fresh, frozen and thawed, or canned chestnuts, chopped, about ¾ cup

2 teaspoons olive oil
¼ red bell pepper, cut into 2 ⅛-inch slices

1 Cut a shallow cross in the base of each sprout to help them cook evenly. Bring a generous amount of water to the boil in a medium saucepan and add 1 teaspoon salt. Add the sprouts and simmer until tender but still bright green, about 10 to 12 minutes. Drain and immediately rinse under very cold running water or plunge into a bowl of ice water (this stops the cooking, keeping the sprouts crunchy and stopping them from turning an unappetizing gray-green color). Drain in a colander.

2 In the same saucepan, boil a generous amount of water, and blanch the fresh chestnuts for 5 minutes or frozen chestnuts for 2 minutes. Drain them in another colander. When they are cool enough to handle, peel them and scrape off the pale brown skin. If using canned chestnuts, skip this step and proceed to step 3.

3 In the same saucepan, heat the oil over medium–low heat. Add the red bell pepper and sauté for 2 minutes. Then add the sprouts and chestnuts and toss very gently to combine and heat through, about 2 minutes. Season with salt and pepper to taste, and serve.

PER 4 LARGE OR 8 SMALL BRUSSELS SPROUTS					
CALORIES	130	CARBOHYDRATES (G)	23	CARBOHYDRATE CHOICES: 1½	
FAT (G)	3	PROTEIN (G)	5	FOOD EXCHANGES PER SERVING: 1 STARCH,	
CALORIES FROM FAT (%)	20	FIBER (G)	7	1 VEGETABLE, ½ FAT	
CHOLESTEROL (MG)	0	SODIUM (MG)	170	LOW-SODIUM DIETS: OMIT SALT AND ADD	
				LEMON.	

CARAMELIZED CARROTS AND PARSNIPS WITH ORANGE ZEST

MAKES 4 SERVINGS

If parsnips are unavailable, you can substitute turnips or rutabagas, or use additional carrots for the half pound of parsnips. Keep in mind that, while very similar to carrots, parsnips tend to be a little tougher, so you might want to consider placing them in boiling water for about 60 seconds before you begin to sauté them. This is blanching, and will make them more tender with less cooking time.

$\frac{1}{2}$ pound carrots, peeled and cut into $\frac{1}{4} \times 1$-inch julienne

$\frac{1}{2}$ pound parsnips, peeled and cut into $\frac{1}{4} \times 1$-inch julienne

1 tablespoon canola oil

$\frac{1}{2}$ cup low-fat, low-sodium chicken broth

2 teaspoons grated orange zest

1 tablespoon fresh lemon juice

1 tablespoon orange juice

1 tablespoon firmly packed brown sugar

4 tablespoons dark rum

$\frac{1}{2}$ teaspoon salt

$\frac{1}{4}$ teaspoon freshly ground black pepper

1 In a medium, heavy saucepan, combine the carrots, parsnips, oil, and stock and bring to a simmer over medium-low heat.

2 Stir occasionally and, as the vegetables begin to wilt, after about 6 to 8 minutes, stir in the orange zest, lemon and orange juices, sugar, and rum.

3 Watching carefully, continue simmering, adding hot water in $\frac{1}{4}$-cup increments as needed, until the liquid has reduced to a glaze and the vegetables are tender, about 20 minutes. Add salt and black pepper, taste for seasoning, and serve.

PER $^{3}/_{4}$-CUP SERVING					
CALORIES	150	CARBOHYDRATES (G)	19	CARBOHYDRATE CHOICES: 1	
FAT (G)	4	PROTEIN (G)	2	FOOD EXCHANGES PER SERVING: 1 STARCH,	
CALORIES FROM FAT (%)	24	FIBER (G)	4	1 VEGETABLE, 1 FAT	
CHOLESTEROL (MG)	0	SODIUM (MG)	320	LOW-SODIUM DIETS: OMIT SALT.	

CHAPTER 24

SMALL DISHES FEATURING GRAINS AND STARCHY VEGETABLES

M om's "square" meal, as you may have experienced it, was traditional meat, starch, and vegetable fare. Where I grew up, the starch was likely to be a serving of plain white rice or mashed potato—about the only ways these staples were served. Now it's time to breathe new life into the grains and starchy vegetables. How? By capitalizing on their versatiltiy. Their very plainness suggests that their only limit is your imagination. Try the Herb-Scented Roasted Potatoes or the medley of Sugar Snap Peas with Potato and Parsley Sauté. Instead of plain white rice, try the Garlicky Seasoned Rice enlivened with cilantro and garlic (known at my house as green rice). I've never served this at a dinner party and not had at least one or two people corner me in my kitchen asking for the recipe. Go multicultural with Caribbean Sweet Potatoes. Or experiment and give your rice color and texture with the brilliant red Beets with Rice and Ham.

If you've moved on to a more vegetarian type of diet, many of these dishes may become entrees. There are recipes for all seasons and all occasions, from an elegant winter dish of Risotto with Red Beans and Sage to Very Wild Rice Salad or Rosemary Polenta Squares. Whatever you do, don't settle on plain old starches. As you can see in these recipes, starches are really more fun than you may remember.

GARLICKY SEASONED RICE

MAKES 6 SERVINGS

Turn plain rice into a lively, colorful side dish by adding only a few simple ingredients. This fragrant rice, known as green rice at my house, is the perfect accompaniment for fajitas (page 256). For a variation, add 1 tablespoon of the sauce from a canned chipotle chile en adobo or 1 roasted, peeled, and diced poblano chile.

3 cloves garlic, coarsely chopped
3 green onions (scallions), white and
   light green parts only, coarsely
   chopped
½ teaspoon salt

6 sprigs cilantro
2¼ cups low-fat, low-sodium chicken
   broth
2 teaspoons canola oil
1½ cups long-grain rice

1 Preheat the oven to 350° F.

2 In a blender or food processor, puree the garlic, green onions, salt, and cilantro with 1 cup of the chicken broth until smooth.

3 In a large ovenproof sauté pan, heat the oil over medium-high heat. Add the rice and sauté, stirring occasionally, for about 4 minutes, until slightly toasted. Add the pureed, seasoned broth and the remaining chicken broth. Bring to a boil, cover the pan, and place in the oven for 20 to 25 minutes, until the rice has absorbed all the liquid.

4 Transfer the rice to a warmed serving platter, stirring with a fork to mix in the seasonings which will have risen to the top during cooking.

PER ⅔-CUP SERVING					
CALORIES	200	CARBOHYDRATES (G)	38	CARBOHYDRATE CHOICES: 2½	
FAT (G)	2.5	PROTEIN (G)	5	FOOD EXCHANGES PER SERVING: 2½ STARCH	
CALORIES FROM FAT (%)	12	FIBER (G)	1	LOW-SODIUM DIETS: OMIT SALT AND COOK	
CHOLESTEROL (MG)	2	SODIUM (MG)	220	IN HOMEMADE CHICKEN STOCK WITH NO	
				ADDED SALT. INCREASE GARLIC, ONIONS,	
				AND CILANTRO TO TASTE.	

SAFFRON-SCENTED BASMATI RICE

MAKES 6 SERVINGS

Basmati is a high-quality long-grain rice used extensively in Indian and Middle Eastern cooking. It is also very popular in England and Europe. It is very aromatic, and must be rinsed well so it doesn't get too sticky. Although it is not absolutely essential to soak basmati rice before cooking, it does produce a fluffier result. Similar domestic varieties such as Texmati and Wehani are much milder in flavor. To make plain basmati, substitute hot water for the saffron-infused broth, and omit the spices, browning the rice in olive oil all alone.

2 cups low-fat, low-sodium chicken broth
1/8 teaspoon saffron threads
1/4 teaspoon salt
1 teaspoon olive oil
1 bay leaf

1/2 teaspoon cumin seeds
1/4 teaspoon black peppercorns, crushed
1 cup basmati rice, rinsed several times in cold water (soaked for 1 hour if time permits)

1 In a medium saucepan, combine the chicken broth, saffron, and salt and bring to a boil. Remove from the heat, pour into a blender, and puree at high speed until the saffron is thoroughly dissolved into the broth. Set aside.

2 In a large heavy saucepan or sauté pan, heat the olive oil over medium-high heat. Add the bay leaf, cumin, and peppercorns and stir together for 30 seconds to release their aroma. Add the rice and sauté, stirring frequently, until slightly browned, about 5 minutes.

3 Pour the hot broth into the pan, stir to mix, and bring to a boil. Reduce the heat to very low, cover the pan and simmer for 30 minutes, or until rice is tender. Fluff with fork, remove the bay leaf, and serve at once.

PER 1/2-CUP SERVING				
CALORIES	150	CARBOHYDRATES (G)	29	CARBOHYDRATE CHOICES: 2
FAT (G)	2	PROTEIN (G)	4	FOOD EXCHANGES PER SERVING: 2 STARCH
CALORIES FROM FAT (%)	12	FIBER (G)	1	LOW-SODIUM DIETS: OMIT SALT.
CHOLESTEROL (MG)	0	SODIUM (MG)	130	

VERY WILD RICE SALAD

MAKES 8 SERVINGS

Wild rice is actually a distant cousin of ordinary rice, slightly higher in protein, but still a complex carbohydrate that will help stabilize blood sugar when eaten within one's carbohydrate goals. It has a greater yield than regular rice: 1 cup of cooked wild rice yields 3½ to 4 cups. Be sure not to overcook the rice for this salad, or it will be mushy. Make this salad well ahead of time to allow the rice to absorb the flavors of the vinaigrette, and if it has been refrigerated, return to room temperature before serving.

Dressing
2 tablespoons balsamic vinegar
½ teaspoon fresh lime juice
Pinch of sugar
Pinch of salt
¼ teaspoon freshly ground black
    pepper
1 tablespoon extra-virgin olive oil

¼ cup currants
2 tablespoons golden raisins
3 ounces (½ cup) wild rice
2 cups cold water
1 medium carrot, peeled and finely
    chopped
1 rib celery, trimmed and finely
    chopped
½ small red bell pepper, cored,
    seeded, and finely chopped
½ small red onion, finely chopped
1½ teaspoons Italian parsley, chopped
Lime wedges, to garnish

1 To make the dressing: In a small bowl, combine the vinegar, lime juice, sugar, salt, and pepper. Whisk in the oil in a thin stream, whisking until the dressing is emulsified. Set aside.

2 In a bowl, cover the currants and golden raisins with warm water and let soak while the rice is cooking, about 30 to 40 minutes, until nice and plump.

3 In a strainer, rinse the rice thoroughly in cold running water. In a large saucepan, combine the rice with the cold water, cover the pan, and bring to a boil. Uncover the pan, regulate the heat so that the water simmers, and cook until the rice is tender on the outside but still has a slightly chewy kernel, about 30 minutes. Drain the rice and let it cool.

4 Drain the currants and golden raisins. In a large bowl, combine the currants, drained wild rice, carrots, celery, red pepper, onion, and parsley. Toss to mix thoroughly. Whisk the dressing again to recombine and pour over the salad. Toss briefly just to mix, garnish with lime wedges and serve.

PER ½-CUP SERVING					
CALORIES	120	CARBOHYDRATES (G)	23	CARBOHYDRATE CHOICES: 1½	
FAT (G)	2.5	PROTEIN (G)	3	FOOD EXCHANGES PER SERVING: 1 STARCH,	
CALORIES FROM FAT (%)	18	FIBER (G)	2	2 VEGETABLE	
CHOLESTEROL (MG)	0	SODIUM (MG)	60	LOW-SODIUM DIETS: ACCEPTABLE	

SEASONED STICKY RICE

MAKES 12 SERVINGS (NOTE: 1 CUP RAW RICE = 3 CUPS COOKED)

Traditional Japanese rice is short-grain. It's stickier than long-grain rice, and therefore is very well suited for sushi and many other Japanese dishes. By rinsing well, and then refrigerating before cooking, you get not only sticky rice, but fluffy rice as well. Baking the rice in the oven allows for more even cooking, and also contributes to fluffiness. Sushi chefs generally add vinegar and sugar after cooking as seasoning.

Nutritionally, this rice is the same as long-grain, both being essentially fat-free and a dense source of carbohydrates. That means it's important to weigh or measure your rice portion so you don't go over your carbohydrate limit for the meal. The added sugar can be deleted, but note that it adds only 1 gram of carbohydrate per half cup and offers a nice flavor.

1¾ cups water
1 teaspoon salt
2 cups short-grain rice

¼ cup seasoned rice vinegar
2 tablespoons sugar

1 In a strainer, rinse the rice thoroughly under cold running water. Strain once or twice, until the water is clear. Refrigerate for 1 hour before cooking.

2 Preheat the oven to 325° F. In a large saucepan, bring the water to a boil and add the salt and the rice (do not stir). When the water returns to a boil, cover the pan and place it in the oven. Cook for 15 to 20 minutes, until all the water has been absorbed and the top of the rice looks dimpled. Remove from the oven and allow to rest, covered, for 10 minutes.

3 Mix the vinegar and the sugar together, add the mixture to the rice, and fluff the rice with a fork, mixing in the seasoning thoroughly.

4 Drape a damp kitchen towel, folded in half, over the top of the pan and cover with the lid. This will keep the rice warm and moist until ready to serve.

PER ½-CUP SERVING					
CALORIES	140	CARBOHYDRATES (G)	32	CARBOHYDRATE CHOICES: 2	
FAT (G)	0	PROTEIN (G)	2	FOOD EXCHANGES PER SERVING: 2 STARCH	
CALORIES FROM FAT (%)	0	FIBER (G)	0.5	LOW-SODIUM DIETS: REDUCE SALT TO	
CHOLESTEROL (MG)	0	SODIUM (MG)	180	½ TEASPOON.	

BEETS WITH RICE AND HAM

MAKES 6 SERVINGS

This recipe is good for parties because it can be made a day in advance. If you're using fresh beets, trim off the tops and the root, and boil about 30 minutes, or until tender. You can easily peel back the skin under cold running water once the beets are cool enough to handle. The beets turn the rice a beautiful, bright pink, making this a very pretty presentation. Garnish with a flower, if you like, and serve at room temperature as an entree salad or side dish.

2 cups diced, cooked beets (fresh or canned, drained)
2 teaspoons red wine vinegar
Salt and freshly ground black pepper, to taste
1½ tablespoons olive oil
½ cup long-grain white rice
1 tablespoon fresh lemon juice
2 teaspoons capers, rinsed and drained

½ cup diced cooked lean ham
¼ cup diced low-fat (or fat-free) Swiss cheese
2½ tablespoons sliced cornichon pickles (about 10 small pickles)
2 tablespoons peas, thawed if frozen
Lemon wedges and whole cornichons, for garnish

1 In a medium bowl, combine the beets with the vinegar, a pinch each of salt and pepper, and ½ tablespoon of the olive oil. Set aside to marinate.

2 Bring a generous amount of water to a boil in a heavy saucepan and add 1 teaspoon salt. Add the rice and simmer uncovered until tender but not mushy, 15 to 20 minutes. Drain and rinse with cold running water, then drain again and shake to remove excess moisture. In a large bowl, toss the rice with the lemon juice and the remaining 1 tablespoon of olive oil.

3 Add the capers, ham, cheese, cornichons, and peas and gently toss together. Add the beets with all of their marinade and toss again. Leave at room temperature for 15 minutes for the flavors to marry, then toss again and taste for seasoning.

PER 1-CUP SERVING				
CALORIES	140	CARBOHYDRATES (G)	19	CARBOHYDRATE CHOICES: 1
FAT (G)	5	PROTEIN (G)	6	FOOD EXCHANGES PER SERVING: 1 STARCH,
CALORIES FROM FAT (%)	30	FIBER (G)	1	1 LEAN MEAT
CHOLESTEROL (MG)	5	SODIUM (MG)	380	LOW-SODIUM DIETS: THIS RECIPE IS NOT
				SUITABLE FOR LOW-SODIUM DIETS.

VEGETABLE FRIED RICE

MAKES 4 SERVINGS

Whenever I make a pot of rice for one meal, I try to cook a cup or two extra in anticipation of making fried rice later in the week. It's a good way to use up whatever vegetables you have in your refrigerator while getting a great-tasting, high-fiber, low-fat dinner. Add fish, chicken, or lean meat for additional variety and protein.

2 teaspoons canola oil
1 large clove garlic, sliced
1 (¼-inch) slice peeled fresh ginger
1 carrot, peeled and cut into ¼-inch matchsticks
1 medium zucchini, quartered lengthwise and cut into ¼-inch matchsticks

6 medium white mushrooms, wiped clean and thinly sliced
2 teaspoons low-sodium soy sauce
1 cup leftover white rice, chilled

1 In a large heavy skillet or a well-seasoned wok, heat the oil over medium-high heat. Add the garlic and ginger and toss for about 30 seconds, until the garlic has released its aroma, then remove them both with a slotted spoon and discard.

2 Add the carrot and toss for 2 minutes, then add the zucchini and mushrooms. Toss for about 4 minutes more until crisp-tender, then add the soy sauce and toss together until all the vegetables are coated. Add the rice and break it up with a spoon. Cook, tossing occasionally, until the rice is golden, about 5 minutes, and serve.

PER 1-CUP SERVING					
CALORIES	90	CARBOHYDRATES (G)	15	CARBOHYDRATE CHOICES: 1	
FAT (G)	2.5	PROTEIN (G)	2	FOOD EXCHANGES PER SERVING: 1 STARCH	
CALORIES FROM FAT (%)	25	FIBER (G)	1	LOW-SODIUM DIETS: ACCEPTABLE	
CHOLESTEROL (MG)	0	SODIUM (MG)	95		

PEAS AND RICE WITH WATER CHESTNUTS

MAKES 4 SERVINGS

Ever wonder what to do with the rice left over from Chinese take-out food? Simply stir-fry with frozen peas and garlic to make a whole new side dish for next night's meal of fish, chicken, beef, or legumes. Add a teaspoon of Chinese 5-spice powder or tablespoon of rice vinegar as variations.

1 tablespoon canola oil
¾ cup fresh peas or thawed
    frozen peas
1 (4-ounce) can water chestnuts,
    drained and sliced
½ medium red bell pepper, cored,
    seeded, and cut into ¼-inch dice

4 cloves garlic, finely chopped
1½ cups left over cooked rice, chilled
Freshly ground black pepper, to taste
1 teaspoon low-sodium soy sauce

1 In a large, heavy skillet or a well-seasoned wok, heat the oil over medium-high heat. Add the peas, water chestnuts, and red pepper and toss for 2 minutes, then add the garlic and toss for 1 minute more.

2 Add the rice and break it up with a spoon. Cook, tossing occasionally, until the rice is golden, about 5 to 7 minutes. Sprinkle the pepper to taste and the soy sauce over the rice, toss to mix, and serve.

PER ¾-CUP SERVING					
CALORIES	170	CARBOHYDRATES (G)	30	CARBOHYDRATE CHOICES: 2	
FAT (G)	4	PROTEIN (G)	4	FOOD EXCHANGES PER SERVING: 2 STARCH,	
CALORIES FROM FAT (%)	20	FIBER (G)	3	½ FAT	
CHOLESTEROL (MG)	0	SODIUM (MG)	75	LOW-SODIUM DIETS: ACCEPTABLE	

RISOTTO WITH RED BEANS AND SAGE

Did you ever wonder what dietitians like to eat? This dish was a favorite of my colleagues at a Christmastime luncheon that I hosted at my home. It's a low-fat version of Marcella Hazan's recipe from her book Marcella's Italian Kitchen. *I reduced the saturated fat by using olive oil instead of butter, and reduced the total fat by using less oil and less cheese. This Italian rice dish requires a lot of stirring, but the creamy end result is well worth the effort.*

1 small head cabbage (about ⅔ pound) quartered and tough outer leaves and core removed
1 tablespoon plus 1 teaspoon olive oil
¼ cup finely chopped onion
1 teaspoon salt
1½ cups arborio rice
10 to 12 fresh sage leaves, coarsely chopped

1 (10-ounce) can red kidney beans, drained and rinsed, or 1¼ cups cooked red beans
Freshly ground black pepper, to taste
½ cup freshly grated Parmesan cheese

1 In a large saucepan, bring a generous amount of lightly salted water to the boil. Cook the cabbage for 5 to 7 minutes, until tender. Drain well, returning 4 cups of the cooking water to the pan and discarding any excess. Slice the cabbage thinly and set the cabbage and the broth aside separately.

2 In a large, heavy casserole, heat 1 tablespoon of the olive oil over medium-low heat. Add the onion and sauté, stirring occasionally, for 8 to 10 minutes or until translucent. Add a tablespoon or two of water, if needed, scraping the glaze from the bottom of the pan, allowing the onion to turn a caramelized golden brown.

3 Meanwhile, bring the cabbage cooking water to a simmer, add the salt, and cover. Keep at a slow simmer at the back of the stove.

4 Add the sliced cabbage to the pan with the onion and cook, stirring frequently, until the cabbage is very well cooked, almost mushy.

5 Add the rice to the onion-cabbage mixture and increase the heat to medium-high. Stir until all the grains of rice are well coated with the oil and just beginning to brown, then immediately add about ½ cup of the simmering cabbage water.

Stir constantly with a wooden spoon until all the liquid has evaporated, then add another ladleful of the simmering liquid. Continue this procedure, adding liquid in ¼-cup increments, stirring until the liquid has evaporated, then adding more liquid, for about 15 minutes.

6 While you are attending to the risotto, heat a small skillet over medium heat and add the remaining teaspoon of olive oil. Cook the sage leaves for about 1 minute on each side, until golden and crisp. Remove with tongs or a slotted spoon and drain on paper towels.

7 Add the beans and the black pepper to the risotto. Stir thoroughly and steadily, as described above, adding another ladleful of liquid if necessary, until the rice is cooked tender, but firm to the bite. You may not need all of the liquid, or you may need a little extra hot water, depending on the rice. Taste for seasoning. The total cooking time will be about 20 minutes.

8 Stir in the grated cheese and the sage and let cook for 1 minute more, just to melt the cheese. Remove from the heat and serve immediately in shallow heated bowls.

PER 1-CUP SERVING				
	BEFORE	AFTER		
CALORIES	400	300	CARBOHYDRATES (G) 51	CARBOHYDRATE CHOICES: 3½
FAT (G)	17	6	PROTEIN (G) 11	FOOD EXCHANGES PER SERVING: 3½ STARCH,
CALORIES FROM FAT (%)	38	19	FIBER (G) 5	½ FAT
CHOLESTEROL (MG)	45	6	SODIUM (MG) 525	LOW-SODIUM DIETS: OMIT SALT AND/OR
				CHEESE. USE HOME-COOKED BEANS WITH
				LITTLE OR NO ADDED SALT. IF USING
				CANNED BEANS, TRY TO FIND THE LOW-
				SODIUM VARIETY OR RINSE VERY WELL
				AFTER DRAINING.

RISOTTO WITH GINGERED BUTTERNUT SQUASH

MAKES 2 SERVINGS

This lightened-up version of risotto uses olive oil instead of butter, and less of it. According to a New York University survey, an order of risotto from a New York restaurant was found to have 1280 calories and 110 grams of fat! Here, the buttery texture of the roasted squash, which is the main component of this dish, coupled with the natural creaminess of the risotto, makes for a very rich and satisfying dish. The squash is a great source of fiber and beta carotene. Serve as a dinner for two, perhaps with a tossed green salad, or as a side dish for four.

1 small butternut squash (about 1 pound)
Vegetable oil cooking spray
Salt and pepper, to taste
3 cups low-fat, low-sodium chicken broth
1 cup water
1 small onion, chopped (about ½ cup)

1 large garlic clove, sliced thin
1¼ teaspoons minced, peeled fresh ginger
1 tablespoon olive oil
½ cup arborio rice
¼ cup dry white wine
2 tablespoons chopped fresh chives
Chopped fresh chives and ¼ cup Parmesan curls, for garnish

1 Preheat the oven to 450° F.

2 Halve the squash lengthwise and discard seeds. Peel one half and cut into ¼-inch dice. Put remaining half, cut side down, with diced squash in a shallow baking pan sprayed with vegetable oil cooking spray and season with salt and pepper. Bake squash in middle of oven, stirring diced squash occasionally, until tender and browned lightly, 15 to 20 minutes. Holding halved squash in a kitchen towel, scoop out flesh and chop coarsely.

3 Bring the broth and water to a simmer in a saucepan, and keep at a very low simmer.

4 In another saucepan, cook onion, garlic, and ginger in oil over moderately low heat, stirring, until softened, about 5 minutes. Add broth to keep from burning, if needed. Stir in the rice and cook over moderate heat, stirring constantly, about 1 minute. Add wine and cook, stirring until absorbed. Stir in ¼ cup broth and cook,

stirring constantly and keeping at a simmer throughout, until absorbed. Continue simmering and adding broth, about ½ cup at a time, stirring constantly and letting each addition be absorbed before adding next, until about half of broth has been added.

5 Stir the diced and chopped squash into rice mixture and continue simmering and adding broth in same manner until rice is tender and creamy-looking but still al dente, 18 to 20 minutes in all. Stir in chives and salt and pepper to taste.

6 Spoon risotto into 2 shallow serving bowls and garnish with chives and Parmesan curls. Serve immediately.

PER 2-CUP SERVING						
	BEFORE	AFTER				
CALORIES	540	460	CARBOHYDRATES (G)	67	CARBOHYDRATE CHOICES: 4½	
FAT (G)	23	15	PROTEIN (G)	11	FOOD EXCHANGES PER SERVING: 4½ STARCH,	
CALORIES FROM FAT (%)	36	28	FIBER (G)	9	2 FAT	
CHOLESTEROL (MG)	45	20	SODIUM (MG)	440	LOW-SODIUM DIETS: OMIT SALT AND	
					PARMESAN CHEESE.	

RISOTTO WITH TOMATOES AND BASIL

MAKES 4 SERVINGS

The classic wide-bottomed French pan called a "sauteuse" is ideal for making risotto, because the liquid can evaporate quickly, while the ingredients at the bottom of the pan are less likely to scorch.

1 (14½-ounce) can low-fat, low-sodium chicken stock

3 cups water

1 tablespoon olive oil

2 cloves garlic, finely chopped

2 large shallots, finely chopped

6 medium ripe tomatoes, peeled, seeded, and chopped

Salt and freshly ground black pepper, to taste

1½ cups arborio rice

⅔ cup freshly grated Parmesan cheese

10 fresh basil leaves, cut into a chiffonade (page 297)

1 In a medium saucepan, combine the stock and the water and bring to a slow simmer. Let the stock simmer at the back of the stove.

2 In a large, heavy saucepan, preferably one with a base narrower than the rim, heat the olive oil over medium-low heat. Add the garlic and shallots and sauté, stirring, until translucent, about 5 minutes. Add the tomatoes and cook for 2 minutes more, until slightly softened. Stir in salt and pepper to taste.

3 Add the rice and stir until it is evenly coated with the oil mixture. Add ½ cup of the simmering broth, and continue stirring the rice until the liquid is almost all absorbed. Continue adding the broth ½ cup at a time, and stirring it in until absorbed, regulating the heat so that the liquid simmers but does not actively boil. It should take approximately 20 minutes to add all of the broth, and the rice, when done, should be tender on the outside but slightly firm at the center, with no chalky "bite." The mixture should still be quite creamy, not dry.

4 Add the Parmesan and the basil. Remove the pan from the heat and stir well. Taste for seasoning and serve immediately, in heated shallow bowls.

PER 1¼-CUP SERVING					
CALORIES	420	CARBOHYDRATES (G)	67	CARBOHYDRATE CHOICES: 4½	
FAT (G)	10	PROTEIN (G)	15	FOOD EXCHANGES PER SERVING: 4 STARCH,	
CALORIES FROM FAT (%)	22	FIBER (G)	3	1 VEGETABLE, 1 MEDIUM-FAT MEAT	
CHOLESTEROL (MG)	15	SODIUM (MG)	380	LOW-SODIUM DIETS: THIS RECIPE IS NOT	
				SUITABLE FOR THOSE ON 500 TO 1000 MG	
				SODIUM DIETS.	

COUSCOUS WITH SHRIMP AND MINT

MAKES 6 SERVINGS

Couscous is a fine-grain pasta, made from semolina flour, and is a staple in the cuisines of the Middle East and North Africa. Save time by buying instant couscous, which is ready in about 5 minutes. Couscous is a naturally low-fat dish and its flavor is enhanced in this recipe by using fresh lemon and mint. This is a great summer recipe, and is best served at room temperature. It can also be made without the shrimp, and the vegetarian version is just as flavorful.

1 cup vegetable broth
½ teaspoon salt
1 tablespoon fresh lemon juice
1 cup instant couscous
2 tablespoons olive oil
2 ripe plum tomatoes, cut into
  ¼-inch dice
2 shallots, finely chopped

1 tablespoon finely chopped parsley
3 tablespoons finely chopped
  fresh mint
Salt and freshly ground pepper, to
  taste
¾ pound cooked medium shrimp
Sprigs of parsley, for garnish
  (optional)

1 Bring the vegetable broth to a simmer and add the salt and lemon juice. Place the couscous in a bowl and pour the hot stock over it. Cover the bowl and leave to sit for 5 minutes.

2 Fluff the grains of couscous with a fork and gently fold in the olive oil, tomatoes, shallots, parsley, mint, and salt and pepper to taste. Cover and refrigerate for 15 minutes.

3 Fold in half of the cooked shrimp, transfer the couscous to a serving platter, and arrange the remaining shrimp on top in a decorative fashion. Serve, garnished with extra sprigs of parsley, if desired.

PER 1-CUP SERVING				
CALORIES	230	CARBOHYDRATES (G)	27	CARBOHYDRATE CHOICES: 2
FAT (G)	6	PROTEIN (G)	17	FOOD EXCHANGES PER SERVING: 2 STARCH,
CALORIES FROM FAT (%)	24	FIBER (G)	3	2 VERY LEAN MEAT
CHOLESTEROL (MG)	85	SODIUM (MG)	450	LOW-SODIUM DIETS: REPLACE VEGETABLE
				BROTH WITH WATER (UNLESS YOU CAN
				FIND LOW-SODIUM VEGETABLE BROTH—I
				COULDN'T) AND DECREASE SALT BY HALF.

POLENTA WITH HOT PEPPER

MAKES 8 SERVINGS

In Italy, particularly in the countryside, polenta is made almost daily, eaten alone with butter and cheese or as a side dish with meat or chicken. When it is cooled and hardened, it can be lightly fried or broiled. Simply press the finished polenta into a lightly oiled 8 × 8-inch baking dish, refrigerate until firm, then cut into squares and sauté in a nonstick pan until brown. Try using simple cookie-cutter shapes, like stars or circles, for an attractive presentation. Keep in mind that if you choose to use water only to cook the polenta, you may want to add more salt for flavor. Polenta is wonderful with stews, such as Weinersaft Gulyass (page 284), when the juices and their flavors seep into the polenta.

4 cups boiling water, or half water and half low-fat, low-sodium chicken broth
¼ teaspoon salt
1 cup cornmeal

1 clove garlic, minced
¼ teaspoon dried red pepper flakes
2 green onions (scallions), minced
¼ cup Parmesan cheese

1 In a large heavy saucepan, bring the water (and chicken broth, if using) to a boil and add the salt. Drizzle the cornmeal into the water in a slow, steady stream, stirring constantly in the same direction with a wire whisk. When the polenta has been added and absorbed, reduce the heat to very low and switch to a wooden spoon. Stir the mixture every minute or two for about 30 minutes, until the polenta is very thick and pulls away from the sides of the pan.

2 Stir in the garlic, pepper flakes, green onions, and Parmesan and serve immediately in warmed bowls.

PER ½-CUP SERVING					
CALORIES	75	CARBOHYDRATES (G)	12	CARBOHYDRATE CHOICES: 1	
FAT (G)	2	PROTEIN (G)	3	FOOD EXCHANGES PER SERVING: 1 STARCH	
CALORIES FROM FAT (%)	22	FIBER (G)	1	LOW-SODIUM DIETS: OMIT OR DECREASE SALT.	
CHOLESTEROL (MG)	4	SODIUM (MG)	160		

ROSEMARY POLENTA SQUARES

MAKES 4 SERVINGS

If you like, serve the polenta hot and creamy, straight from the pan instead of sautéing or broiling it in squares.

1¾ cup low-fat, low-sodium chicken broth
¼ cup nonfat milk
¾ cup polenta or coarse yellow cornmeal
1 tablespoon finely chopped rosemary, or 1 teaspoon dried rosemary, crumbled

1 teaspoon finely chopped thyme, or ½ teaspoon dried thyme, crumbled
¼ cup freshly grated Parmesan
Salt and freshly ground black pepper, to taste

1 In a large heavy saucepan, combine the broth and milk and bring to a boil. Reduce the heat so the liquid is simmering briskly.

2 With one hand, sprinkle in the polenta in a slow, steady stream, stirring with a wire whisk in the other hand as you pour. When the polenta has all been added and absorbed, reduce the heat to low and switch to a wooden spoon. Stir every 1 to 2 minutes (they say that Italian cooks never stop stirring) for 30 to 35 minutes or until very thick.

3 Stir in the rosemary, thyme, cheese, and salt and pepper to taste (if you plan to serve the polenta "creamy," serve immediately, in heated bowls).

4 Quickly scoop the polenta into a lightly oiled 8 × 8-inch or similar-sized roasting pan with sides and spread evenly. Allow to cool completely at room temperature, then cover with plastic wrap and refrigerate for at least 1 and up to 24 hours.

5 Cut into 4-inch squares with a sharp knife and sauté in a nonstick pan for about 2 to 3 minutes on each side, or heat under a hot broiler until golden, about 1 minute on each side.

PER 4-INCH SQUARE				
CALORIES	130	CARBOHYDRATES (G)	19	CARBOHYDRATE CHOICES: 1
FAT (G)	4	PROTEIN (G)	6	FOOD EXCHANGES PER SERVING: 1 STARCH,
CALORIES FROM FAT (%)	24	FIBER (G)	2	1 FAT
CHOLESTEROL (MG)	7	SODIUM (MG)	310	LOW-SODIUM DIETS: OMIT SALT AND DECREASE
				PARMESAN TO 2 TABLESPOONS.

SUGAR SNAP PEAS WITH POTATO AND PARSLEY SAUTÉ

MAKES 6 SERVINGS

When sugar snap peas are in season (look for them in the spring and summer), they're as sweet as candy, making this a great-tasting but simple combination of ingredients. This dish can also be served at room temperature, for a picnic or a potluck. Compared to traditional potato salad, it's a much healthier choice.

1 pound new red potatoes (if they are very small, 1 to 1½ inches in diameter, keep them whole; if not, halve or quarter them)

1 tablespoon olive oil

½ pound sugar snap peas, ends trimmed (about 2 cups)

¼ cup finely chopped parsley, or substitute basil, chives, or green onions (scallions)

Salt and freshly ground black pepper, to taste

1 In a large saucepan, set a steamer over simmering water. Steam the potatoes for about 15 minutes, depending on their size, just until tender. Do not overcook. Remove from the pan.

2 In a large heavy nonstick skillet, heat the oil over medium heat. Add the peas and sauté, stirring occasionally, for 1 minute. Add the potatoes and continue cooking, stirring occasionally, for about 1 minute more or until the potatoes are heated through but not mushy. Take care not to overcook the peas.

3 Stir in the parsley, season with salt and pepper to taste, and serve immediately or at room temperature.

PER ¾-CUP SERVING					
CALORIES	105	CARBOHYDRATES (G)	17	CARBOHYDRATE CHOICES: 1	
FAT (G)	2.5	PROTEIN (G)	4	FOOD EXCHANGES PER SERVING: 1 STARCH,	
CALORIES FROM FAT (%)	20	FIBER (G)	4	1 VEGETABLE	
CHOLESTEROL (MG)	0	SODIUM (MG)	95	LOW-SODIUM DIETS: OMIT SALT; ADD BASIL..	

PARSNIP-POTATO PUREE

MAKES 6 SERVINGS

I first had this dish at the home of my friend Annie Sabroux, where I was invited for a Thanksgiving dinner. When I took the first bite of what I thought was mashed potatoes, I was surprised by the complexity of sweet flavors brought on by the other root vegetable. I now include parsnips in my potato mash and serve it alongside my roast turkey.

1 pound russet potatoes, peeled and
    cut into 1-inch chunks
1 pound parsnips or rutabagas, peeled
    and cut into 1-inch chunks
1 tablespoon olive oil

½ teaspoon salt
¼ teaspoon ground nutmeg
    (optional)
¼ teaspoon white pepper

1 In a large saucepan, combine the potatoes and parsnips. Add enough cold water to cover the vegetables by 1 inch and bring to a boil. Simmer, covered, until the vegetables are very tender, 15 to 20 minutes.

2 Drain in a colander and, in batches, force through a ricer or food mill, fitted with the medium disk, or puree in a food processor or with an electric mixer and return to the pan. Stir in the olive oil, salt, nutmeg, and pepper. Taste for seasoning and serve immediately or keep warm in the top of a double boiler, covered.

PER ½-CUP SERVING				
CALORIES	120	CARBOHYDRATES (G)	23	CARBOHYDRATE CHOICES: 1½
FAT (G)	2	PROTEIN (G)	2	FOOD EXCHANGES PER SERVING: 1½ STARCH
CALORIES FROM FAT (%)	16	FIBER (G)	4	LOW-SODIUM DIETS: OMIT SALT.
CHOLESTEROL (MG)	5	SODIUM (MG)	210	

POTATO GRATIN

MAKES 4 SERVINGS

Bake this in the oven along with the Easy Roast Chicken (page 258). This creamy potato dish is actually a good complement to any roasted meat. For a bit of indulgence, dot the potatoes with a bit of Gruyère.

Vegetable oil cooking spray
1 pound russet potatoes, peeled and
    sliced ¼ inch thick
2 tablespoons olive oil
3 cloves garlic, finely chopped
1 teaspoon salt

Dash of white pepper
1 medium onion, sliced into thin
    rounds
¼ cup grated fat-free Swiss cheese or
    Gruyère cheese (optional)

1 Preheat the oven to 350°F.

2 Spray an 8 × 8 × 2-inch baking or gratin dish with vegetable oil cooking spray. In a bowl, toss potato slices with olive oil, garlic, salt, and pepper. Spread one layer of sliced potatoes, slightly overlapping, in the base of the pan. Scatter some of the onion slices on top and spread with another layer of potatoes, then onion, until all the ingredients have been used.

3 Bake for 45 minutes, covered. Then uncover and sprinkle with the cheese, if desired. Continue to bake for 15 minutes, or until potatoes are tender and the top is golden brown.

4 Remove from oven and allow to rest for about 5 minutes before serving.

PER ½-CUP SERVING				
CALORIES	170	CARBOHYDRATES (G)	24	CARBOHYDRATE CHOICES: 1½
FAT (G)	7	PROTEIN (G)	4	FOOD EXCHANGES PER SERVING:
CALORIES FROM FAT (%)	36	FIBER (G)	2	1½ STARCH, 1 FAT
CHOLESTEROL (MG)	0	SODIUM (MG)	630	LOW-SODIUM DIETS: OMIT SALT.

HERB-SCENTED ROASTED POTATOES

MAKES 8 SERVINGS

I like to serve these unusually presented potatoes alongside a chicken dish. Sliced lengthwise and served facedown, they look so attractive with bits of rosemary peeping out of the slits on the top side of the potato. The flavor of these moist, fragrant potatoes cannot be beat, and it relies heavily on the fresh bay leaves, which are available at most high-end supermarkets, in the fresh herb section of the produce department.

4 large russet potatoes, scrubbed and peeled, halved lengthwise
12 fresh bay leaves, halved crosswise
12 small sprigs rosemary
2 cloves garlic, finely chopped
1 tablespoon olive oil

1 cup low-fat, low-sodium chicken stock, or more as needed
Salt and freshly ground pepper, to taste
Additional sprigs of rosemary, for garnish (optional)

1 Preheat the oven to 350°F. Place the potato halves cut side down on a cutting board. With a sharp knife, cut down into each potato crosswise, making thin slices approximately ½ inch apart, being careful not to cut all the way through the potato.

2 Place pieces of bay leaf and rosemary inside each cut, then place the potato halves flat side down in a rectangular roasting pan just large enough to hold them all.

3 In a small saucepan, combine the garlic, oil, and chicken stock. Bring the mixture to a boil, then drizzle over the potatoes (the liquid should come about halfway up the sides of the potatoes). Season generously with salt and pepper.

4 Bake for 45 minutes to 1 hour, basting every 10 or 15 minutes with the broth, or until tender when pierced with the tip of a knife. If all the stock evaporates, add a little more to the pan. Garnish with additional sprigs of rosemary, if desired. Serve immediately.

PER SERVING				
CALORIES	90	CARBOHYDRATES (G)	16	CARBOHYDRATE CHOICES: 1
FAT (G)	2.5	PROTEIN (G)	2	FOOD EXCHANGES PER SERVING: 1 STARCH
CALORIES FROM FAT (%)	25	FIBER (G)	4	LOW-SODIUM DIETS: ACCEPTABLE
CHOLESTEROL (MG)	LESS THAN 1	SODIUM (MG)	85	

ROASTED, DICED POTATOES WITH CHIPOTLE

MAKES ABOUT 8 SERVINGS

I consider this a delicious alternative to fried potatoes, or French fries. You'll note the fat savings is considerable. The time it takes to get the potatoes crispy and tender like a French fry depends on how small you dice your potatoes and how crispy you like them.

2 pounds waxy potatoes, such as red or white rose
1 tablespoon olive oil
¼ teaspoon cayenne pepper, or to taste
½ small onion, finely chopped
2 teaspoons finely chopped fresh thyme or 1 teaspoon dried, crumbled

1 chipotle chile, stemmed, seeded, and ground in a spice grinder or minced
Salt, to taste

1 Preheat the oven to 375°F. Peel and cut the potatoes into ½-inch dice. In a large saucepan of lightly salted boiling water, simmer the potatoes until just tender, about 5 minutes. Drain well and pat dry with paper towels.

2 In a bowl, combine the potatoes with the olive oil, cayenne, onion, thyme, chipotle chile, and salt, and toss until evenly coated. Transfer to a large baking sheet and spread the potatoes out so that they are barely touching. Roast for 40 minutes, stirring occasionally, until crisp and golden.

PER ½-CUP SERVING					
CALORIES	95	CARBOHYDRATES (G)	15	CARBOHYDRATE CHOICES: 1	
FAT (G)	2	PROTEIN (G)	3	FOOD EXCHANGES PER SERVING: 1 STARCH	
CALORIES FROM FAT (%)	20	FIBER (G)	2	LOW-SODIUM DIETS: OMIT SALT.	
CHOLESTEROL (MG)	0	SODIUM (MG)	70		

CARIBBEAN SWEET POTATOES

MAKES 6 SERVINGS

The maple syrup and currants make this dish a nicely sweet accompaniment to a turkey dinner. Be sure to count carbohydrates, as ½ cup of this dish has twice the carbs of a plain sweet potato.

6 large sweet potatoes, well scrubbed and pierced several times with the tines of a fork
¼ cup reduced-calorie pancake syrup or pure maple syrup (see Note)
¼ cup currants, soaked for 10 minutes in hot water and drained

Salt and freshly ground black pepper, to taste
Pinch of nutmeg
Vegetable oil cooking spray

1 Preheat the oven to 350° F. Lightly oil a baking sheet and place the sweet potatoes on it, not touching one another. Bake for about 1 hour, or until tender. Remove the potatoes to cool and leave the oven on.

2 When the potatoes are cool enough to handle, halve them lengthwise and scoop the pulp into a bowl. Mash with a fork or blend with an electric mixer until fairly smooth.

3 Add the syrup, currants, salt and pepper to taste, and the nutmeg. Mix until smooth and well blended.

4 Spray a large casserole with cooking spray and transfer the sweet potato mixture to the dish.

5 Return the potatoes to the oven for 15 to 20 minutes, until heated through.

Note: Using real maple syrup in place of reduced-calorie pancake syrup increases the carbohydrate level by 5 grams, an insignificant amount.

PER ½-CUP SERVING					
CALORIES	150	CARBOHYDRATES (G)	36	CARBOHYDRATE CHOICES: 2½	
FAT (G)	LESS THAN .5	PROTEIN (G)	2	FOOD EXCHANGES PER SERVING: 2½	
CALORIES FROM FAT (%)	1	FIBER (G)	4	CARBOHYDRATE	
CHOLESTEROL (MG)	0	SODIUM (MG)	120	LOW-SODIUM DIETS: GOOD CHOICE. AVOID ADDING SALT.	

CHAPTER 25

DESSERTS

E veryone loves dessert, including people with diabetes. And while it's true that the 1994 guidelines allow for some sugar in the diet, there are two considerations. First, since desserts contribute more carbohydrates per bite than other starches, they have to be carefully worked into your food plan. For example, if you know you're having dessert, you may want to pass on the starch at your main course so you won't go over your carbohydrate allowance. Remember, its the *amount* and not the *source* of carbohydrate that affects blood glucose levels. Just count those carbohydrate grams and stay within your carbohydrate limit. But exercise moderation: If *all* your carbohydrate is taken in the form of desserts, it may throw your blood sugar into a tailspin.

Second, desserts tend to contribute a significant amount of calories, which you'll want to keep a lid on if weight control is a concern. By making a few key changes in these recipes, I've cut fat and calories yet preserved old-fashioned taste and texture. Several of the recipes call for egg whites instead of whole eggs, all have unsaturated fats, and some call for less sugar, or sugar substitutes, which help to cut back on carbohydrates. All include generous amounts of flavorings, such as vanilla extract, spices, lemon or orange zest, molasses, and brown sugar, to provide a full measure of flavor without fat.

PEARS BAKED IN MARSALA

MAKES 8 SERVINGS

I once saw a T-shirt that read, "Fruit is not dessert," but this one is quite convincing. Here you can have the sweet without the fat, naturally. The standard rule for poaching liquid according to Julia Child is 6 tablespoons of sugar per cup of liquid (water or wine). Half that amount saves 5 grams of carbohydrates per serving and makes a lovely, refreshing, and plenty sweet dessert.

8 small, ripe but firm pears, such as
    Bosc or Anjou (about 3 pounds)
2 tablespoons fresh lemon juice
1 cup Marsala wine

3 tablespoons firmly packed light
    brown sugar
¼ teaspoon ground cinnamon

1 Preheat the oven to 350°F. Peel the pears from the base up with a vegetable peeler, leaving the stems intact. Remove a small slice from the bottom so they will stand upright.

2 Brush the pears with lemon juice and set them in a shallow baking dish that will hold them all just barely touching. Pour the Marsala over and around the pears. Combine the brown sugar and cinnamon and sprinkle the mixture evenly over the tops of the pears.

3 Bake uncovered for 50 to 60 minutes, or until the pears are tender, basting with the wine every 10 minutes or so. Serve warm or at room temperature with the pan juices drizzled over and around them.

PER SERVING WITH 2 TABLESPOONS BAKING LIQUID					
CALORIES	100	CARBOHYDRATES (G)	25	CARBOHYDRATE CHOICES: 1½	
FAT (G)	0.5	PROTEIN (G)	1	FOOD EXCHANGES PER SERVING: 2 FRUIT	
CALORIES FROM FAT (%)	5	FIBER (G)	3	LOW-SODIUM DIETS: THIS RECIPE IS GREAT	
CHOLESTEROL (MG)	0	SODIUM (MG)	0	FOR ANYONE ON A LOW-SODIUM DIET.	
				FRUIT IS NATURALLY SODIUM-FREE.	

GRILLED FRUIT WITH MINT

MAKES 6 SERVINGS

Mix and match seasonal fruits for this high-fiber, fat-free dessert. Be creative; the time of year and your imagination are the only limits. Cooking times will vary; the more ripe a piece of fruit is, the less time it needs to obtain the perfect texture. Nutritional information is based on 2 fruits (2 carbohydrate choices) plus the sweeteners, but you can grill the fruit plain if you like.

Approximately 12 pieces assorted fruit of your choice, such as peaches, apricots, apples, pears, or bananas, washed but not peeled
1 teaspoon honey per piece of fruit as needed, depending on fruits used and quantity

1 teaspoon brown sugar per piece of fruit as needed, depending on fruits used and quantity
1 tablespoon dark rum, or the liqueur of your choice
Sprigs of mint, for garnish

1 Preheat an outdoor grill or a well-seasoned ridged cast-iron griddle pan. If using peaches or apricots, cut them in half and remove the pits. Place ½ teaspoon honey in the center of each half.

2 If using apples or pears, halve and core them. Make 3 shallow cuts in the skin side of each halved fruit. Place ½ teaspoon brown sugar in the hollowed core of each piece of fruit.

3 If using bananas, halve them lengthwise. Keep peels on bananas, especially if they are quite ripe, and remove before serving. Brush the cut side with honey and sprinkle with brown sugar.

4 Place the fruits inside a hinged grilling basket, such as those designed for whole fish, or directly on the grill rack or griddle pan. Grill apples and peaches about 10 minutes skin side down and 2 to 3 minutes on the flesh side. Apricots, bananas, and pears will take about 2 minutes less on the skin side.

5 Transfer an equal portion of fruit to each of six dessert plates. Sprinkle ½ teaspoon dark rum over the grilled fruit and garnish the plate with mint sprigs.

PER SERVING OF ½ BANANA AND ½ PEACH					
CALORIES	100	CARBOHYDRATES (G)	26	CARBOHYDRATE CHOICES: 2	
FAT (G)	LESS THAN .5	PROTEIN (G)	LESS THAN 1	FOOD EXCHANGES PER SERVING: 2 FRUIT	
CALORIES FROM FAT (%)	3	FIBER (G)	2	LOW-SODIUM DIETS: EXCELLENT CHOICE	
CHOLESTEROL (MG)	0	SODIUM (MG)	0		

BANANA ICE CREAM

MAKES 4 SERVINGS

Whenever my bananas are overripe, I peel them, cut them into chunks, place them in a plastic bag, and toss them into the freezer. I use them for smoothies in the morning or ice cream at night. The creamy texture of bananas makes them a great fat-free base for both. I keep other frozen fruit on hand for endless concoctions—strawberries, blueberries, mangos, and on and on. Of course, you could use frozen raspberries for this shocking pink dessert in the winter.

2 ripe bananas, peeled and sliced
½ cup ripe raspberries
½ teaspoon ground cinnamon

Sprigs of mint or cinnamon basil, for garnish

1 Distribute the bananas and the raspberries evenly in the base of a glass or ceramic dish. Cover and freeze for at least 3 hours or overnight.

2 Remove the fruit from the freezer and let rest for 5 minutes at room temperature. In a blender or food processor, combine the bananas, raspberries, and cinnamon. Pulse until evenly mixed, scraping down the sides of the bowl as necessary.

3 Serve the ice cream immediately, garnished with sprigs of mint.

PER ½-CUP SERVING					
CALORIES	60	CARBOHYDRATES (G)	15	CARBOHYDRATE CHOICES: 1	
FAT (G)	LESS THAN .5	PROTEIN (G)	LESS THAN 1	FOOD EXCHANGES PER SERVING: 1 FRUIT	
CALORIES FROM FAT (%)	5	FIBER (G)	2	LOW-SODIUM DIETS: EXCELLENT CHOICE.	
CHOLESTEROL (MG)	0	SODIUM (MG)	0	MOST FRUITS ARE NATURALLY SODIUM-FREE.	

LEMON TART

This simple, lemony tart can also be made in individual tart pans, or in mini-muffin pans and served at "tea." The original recipe is made with whole eggs and butter. Although you can use bottled lemon juice, freshly squeezed lemon juice gives a more intense flavor. Garnish with lemon peel and a sprig of mint.

Crust
1 cup all-purpose flour
¼ teaspoon salt
1 tablespoon cornstarch
½ teaspoon finely chopped
    lemon zest
3 tablespoons canola oil
3 tablespoons ice water
1 teaspoon fresh lemon juice

Filling
⅛ teaspoon salt
3 tablespoons cornstarch
1½ cups boiling water
⅓ cup nonfat liquid egg substitute
1 tablespoon finely chopped lemon
    zest
½ cup fresh lemon juice
Sugar substitute equal to ½ cup sugar

1 Preheat the oven to 425°F.

2 To make the crust, combine the flour, salt, cornstarch, and lemon zest in a bowl. Drizzle with the canola oil and mix gently with a fork until the oil is absorbed. Combine the water and lemon juice and drizzle over the flour-oil mixture. Mix until dough becomes moist and pliable.

3 Form the dough into a ball and press into a 9-inch tart pan with a removable bottom, distributing the dough evenly and crimping off any excess. Place a round of waxed paper in the base of the pan, pour enough dried rice or beans into the pan to cover the base (this weighs down the dough and prevents it from bubbling while it bakes), and bake for 15 to 20 minutes, or until firm and slightly golden. Remove from the oven, remove rice or beans and waxed paper, and allow to cool in the pan while preparing the filling.

4 To make the filling: In a medium saucepan over medium heat, combine the salt and cornstarch with 2 tablespoons of lukewarm water and stir until all of the cornstarch is incorporated. Stir in the 1½ cups boiling water and bring the mixture to a boil. Cook until the mixture thickens and clears, about 2 minutes.

5 Pour the egg substitute into a small bowl, then whisk in 2 tablespoons of the cornstarch mixture to temper the eggs. Pour the eggs back into the pan with the cornstarch and whisk to combine. Add the lemon zest and the juice, and cook for 2 more minutes, stirring constantly. Remove from the heat, place in a bowl, and cool for 20 minutes, stirring occasionally to cool more quickly. Add the sugar substitute, stirring until it has completely dissolved.

6 Pour the lemon mixture into the baked tart shell, smoothing the surface with a rubber spatula, then cover and refrigerate until the lemon filling sets, at least an hour. Cut into wedges and serve.

Note: *Using regular sugar rather than sugar substitute increases carbohydrate to 30 grams, equal to 2 carbohydrate choices.*

PER SERVING						
	BEFORE	AFTER				
CALORIES	410	130	CARBOHYDRATES (G)	17	CARBOHYDRATE CHOICES: 1	
FAT (G)	18	6	PROTEIN (G)	3	FOOD EXCHANGES PER SERVING: 1	
CALORIES FROM FAT (%)	40	39	FIBER (G)	LESS THAN 1	CARBOHYDRATE, 1 FAT	
CHOLESTEROL (MG)	200	0	SODIUM (MG)	120	LOW-SODIUM DIETS: ACCEPTABLE	

APPLE TARTS IN PHYLLO DOUGH

MAKES 4 TARTS

Tender apples, spicy cinnamon, and light, flaky phyllo make this a wonderful treat. Serve these with small scoops of low-fat vanilla frozen yogurt for a tasty—and healthy—version of apple pie à la mode.

Tarts
2 Golden Delicious apples
2 tablespoons packed brown sugar
1 tablespoon fresh lemon juice
1/2 teaspoon ground cinnamon
Vegetable oil cooking spray
4 sheets of phyllo dough, thawed
    according to package instructions
White of 1 large egg, lightly beaten

Topping
1/2 teaspoon ground cinnamon
1 teaspoon sugar

1 Preheat the oven to 350°F and line a baking sheet with parchment paper.

2 Peel, quarter, and core the apples. Cut the apple quarters into thin slices and combine in a bowl with the brown sugar, lemon juice, and cinnamon.

3 Spray each of the phyllo sheets with vegetable oil cooking spray and fold in half lengthwise. Spray again, then fold in half crosswise. Spray once more. Each phyllo dough sheet will be one quarter its original size.

4 Place 2 tablespoons of the apple mixture in the center of each phyllo sheet and fold all 4 corners into the center, overlapping them slightly. Brush with the egg white. For the topping, mix together the cinnamon and sugar; sprinkle it evenly over the tops. Make 4 slits in each envelope to allow steam to escape during cooking.

5 Bake the tarts until slightly golden brown and hot in the center, about 15 minutes. Serve hot or at room temperature.

PER TART					
CALORIES	90	CARBOHYDRATES (G)	19	CARBOHYDRATE CHOICES: 1	
FAT (G)	.5	PROTEIN (G)	2	FOOD EXCHANGES PER SERVING: 1	
CALORIES FROM FAT (%)	6	FIBER (G)	2	CARBOHYDRATE	
CHOLESTEROL (MG)	0	SODIUM (MG)	50	LOW-SODIUM DIETS: EXCELLENT CHOICE	

STRAWBERRIES IN YOGURT AND BROWN SUGAR

MAKES 2 SERVINGS

This is quite a romantic dessert, with no need for a fork or spoon. Balsamic vinegars are very sweet and are often paired with fruits and desserts in Italy. Demerara sugar is raw sugar that flows freely. Brown sugar is a good alternative.

1 to 2 teaspoons balsamic vinegar, or to taste

1 cup nonfat (or low-fat) yogurt

2 tablespoons brown sugar, or raw Demerara sugar, or equivalent sugar substitute (see Note)

1 cup (about 1 basket) ripe strawberries, brushed clean and hulled

1 teaspoon confectioners' sugar

1 In a small bowl, whisk 1 teaspoon of the balsamic vinegar into the yogurt and taste to decide whether you want to add another teaspoon. Place 2 small ramekins on a large oval platter and fill 1 with the yogurt mixture, and the other with the sugar substitute or raw sugar.

2 Arrange the strawberries around the ramekins and dust them lightly with the confectioners' sugar, shaken through a small sieve. Dip the strawberries first in the yogurt mixture, then in the raw sugar.

Note: This recipe was calculated with regular sugar instead of sugar substitute for the purposes of flavor and presentation. If sugar substitute is used, the recipe will have 9 grams less of carbohydrate, equal to ½ carbohydrate choice.

PER SERVING					
CALORIES	140	CARBOHYDRATES (G)	26	CARBOHYDRATE CHOICES: 2	
FAT (G)	LESS THAN .5	PROTEIN (G)	8	FOOD EXCHANGES PER SERVING: 2	
CALORIES FROM FAT (%)	3	FIBER (G)	1	CARBOHYDRATE	
CHOLESTEROL (MG)	LESS THAN 5	SODIUM (MG)	100	LOW-SODIUM DIETS: GOOD CHOICE	

ANGEL FOOD CAKE WITH RASPBERRIES

MAKES ONE 9-INCH CAKE

Angel food cake, my favorite birthday cake, is naturally fat-free. It's primarily made from whipped egg whites blended with flour and sugar. The incredibly easy and truly sensational raspberry sauce makes this cake into a very delicious dessert. When fresh raspberries are in season, I decorate the cake and the plate with them. Strawberries can also be substituted.

1¼ cups sugar, divided
1¼ cups cake flour
Whites of 12 large eggs
¼ teaspoon salt

1½ teaspoons cream of tartar
1 teaspoon vanilla
Raspberry Sauce (recipe opposite)

1 Preheat the oven to 350°F.

2 Have ready, but do not grease, a 9-inch nonstick tube pan.

3 Sift together half the sugar and all of the cake flour and set the mixture aside.

4 In a very large bowl, combine the egg whites, salt, cream of tartar, and vanilla and beat with an electric mixer on medium speed until foamy. Add and beat in the remaining sugar, 1 tablespoon at a time, until stiff peaks form, about 5 minutes.

5 Gradually fold the sifted dry ingredients into the meringue.

6 Gently pour the mixture into the tube pan and bake for 35 to 45 minutes, or until the cake is golden brown and firm to the touch. Invert on a rack and cool completely. Then loosen around the edges of the pan with a small knife and turn the cake out onto a serving platter.

7 Slice the cake into 8 wedges and serve on individual dessert plates with the Raspberry Sauce drizzled over the top.

RASPBERRY SAUCE (makes 2 cups)

2 cups frozen raspberries, defrosted
2 tablespoons Grand Marnier,
    Cointreau, or other fruit liqueur
    (optional)

In a blender or food processor, combine the raspberries and liqueur, if using. Blend until smooth.

PER 1-INCH SLICE WITH 2 TABLESPOONS RASPBERRY SAUCE					
CALORIES	140	CARBOHYDRATES (G)	30	CARBOHYDRATE CHOICES: 2	
FAT (G)	0	PROTEIN (G)	4	FOOD EXCHANGES PER SERVING: 2	
CALORIES FROM FAT (%)	1	FIBER (G)	1	CARBOHYDRATE	
CHOLESTEROL (MG)	0	SODIUM (MG)	75	LOW-SODIUM DIETS: EXCELLENT CHOICE	

ESPRESSO ANGEL FOOD CAKE WITH CHOCOLATE SAUCE

MAKES TWO 9-INCH CAKES, OR 16 SERVINGS

The idea for this recipe came from Dan Bud, when he was pastry chef at the Park Avenue Cafe in New York. He needed a dessert that would please his customers who wanted a fat-free and richly flavored dessert. I have adapted it so that you can make it in your own home.

1¼ cups sugar, divided
1¼ cups cake flour
2 tablespoons finely ground espresso powder
1 tablespoon ground cinnamon

Whites of 12 large eggs
1½ teaspoons cream of tartar
Chocolate Sauce (optional; recipe opposite)

1 Preheat the oven to 350°F.

2 Have ready, but do not grease, two 9-inch nonstick cake pans.

3 Sift together half the sugar, the cake flour, espresso powder, and cinnamon. Set aside.

4 In a very large bowl, whip the egg whites and cream of tartar with an electric mixer on medium speed until foamy. Beat in the remaining sugar 1 tablespoon at a time until stiff peaks form, about 5 minutes.

5 Gradually fold the sifted dry ingredients into the meringue.

6 Divide the mixture evenly between the two pans and bake for about 20 to 25 minutes, or until the cakes are golden brown and firm. Remove from the oven and invert the pans on a rack to cool. Let cool completely in the pans, about 1 hour. Loosen around the edges of the pan with a small knife and turn the cakes out onto a platter.

7 Slice the cakes into 8 wedges each and serve on individual dessert plates with chocolate sauce drizzled on top, if desired.

CHOCOLATE SAUCE

3 ounces semisweet chocolate squares
3 ounces low-fat cream cheese, at
    room temperature

¼ cup nonfat milk, or more as
    needed
½ cup confectioners' sugar

In a nonstick pan on medium-low heat, melt the chocolate squares. Blend together the cream cheese and the milk with a whisk. Combine this mixture and the confectioners' sugar with the melted chocolate and whisk until smooth. If a thinner consistency is desired, add a bit more milk. Spread on the cake with a knife or drizzle over cake.

PER SERVING WITHOUT CHOCOLATE SAUCE					
CALORIES	100	CARBOHYDRATES (G)	22	CARBOHYDRATE CHOICES: 1½	
FAT (G)	0	PROTEIN (G)	3	FOOD EXCHANGES PER SERVING: 1½	
CALORIES FROM FAT (%)	1	FIBER (G)	0	CARBOHYDRATE	
CHOLESTEROL (MG)	0	SODIUM (MG)	55	LOW-SODIUM DIETS: ACCEPTABLE	

PER SERVING WITH CHOCOLATE SAUCE					
CALORIES	150	CARBOHYDRATES (G)	29	CARBOHYDRATE CHOICES: 2	
FAT (G)	2.5	PROTEIN (G)	4	FOOD EXCHANGES PER SERVING: 1½	
CALORIES FROM FAT (%)	15	FIBER (G)	.5	CARBOHYDRATE	
CHOLESTEROL (MG)	LESS THAN 5	SODIUM (MG)	95	LOW-SODIUM DIETS: ACCEPTABLE	

CARROT SPICE CAKE

MAKES 12 SERVINGS

Traditional carrot cake may sound healthy because of the extra beta carotene, vitamin A, and the fiber of the carrots, but those benefits are usually undone by adding a cup or more of oil or butter. But not in my carrot cake, where I replace the butter with buttermilk and a small amount of vegetable oil, and use egg substitute instead of whole eggs. It's moist and flavorful, and your guests will never guess it's anything other than the real thing.

Vegetable oil cooking spray
1 tablespoon all-purpose flour
2½ cups sifted cake flour
2½ teaspoons baking powder
¼ teaspoon baking soda
½ teaspoon salt
1½ teaspoons ground cinnamon
½ teaspoon ground ginger
¼ teaspoon ground nutmeg
⅛ teaspoon ground cloves
1½ cups finely shredded peeled
    carrots (about 3 medium carrots)

½ cup sugar
½ cup firmly packed brown sugar
½ cup nonfat buttermilk
¼ cup nonfat egg substitute, thawed
¼ cup vegetable oil
1 teaspoon vanilla extract
1 (15½-ounce) can crushed
    pineapple in juice, drained, juice
    reserved for Glaze
Whites of 4 large eggs
¼ teaspoon cream of tartar
Glaze (recipe opposite)

1 Preheat the oven to 350° F. Generously coat a 13 × 9 × 2-inch baking dish with cooking spray. Dust with the tablespoon of flour, shaking to distribute it evenly, and set aside.

2 In a large bowl, sift together the cake flour, baking powder, baking soda, salt, cinnamon, ginger, nutmeg, and cloves. Set aside.

3 In a food processor, combine the carrots, white and brown sugars, buttermilk, egg substitute, oil, and vanilla. Pulse until well combined, then add to the dry ingredients and stir until well blended. Stir in the pineapple.

4 In a separate bowl, combine the egg whites and cream of tartar and beat with an electric mixer at high speed until stiff peaks form. Thoroughly stir ½ cup of the egg white mixture into the batter, then gently fold in the remaining mixture.

5 Pour the batter into the prepared pan and bake for 25 to 27 minutes, until golden brown and a toothpick inserted in the center comes out clean. Let cool on wire rack. Poke the cake all over with a fork, and drizzle with the Glaze.

GLAZE (makes about ½ cup)

This glaze requires no cooking, but can be spread directly on the cake.

½ cup confectioners' sugar
¼ teaspoon vanilla extract

1 tablespoon reserved pineapple juice,
or lemon juice

In a bowl, whisk the confectioners' sugar, vanilla, and pineapple juice together thoroughly.

PER 3 × 4-INCH SLICE

	BEFORE	AFTER			
CALORIES	300	250	CARBOHYDRATES (G)	46	CARBOHYDRATE CHOICES: 3
FAT (G)	11	5	PROTEIN (G)	6	FOOD EXCHANGES PER SERVING: 3
CALORIES FROM FAT (%)	33	19	FIBER (G)	2	CARBOHYDRATE, 1 FAT
CHOLESTEROL (MG)	65	0	SODIUM (MG)	280	LOW-SODIUM DIETS: OMIT SALT.

MOCHA ANGEL CAKE ROLL

MAKES 12 SERVINGS

If you prefer your roulade with chocolate, try this light and airy chocolaty filling that tastes creamy without the cream.

Cake
Vegetable oil cooking spray
⅔ cup sugar
⅔ cup all-purpose flour
Whites of 6 large eggs
1 teaspoon vanilla extract
1 teaspoon cream of tartar

Filling
3 tablespoons sugar-free chocolate
    pudding mix
2 teaspoons instant espresso
⅓ cup nonfat milk
6 ounces (about 2 cups) fat-free
    whipped topping
Cocoa powder and/or confectioners'
    sugar, for garnish (optional)

1 For the cake, preheat the oven to 300°F. Lightly spray an 11 × 15-inch jelly roll pan (or cookie sheet with sides) with cooking spray, then line it with parchment paper. Lightly spray the paper and set aside.

2 In a small bowl, sift together 6 tablespoons of the sugar and the flour and set aside.

3 In a large bowl, combine the egg whites, vanilla extract, and cream of tartar. Beat with an electric mixer until foamy, then add the remaining sugar 1 tablespoon at a time, beating the mixture until slightly stiff peaks form. Be careful not to overbeat the egg whites.

4 Sift the flour mixture into the egg white mixture a little at a time, folding carefully, until all of the dry mixture is incorporated. Spread the batter carefully into the prepared pan, making sure the surface is as even as possible.

5 Bake for 20 to 25 minutes, or until golden and springy to the touch. Remove from the oven, transfer to a wire rack, and cover with a damp kitchen towel. Let stand until cool, about half an hour.

6 While the cake is cooling, make the filling. In a small bowl, blend the pudding mix, espresso, and milk until well combined. Add the whipped topping and blend thoroughly. Place in the refrigerator to chill.

7 Place a large sheet of parchment paper on a flat surface. Loosen the edges of the cake with a small knife, and carefully invert it onto the paper. Lift away the pan and gently peel off the parchment paper from the underside of the cake, being careful not to tear the cake.

8 Just before serving, remove the filling from the refrigerator and mix until smooth, then spread evenly over the surface of the cake. Starting from the short end, roll the cake up lengthwise carefully and place on a rectangular serving platter, seam side down. Dust with cocoa powder and/or confectioners' sugar, if desired, and cut into 1-inch-thick slices for serving.

PER SLICE					
CALORIES	85	CARBOHYDRATES (G)	18	CARBOHYDRATE CHOICES: 1	
FAT (G)	0	PROTEIN (G)	2	FOOD EXCHANGES PER SERVING: 1	
CALORIES FROM FAT (%)	0	FIBER (G)	0	CARBOHYDRATE	
CHOLESTEROL (MG)	0	SODIUM (MG)	90	LOW-SODIUM DIETS: ACCEPTABLE	

FRESH STRAWBERRY ROULADE

MAKES 12 SERVINGS

This is basically an angel food cake rolled up with berries and jam.

10 fresh egg whites (about 1¼ cups liquid egg whites)
¾ cup sugar, divided
1 teaspoon vanilla extract
2 teaspoons fresh lemon juice
½ teaspoon grated orange zest
1 cup all-purpose flour
1 cup strawberry preserves
1 pint strawberries, hulled and thinly sliced

1 Preheat the oven to 375° F. Lightly brush the base of an 11 × 15-inch jelly roll pan (or cookie sheet with sides) with oil, then line it with parchment paper (the oil helps the paper adhere to the pan).

2 In a large bowl, combine the egg whites with half the sugar. With an electric mixer, beat the mixture to stiff peaks, gradually adding the remaining sugar. Add the vanilla, lemon juice, and orange zest to the egg white mixture. Sift the flour over the top and fold it in gently, just until thoroughly combined, but do not overmix or you will crush too much air out of the egg white mixture. Using a flat spatula, gently spread the mixture into the prepared pan in an even layer.

3 Bake for 20 minutes, or until golden brown and firm. Remove from the oven, transfer to a rack, and cover with a damp kitchen towel. Cool for 10 minutes.

4 Place a large sheet of parchment on a flat surface. Loosen the edges of the cake with a small knife, and invert it onto the paper. Lift the pan and peel off the parchment paper from the underside of the cake. (Fold one corner back on itself and peel gently downward, not upward.) Keep covered with plastic.

6 Just before serving, spread a thin layer of preserves evenly over the cake. Arrange the strawberries evenly over the cake surface. Roll the cake lengthwise, starting from a longer side, using the edges of the parchment to lift. Place the cake, seam side down, on a rectangular serving plate and slice into rolls just before serving.

PER 1-INCH SLICE					
CALORIES	160	CARBOHYDRATES (G)	35	CARBOHYDRATE CHOICES: 2	
FAT (G)	.5	PROTEIN (G)	5	FOOD EXCHANGES PER SERVING: 2	
CALORIES FROM FAT (%)	2	FIBER (G)	2	CARBOHYDRATE	
CHOLESTEROL (MG)	0	SODIUM (MG)	130	LOW-SODIUM DIETS: ACCEPTABLE	

CHOCOLATE-ORANGE BISCOTTI

MAKES 26 COOKIES

In Italy, these dry, not-too-sweet cookies are served with cappuccino. The classic version contains very little fat and sugar, so you'll notice little difference between these and the traditional biscotti.

2 cups all-purpose flour
⅓ cup sugar
1 teaspoon baking powder
2½ teaspoons fennel seed
¼ teaspoon salt
2 teaspoons finely grated orange zest

3 tablespoons vegetable oil
2 teaspoons vanilla extract
Whites of 3 large eggs, lightly beaten
Vegetable oil cooking spray
¼ cup low-fat chocolate chips

1 Preheat the oven to 350° F.

2 In a large bowl, combine the flour, sugar, baking powder, fennel seed, and salt. In a smaller bowl, combine the orange zest, vegetable oil, vanilla, and egg whites. Add the wet ingredients to the flour mixture. Mix until a soft dough forms. If necessary, add a teaspoon or two of water to help the dough bind.

3 Spray a large cookie sheet with vegetable oil cooking spray. Turn dough out onto the sheet and shape with your hands into a log roughly 12 inches long. Flatten the log to a ½-inch thickness, then bake for 25 minutes.

4 Leave the oven on and transfer the log to a wire rack; allow it to sit until cool enough to handle. While the log is cooling, spray the cookie sheet again with vegetable spray. Then, with a serrated knife, slice the log into ½-inch-thick slices. Place the slices cut side down on the cookie sheet. Bake for 20 minutes more, then transfer to the wire rack to cool completely. The biscotti should be very dry.

5 While the biscotti are cooling, melt the chocolate chips in a double boiler over barely simmering water. Drizzle the chocolate over the cooled cookies and allow it to harden before serving.

PER BISCOTTI						
	BEFORE	**AFTER**				
CALORIES	80	70	CARBOHYDRATES (G)	11	CARBOHYDRATE CHOICES: 1	
FAT (G)	2.5	2	PROTEIN (G)	2	FOOD EXCHANGES PER SERVING: 1	
CALORIES FROM FAT (%)	29	28	FIBER (G)	0	CARBOHYDRATE	
CHOLESTEROL (MG)	15	0	SODIUM (MG)	45	LOW-SODIUM DIETS: ACCEPTABLE	

CHOCOLATE SANDWICH COOKIES

MAKES 50 TO 55 COOKIES OR APPROXIMATELY 25 SANDWICH COOKIES

Every year at Christmastime, my mother-in-law sends me pecans from her own trees in southern Louisiana. This is one of the ways that I use them. It's been called "the best thing I've ever tasted." They are built like an Oreo, but with the complex flavors of nuts, rum, and coffee on the outside and the creamy chocolate mousse inside. Since they can be served frozen, I keep them in the freezer where they are ready for a party or an afternoon snack.

½ cup sugar
¾ cup coarsely chopped pecans
⅓ cup unsweetened cocoa powder
2 tablespoons dark rum
3 teaspoons instant espresso powder

Whites of 3 large eggs
½ cup Chocolate Truffle Mousse
   filling (recipe opposite)
Cocoa or confectioners' sugar, for
   dusting

1 Preheat the oven to 300°F, place the racks in the lower and middle positions, and line 2 baking sheets with parchment paper.

2 In a food processor, combine the sugar, pecans, cocoa, rum, and espresso granules. Process until finely ground. With the machine on, slowly add the egg whites to form a thick, sticky batter, scraping down the sides of the bowl to blend evenly.

3 Drop scant teaspoons of the batter about 2 inches apart on the prepared cookie sheets. Bake for 15 to 18 minutes, switching the pans after 8 minutes to help them cook evenly. When the cookies are puffy and the tops look slightly crackly, remove from the oven and transfer the pans to racks. When cool enough to handle, invert and carefully peel the parchment paper off the backs of the cookies. At this point, you can store the cookies in an airtight container for up to 2 days before finishing.

4 To assemble, arrange 5 of the cookies on a work surface, bottom sides up. Place a heaping teaspoonful of the Chocolate Truffle Mousse onto each cookie and gently press another cookie on top, sandwiching the filling into a flat layer. As you assemble the sandwiches, transfer them to a baking sheet, cover with plastic wrap, and place in the freezer (you will probably need 2 baking sheets). Freeze overnight or for up to 2 months (if you plan to freeze the cookies for longer than 1 day, freeze them overnight first on the baking sheets, then transfer them to an airtight container and separate the layers with sheets of waxed paper or parchment paper).

5 Just before serving, sift a light dusting of cocoa or confectioners' sugar over the cookies. Serve frozen.

CHOCOLATE TRUFFLE MOUSSE FILLING (makes approximately ½ cup)

¼ cup low-fat cream cheese, about
    1½ ounces, at room temperature
Sugar substitute equal to ⅓ cup sugar
3 tablespoons unsweetened cocoa
    powder

1½ teaspoons nonfat milk
½ cup fat-free nondairy whipped
    topping, such as Cool Whip
½ teaspoon vanilla extract

In a medium bowl, using a hand mixer, beat together the cream cheese, sugar substitute, cocoa powder, and milk until smooth. Fold in the whipped topping and vanilla, mixing carefully until well blended. Cover and chill for at least 1 hour before using.

PER SANDWICH COOKIE					
CALORIES	60	CARBOHYDRATES (G)	6	CARBOHYDRATE CHOICES: ½	
FAT (G)	3	PROTEIN (G)	2	FOOD EXCHANGES PER SERVING: ½	
CALORIES FROM FAT (%)	44	FIBER (G)	LESS THAN 1	CARBOHYDRATE, ½ FAT	
CHOLESTEROL (MG)	0	SODIUM (MG)	15	LOW-SODIUM DIETS: ACCEPTABLE	

PUMPKIN PIE

MAKES 8 SERVINGS

Topped with a little fat-free whipped topping, this version of pumpkin pie is a wonderful finish to a traditional turkey dinner, or just a simple way to indulge. As piecrusts go, this one is surprisingly easy, and bakes up golden and crisp.

Crust
1 cup all-purpose flour
¼ teaspoon salt
1 tablespoon cornstarch
3 tablespoons canola oil
3 tablespoons ice water
1 teaspoon fresh lemon juice

Filling
2 cups canned pumpkin puree
Egg substitute equivalent to 2 large eggs, or 2 large, whole eggs lightly beaten
1 cup nonfat evaporated milk
1 teaspoon vanilla extract
½ cup reduced-calorie pancake syrup, with no sugar added
½ cup packed brown sugar
2 tablespoons cornstarch
1 teaspoon ground cinnamon
1 teaspoon ground ginger
¼ teaspoon ground nutmeg
¼ teaspoon salt
Fat-free nondairy whipped topping and candied orange peel, for garnish (optional)

1 Preheat the oven to 425°F.

2 To make the crust: In a large bowl, combine the flour, salt and cornstarch. Drizzle with the canola oil and mix gently with a fork until the oil is absorbed. Combine water and lemon juice and drizzle over the flour-oil mixture, stirring until the dough becomes moist and pliable. Form the dough into a ball and place in 9-inch pie dish. With your fingertips, press the dough evenly out to the edges of the pie dish and crimp any excess dough from the edge. Place the pie dish in the freezer to chill while preparing the filling.

3 To make the filling: In a large bowl, combine the pumpkin, egg substitute, evaporated milk, vanilla, and pancake syrup and whisk until well blended.

4 In a small bowl, sift together the brown sugar, cornstarch, cinnamon, ginger, nutmeg, and salt. Sift the dry ingredients into the pumpkin mixture and whisk until well combined. Carefully pour into the chilled piecrust and bake for 10 minutes. Reduce the heat to 350°F and bake for 40 to 45 minutes more, or until a knife inserted in the center comes out clean. Set on a wire rack to cool. Serve with a dollop of whipped topping and a piece of candied orange peel on top, if desired.

PER SERVING					
CALORIES	230	CARBOHYDRATES (G)	36	CARBOHYDRATE CHOICES: 2½	
FAT (G)	7	PROTEIN (G)	7	FOOD EXCHANGES PER SERVING: 2½	
CALORIES FROM FAT (%)	26	FIBER (G)	3	CARBOHYDRATE, 1 FAT	
CHOLESTEROL (MG)	55	SODIUM (MG)	290	LOW-SODIUM DIETS: NOT ACCEPTABLE ON	
				500 OR 1000 MG SODIUM DIET. THE MILK	
				AND EGG SUBSTITUTE, IN ADDITION TO	
				THE SALT, CONTAIN SIGNIFICANT AMOUNTS	
				OF SODIUM.	

CLASSIC CHEESECAKE

MAKES 12 SLICES

Modern technology, which has brought us nonfat sour cream, cream cheese, and yogurt, allows us to finally have our cake and eat it too. Using these substitutes and eliminating egg yolk and butter gives us a slice of cheesecake with only 2½ grams of fat, and all the taste. Here's the proof. Keep in mind the carbohydrate count is 32 grams, so be sure to save room for it at dinner if you're planning to have it after a meal.

Crust
¾ cup low-fat graham cracker
    crumbs (7 crackers)
2 tablespoons sugar
1 tablespoon unsalted butter, melted

Filling
4 (8-ounce) packages fat-free cream
    cheese, at room temperature
1¼ cups sugar
1 cup nonfat vanilla yogurt

½ teaspoon salt
1 tablespoon vanilla extract
⅓ cup cake flour
1 teaspoon grated lemon zest
1 tablespoon fresh lemon juice
1 cup liquid egg substitute

Topping
2 cups nonfat sour cream
2 tablespoons sugar

1 Preheat the oven to 350°F.

2 To make the crust: In a bowl, stir together the graham cracker crumbs, sugar, and butter. Make sure all the crumbs are evenly moistened. Press the crumb mixture firmly and evenly over the bottom of a 10-inch springform pan (see Note). Bake the crust for 10 minutes. Remove from the oven, place the pan on a baking sheet, and set aside while you prepare the filling.

3 In a large bowl, beat together the cream cheese, sugar, yogurt, salt, vanilla, cake flour, lemon zest, and lemon juice until creamy. Add the egg substitute and continue beating until well combined.

4 Pour the filling into the prepared crust and return it to the oven. Bake for one hour, then remove from the oven, increase the heat to 450°F, and let the cheesecake stand for 10 minutes.

5 To make the topping, whisk the sour cream and sugar together until smooth. Pour it evenly over the top of the cheesecake and bake for 5 minutes more.

6 Remove the cheesecake from the oven and place on a rack to cool completely. Cover well with plastic wrap and refrigerate 3 to 4 hours or overnight.

VARIATION: For a banana cheesecake, substitute 1 mashed banana (½ cup) for ½ cup of the sour cream. This does not affect the calorie, carbohydrate, or exchange values.

Note: Because there is much less butter than in a usual graham cracker crust, you'll find it doesn't quite "mold" in the typical fashion, but don't worry. The crust absorbs liquid from the filling and adheres just fine.

PER 6-OUNCE SLICE						
	BEFORE	AFTER				
CALORIES	360	230	CARBOHYDRATES (G)	32	CARBOHYDRATE CHOICES: 2	
FAT (G)	24	2.5	PROTEIN (G)	18	FOOD EXCHANGES PER SERVING: 2	
CALORIES FROM FAT (%)	60	10	FIBER (G)	0	CARBOHYDRATE, 1 LEAN MEAT	
CHOLESTEROL (MG)	95	10	SODIUM (MG)	490	LOW-SODIUM DIETS: OMIT SALT. MAY BE	
					EATEN OCCASIONALLY ONLY IF SODIUM	
					RESTRICTION IS MILD TO MODERATE.	
					LIMIT TO 1 SERVING.	

VIENNESE BROWNIES

MAKES 16 BROWNIES

If chocolate is what you want, these are a luscious low-fat sweet treat. After many experiments to produce a fat-free brownie with prune puree and date puree—which my tasters unanimously rejected—I came up with a winner. By using egg whites instead of whole eggs, and substituting cocoa powder for part of the chocolate squares, I was able to cut the fat to one-third the amount of a regular brownie.

Vegetable oil cooking spray
2 ounces unsweetened chocolate
   (2 squares)
2 tablespoons canola oil
¾ cup water (only if using powdered
   egg white)
2 teaspoons vanilla extract
3 egg whites

1 cup sugar
½ cup all-purpose flour
⅓ cup unsweetened cocoa
¼ teaspoon baking powder
⅛ teaspoon salt
2 teaspoons sifted confectioners'
   sugar

1 Preheat the oven to 350°F and coat an 8-inch square baking pan with vegetable oil cooking spray.

2 Place chocolate squares in a small glass bowl with the oil and melt in the microwave (or in a double boiler on the stovetop). Remove from heat and add the water and vanilla.

3 In a separate bowl, combine the sugar, flour, cocoa, baking powder, and salt. Blend thoroughly. Fold in the melted chocolate mixture, stirring until just moist. Add the egg whites and blend well.

4 Pour batter into a prepared pan and bake for 25 to 30 minutes, or until a wooden pick comes out clean. Let stand to cool and sprinkle with confectioners' sugar.

PER BROWNIE	BEFORE	AFTER				
CALORIES	180	110	CARBOHYDRATES (G)	18	CARBOHYDRATE CHOICES: 1	
FAT (G)	13	4	PROTEIN (G)	2	FOOD EXCHANGES PER SERVING: 1	
CALORIES FROM FAT (%)	60	31	FIBER (G)	1	CARBOHYDRATE, ½ FAT	
CHOLESTEROL (MG)	40	0	SODIUM (MG)	35	LOW-SODIUM DIETS: ACCEPTABLE	

NONFAT EGGNOG

MAKES 6 SERVINGS

Holiday get-togethers often include a festive glass of eggnog blended with a bit of rum and sprinkled with a dash of nutmeg. My fat-free rendition has been thoroughly tested by eggnog lovers and not only wins the taste test, but uses powdered egg white in place of raw eggs, so there's no need to worry about salmonella, and you cut the calories, fat, and cholesterol. (See page 422 for information on mail-ordering powdered egg white.)

1 (12-ounce) can nonfat
  evaporated milk
2 tablespoons powdered egg white
4 tablespoons sugar
1 cup nonfat milk

1 teaspoon vanilla extract
1 teaspoon rum flavoring, or 6
  tablespoons rum or brandy
Ground nutmeg, for serving

1 In a small saucepan, warm ½ cup of the evaporated milk until hot but not boiling.

2 Pour the milk into a medium mixing bowl and add the powdered egg white. With an electric mixer, beat the mixture until foamy. Begin adding the sugar gradually, and continue beating until soft peaks begin to form.

3 Fold in the remaining evaporated milk, the nonfat milk, vanilla, and rum until combined.

4 Serve immediately, sprinkling each glass with ground nutmeg or, for best results, refrigerate for 1 day and reheat gently before serving.

PER ½-CUP SERVING					
	BEFORE	AFTER			
CALORIES	180	90	CARBOHYDRATES (G) 15	CARBOHYDRATE CHOICES: 1	
FAT (G)	9	0	PROTEIN (G) 8	FOOD EXCHANGES PER SERVING: 1	
CALORIES FROM FAT (%)	45	1	FIBER (G) 0	CARBOHYDRATE	
CHOLESTEROL (MG)	125	5	SODIUM (MG) 125	LOW-SODIUM DIETS: ACCEPTABLE	

APPENDIXES

EXCHANGE LISTS FOR MEAL PLANNING

The following exchanges lists can serve as a tool to help people with diabetes plan meals. Even if you use the carbohydrate counting system, you and your dietitian may refer to the exchange lists for guidelines when you work out your meal plan. If you have diabetes, consistency is one of your main goals—eating the same amount of food at the same time each day, without skipping meals or snacks. This will help you avoid large swings in your blood glucose level. The exchange lists will help you eat a variety of foods.

What Is an Exchange?

Exchanges are foods listed together because they are alike. Each serving of a food has about the same amount of carbohydrate, protein, fat, and calories as the other foods on the same list. When your meal plan calls for a food on a particular list—say, the Starch list—you can "exchange" or trade it for any food on the list: a slice of bread or an 8-inch tortilla, for example. Each of these foods equals one starch exchange or one starch choice.

The exchange system is based on dividing foods into three main groups: carbohydrates, meat and meat substitutes, and fats. The carbohydrate group includes starch, fruit, milk, other carbohydrates, and vegetable lists. Since most foods in the carbohydrate group have about the same amount of carbohydrate per serving (15 grams), you can exchange starch, fruit, or milk choices in your meal plan. Vegetables are in this group but contain only about 5 grams of carbohydrates, so three vegetable servings equals one carbohydrate exchange or 15 grams.

Some foods appear on two lists. For example, dried beans and peas can be counted as a starch or a protein, which is particularly helpful if you choose a vegetarian style of eating. You'll note that some of the starchy vegetables appear in the starch group rather than the vegetable group as you might expect. That's because their carbohydrate value is closer to that of grains than it is to that of vegetables.

The foods are listed in groups along with their serving sizes. In the beginning, and again from time to time, you'll want to weigh or measure your food choices so that you're eating the amount of carbohydrates, protein, and fat in your food plan. Eventually you'll be better able to eyeball correctly, at home or in a restaurant. For example, by measuring ½ cup of pasta, you'll know what one starch exchange looks like.

You and your dietitian will work together to determine how many servings from each list are best for you at breakfast, lunch, dinner, and snacks. For example, you may have 3 starches at dinner and choose to have those as pasta. Since one exchange is ½ cup of pasta, you'll want to measure 1½ cups of pasta to get 3 servings, or 45 grams of carbohydrate. The next night, you may decide to choose a small potato, a half cup of corn, and a slice of bread. Each of these choices is 1 starch exchange, with 15 grams of carbohydrates in each, or a total of 45 grams of carbohydrates.

These exchange lists (© 1995 American Diabetes Association and The American Dietetic Association) have been reprinted with permission. They have been designed to help people with diabetes plan special diets and are often used by others who must follow special diets or simply want to lose weight. Occasionally you'll find brand names in exchange lists as in other parts of this book. These are included in order to help identify food products and do not constitute an endorsement by the associations, publisher, or author.

Exchange lists are based on specific portion sizes of each food listed, so make sure you use proper measuring tools including a set of measuring spoons, measuring cups, a ruler, and a food or postage scale.

CARBOHYDRATE CHOICES
STARCH LIST

One starch exchange equals approximately
    15 grams of carbohydrate,
    3 grams of protein,
    0 to 1 gram of fat, and
    80 calories

Cereals, grains, pasta, breads, crackers, snacks, starchy vegetables, and cooked dried beans, peas, and lentils are starches. In general, one starch is:

- ½ cup of cereal, grain, pasta, or starchy vegetable
- 1 ounce of a bread product
- ¾ to 1 ounce of most snack foods (Some snack foods also have added fat.)

Nutrition Tips

- Most starch choices are good sources of B vitamins.
- Foods made from whole grains are good sources of fiber.
- Dried beans and peas are a good source of protein and fiber.

Selection Tips

- Choose starches made with little fat as often as you can.
- Starchy vegetables prepared with fat count as one starch and one fat.
- Bagels or muffins can be 2, 3, or 4 starch choices. Check the size you eat.
- Dried beans, peas, and lentils are also found on the Meat and Meat Substitutes list.
- Regular potato chips and tortilla chips are found on the Other Carbohydrates list.
- Most of the serving sizes are measured after cooking.
- Always check Nutrition Facts on the food label.

One starch exchange equals 15 grams carbohydrate, 3 grams protein, 0 to 1 gram fat, and 80 calories.

FOOD	EXCHANGE

Bread

Bagel	½ (1 ounce)
Bread, reduced calorie	2 slices (1½ ounces)
Bread, white, whole wheat, pumpernickel, rye	1 slice (1 ounce)
Bread sticks, crisp, 4 inches long × ½ inch	2 (⅔ ounce)
English muffin	½
Hot dog or hamburger bun	½ (1 ounce)
Pita, 6 inches across	½
Raisin bread, unfrosted	1 slice (1 ounce)
Roll, plain, small	1 (1 ounce)
Tortilla, corn, 6 inches across	1
Tortilla, flour, 7 to 8 inches across	1
Waffle, 4½ inches square, reduced-fat	1

Cereals and Grains

Bran cereals	½ cup
Bulgur (cooked)	½ cup
Cereals (cooked)	½ cup
Cereals, unsweetened, ready-to-eat	¾ cup
Cornmeal (dry)	3 tablespoons
Couscous	⅓ cup
Flour	3 tablespoons
Granola, low-fat	¼ cup
Grape-Nuts	¼ cup
Grits (cooked)	½ cup
Kasha	½ cup
Millet	¼ cup
Muesli	¼ cup
Oats	½ cup

Cereals and Grains *(cont'd)*

Pasta (cooked) ....½ cup

Puffed cereal ....1½ cups

Rice milk ....½ cup

Rice, white or brown (cooked)..⅓ cup

Shredded wheat ....½ cup

Sugar-frosted cereal ....½ cup

Wheat germ ....3 tablespoons

Starchy Vegetables

Baked beans ....⅓ cup

Corn..½ cup

Corn on cob, medium...1 (5 ounces)

Mixed vegetables with corn, peas, or pasta.........................1 cup

Peas, green ....½ cup

Plantain..½ cup

Potato, baked or boiled ....1 small (3 ounces)

Potato, mashed ....½ cup

Squash, winter (acorn, butternut) ....1 cup

Yam or sweet potato, plain..½ cup

Crackers and Snacks

Animal crackers..8

Graham crackers, 2½-inch square 3

Matzo..¾ ounce

Melba toast..4 slices

Oyster crackers...24

Popcorn (popped, no fat added or low-fat microwave) ....3 cups

Pretzels..¾ ounce

Rice cakes, 4 inches across...2

Saltine-type crackers 6

Snack chips, tortilla or potato (fat-free) ....15 to 20 (¾ ounce)

Whole wheat crackers (no fat added)..........................2 to 5 (¾ ounce)

Dried Beans, Peas, and Lentils

Count as 1 starch exchange plus 1 very lean meat exchange

Beans and peas: garbanzo, pinto, kidney, white, split, black-eyed.................½ cup

Lentils...½ cup

Lima beans...⅔ cup

Miso...3 tablespoons

Starchy Foods Prepared with Fat

Count as 1 starch exchange plus 1 fat exchange

Biscuit, 2½ inches across 1

Chow mein noodles...½ cup

Cornbread, 2-inch cube ....1 (2 ounces)

Crackers, round butter type 6

Croutons..1 cup

French-fried potatoes ....16 to 25 (3 ounces)

Granola..¼ cup

Muffin, small...1 (1½ ounces)

Pancake, 4 inches across..2

Popcorn, microwave ....3 cups

Sandwich crackers, cheese filling 3

Sandwich crackers, peanut butter filling...3

Stuffing, bread (prepared)...⅓ cup

Taco shell, 6 inches across..2

Waffle, 4½ inches square 1

Whole wheat crackers, fat added.............................4 to 6 (1 ounce)

Planning for Cooked Starches

Some food, bought uncooked, will weigh less after you cook it. Starches, in contrast, often swell in cooking. A small amount of uncooked starch will become a much larger amount of cooked food. The following table shows some of the changes.

FOOD	EXCHANGE AMOUNT	EXCHANGE AMOUNT
	Uncooked	Cooked
Oatmeal	3 tablespoons	½ cup
Cream of Wheat	2 tablespoons	½ cup
Grits	3 tablespoons	½ cup
Rice	2 tablespoons	⅓ cup
Spaghetti	⅓ cup	½ cup
Noodles	¼ cup	½ cup
Macaroni	¼ cup	½ cup
Dried beans	¼ cup	½ cup
Dried peas	¼ cup	½ cup
Lentils	3 tablespoons	½ cup

FRUIT LIST

One fruit exchange equals 15 grams carbohydrate and 60 calories.

The weight for fresh fruit includes skin, core, seeds, and rind. Fresh, frozen, canned, and dried fruits and fruit juices are on this list. In general, one fruit exchange is:
- 1 small to medium fresh fruit
- ½ cup canned or fresh fruit or fruit juice
- ¼ cup dried fruit

Nutrition Tips
- Fresh, frozen, and dried fruits have about 2 grams of fiber per choice. Fruit juices contain very little fiber.
- Citrus fruits, berries, and melons are good sources of vitamin C.

Selection Tips

- Count ½ cup cranberries or rhubarb sweetened with a sugar substitute as free foods.
- Read the Nutrition Facts on the food label. If one serving has more than 15 grams of carbohydrate, you will need to adjust the size of the serving you eat or drink.
- Portion sizes for canned fruits are for the fruit and a small amount of juice.
- Whole fruit is more filling than fruit juice and may be a better choice.
- Food labels for fruits may contain the words "no sugar added" or "unsweetened." This means that no sucrose (table sugar) has been added.
- Generally, fruit canned in extra-light syrup has the same amount of carbohydrate per serving as the "no sugar added" or the juice pack. All canned fruits on the fruit list are based on one of these three types of pack.

FOOD	EXCHANGE
Fruit	
Apple, unpeeled, small	1 (4 ounces)
Apples, dried	4 rings
Applesauce, unsweetened	½ cup
Apricots, fresh	4 whole (5½ ounces)
Apricots, dried	8 halves
Apricots, canned	½ cup
Banana, small	1 (4 ounces)
Blackberries	¾ cup
Blueberries	¾ cup
Cantaloupe, small	⅓ melon (11 ounces) or 1 cup cubes
Cherries, sweet, fresh	12 (3 ounces)
Cherries, sweet, canned	½ cup

Fruit *(cont'd)*

Dates 3

Figs, fresh ....1½ large or 2 medium (3½ ounces)

Figs, dried..1½

Fruit cocktail ....½ cup

Grapefruit, large ....½ (11 ounces)

Grapefruit sections, canned..¾ cup

Grapes, small ....17 (3 ounces)

Honeydew melon...........................1 slice (10 ounces) or 1 cup cubes

Kiwi ....1 (3½ ounces)

Mandarin oranges, canned ....¾ cup

Mango, small...............................½ fruit (5½ ounces) or ½ cup

Nectarine, small...1 (5 ounces)

Orange, small ....1 (6½ ounces)

Papaya ....½ fruit (8 ounces) or 1 cup cubes

Peach, medium, fresh ....1 (6 ounces)

Peaches, canned...½ cup

Pear, large, fresh...½ (4 ounces)

Pears, canned...½ cup

Pineapple, fresh...¾ cup

Pineapple, canned...½ cup

Plums, small ....2 (5 ounces)

Plums, canned ....½ cup

Prunes, dried...3

Raisins ....2 tablespoons

Raspberries ....1 cup

Strawberries ....1¼ cups whole berries

Tangerines, small ....2 (8 ounces)

Watermelon.............................1 slice (13½ ounces) or 1¼ cups cubes

Fruit Juice

Apple juice/cider ....½ cup

Cranberry juice cocktail..⅓ cup

Cranberry juice cocktail, reduced calorie ....1 cup

Fruit juice blends (100% juice) ....⅓ cup

Grape juice ....⅓ cup

Grapefruit juice...½ cup

Orange juice ....½ cup

Pineapple juice..½ cup

Prune juice ....⅓ cup

MILK LIST

1 milk exchange equals 12 grams of carbohydrate and 8 grams of protein.

Different types of milk and milk products are on this list. Cheeses are on the Meat list and cream and other dairy fats are on the Fat list. Based on the amount of fat they contain, milks are divided into skim/very low-fat milk, low-fat milk, and whole milk. One choice of these includes:

	Carbohydrate (grams)	Protein (grams)	Fat (grams)	Calories
Skim, very low-fat	12	8	0 to 3	About 90
Low-fat	12	8	5	120
Whole	12	8	8	150

Nutrition Tips
- Milk and yogurt are good sources of calcium and protein. Check the food label.
- The higher the fat content of milk and yogurt, the greater the amount of saturated fat and cholesterol. Choose lower-fat varieties more often.

Nutrition Tips (*cont'd*)

- For those who are lactose-intolerant, look for lactose-reduced or lactose-free varieties of milk.

Selection Tips

- One cup equals 8 fluid ounces or ½ pint.
- Look for chocolate milk, frozen yogurt, and ice cream on the Other Carbohydrates list.
- Nondairy creamers are on the Free Foods list.
- Look for rice milk on the Starch list.
- Look for soy milk on the Medium-fat Meat list.

FOOD	EXCHANGE
Skim and Very Low-Fat Milk	
(0 to 3 grams fat per serving)	
Skim milk	1 cup
½% milk	1 cup
1% milk	1 cup
Nonfat or low-fat buttermilk	1 cup
Evaporated skim milk	½ cup
Nonfat dry milk (dry)	⅓ cup
Plain nonfat yogurt	¾ cup
Nonfat or low-fat fruit-flavored yogurt, sweetened with aspartame or other nonnutritive sweetener	1 cup
Low-Fat Milk	
(5 grams fat per serving)	
2% milk	1 cup
Plain low-fat yogurt	¾ cup
Sweet acidophilus milk	1 cup

| FOOD | EXCHANGE |

Whole Milk
(8 grams fat per serving)

Whole milk ....1 cup

Evaporated whole milk ....½ cup

Goat's milk ....1 cup

Kefir ....1 cup

OTHER CARBOHYDRATES LIST

One exchange equals 15 grams of carbohydrate, or 1 starch, or 1 fruit, or 1 milk.

You can substitute food choices from this list for a starch, fruit, or milk choice on your meal plan. Some choices will also count as one or more fat choices.

Nutrition Tips
- These foods can be substituted in your meal plan, even though they contain added sugars or fat. However, they do not contain as many important vitamins and minerals as the choices on the Starch, Fruit, and Milk lists.
- When planning to include these foods in your meal, be sure to include foods from all the lists to eat a balanced meal.

Selection Tips
- Because many of these foods are concentrated sources of carbohydrate and fat, the portion sizes are often very small.
- Always check Nutrition Facts on the food label. It will be your most accurate source of information.
- Many fat-free or reduced-fat products made with fat replacements contain carbohydrate. When eaten in large amounts, they may need to be counted. Talk with your dietitian to determine how to count these in your meal plan.
- Look for fat-free salad dressings in smaller amounts on the Free Foods list.

FOOD	SERVING SIZE	EXCHANGE(S) PER SERVING
Other Carbohydrates		
Angel food cake, unfrosted	⅟₁₂ cake	2 carbohydrates
Brownie, small, unfrosted	2-inch square	1 carbohydrate, 1 fat
Cake, unfrosted	2-inch square	1 carbohydrate, 1 fat
Cake, frosted	2-inch square	2 carbohydrates, 1 fat
Cookie, fat-free	2 small	1 carbohydrate
Cookie	2 small	1 carbohydrate, 1 fat
Cookie sandwich with cream filling	2	1 carbohydrate, 1 fat
Cranberry sauce, jellied	¼ cup	2 carbohydrates
Cupcake, frosted	1 small	2 carbohydrates, 1 fat
Doughnut, plain cake	1 medium (1½ ounces)	1½ carbohydrates, 2 fats
Doughnut, glazed	3¾ inches across	2 carbohydrates, 2 fats
Fruit juice bars, frozen, 100% juice	1 bar (3 ounces)	1 carbohydrate
Fruit snacks, chewy (pureed fruit concentrate)	1 roll (¾ ounce)	1 carbohydrate
Fruit spreads, 100% fruit	1 tablespoon	1 carbohydrate
Gelatin, regular	½ cup	1 carbohydrate
Gingersnaps	3	1 carbohydrate
Granola bar	1	1 carbohydrate, 1 fat
Granola bar, fat-free	1	2 carbohydrates
Hummus	⅓ cup	1 carbohydrate, 1 fat
Ice cream	½ cup	1 carbohydrate, 2 fats
Ice cream, light	½ cup	1 carbohydrate, 1 fat
Ice cream, fat-free, no sugar added	½ cup	1 carbohydrate
Jam or jelly, regular	1 tablespoon	1 carbohydrate
Milk, chocolate, whole	1 cup	2 carbohydrates, 1 fat
Pie, fruit, 2 crusts	⅙ pie	3 carbohydrates, 2 fats

FOOD	SERVING SIZE	EXCHANGE(S) PER SERVING
Pie, pumpkin or custard	⅛ pie	1 carbohydrate, 2 fats
Potato chips	12 to 18 (1 ounce)	1 carbohydrate, 2 fats
Pudding, regular, made with low-fat milk	½ cup	2 carbohydrates
Pudding, sugar-free, made with low-fat milk	½ cup	1 carbohydrate
Salad dressing, fat-free or low-fat, French, ranch, Thousand Island	¼ cup	1 carbohydrate
Sherbet or sorbet	½ cup	2 carbohydrates
Spaghetti or pasta sauce, canned or bottled	½ cup	1 carbohydrate, 1 fat
Sweet roll or Danish	1 (2½ ounces)	2½ carbohydrates, 2 fats
Syrup, light	2 tablespoons	1 carbohydrate
Syrup, regular	1 tablespoon	1 carbohydrate
	¼ cup	4 carbohydrates
Tortilla chips	6 to 12 (1 ounce)	1 carbohydrate, 2 fats
Vanilla wafers	5	1 carbohydrate, 1 fat
Yogurt, frozen, low-fat or fat-free	⅓ cup	1 carbohydrate, 0 to 1 fat
Yogurt, frozen, fat-free no sugar added	½ cup	1 carbohydrate
Yogurt, low-fat with fruit	1 cup	3 carbohydrates, 0 to 1 fat

VEGETABLE LIST

One vegetable exchange equals 5 grams carbohydrate, 2 grams protein, 0 grams fat, and 25 calories.

Vegetables that contain at least 400 milligrams sodium per serving are identified with the symbol ♜.

Vegetables that contain small amounts of carbohydrates and calories are on this list. Vegetables contain important nutrients. Try to eat at least 2 or 3 vegetable choices each day. In general, 1 vegetable exchange is:

- ½ cup cooked vegetables or vegetable juice
- 1 cup raw vegetables

If you eat 1 to 2 vegetable choices at a meal or snack, you do not have to count the calories or carbohydrates because they contain small amounts of these nutrients.

Nutrition Tips

- Fresh and frozen vegetables have less added salt than canned vegetables. Drain and rinse canned vegetables if you want to remove some salt.
- Choose more dark green and dark yellow vegetables, such as spinach, broccoli, romaine, carrots, chiles, and peppers.
- Broccoli, Brussels sprouts, cauliflower, greens, peppers, spinach and tomatoes are good sources of vitamin C.
- Vegetables contain 1 to 4 grams of fiber per serving.

Selection Tips

- A 1-cup portion of broccoli is a portion about the size of a lightbulb.
- Tomato sauce is different from spaghetti sauce, which is on the Other Carbohydrates list.
- Canned vegetables and juices are available without added salt.
- If you eat more than 4 cups of raw vegetables or 2 cups of cooked vegetables at one meal, count them as 1 carbohydrate choice.
- Starchy vegetables such as corn, peas, winter squash, and potatoes that contain larger amounts of calories and carbohydrates are on the Starch list.

VEGETABLES

Artichoke
Artichoke hearts
Asparagus
Beans (green, wax, Italian)
Bean sprouts
Beets
Broccoli
Brussels sprouts
Cabbage
Carrots
Cauliflower
Celery
Cucumber
Eggplant
Green onions or scallions
Greens (collard, kale, mustard, turnip)
Kohlrabi
Leeks
Mixed vegetables (without corn, peas, or pasta)
Mushrooms
Okra
Onions
Pea pods (snow peas, sugar snaps)
Peppers (all varieties)
Radishes
Salad greens (endive, escarole, lettuce, romaine, spinach)
Sauerkraut ⚕
Spinach
Summer squash

Tomato
Tomatoes, canned
Tomato sauce ⚕
Tomato/vegetable juice ⚕
Turnips
Water chestnuts
Watercress
Zucchini

PROTEIN CHOICES
MEAT AND MEAT SUBSTITUTES LIST

Meat and meat substitutes that contain both protein and fat are on this list. In general, 1 meat exchange is:
- 1 ounce meat, fish, poultry, or cheese
- ½ cup dried beans, peas, or lentils

Based on the amount of fat they contain, meats are divided into very lean, lean, medium-fat, and high-fat lists. This is done so you can see which ones contain the least amount of fat. One ounce (one exchange) of each of these includes:

	Carbohydrate (grams)	Protein (grams)	Fat (grams)	Calories
Very lean	0	7	0 to 1	35
Lean	0	7	3	55
Medium-fat	0	7	5	75
High-fat	0	7	8	100

Nutrition Tips
- Choose very lean and lean meat choices whenever possible. Items from the high-fat group are high in saturated fat, cholesterol, and calories and can raise blood cholesterol levels.
- Meats do not have any fiber.
- Dried beans, peas, and lentils are good sources of fiber.
- Some processed meats, seafood, and soy products may contain carbohydrates when consumed in large amounts. Check the Nutrition Facts on the label to see if the amount is close to 15 grams. If so, count it as a carbohydrate choice as well as a meat choice.

Selection Tips

- Weigh meat after cooking and removing bones and fat. Four ounces of raw meat is equal to 3 ounces of cooked meat. Some examples of meat portions are:
  - —1 ounce cheese = 1 meat choice and is about the size of a 1-inch cube
  - —2 ounces meat = 2 meat choices, such as small chicken leg or thigh, ½ cup cottage cheese or tuna
  - —3 ounces meat = 3 meat choices and is about the size of a deck of cards, such as 1 medium pork chop, 1 small hamburger, ½ of a whole chicken breast, or 1 unbreaded fish fillet
- Limit your choices from the high-fat group to three times per week or less.
- Most grocery stores stock Select and Choice grades of meat. Select grades of meat are the leanest meats. Choice grades contain a moderate amount of fat, and Prime cuts of meat have the highest amount of fat. Restaurants usually serve Prime cuts of meat.
- "Hamburger" may contain added seasoning and fat, but ground beef does not.
- Read labels to find products that are low in fat and cholesterol (5 grams or less of fat per serving).
- Dried beans, peas, and lentils are also found on the Starch list
- Peanut butter, in smaller amounts, is also found on the Fats list.
- Bacon, in smaller amounts, is also found on the Fats list.

Meal-Planning Tips

- Bake, roast, broil, grill, poach, steam, or broil these foods rather than frying.
- Place meat on a rack so the fat will drain off during cooking.
- Use a nonstick spray and a nonstick pan to brown or fry foods.
- Trim off visible fat before or after cooking.
- If you add flour, bread crumbs, coating mixes, fat, or marinades when cooking, ask your dietitian how to count it in your meal plan.

VERY LEAN MEAT AND MEAT SUBSTITUTES

One exchange equals 0 grams carbohydrate, 7 grams protein, less than 1 gram fat, and 35 calories.

Items that have 400 milligrams or more of sodium per exchange are marked with the symbol ⚑.

One very lean meat exchange is equal to any one of the following items.

FOOD	EXCHANGE
Poultry	
Chicken or turkey (white meat, no skin) or Cornish hen (without skin)	1 ounce
Fish	
Cod, flounder, haddock, halibut or trout (fresh or frozen) or tuna (fresh or canned in water)	1 ounce
Shellfish	
Clams, crab, lobster, scallops, shrimp, or imitation shellfish	1 ounce
Game	
Duck (no skin), pheasant (no skin), venison, buffalo, or ostrich	1 ounce
Cheese with less than 1 gram fat per ounce	
Nonfat cottage cheese or low-fat cottage cheese	¼ cup
Fat-free cheese	1 ounce
Other	
Processed sandwich meats with less than 1 gram fat per ounce, such as deli thin, shaved meats, chipped beef ⚑, turkey ham	1 ounce
Egg whites	2
Egg substitutes, plain	¼ cup
Hot dogs with less than 1 gram fat per ounce ⚑	1 ounce
Kidney (high in cholesterol)	1 ounce
Sausage with less than 1 gram fat per ounce	1 ounce
Count as 1 Very Lean Meat plus 1 Starch Exchange:	
Dried beans, peas, lentils (cooked)	½ cup

LEAN MEAT AND SUBSTITUTES

One exchange equals 0 gram carbohydrates, 7 grams protein, 3 grams fat, and 55 calories.

One lean meat exchange is equal to any one of the following items.

FOOD	EXCHANGE
Beef	
USDA Select or Choice grades of lean beef trimmed of fat, such as round, sirloin, and flank steak; tenderloin; rib, chuck, and rump roast; T-bone, porterhouse, and cubed steak; ground round	1 ounce
Pork	
Lean pork, such as fresh ham; canned, cured, or boiled ham; Canadian bacon ✴; tenderloin; center loin chop	1 ounce
Lamb	
Roast, chop, leg	1 ounce
Veal	
Lean chops and roasts	1 ounce
Poultry	
Chicken or turkey dark meat (without skin), chicken white meat (with skin), or domestic duck or goose (well drained of fat, with skin)	1 ounce
Fish	
Herring, uncreamed or smoked	1 ounce
Oysters	6 medium
Salmon, fresh or canned, or catfish	1 ounce
Sardines, canned	2 medium
Tuna, canned in oil, drained	1 ounce
Game	
Goose (without skin) or rabbit	1 ounce

FOOD	EXCHANGE

Cheese

4.5% cottage cheese	¼ cup
Grated Parmesan	2 tablespoons
Cheese with about 2 to 3 grams fat per ounce	1 ounce

Other

Hot dogs with 3 grams or less fat per ounce ☀	1½ ounces
Processed sandwich meat with about 3 grams fat per ounce, such as turkey pastrami or kielbasa	1 ounce
Liver or heart (high in cholesterol)	1 ounce

MEDIUM-FAT MEAT AND SUBSTITUTES

One exchange equals 0 gram carbohydrate, 7 grams protein, 5 grams fat, and 75 calories.

One medium–fat meat exchange is equal to any one of the following items.

FOOD	EXCHANGE

Beef

Most beef products, including ground beef, meat loaf, corned beef, short ribs, prime grades of meat, trimmed of fat, such as prime rib	1 ounce

Pork

Top loin, chop, Boston butt, cutlets	1 ounce

Lamb

Rib roast, ground	1 ounce

Veal

Cutlet (ground or cubed, unbreaded)	1 ounce

Poultry

Chicken dark meat (with skin), ground turkey or chicken, fried chicken (with skin)	1 ounce

FOOD	EXCHANGE

Fish

Any fried fish products...1 ounce

Cheese

Skim- or part-skim-milk cheese, with about 4 to
5 grams fat per ounce...1 ounce

Feta ....1 ounce

Mozzarella...1 ounce

Ricotta..¼ cup (2 ounces)

Other

Egg (high in cholesterol; limit to 3 per week).........................1 ounce

Sausage with about 5 grams or less fat per ounce.....................1 ounce

Soy milk...1 cup

Tempeh..¼ cup

Tofu ....½ cup (4 ounces)

HIGH-FAT MEATS AND SUBSTITUTES

One exchange equals 0 gram carbohydrate, 7 grams protein, 8 grams fat, and 100 calories.

Remember, these items are high in saturated fat, cholesterol, and calories and may raise blood cholesterol levels if eaten on a regular basis. One high-fat meat exchange is equal to any one of the following items.

FOOD	EXCHANGE

Pork

Spareribs, ground pork, or pork sausage......................................1 ounce

Cheese

All regular cheeses, such as American ☀, cheddar,
Monterey Jack, Swiss ....1 ounce

FOOD	EXCHANGE

Other

Processed sandwich meats with about 6 to 8 grams fat
per ounce, such as bologna, pimiento loaf, or salami ....1 ounce

Sausage, such as bratwurst, Italian, knockwurst,
Polish, smoked...1 ounce

Hot dog (turkey or chicken) ⍟...1 (10 per pound)

Bacon...3 slices (20 slices per pound)

Count as 1 high-fat meat plus 1 fat exchange:

Hot dog (beef, pork, or combination) ⍟.....................................1 (10 per pound)

Peanut butter (contains unsaturated fat)...2 tablespoons

FAT CHOICES

One fat exchange equals 5 grams fat and 45 calories.

Items that have 400 milligrams or more of sodium per exchange are marked with the symbol ⍟.

FAT LIST

Fats are divided into three groups based on the main type of fat they contain: monounsaturated, polyunsaturated, or saturated. Small amounts of monounsaturated and polyunsaturated fats in the foods we eat are linked with good health benefits. Saturated fats are linked with heart disease and cancer. In general, one fat exchange is:

- 1 teaspoon butter, margarine, or vegetable oil
- 1 tablespoon salad dressing
- 2 to 3 tablespoons light or reduced-calorie salad dressing

Nutrition Tips

- All fats are high in calories. Limit serving sizes for good nutrition and health.
- Nuts and seeds contain small amounts of fiber, protein, and magnesium.
- If blood pressure is a concern, choose fats in the unsalted form to help lower sodium intake, such as unsalted peanuts.

Selection Tips

- Check the Nutrition Facts on food labels for serving sizes. One fat exchange is based on a serving size containing 5 grams of fat.
- When selecting regular margarine, choose those with liquid vegetable oil as the first ingredient. Soft margarines are not as saturated as stick margarines. Soft margarines are healthier choices. Avoid those listing hydrogenated or partially hydrogenated fat as the first ingredient.
- When selecting low-fat margarines, look for liquid vegetable oil as the second ingredient. Water is usually the first ingredient.
- When used in smaller amounts, bacon and peanut butter are counted as fat choices. When used in larger amounts, they are counted as high-fat meat choices.
- Fat-free salad dressings are on the Other Carbohydrates list and the Free Foods list.
- See the Free Foods list for nondairy coffee creamers, whipped topping, and fat-free products, such as margarines, salad dressings, mayonnaise, sour cream, cream cheese, and nonstick cooking spray.

FOOD	EXCHANGE
Monounsaturated Fats	
Avocado, medium	⅛ (1 ounce)
Oil (canola, olive, or peanut)	1 teaspoon
Olives, ripe (black)	8 large
Olives, green, Spanish stuffed ⍓	10 large
Nuts	
Almonds or cashews	6 nuts
Mixed nuts (50 percent peanuts)	6 nuts
Peanuts	10 nuts
Pecans	4 halves
Peanut butter, smooth or crunchy	2 teaspoons
Sesame seeds	1 tablespoon
Tahini (sesame paste)	2 teaspoons

Polyunsaturated Fats

Margarine (stick, tub, or squeeze) ....1 teaspoon

Margarine, lower-fat (30 to 50 percent vegetable oil).........................1 tablespoon

Mayonnaise, regular ....1 teaspoon

Mayonnaise, light or reduced-fat ....1 tablespoon

Miracle Whip salad dressing, regular ....2 teaspoons

Miracle Whip salad dressing, light..1 tablespoon

Oil (corn, safflower, or soybean) ....1 teaspoon

Salad dressings, regular ⁂...1 tablespoon

Salad dressings, reduced-fat ....2 tablespoons

Seeds, pumpkin, or sunflower..1 tablespoon

Walnuts, English ....4 halves

Saturated Fats

Bacon, cooked..1 slice (20 per pound)

Bacon grease ....1 teaspoon

Butter, stick ....1 teaspoon

Butter, whipped...2 teaspoons

Butter, reduced-fat..1 tablespoon

Chitterlings, boiled ....2 tablespoons (½ ounce)

Coconut, sweetened, shredded ....2 tablespoons

Cream, half-and-half...2 tablespoons

Cream cheese, regular ....1 tablespoon (½ ounce)

Cream cheese, light or reduced-fat ....2 tablespoons (1 ounce)

Fatback or salt pork ....See Note

Shortening or lard ....1 teaspoon

Sour cream, regular...2 tablespoons

Sour cream, light or reduced-fat...3 tablespoons

Sour cream, fat-free ....See Free Foods list

Note: A piece 1 inch × 1 inch × ¼ inch is 1 fat exchange if you plan to eat the fat-back cooked with vegetables.

A piece 2 inches × 1 inch × ½ inch is 1 fat exchange if you eat only the vegetables with the fatback removed.

FREE FOODS

Many processed foods now come in sugar-free or fat-free forms or in reduced-fat varieties that can be used as Free Foods. Sugar substitutes and most sugar-free beverages are Free Foods. Most seasonings are Free Foods, but be careful when using seasonings and condiments that contain sodium. They are marked on the list with the salt symbol ⍒.

A Free Food is any food or drink that contains less than 20 calories or less than 5 grams carbohydrate per serving. Foods with the serving size listed should be limited to three servings per day and spread out throughout the day. Foods listed without a serving size can be eaten as often as you like. Items that have 400 milligrams or more of sodium per choice are marked with the symbol ⍒.

FOOD	EXCHANGE
Fat-free or Reduced-fat Foods	
Cream cheese, fat-free	1 tablespoon
Creamers, nondairy, liquid	1 tablespoon
Creamers, nondairy, powdered	2 teaspoons
Mayonnaise, fat-free	1 tablespoon
Mayonnaise, reduced-fat	1 teaspoon
Margarine, fat-free or nonfat	4 tablespoons
Margarine, reduced-fat	1 teaspoon
Miracle Whip salad dressing, nonfat	1 tablespoon
Miracle Whip salad dressing, reduced-fat	1 teaspoon
Nonstick cooking spray	
Salad dressing, fat-free, ranch, or French	1 tablespoon
Salad dressing, Italian fat-free	2 tablespoons
Salsa	¼ cup

Fat-free or Reduced-fat Foods *(cont'd)*

Sour cream, fat-free or reduced-fat....................................1 tablespoon

Whipped topping, regular or light..................................2 tablespoons

Sugar-free or Low-sugar Foods

Candy, hard, sugar-free ....1 candy

Gelatin dessert, sugar-free

Gelatin, unflavored

Gum, sugar-free

Jam/jelly, low-sugar or light ....2 teaspoons

Sugar substitutes★

Syrup, sugar-free ....2 tablespoons

> **★*Sugar Substitutes:*** *Sugar substitutes, alternatives, or replacements that are approved by the Food and Drug Administration (FDA) are safe to use. Common brand names include:*
>
> | | |
> |---|---|
> | *Equal (aspartame)* | *Sweet-10 (saccharin)* |
> | *Sprinkle Sweet (saccharin)* | *Sugar Twin (saccharin)* |
> | *Sweet One (acesulfame-K)* | *Sweet'n Low (saccharin)* |

Drinks

Bouillon, broth, or consommé ⵜ

Bouillon or broth, low-sodium

Carbonated or mineral water

Cocoa powder, unsweetened..1 tablespoon

Coffee

Club soda

Diet soft drinks, sugar-free

Drink mixes, sugar-free

Tea

Tonic water, sugar-free

| **FOOD** | **EXCHANGE** |

Condiments

Ketchup...1 tablespoon

Horseradish

Lemon juice

Lime juice

Mustard

Pickles, dill ⚲ ....1½ large

Soy sauce ⚲

Soy sauce, light ⚲

Taco sauce ....1 tablespoon

Vinegar, flavored vinegars

Seasonings

Be careful with seasonings that contain sodium or are salts,
   such as garlic or celery salt, and lemon pepper.

Flavoring extracts

Garlic

Herbs, fresh or dried

Pimiento

Spices

Tabasco or other hot sauces

Wine, used in cooking..¼ cup

Worcestershire sauce

COMBINATION FOODS

Many of the foods we eat are mixed together in various combinations. These combination foods do not fit into any one exchange list. Often it is hard to tell what is in a casserole dish or prepared food item. This is a list of exchanges for some typical combination foods. This list will help you fit these foods into your meal plan. Ask your dietitian for information about any other combination foods you would like to eat.

FOOD		EXCHANGE
Entrees		
Tuna noodle casserole, lasagna, spaghetti with meatballs, chili with beans, macaroni and cheese ⚱	1 cup (8 ounces)	2 carbohydrates, 2 medium-fat meats
Chow mein (without noodles or rice)	2 cups (16 ounces)	1 carbohydrate, 2 lean meats
Pizza, cheese, thin crust	¼ of 10-inch pizza (5 ounces)	2 carbohydrates, 2 medium-fat meats, 1 fat
Pizza, meat topping, thin crust	¼ of 10-inch pizza (5 ounces)	2 carbohydrates, 2 medium-fat meats, 2 fats
Pot pie ⚱	1 (7 ounces)	2 carbohydrates, 1 medium-fat meat, 4 fats
Frozen Entrees		
Salisbury steak with gravy, mashed potato ⚱	1 (11 ounces)	2 carbohydrates, 3 medium-fat meats, 3 to 4 fats
Turkey with gravy, mashed potato, dressing ⚱	1 (11 ounces)	2 carbohydrates, 2 medium-fat meats, 2 fats
Entree with less than 300 calories	1 (8 ounces)	2 carbohydrates, 3 lean meats
Soups		
Bean ⚱	1 cup	1 carbohydrate, 1 very lean meat
Cream (made with water)	1 cup (8 ounces)	1 carbohydrate, 1 fat

FOOD		EXCHANGE
Split pea (made with water) ⚲	½ cup (4 ounces)	1 carbohydrate
Tomato (made with water) ⚲	1 cup (8 ounces)	1 carbohydrate
Vegetable, beef, chicken, noodle, or other broth type ⚲	1 cup (8 ounces)	1 carbohydrate

Fast Foods

Burritos with beef ⚲	2	4 carbohydrates, 2 medium-fat meats, 2 fats
Chicken nuggets ⚲	6	1 carbohydrate, 2 medium-fat meats, 1 fat
Chicken, breaded, fried side breast and wing ⚲	1 each	1 carbohydrate, 4 medium-fat meats, 2 fats
Fish sandwich with tartar sauce ⚲	1	3 carbohydrates, 1 medium-fat meat, 3 fats
French fries, thin	20 to 25	2 carbohydrates, 2 fats
Hamburger, regular	1	2 carbohydrates, 2 medium-fat meats
Hamburger, large ⚲	1	2 carbohydrates, 3 medium-fat meats, 1 fat
Hot dog with bun ⚲	1	2 carbohydrates, 1 high-fat meat, 1 fat
Individual pan pizza	1	5 carbohydrates, 3 medium-fat meats, 3 fats
Soft-serve cone	1 medium	2 carbohydrates, 1 fat
Submarine sandwich ⚲	1 sub (6 inches)	3 carbohydrates, 1 vegetable, 2 medium-fat meats, 1 fat
Taco, hard shell ⚲	1 (6 ounces)	2 carbohydrates, 2 medium-fat meats, 2 fats
Taco, soft shell ⚲	1 (3 ounces)	1 carbohydrate, 1 medium-fat meat, 1 fat

EXCHANGES FOR ALCOHOLIC BEVERAGES

Beverage	Serving	Alcohol (grams)	Carbohydrate (grams)	Calories	Exchanges
Beer					
Regular	12 ounces	13	13	150	1 starch 2 fats
Light	12 ounces	11	5	100	2 fats
Near	12 ounces	1.5	12	60	1 starch
Distilled Spirits					
80 Proof (gin rum, vodka, whiskey, or scotch)	1½ ounces	14	trace	100	2 fats
Dry brandy or cognac	1 ounce	11	trace	75	1½ fats
Table Wines					
Dry white	4 ounces	11	trace	80	2 fats
Red or rosé	4 ounces	12	trace	85	2 fats
Sweet	4 ounces	12	5	105	⅓ starch 2 fats
Light	4 ounces	6	1	50	1 fat
Wine cooler	4 ounces	13	30	215	2 fruits 2 fats
Sparkling Wines					
Champagne	4 ounces	12	4	100	2 fats
Sweet kosher	4 ounces	12	12	132	1 starch 1 fat

Beverage	Serving	Alcohol (grams)	Carbohydrate (grams)	Calories	Exchanges
Appetizer/Dessert Wines					
Sherry, dry or sweet	2 ounces	9	2	74	1½ fats
Port or muscatel	2 ounces	9	7	90	½ starch 1½ fats
Cordials or liqueurs	1½ ounces	13	18	160	1 starch 2 fats
Cocktails					
Bloody Mary	5 ounces	14	5	116	1 vegetable 1 fat
Daiquiri	2 ounces	14	2	111	2 fats
Manhattan	2 ounces	17	2	178	2½ fats
Martini	2½ ounces	22	trace	156	3½ fats
Old-fashioned	4 ounces	26	trace	180	4 fats
Tom Collins	7½ ounces	16	3	120	2½ fats
Mixers					
Mineral water	Any	–	0	0	Free
Sugar-free tonic	Any	–	0	0	Free
Club soda	Any	–	0	0	Free
Diet soda	Any	–	0	0	Free
Tomato juice	½ cup	–	5	25	1 vegetable
Bloody Mary mix	½ cup	–	5	25	1 vegetable
Orange juice	½ cup	–	15	60	1 fruit
Grapefruit juice	½ cup	–	15	60	1 fruit
Pineapple juice	½ cup	–	15	60	1 fruit

The Exchange Lists are the basis of a meal-planning system by a committee of the American Diabetes Association and The American Dietetic Association. While designed primarily for people with diabetes and others who must follow special diets, the Exchange Lists are based on principles of good nutrition that apply to everyone. Copyright © 1995 American Diabetes Association, Inc., The American Dietetic Association.

HEALTH TERMS NOW DEFINED ON FOOD LABELS

In 1990, the Food and Drug Administration overhauled food labeling, and gave quantitative definitions to words used to describe the nutrient composition of foods and food products. The new labels offer more useful nutrition information but can be confusing. The following review will help shoppers decipher the descriptors.

Calorie-free: Less than 5 calories per serving

Low-calorie: 40 calories or less per serving

Salt-free or Sodium-free: Less than 5 milligrams sodium per serving, and does not contain sodium chloride (table salt)

Very Low Sodium: 35 milligrams or less sodium per serving

Low Sodium: 140 milligrams or less sodium per serving

Fat-free: Less than 0.5 gram fat per serving

Low-fat: 3 grams or less fat per serving

Cholesterol-free: Less than 2 milligrams cholesterol and 2 grams or less saturated fat per serving

Low cholesterol: 20 milligrams or less cholesterol and 2 grams or less saturated fat per serving

Saturated Fat–free: Less than 0.5 gram saturated fat per serving, and the level of trans-fatty acids does not exceed 1 percent of total fat

Low Saturated Fat: 1 gram or less saturated fat per serving, and not more than 15 percent of calories from saturated fat

Lean: Meat, poultry, seafood, and game meat with less than 10 grams fat, 4 grams saturated fat, and 95 milligrams cholesterol per serving and per 100 grams

Extra Lean: Meat, poultry, seafood, and game meat with less than 5 grams fat, 2 grams saturated fat, and 95 milligrams cholesterol per serving and per 100 grams

Good Source of . . . or Contains . . . or Provides . . . : 10 to 19 percent of the Daily Value per serving. Example: A good source of iron contains between 1.8 and 3.4 milligrams iron per serving.

Excellent Source of . . . or High in . . . or Rich in . . . : 20 percent or more of the Daily Value per serving. Example: An excellent source of fiber contains 5 grams or more fiber per serving.

Light or Lite: ⅓ fewer calories or 50 percent less fat than the higher-calorie, higher-fat version

Reduced in . . . : A nutritionally altered food that contains at least 25 percent less of a nutrient than a reference food

Healthy: A food that is low in fat and saturated fat, contains 480 milligrams or less sodium per serving, and provides at least 10 percent of the Daily Value for one of these nutrients: Vitamin A, Vitamin C, calcium, iron, protein, and fiber.

So the next time you describe one of your recipes as *lean* or *lite* or *low-fat,* check out the definition first to make sure it meets FDA rules. Voluntary compliance helps assure a consistent message for consumers.

MAIL-ORDER SOURCES

American Spoon Foods Inc.
1668 Clarion Avenue, PO Box 566
Petoskey, MI 49770-0566
(800) 222-5886, fax (800) 647-2512
www.spoon.com
•*no-sugar fruit butters, jams, and pie fillings; dried cherries*

Coyote Cafe General Store
132 West Water Street
Santa Fe, NM 87501
(800) 866-4695
•*dried chiles, southwestern spices, specialty foods, salsas, sauces, cookbooks*

Dean and DeLuca
Mail Order Department
560 Broadway
New York, NY 10012
(800) 221-7714
•*specialty foods, grains, beans, dried chiles, canned chipotle peppers, extra-virgin olive oil*

Deb-El Foods
2 Papetti Plaza, PO Box 876
Elizabeth, NJ 07207
(908) 351-0330, (800) 421-EGGS
•*Just Whites: powdered egg whites to replace egg whites in cooking and baking*
•*Scramblettes: Healthy real-egg product, dried, for use as whole egg replacer in omelettes, scrambled eggs, cookies, cakes, muffins, etc.*

Ideal Cheese
1205 Second Avenue
New York, NY 10021
(212) 688-7579
•*low-fat cheeses, low-fat goat cheese*

Josie's
2600 Camino Entrada
Santa Fe, NM 87505
(505) 473-3437
•*dried chiles, blue cornmeal*

Los Chileros de Nuevo Mexico
PO Box 6215
Santa Fe, NM 87502
(505) 471-6967
•*dried chiles, white posole, blue popcorn*

Meadowbrook Herb Gardens
RR Box 138
Wyoming, RI 02898
(401) 539-7603
•*dried herbs and seasonings, peppercorns*

NutraSweet Center
PO Box 2986
Chicago, IL 60654
(312) 840-5000
•*recipes*

Quaker Oats Company
321 North Clark Street
Chicago, IL 60610
www.quakeroatmeal.com
•*recipes for people with diabetes*

Rafal Spice Co.
2521 Russell Street
Detroit, MI 48207
(313) 259-6373
•*spices, seasoning mixes, peppercorns*

San Francisco Herb Co.
250 Fourteenth Street
San Francisco, CA 94103
(800) 227-4530
www.sfherb.com
•*dried herbs, spices*

Vanilla Saffron Imports, Inc.
949 Valencia Street
San Francisco, CA 04110
(415) 648-8990
•*dried mushrooms, herbs, peppercorns*

Walnut Acres
Penns Creek, PA 17862
(717) 837-0601
•*stone-ground flours, oils, exotic rice*

Wax Orchards
22744 Wax Orchards Road, SW
Vashon, WA 98070
(206) 463-9735, (800) 634-6132
•*no-sugar condiments, chutneys, fruit jams, fruit syrups, fruit butters, berry spread; low-fat, no-cholesterol, no-sugar fudge toppings*

Williams-Sonoma
PO Box 7456
San Francisco, CA 94120-7456
(800) 541-2233
•*specialty oils, extra-virgin olive oil, vinegars, specialty foods*

RESOURCES

BOOKS

American Dietetic Association. *Carbohydrate Counting,* Levels 1, 2, and 3.

American Diabetes Association. *Exchange Lists for Meal Planning.* The American Diabetic Association, 1995. To order, call (800)-ADA-ORDER.

Brackenridge, Betty. *Counting Carbohydrates—How to Zero In on Good Control.* Mini-Med Technologies, 1995. To order, call (800) 933-3322.

Corporate Sponsors, *Brand Name Diabetic Meals.* American Diabetes Association, June 1997. To order, call (800) ADA-ORDER.

Environmental Nutrition. *The Healthy Eating Guide to Over 800 Brand Name Foods.* Franklin Publishing, 1994. Environmental Nutrition, PO Box 221018, Beachwood, OH 44122-9846.

Franz, Marion. *Exchanges for All Occasions.* International Diabetes Center, Inc., 1993.

———. *Fast Food Facts.* International Diabetes Center, Inc., 1994.

Guiducci, Lynn. *Nutrition and Kids.* For more information, call (503) 848-0898; fax (503) 649-1056. e-mail: nutrkid@teleport.com

Holzmeister, LeaAnn. *Diabetes Carbohydrate and Fat Gram Guide: Quick Easy Meal Planning Using Carbohydrate and Fat Gram Counts (with Exchanges).* American Diabetic Association, June 1997.

Kraus, Barbara. *Calories and Carbohydrates.* 10th ed. Penguin, 1993.

———. *Carbohydrate Guide to Brand Names and Basic Foods.* New American Library, 1992.

Netzer, Corrine. *Carbohydrate Gram Counter.* Dell, 1994.

———. *The Complete Book of Food Counts.* Dell, 1994.

Pennington, J. *Food Values of Portions Commonly Used*. J. B. Lippincott, 1994.

Resch, Elyse, and Evelyn Tribole. *Intuitive Eating*. St. Martin's, 1996.

Walsh, John. *Pumping Insulin*. Torry Pines Press, 1994; new edition to be released 1998. To order, write: 1030 West Upas Street, San Diego, CA 92103 or call (800) 988-4772. www.diabetesnet.com

Warshaw, Hope. *Diabetes Meal Planning Made Easy*. The American Dietetic Association, 1996.

————. *The Restaurant Companion: A Guide to Healthier Eating Out*. Surrey Books, 1995.

ORGANIZATIONS

American Association of Diabetes Educators
(800) 832-6874
444 North Michigan Avenue, Suite 1240
Chicago, IL 60611-3901
www.aadenet.org/
Provides referrals to certified diabetes educators in your area.

The American Diabetes Association
(800) ADA-ORDER
    or (703) 549-1500
1660 Duke Street
Alexandria, VA 22314
www.diabetes.org or
    www.ada.judds.com

The American Dietetic Association
(800) 877-1600
National Center for Nutrition and Dietetics
216 West Jackson Boulevard
Chicago, IL 60606-6995
www.eatright.org
•*To speak to a dietitian directly, call
    1-900-CALL-AN-RD
    or 1-900-225-5267.*
•*For a referral to a registered dietitian in
    your area, call 1-800-366-1655.*

American Heart Association
(800) 242-8721
7272 Greenville Avenue
Dallas, TX 75231
www.amheart.org

Canadian Diabetes Association
(416) 214-1900
15 Toronto Street, Suite 500
Toronto, ON M5C 2E3
Canada
www.diabetes.ca/

International Diabetes Center
(612) 993-3393
3800 Park Nicollet Boulevard
Minneapolis, MN 55416
www.idc.org

International Diabetic Athletes
    Association
(602) 433-2113
1647-B West Bethany Home Road
Phoenix, AZ 85015
www.getnet.com/~idaa/

Joslin Diabetes Center
(617) 732-2400
1 Joslin Place
Boston, MA 02215
www.joslin.harvard.edu

Juvenile Diabetes Foundation
(212) 689-2860
432 Park Avenue
New York, NY 10016
www.jdfcure.com

National Diabetes Information
    Clearinghouse
(301) 654-3327
1 Information Way
Bethesda, MD 20892
www.niddk.nih.gov

PERIODICALS

Cooking Light
PO Box 1748
Birmingham, AL 35201
cookinglight@pathfinder.com

Eating Well
Subscriptions:
PO Box 54263
Boulder, CO 8032-4263
(303) 604-1464
Editorial: (802) 425-3961
EWellEdit@aol.com

Diabetes Forecast
(800) 232-3472
American Diabetes Association
1660 Duke Street
Alexandria, VA 23314
Automatic subscription with membership

Diabetes Self-Management
(212) 989-0200
Rapaport Publishing, Inc.
150 West 22nd Street
New York, NY 10011
www.diabetes/self/mgmt.com

The Diabetic Reader
(800) 735-7726
5623 Matilija Avenue
Van Nuys, CA 91401

Two Types
(404) 467-9700
Patients Publishing Co., Inc.
454 East Paces Ferry Road
Atlanta, GA 30305
editor@twotypes.com
www.twotypes.com

INDEX

CONVERSION CHART

EQUIVALENT IMPERIAL AND METRIC MEASUREMENTS

American cooks use standard containers, the 8-ounce cup and a tablespoon that takes exactly 16 level fillings to fill that cup level. Measuring by cup makes it very difficult to give weight equivalents, as a cup of densely packed butter will weigh considerably more than a cup of flour. The easiest way therefore to deal with cup measurements in recipes is to take the amount by volume rather than by weight. Thus the equation reads:

1 cup = 240 ml = 8 fl. oz.   ½ cup = 120 ml = 4 fl. oz.

It is possible to buy a set of American cup measures in major stores around the world.

In the States, butter is often measured in sticks. One stick is the equivalent of 8 tablespoons. One tablespoon of butter is therefore the equivalent to ½ ounce/15 grams.

Solid Measures

U.S. and Imperial Measures		Metric Measures	
Ounces	Pounds	Grams	Kilos
1		28	
2		56	
3½		100	
4	¼	112	
5		140	
6	‘	168	
8	½	225	
9		250	¼
12	¾	340	
16	1	450	

Liquid Measures

Fluid Ounces	U.S.	Imperial	Milliliters
	1 teaspoon	1 teaspoon	5
¼	2 teaspoons	1 dessertspoon	10
½	1 tablespoon	1 tablespoon	14
1	2 tablespoons	2 tablespoons	28
2	¼ cup	4 tablespoons	56
4	½ cup		110
5		¼ pint or 1 gill	140
6	¾ cup		170
8	1 cup		225
9			250, ¼ liter
10	1¼ cups	½ pint	280
12	1½ cups		340
15		¾ pint	420
16	2 cups		450
18	2¼ cups		500, ½ liter
20	2½ cups	1 pint	560

Oven Temperature Equivalents

Fahrenheit	Celsius	Gas Mark	Description
225	110	¼	Cool
250	130	½	
275	140	1	Very Slow
300	150	2	
325	170	3	Slow
350	180	4	Moderate
375	190	5	
400	200	6	Moderately Hot
425	220	7	Fairly Hot
450	230	8	Hot
475	240	9	Very Hot
500	250	10	Extremely Hot

Any broiling recipes can be used with the grill of the oven, but beware of high-temperature grills.

Equivalents for Ingredients

all-purpose flour—plain flour
arugula—rocket
beet—beetroot
coarse salt—kitchen salt
confectioners' sugar—icing sugar
cornstarch—cornflour
eggplant—aubergine
fava beans—broad beans
granulated sugar—caster sugar
lima beans—broad beans

scallion—spring onion
shortening—white fat
snow pea—mangetout
sour cherry—morello cherry
squash—courgettes or marrow
unbleached flour—strong, white flour
vanilla bean—vanilla pod
zest—rind
zucchini—courgettes or marrow

light cream—single cream
heavy cream—double cream
half and half—12% fat milk
buttermilk—ordinary milk

baking sheet—oven tray
cheesecloth—muslin
parchment paper—greaseproof paper
plastic wrap—cling film